ONE NIGHT ON TV IS WORTH WEEKS AT THE PARAMOUNT

Console-ing Passions

Television and Cultural Power

Edited by Lynn Spigel

ONE NIGHT ON TV

IS WORTH WEEKS

AT THE PARAMOUNT

Popular Music on Early Television

MURRAY FORMAN

Duke University Press   Durham and London   2012

© 2012 Duke University Press

All rights reserved

Printed in the United States of America on acid-free paper ∞

Designed by Heather Hensley

Typeset in Garamond Premier Pro by Tseng Information Systems, Inc.

Library of Congress Cataloging-in-Publication Data appear
on the last printed page of this book.

"TV Is the Thing." Written by Phil Medley and William Sanford.
© 1985 Straylight Music (ASCAP), You Look Good Music
Publishing (ASCAP). All Rights Reserved. Used by Permission.
International Copyright Secured.

"Dear Mr. Godfrey." Written by Ruth Wallis, 1953. Courtesy
of Alan Pastman.

IN MEMORY OF MY FATHER,

WITH GRATITUDE TO MY MOTHER.

CONTENTS

ACKNOWLEDGMENTS ★ XI

Popular Music and the Small Screen Frontier:
An Introduction ★ 1

1. Music, Image, Labor: Television's Prehistory ★ 17

2. "Hey TV!": Musical Pioneers and Pessimists ★ 51

3. Harmonizing Genres ★ 115

4. The Look of Music ★ 169

5. Music in a "Sepia" Tone ★ 231

6. Maracas, Congas, and Castanets ★ 273

CONCLUSION Rocking the TV Conventions ★ 319

APPENDIX ★ 341

NOTES ★ 343

BIBLIOGRAPHY ★ 363

Index ★ 389

ACKNOWLEDGMENTS

This project has long been in the works, and at times it seemed that its completion might take as long as it took to invent and perfect the television. My work benefited immeasurably from the funding support of the City University of New York (CUNY-PSC Grant), the Marion and Jasper Whiting Memorial Foundation, the Faculty-Undergraduate Research Initiative (FURI) at Northeastern University, and the Office of the Provost at Northeastern University. Also at Northeastern, the former dean of arts and sciences James Stellar, and the former vice provost Patricia Maguire Meservey facilitated project funding and a valuable research leave, for which I am grateful. Stuart Liebman was similarly helpful at Queens College–CUNY. I am especially indebted to the National Endowment for the Humanities, which awarded me a research fellowship for this project in 2003–4.

My sincere thanks to the staff at the libraries and archives where I conducted my core research: Snell Library at Northeastern University, Boston University's Mugar Library (microfiche division), the New York Museum of Television and Radio (now the Paley Center for Media), The Museum of Broadcast Communications in Chicago, the Wisconsin State Historical Archives, the UCLA Film and TV Archive, the Library of American Broadcasting at the University of Maryland, the Smithsonian Institution, and the Museum of American History. I was also assisted by the librarians of the Boston Public Library, the Free Library of Philadelphia, and by those of the New York Public Library system at the library's main branch as well as at the Schomburg Center for Research in Black Culture, the Science,

Industry, and Business section, and the New York Public Library for the Performing Arts.

Ray Faiola and John Behrens at CBS Television kindly assisted me during my brief research foray at the network's New York headquarters. Mark Cantor (Los Angeles) and J. Fred MacDonald (Chicago) took time to discuss my project and to share rare video materials from their extensive personal collections of music on early television. The experience (and the footage) was very useful; special thanks to each of you.

Numerous bright minds in Canada and the United States assisted me with this project. Some provided books and articles or other archival materials, others sent along the written fruits of their own research labor, while others provided editing and organizational suggestions. Thanks to Doug Battema, Elaine Hayes, Michele Hilmes, Steve "The Machine" Kosareff, Jason Mittel, Keith Negus, Elena Razlogova, Brian Rose, Lynn Spigel, Haidee Wasson, David Weinstein, and Mark Williams. Keir Keightley, Vincent Rocchio, David Sanjek, and Matt Stahl went above and beyond what was asked of them, taking time away from their own brilliant research projects to read and comment on sections of this book. Omar Arenas also provided helpful comments for chapter 6. Gentlemen, I thank you. Norma Coates is a kindred scholar (her work on television music after 1956 is the bomb!) and she too read several sections of the manuscript while freely sharing segments of her own excellent research directly and on conference panels; thanks, Norma. You're up! Finally, Ken Wissoker was a perfect editor throughout the process, offering encouragement and guidance at just the right times; thanks also to Leigh Barnwell at Duke University Press for helping with the details and getting the answers when I asked and Neal McTighe who assisted with the final production work.

I am indebted to many colleagues and dear friends for their ongoing encouragement in this undertaking and all else. The initial inspiration for the book you now hold can be indirectly traced to George Szanto. Whenever daunting challenges in the research or writing emerged I could always blame George . . . or thank him, which I do here. At Northeastern University many of my past and present colleagues in the Communication Studies Department have been extremely supportive; a special shout out to Jayson Harsin, Alison Hearn, P. David Marshall, David Monje, Joanne Morreale, Craig Robertson, Vincent Rocchio, Kumarini Silva, Marcus Breen, Michael Woodnick, and Alan Zaremba. Noah Danoff proved to be an excellent research assistant while providing fine company in the microfiche trenches;

big up, Noah! My intellectual fire was also fueled by my former coeditors at the *Journal of Popular Music Studies*, Reebee Garofalo, Jeff Melnick, Deborah Pacini Hernandez, Emmett Price III, and Rachel Rubin; thanks, guys!

I enjoy the unqualified love and support of my family; a tip of the hat and a raised glass to Jan, Shawn, and Dave. La familia Arenas en Caracas, Venezuela, shared music, laughter, arepas, and rum; muchas gracias a todo la familia. My daughter Bayla Metzger patiently listened to me explain the joys of screening a Peggy Lee performance or the ongoing struggle to attain writer's eloquence; thanks for all that and more, Bay. As ever, Zamawa Arenas offered unfailing encouragement and "held the fort on Fort" while I was away doing research (or locked in mortal combat with an uncooperative computer). Strong of mind and character, tender of heart, Zamawa is a pillar in my world. Maybe now we can get back to that bolero, "polishing the buckle." Te amo, mi amor.

Finally, it was my parents who first introduced me to many of the musicians referenced in these pages. They each shared their recollections of postwar popular music and early television, providing important "real world" testimonies for some of my more uncertain ponderings. It is to them that I dedicate this book. My father passed away before this manuscript was complete, but he heard enough about it to know where it was heading. Perhaps, like Glenn Miller, he's still out there, eternally flying in his Lancaster, navigating to the dulcet strains of the band.

Popular Music and the Small Screen Frontier

*

AN INTRODUCTION

Shortly after the launch of MTV in 1981, when advertisers, recording industry corporations, and teen television viewers each
applauded the network's debut, there was a surge in critical
assessments about its impact and the shifting role of the contemporary popular musician. Music television was the topic of
intense debate across varied sectors of the entertainment industry and among the questions raised was how a twenty-four-
hour all-music network might alter the status of musicians
whose recorded sounds were heard widely and whose appearances in magazines, as television guest performers or hosts of
TV "specials," in films (often documentaries), or in live concerts,
extended their public recognition and celebrity presence. While
some artists such as Joe Jackson (who, it was wryly noted, "has
a face for radio") expressed exasperation at the music industry's
growing reliance on videos as promotional vehicles, many other
established and rising artists leapt at the chance to advertise
their sound and image over the music television network. The
network's publicity slogan "I Want My MTV" quickly became a
clarion call among eager young viewers across the nation.

When MTV was introduced with a barrage of advertising,

cultural critics and television historians cited some of the network's more pertinent television precedents. These included U.S. shows from the 1950s, 1960s, and 1970s such as *American Bandstand, Shindig!, Hullabaloo, Soul Train, Don Kirshner's Rock Concert,* or *The Midnight Special,* and such historic televised musical events as Elvis Presley's spate of 1956 broadcast performances, the Beatles' first guest spots on *The Ed Sullivan Show* in 1964, or Presley's truly engaging 1968 NBC "comeback" special. In these examples, the benefits of "breaking" new acts on television were readily apparent, as were the potentials for veteran artists to introduce new material or to rehabilitate their careers by transforming their image or popular profile. Since its debut, MTV (and other music television networks in North America and internationally) has delivered countless groundbreaking musical telecasts, attaining its own status as a recognized cultural icon and trendsetter (something that continues even as the network has reduced its reliance on music videos in the United States). Many of MTV's successes were recalled in 2001 and again in 2011, the network's twentieth and thirtieth anniversaries, briefly spurring renewed discussion about the phenomenon of "music television" and "music videos."

Scholars agree in principle that, despite shared and overlapping elements within the entertainment industries (especially in view of tendencies toward concentration of ownership, industrial convergence, and corporate synergy), the music and television sectors are not precisely alike, nor do they adhere to the same institutional forces or practices (Deaville, 2011). Norma Coates is critical of the term "music television," suggesting that, "it is premised on two separate realms, that of music and television, and in this instance the second term is engulfed by the first, given the cultural weight placed upon 'music'" (2007: 22). For Coates, the intensified interest in "music television" since MTV's inception has often ignored the television component. In what amounts to a manifesto, Coates provides a powerful corrective to what she regards as an inaccurate and improper analytical framework:

> This requires a conceptual shift to the study of *television music,* not music television. This is not an attempt at clever wordplay, but a call for change of the object and focus of analysis. Such a change of emphasis forces scholars to think about television music as television, to foreground the corresponding industrial, economic, programming, production, and business aspects of the medium as informed by the engagement of popular music. The deployment of television music as an analytical frame gen-

erates a different set of questions and conclusions than those previously posed and answered. It engenders inquiries into the impact of popular music on television conventions, styles, genres, writing, direction, lighting, and dance, to name a few. (ibid.: 23)

With Coates's perspective close at hand and remaining mindful of the many scholarly discussions and academic publications devoted to music videos in the wake of MTV's debut,[1] *One Night on TV is Worth Weeks at the Paramount* addresses the conjoined histories of popular music and television during the earliest phase of TV broadcasting. This book places music and television on equal footing, affirming the claim that television affected popular music in the immediate postwar era while substantiating the accompanying claim that music also affected the development of television through its embryonic stage.

Despite abundant historical evidence attesting to the importance of popular music in television's early development there remain several noticeable gaps in the research on these linked cultural sectors. Few historians, it seems, have isolated the musical aspects of television's emergent phase for close and detailed study, although examples such as Horace Newcomb's (1997) critical appraisal of the musical passages in a single 1951 episode of *The Texaco Star Theater* (featuring host Milton Berle) offer rich analyses for consideration. Keith Negus (2006) also explores some of the early musical forays in television, simultaneously addressing the immediate postwar era and the contemporary period, identifying important threads of connection across roughly sixty years. As Negus notes, "Histories of twentieth-century music have, in general, tended to ignore television. . . . Equally, studies of television have often devoted little attention to music" (2006: 20–21). Existing entries on the history of television or the evolution of program genres almost never fully address popular music's central role in early program content, nor do historical studies of popular music grant sufficient attention to the multiple ways that music was introduced to the small screen in television's formative stages, with a few exceptions (e.g., Eberley 1982; Shumway 1997; Burns 1998; Rodman 2010).

John Mundy, for example, offers valuable analytic insight onto the conjunctural relations between popular music and television at various stages of its development in Britain and the United States, appropriately situating popular music in the postwar era within a general framework of "the screen" encompassing both cinema and television. Yet his suggestion that there was "an initial reluctance to programme popular music" (1999: 179) in the early television industry misrepresents the historical record of TV programming and content decisions in the United States since at least 1930, overlooking the many forms of musical presentation that existed on the small screen since the medium's early experimental stages. Such a claim defies the evidence of extant corporate memoranda, industrial documentation, or television kinescopes that testify to just the opposite conclusion, that there was, in fact, an intense need, desire, and effort to program popular music.

In scholarly studies, music programs airing through the late 1940s and early 1950s, such as *Peter Potter's Jukebox Jury*, *The Dinah Shore Show*, *The Perry Como Show*, *Toast of the Town*, or *Your Hit Parade* may be referred to in passing, but seldom is there rigorous analysis of the character and content of the musical element on these early television shows. Gary Burns (1998) offers close analysis of the style and aesthetics of *Your Hit Parade* in the early 1950s, but he employs a curious analytical approach foregrounding much later aesthetic standards associated with MTV-era video practices that obscures rather than explains the idiosyncrasies of these early broadcasts. Nor does Burns answer questions about the program's aesthetic construction and its significance in relation to music promotion or public taste and audience consumption at the time.

Scholars seldom focus explicitly on the visual medium's impact as it rippled through the popular music sector of the wider entertainment industry at its inception. In this regard, Russell Sanjek and David Sanjek (1991) admirably address many significant factors that arose in the music industry with television's advent, yet their unrelenting emphasis on wider industrial issues forecloses the analysis of TV program content and production formats or other aspects of the medium that might be more broadly conceived as *cultural*. Among popular music scholars, then, the full range of music programming on television, spanning musical genres, performance styles, promotional strategies, and television production has generally been poorly acknowledged.

In a similar context, though countless studies may isolate early television's musical or comedy variety shows as distinct and important genres they seldom explore music as a primary genre component of the medium in its nascent phase. Such scant attention to the role and importance of music on TV among television historians stands in marked contrast to the depth of critical study and analysis devoted to, for instance, television's technological progress, policy development and industrial growth, and its dramatic or narrative content, or to various other influential TV genres such as the situation comedy or televised news broadcasting. Music on early television has all too often been an afterthought.

In *TV a-Go-Go*, a general market book about televised musical performance, Jake Austen (2005) offers a rather common perspective on early televised music. Austen reviles the earliest broadcasts of popular music (and, apparently, television itself, describing the medium as either "the boob tube" or "idiot box") and berates most of the musical fare that was screened prior to the mid-1950s. Austen's explicit disdain for early televised musical content also informs his negative assessment of audiences at the time (especially female viewers) that in his estimation lacked sufficiently discerning taste. His narrow perspective, glorifying the emergence of rock 'n' roll on mid-fifties TV, leads Austen to denigrate the musical performances of programs such as *The Perry Como Show*, *Ted Mack's Original Amateur Hour*, or *Your Hit Parade*, shows that in his opinion consisted of "bland, reliable favorites of America's housewives" (2005: 4).

While the musical selections on these programs were undeniably oriented toward the popular mainstream, his curmudgeonly stance obliterates the opportunity to probe the relevant aspects of performance aesthetics, modes of production and staging, industry discourse, or viewer responses to what they were watching. More strikingly, Austen never inquires as to why so many people — including droves of "America's housewives" — watched and apparently enjoyed these programs. Like many others, Austen overlooks the fundamental elements that might have rendered these early programs and musical performances distinctive or entertaining. What, we might ask, made televised musical performances important and/or pleasurable?

Most critical studies of popular music and television seem to underanalyze television's first broadcast years, picking up the thread and focusing intensely on the evolution of televised music after 1955 (Shumway 1997; Mundy 1999; Frith 2002). This period encompasses the rapid rise of rock 'n' roll and is frequently associated with Elvis Presley's 1956–57 assault on the small screen, roughly concurrent with his departure from the independent Sun Records label after signing a new contract with the major RCA Victor label (a contract that included a requirement of at least ten "personal appearance performances" annually in support of his recordings).

While briefly acknowledging television's prior music broadcasts from the late 1940s to the mid-1950s (mainly in the United Kingdom), Simon Frith regards the period after 1955 as being of particular significance because, in his view, the relatively new television medium was an essential factor in the development of the even newer rock 'n' roll form and the ascendance of its music celebrities, including Presley. Frith writes, "It certainly could be argued that the visual conventions of rock performance were shaped by television — because it was there — in ways that do not apply to musical genres which pre-dated television" (2002: 283). It is significant in this context, however, to acknowledge that to varying degrees, television was also "there" in 1936 and 1946, as well as in 1956, when Presley emerged with particular force. Though television was negligible through the 1930s and 1940s and the industry infrastructure was still under construction, networks were then also actively exploring the best ways to integrate popular music performances into TV production processes.

As I will argue in the following pages, despite his cogent argument for television's significant influences on the evolution of rock 'n' roll (and virtually all pop music since), Frith's historical account falls slightly short by suggesting that earlier popular music broadcasts "were more about bringing stage acts into the living room than about changing their performance conventions" (ibid.). In this book I assert that, while television's presentational power was more fully realized in the period after rock 'n' roll's emergence as Frith contends, the transformations of musical performance and broadcasting conventions were already well under way by the time Presley hit the screen.

Addressing the broadcast of R & B musicians over southern radio in the 1940s and 1950s, the Turkish expatriate and influential record industry executive Ahmet Ertegan posed the question, "Young white teenagers heard them on those top-of-the-dial stations and began requesting them. What the hell was Elvis listening to when he was growing up?" (Szatmary 1991: 36). Turning such queries toward the visual broadcast medium, although Presley's TV presence and his jarring performance style generate considerable attention (Rodman 1996; Shumway 1997; Mundy 1999; Austen 2005) never, *ever* is it suggested that by 1956 Presley was, like Americans far and wide, also well acquainted with television, absorbing the medium's aesthetic forms and visual lessons that were on display nightly. We should also, therefore, pose the question, What the hell was Elvis *watching* when he was growing up?

The particulars of Presley's teen TV viewing patterns are not well established, although numerous interviews and observations attest to the extent of his engagement with the medium, allowing for speculation about his viewing habits and TV influences. Presley was a product of a cultural moment when television emerged as a new and influential medium along-side more established and traditional facets of the entertainment industry, including recording, radio broadcasting, jukeboxes, film, and clubs and theater concerts. By all accounts he was an eager consumer in all mediums. He moved with his parents from Tupelo, Mississippi, to Memphis, Tennessee, in 1948 when he was thirteen years old, graduating from high school in 1953. Philip Ennis writes that in Presley's Memphis, "The four radio stations founded in the 1920s were augmented by five more, along with two TV stations" (1992: 232). Because he was raised in lower-class economic conditions through the late 1940s, television viewing was most likely something that occurred outside the family home, yet by 1956 Presley was a professional touring musician who was comfortable in finer hotels and other sites where televisions were standard.

The photographer Alfred Wertheimer (1979) recounts that, in mid-1956, Presley's new home at 1034 Audubon Drive in Memphis was outfitted with *three* TV sets, along with a hi-fi stereo console. Presley's bedroom television set was also equipped with a Zenith remote control device (a unit that, having only reached the commercial market in 1956, made for a higher-priced TV set), suggesting that Presley was both familiar with the medium and an early adopter of new TV technology (Ritz 2005). Apart from Presley's status as a vibrant performer, rock 'n' roll pioneer, and sensitive interpreter of ballads and country spirituals, therefore, it is appropriate to assert that by mid-decade he was also a seasoned TV viewer. Television was, for him and a vast number of his teenage fans, *normal*. *One Night on TV* presents a detailed historical account and analysis of television's early musical programming, encompassing the content that was available to Presley and the emergent rock 'n' roll generation.

To fully comprehend the implications of the intersection of popular music and television it is consequently necessary to evaluate their dynamics and interaction over a longer duration, assessing evolutionary processes that include practices of experimentation and the ongoing refinement of aesthetic or programming strategies, as well as other more expansive cultural factors that came to bear on the character of both music and television. Without delving into this formative era and adopting an extended view of the emergent television industry's accommodation of music and musical performance, there is a risk of neglecting the rich and convoluted tale of how popular music and television were merged in deliberate fashion and adopted by audiences in unique and decidedly nonpassive ways; in contemporary terminology this might be described as a matter of "media convergence" (Jenkins 2006).

In another account of popular music on television in the mid-1950s, Kevin Donnelly emphasizes Elvis Presley's importance, writing, "Live television broadcasts relied upon the performance of musical numbers as much as they relied upon other 'turns' from the stage, offering the opportunity for audiences to see stars from close quarters. With the arrival of rock 'n' roll, popular music became more stridently visual, embodied by the impact (both real and imagined) of Elvis swinging his hips" (2001: 89). Donnelly's account is fairly standard of the writing on musical presentation and early television; there is nothing necessarily out of order in his brief overview of the broadcast industry's shift from radio to television and the rise of a new visual emphasis on musical performance. Yet the suggestion that music was merely "relied upon" is inadequate for an elaborated understanding of the ways in which television either embraced or alienated musicians and others associated with the music and entertainment industries. This description displaces the actual labor of unionized musicians who appeared on early television, and it understates the artistry that eventually led to superior television performances, basically discounting the thick tangle of industrial *and* cultural circumstances that influenced the convergence of popular music and early television.

A certain analytical orthodoxy tends to seep into many of the narratives about early TV's musical performances, obscuring the complex processes involved in the evolution of presentational norms and standards. Such narrative portrayals (for example, the stock references to Presley's scandalously physical performance style) remain relevant to our contemporary understanding of broadcasting history, yet they also tend to reinforce or fix certain "common sense" facets of broadcasting lore without fully exploring the various resonant historical factors relating to industrial, aesthetic, and more broadly cultural issues. This is ultimately how rock 'n' roll mythology has been forged. If the general perception maintains that, for example, Presley's televised performances were somehow radical and revolutionary for the medium in 1956, that with his arrival television somehow "became more stridently visual," then there is also need for careful explanation of why this is so.

The customary account of a powerful and sudden rupture, rooted in Presley's television year, seems ill conceived when roughly eight years of prior musical broadcasts are taken into consideration. The prevailing views of Presley's arrival and televised portrayal diminish the "strident" visuality of (to cite only a very partial set of exemplary performers) Desi Arnaz, Cab Calloway, Lorraine Cugat, Ina Ray Hutton, Spike Jones, Big Jay McNeely, Johnnie Ray, and literally scores of other musicians who appeared on television as musical guests or hosted their own TV programs after 1948. This emphasis on Presley and his particular mode of visual performance also implies that the incredibly nuanced music and performance styles of established TV mainstays that I analyze in the following pages, including Perry Como, Frankie Laine, Liberace, Peggy Lee, Tony Martin, Dinah Shore, and Lawrence Welk, are somehow of lesser value or importance, ignoring the rewards of a performance aesthetic that is frequently registered in the combination of gentle-hued ballads, softly cast vocal phrasing, restrained orchestral rhythmic structures, and subtle physical gestures. Indeed, Presley's televised performances of ballads or southern spiritual numbers shared much in their presentational style with many of TV's leading musical program hosts of the day, and he openly professed his respect and appreciation of the TV veterans Perry Como and Eddie Fisher. The performances by Presley's predecessors might also be considered "stridently visual" if one is attuned to the more gentle and innocuous shadings of musical performance and television presentation.

In order to understand the important distinctions among musical broadcasts, it requires more than the mere assertion that vocalists such as Perry Como or Dinah Shore reflect average or "bland" cultural tastes or that they represent insignificant mainstream musical values as many historians and critics comfortably claim. Rather, it is of vastly greater interest to acknowledge the importance of these individuals and to tease out the differences between, for example, Shore and her television contemporaries Hutton and Lee or to analyze the distinctions between male vocalists such as Como, Martin, Laine, Frank Sinatra, or Vaughn Monroe. The industry certainly registered such distinctions. This approach involves observing how production processes (including camera placement, set design, and stage lighting), song selection, brief comedy skits, costumes, and physical comportment combine to orient the performances toward distinct and varying social spaces (i.e., the domestic or public spheres) and, accordingly, varied cultural values and identities (encompassing simple virtue, exoticism, feminine sexual allure, masculine vulnerability or virility, nostalgia, etc.). Auxiliary sources such as contemporaneous media and industry analyses of musical programs or performances and, where possible, audience commentary, enrich the understanding of the evolution of televised musical performances.

In order to more fully comprehend how popular music was integrated into early television at its inception and how musical presentation developed through TV's first years, it is necessary to illuminate a wide range of factors that include industry motivations, aesthetic innovations, and cultural transformations in the period immediately prior to Presley's ostensibly outrageous gyrations. This book seeks to identify and analyze the dominant performance and broadcast conventions within which a twenty-one-year-old Elvis Presley was working when he made his television debut in January 1956. As I will illustrate, the evidence suggests that Presley was conventional *and* revolutionary, conformist *and* innovative. His TV appearances between January 1956 and January 1957 sustained certain standards of performance and presentation that had evolved over roughly a decade even as he introduced a unique, idiosyncratic style that broke from many of television's established patterns.

The television studies theorist John Corner writes, "Study of television has often been preoccupied with the contemporary moment; it has been the study of the perpetual present. The limitations of this when, among other things, we now need a steady sense of the past in order to understand the significance of imminent and future change, will quickly become apparent" (1999: 121). Taking Corner's emphasis on historical research to heart, my main claim is that popular music was never peripheral to the early conception of television programming and content at the medium's inception; it was, in fact, of central concern and was deemed essential to television's public acceptance and the industry's commercial viability. Even in television's most primitive stages, from the early 1930s to the late 1940s, executives and program developers in the emergent broadcasting sector were convinced that the medium's success required popular music performances with a pronounced visual component. It can be stated without ambiguity that popular music has been part of television from the beginning.

Drawing on original archival materials from the music and television industries from the 1930s, 1940s, and 1950s (trade journals, executive memoranda, press releases and other promotional materials) and from contemporaneous mainstream press articles (including TV program reviews, celebrity profiles, industry analyses),[2] this book explores how popular music was integrated into early television and how television (as an industry, as a medium, and as a cultural institution) accommodated music in its broad range of genres and performance styles. It analyzes the means by which musical presentation gradually became a standardized facet of television broadcasts.

Throughout the following pages I scrutinize the discussions, debates, and industry decisions that influenced popular music's role in television broadcasting and the deliberate processes through which popular music presentation gradually adhered to ever-more familiar broadcasting conventions. I take much inspiration from Kay Dickinson, whose research on music and film and the interrelations between aesthetic and industrial issues provides abundant insight. She writes: "We should interrogate the labor expended on maintaining horizontal integration across entertainment industries like music and cinema, not only that leisure commodities might somehow speak to and of greater fractures in how more everyday employment functions, but also that the *work* of the media, in all sorts of senses, should figure more prominently in academic inquiry" (2008: 4).

After 1948, when television sales accelerated and the medium's influence became more distinct, musicians and others working in the entertainment industries more frequently offered their own detailed industry assessments, attempting to understand television's value and effects in its ascendance as a cultural force. In these instances, the terms and structure of debate often illustrate wider social and cultural concerns of the postwar period, revealing diverse interests and ideals that were implicated in individuals' pursuit of leisure and entertainment as well as the search among musicians for employment or the expression of artistry.

The challenge from the present juncture is to identify the specific means through which television's musical programs were defined and to carefully document and analyze the aesthetic influences and the industrial approaches that were employed as televised musical performances occupied a new and pervasive role in American culture. Instead of approaching the medium and its first several years of musical presentation as a set of easily recognizable and commonly accepted achievements, it has proven to be more productive — and accurate — to approach 1940s and early 1950s television as an incomplete project, very much part of "a work in progress" that was prone to errors, miscues, and foibles in both a broader institutional orientation and in its regular daily programming. This is how many observers, both within and outside the music and television broadcasting industries, understood it at the time.

Lest we forget exactly how uncharted the television terrain was in this formative period, even the terminology used to describe the medium was uncertain: congratulating the dance band leader Fred Waring on his first "official" broadcast on NBC during the network's launch of a regular program schedule during the New York World's Fair in May 1939, the network president John Royal proclaimed, "You caught the tempo of television better than anybody we've seen on the thingamajig — whatever we decide to call it" (Royal 1939). Even by 1948, the language surrounding the medium was apparently indeterminate, as reported in *Modern TV and Radio*: "People inside and outside the broadcasting field are looking around for a new word for television — which is considered too long and cumbersome. 'Video' and 'TV' have been tried out, but they don't seem to catch the public fancy. A London newspaper recently asked its readers for suggestions and some of the words they came up with are 'Telio,' 'Luksee,' 'Oculo,' 'C-U,' and 'Lookies'" (December 1948: 12).

In 1950, James C. Petrillo, the president of the American Federation of Musicians, acknowledged, "Television is here to stay"; yet he also admitted to puzzlement about the trajectory of television and the networks' plans for its ongoing development:

> The disagreement among the employers themselves as to what television is going to do is unbelievable. They have so many different ideas and predictions that most of them contradict each other, and after listening to them for a couple of years, I find myself a little confused as to who has the right ideas and predictions. . . . When you really pin them all down, the answer is the same — they just don't know. ("TV Only Job Hope" 1950: 18)

With these contemporaneous perspectives I endeavor in this book to analyze televised musical performances and the evolution of musical programming in the spirit of an era when public skepticism, awe, or inspiration for the new broadcast medium were widespread, when the consequences of television's arrival were yet unknown, and the possibility of its failure still remained quite real.

Today, music and television are closely linked as components of cultural industry and artistic enterprise and it is standard practice that musicians' contracts include obligations to appear in videos and other televised promotional endeavors. The images and sounds of contemporary pop, rock, rap, metal, emo, R & B, country, and countless other genres or subgenres (that are associated with varying cultural environments and different temporal eras) emit from the television on a twenty-four-hour cycle, framed within an array of program formats and presentational styles that attest to the incredible success of televising music. Clearly the institution of television did not fail, and it is a given today that television and popular music are tightly entwined. It is from this vantage that I look back on television's formative stages.

Chapter 1 focuses on television's early history largely before 1948. It isolates the industrial considerations that emerged as executives developed the new medium, and it profiles several documented musical performances that occurred in the contexts of television laboratory experiments or network demonstrations through the 1930s and 1940s. These first tentative performances — not TV *broad*casts as such, since they were often in-house affairs sent over closed-circuit systems — indicate that popular music was always a prominent consideration among television executives and that there was active effort involved in developing suitable presentational techniques through which music would be made viable for the small screen. This discussion encompasses early predictions and informed critical views on television's implementation of music. I end this chapter with a detailed assessment of the role of the American Federation of Musicians and its controversial chief, James C. Petrillo, as professional union musicians approached television as an emergent industrial labor sector.

In chapter 2, I analyze the themes of opportunity and optimism and the concurrent perceptions of risk or anxiety that arose when television was introduced to working musicians within the popular music sector. With television's development, artists throughout the performing arts were confronted with a critical professional dilemma: many questioned how they could benefit from the new opportunities offered by television, whether acquiring access to a vast, dispersed audience or tapping the medium's unknown potentials as an effective promotional or marketing vehicle. For them, television was a dynamic environment within which they might thrive. Conversely, others, including music industry veterans and employees in related entertainment sectors, asked how television might potentially damage their carefully managed reputations or undermine their professional livelihoods. Unfounded speculation and anxiety were, in many instances, reinforced by actual data figures as television's impact became clearer. Television's rapid rise as a powerful new force competing for capital, talent, and audience attention produced positive *and* negative effects that reverberated throughout the music industry. Drawing from the ample resources available in music and entertainment industry trade papers from the period, this chapter monitors the discursive patterns that emerged in the wider entertainment industry with television's advent and it assesses the implications of shifting industrial practices across various sectors of the music business.

The evolution and establishment of various musical program genres with their accompanying conventions comprises the focus of chapter 3. Although popular music was assumed to be an indispensable component of early television programming even before the technical bugs had been engineered out of the system, the methods of successfully presenting music were by no means assured. While the character and aesthetics of vaudeville and the music halls of the early twentieth century, Tin Pan Alley song styles, and film, nightclub or Broadway-style musical performances dominated, programming directors and other television executives were eagerly intent on designing something new and different, something distinctly *televisual*. Isolating examples of televised musical programming and the emergence of recognizable genre formulas (with specific attention to nightclub-oriented programs and DJ/teen dance shows), I critically examine the issues and aspects that informed their production and standardization.

Chapter 4 addresses the aesthetics of musical performance on television. The chapter scrutinizes specific televised musical performances across network programs as well as analyzing musicians' disparate views about performance practices and television's emergent presentational conventions. Included here is the acknowledgment that performance is inextricably related to an artist's persona, a relationship that necessitates the identification of specific performance traits if we expect to comprehend the connection between artistic reputations and performance mannerisms. I explain how television's much-vaunted demand for distinct, expressive visual routines created considerable rancor among musicians. Many artists struggled in their attempts to transition into television, recoiling when they were suddenly called upon to participate in onscreen shtick and comedic skits that were dismissively dubbed "funny hats routines." With television producers' increased demands for visual and comedic performances, a discourse of authenticity, seriousness, and artistic integrity surfaced as musicians attempted to maintain their reputations in the face of television's unprecedented visual stipulations.

Chapters 5 and 6 identify the unique contributions of black and Latino musicians in an era when racial and ethnic representation in the mainstream media was a point of dispute and struggle. As we see in chapter 5, despite the prevailing notion that African American actors were underrepresented in early television, the historical evidence indicates a relatively lively and robust presence of *musicians* in various program contexts. The networks strived to incorporate black musical performances in their broadcasts, devising new internal policies that, gradually, integrated the networks and their program schedules. As television established itself in the nation's major urban hubs, black musicians were essential in ensuring that there was sufficient high-caliber talent on the air, though the racial "sensibilities" of the U.S. South presented a broadcasting dilemma for the national networks. While numerous musicians forged successful careers in television, few were assigned their own programs, creating substantial backlash among the nation's cultural critics and community watchdogs.

Latin music on TV comprises the content of chapter 6. Throughout the 1930s and 1940s, South American cultural motifs were grafted onto U.S. Tin Pan Alley compositions and many stereotypical representations appeared in Hollywood cinema, providing a foundation for television's program content. U.S. foreign policy, coupled with corporate expansion into new international markets also drew the United States closer to Latin America throughout the war years and afterward. With television's inception, Latin music found a new site where musicians could perform the rumba, conga, and most important, the mambo, in the latter case helping to fuel a surging dance and music trend that swept the nation. The performances gradually displayed several conventional production traits that included standard costumes, spatial references, and dance flourishes that communicated an indelible "Latin flavor."

In his theoretical analyses of television performance and popular music, Philip Auslander advocates "doing close readings of particular performances" in order to better understand the complicated relationships between musical artists and the various industrial and cultural forces that are in motion at any given period (2004: 9). This calls for the screening of actual televised musical performances as a means of augmenting the theoretical and original/primary materials that also offer context and data about music and early television. Taking Auslander's cue, in the course of researching this book I meticulously viewed roughly two hundred tapes of televised musical broadcasts in order to determine how popular music was staged in various presentational modes and the many ways that musical acts were contextualized as TV program genres evolved and broadcast formulae matured. Initially saved on kinescope tapes and, later, transferred to videotape by archivists, early TV programs are, with increasing frequency, also broadcast on contemporary cable television networks such as TV Land and made available through online nostalgia brokers that market videotapes and DVD copies of classic programs, or they are available for screening through web options including YouTube or dedicated websites maintained by independent history buffs.

These tapes offer visual corroboration for the contemporaneous views expressed in published articles, artist interviews, and TV program reviews that describe specific programs and performances or that generally address televised musical presentations from the late 1940s and early 1950s. The visual material also confirms that, despite the rudimentary nature of television in its formative phase, its content and character was heterogeneous and, at times, extremely sophisticated in its formal construction. Images reveal many of the mannerisms and cultural mores of the immediate postwar era, thus exposing wider aspects of social value and meaning—elements of *social significance*—and the role of music as a communicative force.

One Week on TV Is Worth Weeks at the Paramount, therefore, directly engages themes and issues from a period when television was still new and very much in its experimental mode. It probes the evolution of the emergent TV industry as corporate executives, engineers, and producers navigated the technical and aesthetic aspects of musical presentation in their struggle to establish content and programming conventions. It foregrounds the dominant issues and anxieties within the music industry in the postwar period, detailing the means by which musicians and those with stakes in the music industry (financial or otherwise) encountered the new broadcast medium and integrated it into their professional strategies and artistic practices.

1

Music, Image, Labor

*

TELEVISION'S PREHISTORY

Popular music and television are inextricably entwined. When television was nothing more than a dream in the mind of visionaries or a conundrum troubling scientists around the world, there was a clear sense that the sounds and images of musical performance would one day converge in a single broadcast transmission. The widely circulated notion of "radio with pictures" in the 1920s made sense then since much of television's invention, financing, and program planning emerged directly from the radio broadcasting industry. As countless historians have explained since, even though radio was less than a decade old and still developing as a standard facet of daily life at the end of what was termed "the roaring twenties" or "the jazz age," the earliest television broadcast experiments regularly incorporated musical performances (Fisher and Fisher 1996; Koszarski 2008; Magoun 2009; Rodman 2010). Documents show that many radio network executives believed that their approaches to programming and scheduling (with popular music prominently featured) would prevail although they could not forecast what television's content might actually look like. The issue of visualizing popular music consequently presented an early dilemma in TV content development.

When synchronized sound was still relatively new in cinema (having been successfully launched in 1927 following the release of a series of short synch-sound films) musicals quickly won public favor (Gabbard 1996; Mundy 1999; Koszarski 2008). Featuring spectacular imagery structured upon the thinnest of narrative scaffolding and musical performances by some of the era's most popular artists, the early film musicals were indebted to Broadway's presentational logic. Yet by the mid-1930s there was still nothing that could be described as a *tradition* of film musicals that television pioneers might emulate.

Television's early indeterminacy presented a major conceptual barrier but, of course, the challenges accompanying such indeterminacy can also inspire expansive thinking and lead to incredible innovation. Broadcast executives were expected to project how television might fit within their existing range of services and those in charge of radio programming and content development attempted to predict how abstract audience formations would respond to hypothetical TV shows. Imagining television — what it would be, whom it would be for — necessitated deep and probing analysis of an array of cultural factors encompassing the spirit and conditions of an era.

Somehow, during an economic depression and throughout a horrific war, the television industry continued to grow and evolve even as various other industrial sectors stalled and a great many original ideas withered on the vine. And while television's creators worked to improve the medium, musicians were intrinsically involved in the ongoing television experiment, at times toiling as full-fledged collaborators. After the war there was a remarkable burst of invention with several crucial developments facilitating the convergence of popular music and television.

In each of TV's transitional phases, discussions always incorporated popular music and the broadcast value of musical performances. The dominant discourses and public debates concerning early television and the role of popular music are noteworthy for they often illuminate other important features of the period, revealing a dynamic cultural vortex. By exploring some of the key sociocultural elements at television's inception (involving art and aesthetics, technology, and institutional entities) and the ways in which television was positioned among them, we might generate a better sense of the underlying values that informed the nation's cultural expression and leisure practices and the concurrent stakes for popular music and its performers.

In a December 1930 corporate memorandum, George Engles, National Broadcasting Corporation (NBC) vice president in charge of programs, wrote that with the emergence of visual broadcast capabilities it would be increasingly necessary to review and vet the physical or *telegenic* attributes of the singers hired by the network. Engles gently upbraided Bertha Brainard of the network's Program Department, reminding her that with "the forecast of oncoming television and the new requirements it would demand in the pictorial quality of our artist personnel" there was intensifying pressure to "revamp" the musical talent under contract "with a view to having when needed a picture that would pass the censors" (1930a). In this context, the "censors" to which Engles refers were internal network executives charged with evaluating the look and comportment of prospective TV talent, ensuring that no one deemed to be of sub-par physical appearance would be hired as television broadcasting progressed.

Brainard was the extremely rare woman in an organizational cadre dominated by men, having entered radio broadcasting in the early 1920s and risen in NBC's Program Department, where she worked closely with senior executives including Engles and John F. Royal (Halper 2001). Memoranda from the 1930s reveal Brainard's firm principles, shrewd mind, and sharp wit, and in her reply to Engles she subtly requested examples of any incidents where she and her programming unit may have failed to adequately assess the visual potential of vocalists, further suggesting that such a process of judgment requires an agreed-upon set of criteria. Noting the apparently subjective nature of such visual appraisals, she writes, "I find, unfortunately, a question of who is and who is not good looking, arising in the men's minds" (Brainard 1930).

As these exchanges indicate, during television's earliest phase no one had a clear sense of how the medium would accommodate the various expressions of art and culture, including musical performance, nor was there a stable notion of a visual standard for musical presentation. The discussions were fully in the realm of abstraction. Those such as Brainard and Engles (as well as countless engineers, directors, and programmers who were tasked with designing television) strived to meet as-yet-undefined broadcasting goals, to predict and then fulfill viewer expectations. Profoundly lacking rules and formal guides, television's first decision-makers — both independents and those working under the aegis of corporate broadcasters — stumbled forward with speculation more than fact at their disposal. In retrospect, theirs seems an almost impossible undertaking.

The dialogue between Engles and Brainard points to an emergent visual strategy at the network. It articulates the beginning of an industrial process that involved TV's appropriation and instrumental attitudes toward popular music and musicians that would only intensify over the next twenty-five years. Their interaction also indicates that the visual regime championed by Engles evolved at the network as a source of pressure and even coercion, challenging the prevailing practices and audio supremacy associated with radio broadcasting. Brainard's push back against Engles should not, therefore, be regarded as insubordination but as an example of two paradigms colliding within the specific contexts of 1930s corporate broadcasting.

Engles further outlined the problem of visualizing music in a lengthy response to Brainard, explaining, "Several rumors had come to me that various members of the Program Department were pushing artists whose sole claim to distinction lies in their voices" (1930b). His barely contained ire was based on the belief that employees in the network's Program Department evidently remained committed to the established talent recruitment and hiring practices of radio broadcasting. In his view, Brainard and her colleagues in the Program Department lacked proper foresight as plans for the network's television broadcasting branch evolved, as well as falling short of NBC's corporate objectives. David Sarnoff, president of NBC's parent company Radio Corporation of America (RCA) and a driving figure responsible for the formation of NBC in 1926, was an early and constant supporter of television. The network's executives and middle management were exposed to a stream of directives and corporate statements from Sarnoff addressing the medium's development. Indeed, Sarnoff staked much of his reputation on television's success. The issue of musicians' image and appearance developed into a central topic as television evolved, creating conflict and debate about visual or aural primacy in musical presentation.

The interaction between Engles and Brainard conveys a pressure that is common within hierarchical, top-down structures of power. As an executive representative, Engles exerted a coercive force extending institutional authority. He communicated NBC's corporate line within a chain of command and as volumes of published records confirm, his emphasis on television reflects Sarnoffs priorities at the time. Sarnoff's corporate support for technical research and his aggressive legal maneuvering pertaining to TV patent issues represent two fronts in an effort to dominate early television; programming represents a third front. Engles and Brainard were not merely encountering an insignificant impasse but, rather, they were engaged in a discussion about the process through which the corporation would integrate music in the manifestation of television.

In urging the Program Department to consider television's particular visual demands pertaining to singers, Engels introduced the terms "salable outstanding radio artists" or "salable talent" to his discourse about musical performances. The implication was that the commercial practicality of any given artist and, by extension, any given television program would eventually be judged according to the combined standards of performers' appearances *and* their musical talent, drawing television nearer to stage performances and cinema than to radio. In one sense, Engles's reference to salability points to a perceived need for musical artists to make a solid impression; to "sell" a song was a common expression among entertainers, referring to a quality performance that registered positively.

Engles implies more, however. He also addresses the need for musical artists to essentially sell themselves to audiences through their engaging performances and innate visual appeal. Here we get closer to the evolving notions of artists' commodified congeniality and television presence that was regularly attached to the concept of television in its nascent period. In yet another related sense germane to the era, the commercially oriented terminology suggests that it is television itself that must be "sold" to a public that was, by the mid- to late 1930s, highly familiar with radio broadcasting and with the performance aesthetics of film musicals and live theater or nightclubs but that was also skeptical of the early TV industry's promise of a fuller, visually enhanced entertainment experience (especially one that necessitated the purchase of an expensive new electrical appliance). Music was going to help sell the concept of television to the public.

The discourse of commercial/commodity value and televised musical performances speaks to the extent to which culture was ensconced within a capitalist logic at this historical moment but it also reflects how deeply invested in commercial media and music industry economics NBC, television's industry leader, was at the time. Russell and David Sanjek (1991) explain how Sarnoff oversaw both the implementation of NBC's nationwide broadcast network and the acquisition of the Radio-Keith-Orpheum (RKO) theater chain and film production company in 1928 and spearheaded RCA's purchase of the Victor Talking Machine Company (creating the RCA Victor phonograph company) in 1929. After the 1930s, popular music lay at the center of each of these sectors and the corporate jockeying for dominance notably affected television's trajectory.

Industry executives injected a pronounced capitalist sensibility into television's development even though the programming structure and content — the medium's main selling point — had not fully congealed. The popular music sector had by this point already proven its strengths and value in relation to the commercial culture industries and radio, too, was confirmed as a valid medium within purely corporate and capitalist ideals. By conceiving TV's programming content in relation to abstract commodity values before any norms or standards existed the industry was operating within a symbolic realm whereby cultural texts are understood as objects with commercial worth. The programs and the musical performances were all oriented toward the logic of commodification and consumption, setting a pattern for the entire future of the medium.

Establishing a workable program schedule and ensuring top-quality performances was a prime objective if the public was to be "sold" on the new medium. In this reading, televised musical performances can be attached to a range of other commercial interests, and, in fact, the whole notion of TV viewer expectation, pleasure, or satisfaction can be linked to commercial and commodity values. Engles and other executives were, thus, dedicated to creating a commercial medium that could deliver consistently engaging and pleasurable shows that featured visually attractive musical performers.

The industry's early deliberations surrounding the role of popular music on television indicate a tendency toward the brute appropriation of musical talent, reflecting attitudes that prevailed throughout the medium's developmental phase and over the next quarter century. Without explicitly declaring that an artist's visual appearance and telegenic qualities trumped his or her musicality, Engles (among others) seems to place these attributes at least on par in the commercial contexts of television broadcasting. Although this position may have seemed contentious to some at the time, the perspective was not unknown in the realm of musical theater or cinema where physical appearances were crucial in casting. Such concerns were also an integral factor in the production of modern icon status; good-looking actors or musicians fared inordinately well in the nascent celebrity culture of the early twentieth century.

The film industry had confronted somewhat similar issues, if in reverse. When synchronized sound technology facilitated the "talkies" in the 1920s (the first feature-length film with synchronized musical selections being *The Jazz Singer*, in 1927), a host of attractive screen actors quickly found that, despite their acting talent, physical attributes, or film experience, their vocal abilities were under close scrutiny and subject to intensified critique as dialogue-laden scripts and musical scenes were popularized. For some (rumored to include the top silent film stars John Gilbert and Norma Talmadge), looking good or moving well onscreen was not always enough; they had to sound good as well in order to "sell" both the individual movie and the concept of the talkies. For artists faced with imminent irrelevance, the enlistment of vocal coaches and elocution lessons was a desperate attempt to maintain a footing in the changing industry. Musicians hired to provide musical accompaniment for the silent films in the nation's movie houses were also summarily dismissed with the advent of synch-sound. With the prospect of television, NBC's Engles expressed an apparent willingness to hire marginally inferior musical talents possessing better-than-average physical traits, urging his staff to identify appropriate-looking singers, especially those already under contract with NBC's radio branch, who could be efficiently plucked from the existing talent roster on the network's payroll.

The rather blunt exchanges that flitted between NBC executives over musical talent and telegeneity in the 1930s align with two of Simon Frith's observations, that "the dominant use of music on television, one might conclude, is to sell things" and "looking good on television has always been essential for success" (2002: 281–84). It is important to acknowledge, however, that the social practices and the discourses informing early television's commercial trends and its visual character also have their own unique histories. Each evolved in a nonlinear fashion as various industrial and cultural factors ebbed and surged. As television progressed through the 1930s, there was never a doubt that it would be anything other than commercial (the balance between culturally edifying content, strictly educational fare, and popular entertainment remained a point of considerable debate), yet in this early instance, television was not a fully realized technological medium *or* a commercially viable broadcast option. Much of the commentary in the 1930s was subsequently hypothetical, projecting various cultural values, hopes, and ideals as much as solid plans for television's future.

From the 1920s to the late 1940s prominent inventors (in the United States, Allen B. Du Mont, Philo T. Farnsworth, C. Francis Jenkins, and Vladimir Zworykin among them) or teams of comparatively anonymous scientists in corporate laboratories (A.T.T., General Electric, and Westinghouse were most prominent) worked to construct reliable TV studio production equipment or reception appliances while executives applied themselves to building an efficient television broadcasting system. For the science and engineering wizzes, content was a subordinate concern that served a purpose for the testing of transmission and reception. Jonathan Sterne identifies similar tendencies in sound reproduction experiments of the late eighteenth and early nineteenth centuries (involving recordings on phonograph cylinders), observing that the content of the recordings were "clearly aimed at the middle-class market" (featuring musical pieces that echoed "the range of subject matter in other middle-class entertainment") and that "the recordings were very much limited by the parameters of the available technology" (2003; 244). In reproducing and transmitting sound, simple phrases and familiar musical ditties (or, at least, familiar musical genres such as marches) were the standard for laboratory experiments and for public demonstrations.

According to Richard Koszarski (2008), in their rudimentary broadcasts the engineer-headed experimental TV stations in New York City and the surrounding environs all at one time or another featured children's vocal choruses and adult soloists, piano players and instrumentalists, and the occasional Broadway performer. The CBS network launched its television station W2XAB with much fanfare in July 1931; while still very much an experimental station, the launch featured musical performances by the talented radio and recording vocal trio the Boswell Sisters,[1] the newcomer Kate Smith (her radio and recording career still ahead of her), and the inestimable George Gershwin, who performed the song "Liza," composed two years earlier. With the technological barriers rapidly falling away in the 1930s, television's content and the accompanying issues of visual allure were reprioritized among the broadcast industry's executive decision-makers, who turned their focus toward presentational aesthetics and programming strategies that, like the prior sound reproduction trials, might appeal to middle-class values and middlebrow tastes.[2]

In 1935, NBC's Bertha Brainard again figured in discussions about the intensifying need to define television's programming and refine the visualization of popular music. She received a memorandum from William Fairbanks of the network's Statistical Department, who referred to an experimental demonstration on June 3, 1935, at the NBC television laboratory located in Camden, New Jersey, that, as he explains, included "a very ambitious sight and sound reproduction of Fred Waring's rendition of 'Lullaby of Broadway' as a production number" (1935). The decision to emphasize Waring's performance was surely based in his general popularity as a bandleader and his prior film experience: he and his band The Pennsylvanians had participated in the production of Vitaphone musical shorts in the late 1920s and in 1929 they headlined in the film *Syncopation*, "the first feature-length musical made in New York" (Koszarski 2008: 170).

Fairbanks enclosed a copy of the script from the Camden demonstration detailing a forty-five-minute musical production structured upon a recognizable Broadway theater format featuring music selections sung by the cast (composed of Billy Milton, Sara Allgood, Rose Walker, Reita Nugent, Georgie Harris, Charlie Woods, and a dance chorus aptly called The Eight Good Lookers) with musical accompaniment by Sydney Jerome's seven-piece band. The 1935 demonstration featured typical production numbers and popular songs associated with Tin Pan Alley, Broadway theater, and Hollywood films such as "Rock and Roll," "Zing Went the Strings of My Heart," "Sady O'Grady," "Forty-Second Street," "Sidewalks of Cuba," "Here Comes That Rainbow," "I'm on the Crest of a Wave," "When Love Comes Swinging Along," "Limehouse Blues," "Old Folks at Home," "It's an Old Southern Custom," "The Man from Harlem," "Mood Indigo," and the aforementioned "Lullaby of Broadway."

Though no visual record remains of this television experiment, the script reveals several key production considerations with a pronounced reliance on established theatrical and cinematic performance conventions encompassing repertoire, staging, and (to lesser extent) interstitial dialogue. The show's loosely structured narrative and musical performances portrayed ersatz versions of various New York City locales in all of their cultural and spatial diversity: Broadway, China Town, Harlem, and the swank Rainbow Room nightclub (which had opened less than a year earlier on the sixty-fifth floor of the GE Building at Rockefeller Center, where the NBC corporate headquarters are also housed). Interestingly, the influence of radio is entirely absent in the discussion; the production logic was anchored in visual performance styles that immersed audience members in a fantasy spectacle, promising a generally pleasant experience while virtually "transporting" them to other cultural locales. The TV demonstration also harbored latent similarities with filmed travelogues that displayed exciting or exotic Otherness cohering within recognized cultural sites. We can see here that the aesthetic push-and-pull between the existing communication media and various performance sites and forms was not yet resolved, and TV's early experimental process explored the potentialities of each option for future musical productions.

Script notes explain the character of the studio set designs for each musical number, describing the construction of ersatz urban spaces and props that reflect the highly staged aspect of the broadcast production. Offering basic stage directions with cast entrances and exits, the script also illustrates how, even in 1935, there was careful forethought about television's onscreen action, camera placement, and shot composition, and the communication of presentational intimacy forged in the dynamics between musical talent and the camera. Simultaneity, immediacy, and a sense of presence were as crucial to early television as they were to theater.

Lynn Spigel addresses these representational issues and television's distinguishing characteristics with the observation,

> Television, it was constantly argued, would be a better approximation of live entertainment than any previous form of technological reproduction. Its ability to broadcast direct to the home would allow people to feel as if they really were at the theater. . . . According to the popular wisdom, then, television was able to reproduce reality in a way no previous medium could. Whereas film allowed spectators imaginatively to project themselves *into a scene*, television would give people the sense of being *on the scene* of presentation — it would simulate the entire experience of being at the theater. (1992: 138–39)

Proximity, intimacy, liveness, and an ideal perspective or "perfect view" (ibid.: 140) that privileged the audience member were important features of early TV broadcasting even as the medium experienced programming and technical modifications. Although television had yet to fully mature, by 1935 the conceptual framework and representational principles that eventually came to dominate were already discernible and many of the general qualities inscribed in this early "TV laboratory" trial remained more or less intact when television was finally introduced on a massive commercial scale at the end of the 1940s.

Though the Camden experiment stands out for its detail and complexity,

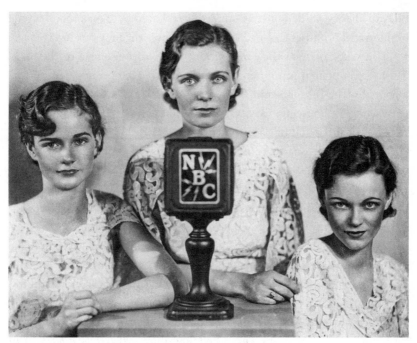

The Pickens Sisters. NBC radio, circa mid-1930s. COURTESY OF PHOTOFEST.

similar experiments involving popular music performances continued throughout the 1930s. In 1936, the television pioneer Philo T. Farnsworth hired the Nick Ross Orchestra to appear on his self-operated experimental station W3XPF in Philadelphia, where he also featured preadolescent amateurs in televised song and dance routines (Fisher and Fisher 1996: 253). Also in 1936, NBC introduced musical artists including the popular radio trio the Pickens Sisters in a promotional demonstration that was narrowly beamed to televisions viewed by invited network insiders, advertising executives, and select members of the press corps.

Later that year, a further demonstration was conducted for the press under what NBC and RCA jointly termed "practical working conditions. . . . It represented the first showing of a complete program built for entertainment value as well as a demonstration of transmission" ("Television Developments" 1936). The network's explicit announcement of "practical working conditions" implies that this was more than a simple experiment, rather, something akin to a product roll-out; its purpose was not merely to titillate reporters with a vision of what TV broadcasting *may one day be* but was a much more grounded presentation asserting what TV *is*. In terms of corporate expediency the demonstration was also an attempt to make good on the promotional promises that had accumulated over the previous several years while serving notice to the competition that NBC was ahead of the pack. Music again figured prominently and the demonstration featured performances by The Inkspots and Hildegarde, a likable if unremarkable chanteuse whose in-house moniker was "The Television Girl" on account of her telegenic qualities and frequent participation in NBC's early experiments.

A young Frank Sinatra, recognized as an emerging star during his tenure with the Harry James Orchestra (and soon to join forces with the Tommy Dorsey Orchestra), was invited to participate in NBC's experimental TV broadcasts in 1939, but he demurred. Broadcast experiments continued without Sinatra in NBC's cramped and overheated studio 3H in midtown Manhattan, with Dinah Shore singing for the closed circuit system well before she reached full blossom as a top recording, film, and television star ("Dinah in Blackface" 1949; Ritchie 1994; Kisseloff 1995: 56). At the DuMont studios, the program host Dennis James (a former radio disk jockey with WNEW in New York who went on to define the role of the TV host) was also tentatively exploring the new medium with a fledgling show called *Television Roof* in 1939. The show featured the vocal group The Pied Pipers, which included Jo Stafford (Kisseloff 1995: 68). In these instances musicians served a primarily functional role since their performances fulfilled the network's demonstration objectives yet demanded minimal scripts or none at all, making them a cheap and effective solution to the medium's content dilemma. Demonstrational presentations at this stage featured popular songs as a rule, not as an exception, and in so doing they primed the public for a visual medium that included popular music as a vital component.

Music's central significance in television development continued when NBC made its grand—and ultimately premature—announcement of regular television programming at the 1939 New York World's Fair (the subsequent broadcasts originated from station W2XBS in mid-town Manhattan). The company introduced the famed Broadway composer Richard Rogers (accompanying the theater singer Mary Wescott on piano), as well as Fred Waring and his Pennsylvanians, broadcasting their well-known dance band selections to those on the fairgrounds and to the roughly 250 television households in the New York area; according to NBC's estimates, this number eventually climbed to roughly 2,000 set owners by the end of the year ("RCA and NBC" 1940). The World's Fair broadcasts were proudly touted as the official launch of NBC's television division, although critics at the time were divided on the achievement: on the one hand there was much excitement and anticipation about the prospect of regular TV entertainment, but on the other hand reporters were generally unimpressed, commenting in exquisite detail about the abysmal quality of the broadcast performances.

In retrospect it was perhaps providential that television's progress was interrupted by the outbreak of war in the early 1940s since the public was not yet fully convinced about TV's value and there was much room for improvement. James Von Schilling (2003) explains how the cost of television sets (around $500) during the 1939 Fair remained prohibitive for many families. Purchasing a TV set was not a priority when fine musical entertainment could be had for free over cheaper radio sets or, for a reasonable cost, at public theaters and nightclubs. Phonograph players and records, too, were both less expensive and already established as a consumer item. The Federal Communications Commission (FCC) also voiced concern that consumers would be enticed to spend on televisions before the technology or the programming reached a standard of acceptability. Though the cost of TV sets was sharply reduced as part of an aggressive marketing campaign, the content still did not justify the expense; according to Richard Koszarski, "The public expected value for money" (2008: 465).

With the buildup to the war, more urgent issues beset all the major players in television development, including the TV set manufacturers, the networks, and the government's policy makers. Philip Auslander writes of this period: "The first television era in the United States . . . occurred between 1939 and 1945, for although programming and the industrial development of television were truncated by the war effort, the discourse on television remained lively during the war years" (1999: 14). Auslander's assessment is generally accurate; broadcasting experiments and demonstrations involving popular music performances did not completely halt during the war years even though the mission and priorities at the networks were seriously altered. Both CBS and NBC briefly suspended their operations in 1942, yet the General Electric studio in Schenectady, New York, and the fledgling DuMont network continued their studio experiments. In fact, television's technical development was assisted by various spin-off benefits from electronic engineering and scientific research oriented toward the war effort. While the greatest progress during the war was in the technical realm, production and programming work also advanced, albeit within a reduced scope and with lesser aspirations.

Photographs published between 1944 and 1945 in the DuMont corporation's monthly newsletter *The Raster* depict musical artists in the network's New York television studio working on performance and broadcast productions while the war raged. The musicians represent a remarkable range of genres, including the celebrity bandleader Waring accompanied by members of his Glee Club vocal group, the "negro" folk singer Josh White, Margaret Johnson (wearing a cowboy hat, singing the western classic "Don't Fence Me In"), and two unnamed Latin music trios. James Von Schilling also cites a 1944 NBC broadcast featuring the wide-eyed song-and-dance man Eddie Cantor, who encountered the first documented case of network censorship while performing "We're Having a Baby, My Baby and Me" that featured arguably suggestive lyrics (Von Schilling 2003: 53). As these examples illustrate, popular music was central in television's ongoing (and very local) broadcast trials while the nation was at war, even though the music industry and many of the top orchestras of the period were rent apart by enlistment, fuel rationing, and other constraints.

The diversity of acts appearing on television through the war years, spanning a musical and cultural spectrum, defies the still relatively common notion that early television was relentlessly homogeneous. The fact that televised musical performances cleaved toward mainstream, middlebrow tastes (Mundy 1999) is not to say that the broadcasts were uniform in their musical content or performance aesthetics. In many ways, television was more consistently varied in its formative phase than it was in later decades. Television producers who were still toiling to perfect the medium tapped into an assortment of musical forms representing an array of cultural sensibilities and ethnic or racial backgrounds. These industry architects were intent on honing their facility with different music and performance styles in the quest to introduce a broad range of musical performances to the slowly growing ranks of television viewers.

Aesthetic Ideals and Critical Predictions

Citing television's promise and predicting its positive cultural influence during the war years, Robert Lee wrote in 1944, "Everybody should know about television, because it's going to be 'everybody's art.' Television belongs to the people — more than motion pictures, or even radio. There isn't one person in the United States who won't be affected by television" (1944: 6). Lee's optimism was rooted in what he believed were television's democratic and artistic potentials as a medium (following the rhetoric of TV's more ardent promoters), although history reveals that, apart from his final remark, his views were rather naive.

In his assessment and predictions specifically about music, Lee curiously undermined TV's distinguishing visual element, stressing that the images should remain secondary to the aural experience of any televised musical performance. His comments reflect an outlook that was likely influenced by the prevailing modes of reception and audience listening demeanor at classical music concerts or the comfort and familiarity associated with electrical home entertainment appliances: "In presenting music, the sight channel must always be the hand-maiden to sound. When the video screen cannot conceivably add anything to a musical effect, producers must have the courage to leave it blank. This is true of much of the world's music. As a matter of fact, most great music can be best enjoyed in darkness; any activity on the screen would be distracting" (ibid.: 10). As Lee envisioned it, capable musicians would be called upon to perform in their standard manner, but it was, in his opinion, improperly left to the television producers, camera crews, and technicians to coax and shape the performance's compelling elements according to the medium's visual capacity. The studio experiments up to this point showed that musicians' expertise and talent were overwhelmed by the comparatively inexperienced and clumsy efforts of the TV production units. Despite his enthusiasm and support for the primacy of the musical performance, Lee's particular misgivings were soon realized: the visual regime of television proved to be a formidable force and music's aural qualities were regularly subordinated to the scopic pleasures offered by handsome male and beguiling female performers or to the spectacular production numbers that quickly became television staples.

Lee's perspective also seemed to rely on TV sounds being of acceptable, if not necessarily pristine quality, yet the poor-to-mediocre sound of most early television sets (roughly on par with those of the average mid-price radio receiver) conspired with the low-resolution images of the tiny screens to produce what were reported to be a less-than-rewarding audience experience (VanCour 2011). Whereas the voice carried reasonably well in early television's dramatic performances (depending on proper microphone placement and related staging aspects) or on sports broadcasts under normal circumstances, musical performances, especially those involving multi-instrumental arrangements and nuanced orchestral presentations, were poorly served.

Lee was more accurate, however, in his predictions when he noted, "Top name-bands — especially when enhanced by interesting camera-handling — are especially adaptable: the solid showmanship of Fred Waring's Pennsylvanians; leaders with singularly visual personalities, such as Kay Kyser and Cab Calloway; or Xavier Cugat, whose talents as a cartoonist can add a whimsical touch to his telecasts of South American melodies" (ibid.: 107). Lee identifies specific musicians whose performance skills and spectacular excesses were already well-established facets of their performance aesthetic, lending them additional cachet as the new industry sought feasible talent-as-content. Each of the musicians Lee mentions did, in fact, go on to active television careers as invited guests or as program hosts. Of those listed, it was the comparatively subdued Waring (who had already performed in front of TV cameras and under the blazing hot studio lights in prewar and wartime experimental broadcasts with NBC and Du Mont) who would enjoy the greatest success, eventually hosting his own show featuring a sixty-member musical agglomeration on CBS from 1949 to 1954 and again, briefly, in 1957.

Anticipating enhanced artistic innovation in the combination of music and images, several commentators in the 1940s focused on the promising experiments in *synaesthesia* (a condition whereby the senses are involuntarily stimulated by a single catalyst; for example, one may experience an overwhelming sensation of visual shape and color while hearing a musical passage). Kay Dickinson defines the condition as "the transportation of sensory images from one modality into another. Synaesthetes claim the ability to see music (usually in terms of color) or to taste shapes, with the former being the most common of its manifestations and the most pertinent to the study of music video" (2007: 14).

Animators and other visual artists (Thomas Wilfred or Oskar Fischinger among them)[3] attempted to merge the sensory experiences of sound and sight, creating free-form nonnarrative films involving abstract electronic images that throb and glow in varying intensities, matching transitions in the musical arrangements. Robert Lee also described such possibilities for television, referring in 1944 to the mechanical "image-organ" — consisting of a cyclorama "upon which appears a kaleidoscopic whirling of patterns and shadows in cadence with the music" (1944: 109).

Seeking a different model for TV emulation, Mildred Steffens (1945) identified *Fantasia*, Walt Disney's animated film released in 1940, as an ideal example of tasteful, artistic musical presentation. She suggested that television's visual artists might create animated accompaniment à la Disney or design abstract and symbolic light and image renderings of classical music performances for television broadcast. Steffens's references to "optical accompaniment" were not, however, entirely accommodating of "popular" music; instead, she framed her preferences within a discourse of musical aesthetics and quality that unambiguously favored classical music. Steffens explained, "When television promotion again goes forward following 'V' day, a maturer, more thoughtful public will demand serious programs of good variety. And it will insist upon music—'good' music. . . . Although we are limiting ourselves here to a discussion of good music, even 'swing' can be visualized with tremendous effect" (1945: 9). It is worth emphasizing that, like Lee, Steffens regarded musical instrumentation as the dominant element, with TV's visual effects accentuating or otherwise reinforcing the arrangement in a secondary role.

Addressing the artistic creation of what he termed "audivisual music," Ralph Potter also cited the brilliance of Disney's *Fantasia*, although his interests at the time lay within the wartime development of electronic rather than mechanical technologies, including light response mechanisms such as "the sound spectograph" that "picture musical notes in action . . . with visuals accompanying sound in unison" (1947: 74). Praise for *Fantasia*, with its soaring classical soundtrack, was widespread in this period, and if there were any doubts about the high-art pretensions of Disney's animated extravaganza, these were allayed by the film's narrative voice, provided by Deems Taylor, the composer, music critic, and first radio announcer of the New York Metropolitan Opera's radio broadcasts (in 1931, on NBC), who added experience and gravitas to the film's renderings of familiar symphonic compositions (Pegolotti 2003: 188–90).

It is striking that, while music is the chief interest in these assessments and proposals, there is little effort to address the portrayal of actual musical performances. The musicians are relegated to the background or, worse, they are merely assigned to the soundtrack while the image-music correlation is achieved via technical or graphic means. Notwithstanding these predictions and appraisals for the visualization of music, the television networks showed little inclination to adopt them or to reproduce *Fantasia*'s animated style for the small screen.

The home television, it was suggested, would eventually provide an entertaining visual appliance that either augmented or surpassed the basic aural experience of listening to radio broadcasts or phonograph recordings. There were also occasional debates about the hierarchy of the human senses, displaying a prevailing set of social values and a latent belief that sight is of a higher sensual rank than hearing. In the music trade magazine *Billboard* this visual privileging produced the interesting term "em-see" (instead of MC or emcee) to describe television program hosts, with the term "fem-see" applying to female show hosts. Through the postwar years, expert predictions, industry proclamations, and media speculation about television accelerated, with many touting the medium as a logical and welcome cultural achievement or an avatar of progress, in the process fanning the flames of public anticipation for television's new pleasures.

Another set of descriptions at the time compared television to public (or nondomestic) entertainment contexts, most frequently relating television entertainment to existing options of the cultural arena, notably the cinema or performances in theaters or nightclubs. This comparison implicitly acknowledged that these leisure pastimes had achieved ritual status within American culture and were, thus, a standard aspect of everyday life for many Americans. Cast in this light, television's most aggressive promoters (including network executives and television set manufacturers) sought to discursively normalize television, aligning it with typical entertainment interests and leisure patterns.

Viewers were promised "the best seat in the house" (reinforcing ideals of individualized reception), or else audiences were assured that the medium would deliver quality entertainment in the style and form of familiar musical showcases while freeing them from the cost and effort of attending actual public events. In the midst of this promotional phase it seems that few people asked the question whether American entertainment was such a priority or if people sought or demanded alternative leisure options. That they did was a largely unchallenged assumption on the part of broadcasting and advertising industries. Indeed, this underlying assumption has been maintained throughout the years since television's introduction and continues to inform the development of many subsequent leisure and entertainment commodities.

While prevailing attitudes invoked the element of convenience, television's development was also explained as a matter of rational economics as the TV industry's executive deliberations and public promotional strategies often framed a TV set purchase as a one-time financial outlay for years and years of home-based entertainment. As one early advertising campaign declared, television was "the greatest free show on earth!" although, by 1953, this same phrase was cynically employed in *Variety* as the industry lamented the rising costs of TV talent and the rapidly increased expense of producing musical programs (Rosen 1953: 1). Such claims for TV's contributions to leisure and entertainment were initially a matter of faith since the early programming schedule did not offer much upon which to form an opinion and what did exist was, as many reviews of the day indicated, of dubious quality.

The TV set manufacturers and networks promised potential consumers and audiences that television would eventually flourish, although the promises had been forthcoming for over a decade and the medium still remained far beneath the praises heaped upon it. Cultural critics and industry watchdogs reported on each new development and innovation, providing considerable publicity for the burgeoning medium yet granting no quarter to the industry when the actual product lagged so far behind the promotional hype. Slow TV set sales were a major concern for the industry, especially as manufacturers repeatedly fell short of their sales projections and sweated over the corporate costs and the pressure from increasingly impatient investors and shareholders (Baughman 2007). Over time, as the television networks established a track record by offering increased programming (including a shift away from remote broadcasts of sports events or simple roundtable discussions featuring various "experts," community leaders, or authorities) and demonstrating a new production savvy, they could point to their mounting achievements as proof that the medium was indeed able to provide solid musical entertainment and, thus, offer value to viewers.

By the end of the war, television was far more than "an eccentric idea offered by a few esoteric inventors" as William Chafe (1986) and Constance Hill (2000) each claim. After almost twenty years of development and continual technical improvement, it was about to erupt as a full-fledged industrial sector. While there remained substantial doubts about how television might fare, the corporate broadcast networks and TV set manufacturers were gearing up for a concentrated thrust into the market. Given the sheer scale of the industry buildup, there was little to suggest that this was simply an "eccentric idea" but, rather, a major incursion into American business and cultural life. With greater technological consistency and production reliability in the late 1940s, television programming and content issues were prioritized. The specific question of musical presentation rose as a regular topic, spilling into the entertainment trade papers such as *Billboard*, *Down Beat*, *Metronome*, and *Variety*. The popular press also weighed in on television's programming developments, and reporters such as John Crosby at the *New York Herald Tribune* and Jack Gould of the *New York Times*, among others, soon emerged as important monitors of the rising television industry, providing astute analysis of policies and technical developments as well as offering keen criticism of TV's musical content.

American Federation of Musicians and James C. Petrillo

During the Depression and the war years, American laborers found solace and support among unions and the steady rise of both union organizing and membership inexorably influenced the country's economic and social character. In this period the American Federation of Musicians (AFM) effectively secured standard wage scales and employee protection for professional musicians, but the changing patterns of radio broadcasting, jukebox production, and phonograph recording in the 1930s and 1940s intensified the AFM's role and enhanced its status.

Throughout the 1940s, the AFM, under the fiery leadership of its president, James C. Petrillo (who took over the union presidency in 1940), confronted a complex scenario in which musical styles, audience tastes, and commercial demand each underwent substantial change. The influences of war presented several serious challenges to musicians and to their union; after the war, the union played a pivotal role in the concurrent evolution of popular music and television as the union battled with the recording, radio broadcast, and television industries. The AFM had always remained attuned to developments across the entertainment and broadcast industries and Petrillo was cognizant of television's significance and its potential consequences for the nation's musicians, especially after NBC's 1939 New York World's Fair debut when the network's premiere broadcasts prominently featured musical performances. Although the union set a preliminary television wage scale as early as 1943, signing a contract with the emerging networks that permitted union musicians to perform on TV programs, the arrangement proved to be premature since television was insufficiently evolved at the time and the war's effects constituted a barrier to its development.

The AFM engaged in heated squabbles with the recording and broadcasting industries during the war years, even going so far as to ban recording altogether in 1942–44 in an attempt to secure a fair and manageable royalty system and to restrict reproduction without remuneration from radio broadcasters. Paul Chevigny recounts that "the ban made Petrillo's name synonymous in the press with 'dictatorial' and 'featherbedding' labor tactics" (1993: 24). Showing a fighter's resolve, Petrillo also rescinded the union's permission for its members to appear on television in 1945, with the pugnacious union man expressing the view that it was ill advised to commit to an industry that had yet to fully mature.

The ban on televised musical performances lasted for three years, just when the television networks and set manufacturers were preparing to launch their ventures in earnest. Chevigny explains, "More importantly, the bans resulted in national outcry against Petrillo, and in legislation directed against organized labor in general and the musicians union in particular" (ibid.). With musicians surging back into society after their military service, the AFM's importance was reinforced and Petrillo wielded his authority and influence with what his critics denounced as imperiousness, sarcastically citing his middle name, "Caesar," as an appropriate character metaphor. Nonetheless, Petrillo proved to be a wily and tireless adversary as he negotiated with government policy makers and with corporate executives from the recording and broadcast sectors.

Petrillo accurately predicted radio's gradual reliance on recorded music, a trend that emerged throughout the 1940s, and he confronted the radio broadcast industry by seeking suitable compensation as "live" musical performances, studio orchestras, and remote dance band broadcasts were scaled back. Among his demands was that radio networks pay musicians on a retainer basis rather than hiring them under sporadic contracts or on a part-time basis. He also expressed serious concerns about the television networks' plans; with kinescope and film technologies at their disposal, televised music performances could, like any record, potentially be stored and replayed at will with virtually no additional cost to the networks and without proper guaranteed remuneration (what came to be termed residual payments or "residuals") for the musicians involved. It was this aspect of television, not the airing of live musical performances, that most irked Petrillo.

In an open letter to the AFM national membership in 1946 Petrillo voiced a three-part rationale for the TV appearance ban, citing the possibility that television could decimate the radio jobs currently available to union musicians; that the medium might ignore active musicians by relying substantially on kinescopes or films featuring prerecorded musical soundtracks; and that television-radio simulcasts should require dual contracts covering musician performance fees on each medium rather than acquiescing to the broadcasters' desire to pay only a single fee (Petrillo 1946). Stating his position, he wrote to the union rank-and-file members: "Television is not going to grow at the expense of the musicians. As television grows, the musician is

President Harry Truman playing piano, accompanied by James C. Petrillo, president, American Federation of Musicians. June 15, 1954. COURTESY OF THE HARRY S. TRUMAN LIBRARY.

going to grow with it, or we are not going to assist in its development. The sooner our critics — I should say our 'severe' critics — understand that musicians, who have been exploited for years, studied their instruments for a livelihood and not just to play for the love of it, the better off we will all be" (ibid.).

Notwithstanding the criticism leveled at Petrillo for his clashes with the expanding entertainment industries (including interunion conflicts with the American Federation of Television-Radio Actors/AFTRA and, occasionally, discord with his own union's locals), he was always fiercely committed to his union as well as to fortifying his own strength and authority at the helm of the AFM. In his brawls with the radio and recording companies and, later, the television networks, Petrillo's actions also exhibited shrewdly conceived political agendas that were important to his wider public profile while improving his stature within the union. He benefited in no small way from a close personal friendship with President Harry Truman, who was a piano player of modest talent and considered as someone who might sympathize with the plight of unemployed or underpaid musicians (Petrillo gave the president a gold "honorary lifetime member" union card in 1949).[4]

In a trend beginning almost immediately following the war's end, the market for the once reigning touring orchestras and dance bands dwindled. The demise of several "name" orchestras in December 1946 (including, as Lewis Erenberg itemizes them, those of Les Brown, Benny Carter, Tommy Dorsey, Benny Goodman, Woody Herman, Ina Ray Hutton, Harry James, and Jack Teagarden) stunned the popular music industry, corroding the foundation of the commercial music business. Erenberg summarizes the situation and its dire implications when he explains, "The growing funeral parade of bands sent shock waves through the music world. . . . The end of so many top orchestras ran counter to people's hopes for the postwar music scene. . . . The postwar depression that so many had feared became a reality in the band business; bright hopes turned dark" (1998: 213–14).

The costs associated with maintaining the large orchestras was certainly a factor, as was the reality that audiences were encountering a major case of aesthetic fatigue, growing weary of swing and big-band jazz, which had been the dominant musical form for over a decade. Moreover, with the war's end, the music business was flooded with talent, creating a deluge of available musical labor for a limited professional market.

Musicians who had relied on nightclub employment during the 1930s and throughout the war years also faced dire conditions in the postwar period and individuals working in the music industry or in related cultural sectors were understandably fretful about their professional prospects. *Life* magazine cited a 30 percent drop in nightclub attendance in 1947: "Nightclubs are a surprisingly accurate barometer of U.S. luxury spending. Fewer surplus dollars jingled in the public pocketbook and nightclubs were first to feel the pinch. . . . [I]n New York impresarios were suffering from what the trade calls 'snow-blindness,' an occupational disease brought on by staring at too many white tablecloths uncluttered by customers" ("Nightclubs" 1947: 109). Considering the declining economics of the music industry, there was a latent optimism that television broadcasting could evolve as an important source of musical employment. In the view of many struggling musicians, television couldn't have come at a better time since it was beyond comprehension to think that they would not be hired as an essential facet of television's entertainment package.

Along with fluctuations in the band business, the immediate postwar period also saw the rise and entrenchment of a powerful labor base across the nation's production sectors as the gains of a wartime economy were transferred to peacetime prosperity. Marty Jezer explains that membership in the nation's major union organizations was at a historical high and, flush with membership dues, the unions were well positioned to skirmish with corporate employers while continuing to fund organizing initiatives and membership drives (1982: 78). William Chafe explains, "No group had greater optimism at the end of the war than organized labor. . . . Indeed, the surge of labor organization prompted one scholar to suggest that the United States was 'gradually shifting from a capitalistic community to a laboristic one' — that is, to a community in which employees rather than businessmen are the strongest single influence" (1986: 92).

The AFM was similarly strengthened in this period, yet union members were severely affected by the combined flux in the nation's economy and in audience tastes, and in several locals a sense of frustration set in. Despite his steadfastness on their behalf, among struggling union musicians there existed a creeping sense that Petrillo's confrontational approach to the music and broadcasting industries was counterproductive to their employment interests, antagonizing potential employers and narrowing their performance options. His intransigence, based on principle, politics, or personal style mattered little to the union's economically disenfranchised musicians. Petrillo also lost several key battles.

For instance, Petrillo's demand that radio broadcasters maintain studio musicians and orchestra members on a retainer basis whether they intended to use them or not was regarded by broadcasters — and the government — as tantamount to extortion, and Petrillo's critics regarded his actions as little more than criminal racketeering. His attempt to impose a levy on recordings that might be broadcast on the radio was similarly castigated. After extensive hearings of the Congressional House Committee on Interstate and Foreign Commerce under the guidance of Chairman Clarence F. Lea, the U.S. Congress passed the Lea Act in 1946 as an unambiguous response to Petrillo's uncompromising stance toward the radio broadcasting industry (and, as Lea explained in a letter written in 1946 to the National Association of Broadcasters, a handful of other "practices").[5] The congressional action — unofficially known as the "Anti-Petrillo Act" — refuted the AFM's power of coercion in the radio sector and among the act's immediate outcomes was the dismissal of hundreds of musicians from broadcasters' payrolls and the gradual eradication of radio studio orchestras with the end of the union's "standby" contract provision.

The advertising and broadcast industry trade paper *Sponsor* reported in early 1947 that regional radio disk jockeys were also contributing to transitions in the music industry, gaining new ground by spinning records by top artists while the major networks' "live" performance broadcasts of the same musicians often fared less well: "Dinah Shore platters compete with the *Ford Show* with Dinah Shore; Old Gold's Frank Sinatra session on CBS fights a number of 'Frankie' sessions on turntables all over the nation; and so on through the night" ("Music Sells" 1947: 21). The main music industry trade papers, *Billboard*, *Down Beat*, and *Variety*, described a rather dire set of conditions, acknowledging that a growing number of union musicians faced an indeterminate future. Petrillo saw corporate broadcast practices as being harmful to his union and its collective interests and, accordingly, he attempted to reassert the AFM's power by establishing the Recording and Transcription Fund, a fee charged to broadcasters and transcription companies by the union regardless of whether the recordings were ever actually replayed on radio or not. Petrillo imposed the fees preemptively as a precaution against the broadcasting industry's proven inclination to avoid additional recompense for subsequent or repeat airings of recorded material.

His efforts on behalf of the union were once again thwarted by direct and decisive federal involvement. In August 1947, The Labor-Management Relations Act, known as the "Taft-Hartley Act" (sponsored by Senator Robert Taft and Representative Fred Hartley Jr.), was written into law. The act was a biting piece of federal legislation with the stated intent to protect both employers and workers by ensuring, among other things, that the nation's business productivity would not be interrupted by strikes, picketing, boycotts, or other "disorderly" activities, especially involving secondary strikes by sympathetic unions. The unwritten intent was to curb the power of American labor unions. The act's various clauses also collided with the AFM's practice of collecting fees through its Recording and Transcription Fund as well as tempering Petrillo's constant threat of a nation-wide AFM strike against the broadcasting and recording industries. Though Petrillo's old friend President Harry Truman attempted to veto the act, his effort was defeated after an extended Senate filibuster. As the Taft-Hartley Act, section 302, states, it is forbidden to "cause or attempt to cause an employer to pay or deliver or agree to pay or deliver any money or other things of value, in the nature of an extraction for services which are not performed or not to be performed," a ruling that effectively rendered the AFM's Recording and Transcription Fund illegal.

With television's imminent commercial breakout, the instinctive fear within the AFM in 1947 was that any reliance on recorded material could further harm musicians, reducing employment and negatively impacting revenues that traditionally accrued to them from performances. Additionally, the union was concerned that television broadcasting might erode finances deriving from jukeboxes and radio broadcasts if audiences switched to television for their entertainment. Such apprehensions were not unreasonable (as rudimentary audience and consumer research surveys indicated) and though no single factor can be identified as the main culprit, television *did* quickly challenge other established entertainment options by creating new competition for audience attention.[6] Petrillo was keenly aware that, as dues-paying members, working musicians contributed to a stronger and more financially empowered union over which he presided. Television was sure to add to the estimated $25 million that radio already contributed to the AFM coffers by the late 1940s.

Petrillo's staunchest detractors hoped that the governmental edicts would alleviate his renowned belligerence and combativeness; they were to be disappointed. Following the signing of the Lea Act and the Taft-Hartley Act, the angered but unrepentant AFM leader imposed the second recording ban in less than a decade in January 1948. By instating the 1948 AFM recording ban, Petrillo sought to ensure that musicians were not financially compromised as the radio stations continued their trend away from remote or studio music performances by turning toward the nefarious disk jockey; DJs spinning recorded songs were on the cusp of attaining a new and powerful role as sales motivators and musical tastemakers and without a responsive royalty system in place, the AFM regarded them as the enemy. Although in the long run DJs helped to spur music sales among the youth demographic, promoting R & B and the soon-to-emerge rock 'n' roll genre, in the late 1940s the outcomes could not be predicted.

As Russell Sanjek and David Sanjek (1991: 83) recount, the prospect of yet another AFM recording ban sent the major record companies into a frenzy of studio recording sessions. They hurried to produce an archive of unreleased material that would provide a cushion during the ban since songs recorded prior to the ban were not restricted from the market. Whereas the first ban in 1942 had caught the labels shorthanded and, in some instances, without sufficient recorded material to see them through the ban (or reduced to releasing vocal/acappella recordings—vocalists were exempt from the ban), the situation was different in 1948 when the major labels anticipated Petrillo's actions.

With vaults of recordings in place they were better prepared to fight Petrillo while continuing to release new material to the market. Staying the course, the record industry was able to outwait Petrillo with negligible damage. The ban extended almost a full year, until late 1948, when the AFM and recording companies finally agreed to the formation of the Music Performance Trust Fund, through which industry monies were paid into a separate nonunion account and then reallocated to the union to pay musicians to perform in free public concerts and musical exhibitions. The fund differed from the earlier Recording and Transcription Fund in that it was administered by an impartial trustee agreed upon by the record labels and the union (*Music Performance Trust Fund* 1949).

While the recording companies were mostly able to circumvent Petrillo's commanding decrees, television broadcasters were in a fix. With his ban on TV performances by union members, Petrillo held up the broadcasters, who were now certain that their new medium would rely heavily on musical programming. The AFM announcement came just as the nation's industrial manufacturers began to produce electrical home appliances (including radios and phonographs) in unprecedented volume and as the budding television industry hastened its program development and promotions for a nationwide market. The television networks attempted to maneuver around the union's TV ban as numerous extant NBC memoranda reveal. In response to the AFM's music restrictions, a memorandum sent by Ray O'Connell to the NBC national program manager, Thomas McCray, in late 1947 presents an extensive list describing a series of network programs with status reports on their musical material, designating programs within categories, "not affected by strike," "substitute program required," "could be done by using recorded musical background and bridges," "show could be done without music," and "program would require extensive revision."

With no clear sense of when the AFM would relent, the entire 1948 season program schedule was cast into doubt, necessitating alternative musical strategies and in some cases the dissolution of TV studio orchestras or cancellation of shows. In his statements to the House Committee on Education and Labor in January 1948, Justin Miller, the president of the National Association of Broadcasters excoriated Petrillo (a nemesis whom he loathed), explaining, "If as a result of this artificial restriction television is permitted to develop without musicians, musicians may lose potential jobs. If this happens, the result will be ascribable, not to the development of a new technology and not to the desire of employers, but solely to Mr. Petrillo's own ruling." With emphatic clarity, Miller declared, "Mr. Petrillo is educating a generation of television broadcasters in how to program television without the use of musicians" (1948).

These numerous overlapping clashes again revealed Petrillo's stubborn character as a negotiator. Obviously unafraid to confront the large entertainment corporations, major broadcast associations, or the government, he was unapologetic about revoking the networks' access to unionized musical talent. It was by this point inconceivable to either television's advocates or its critics that the medium could advance without featuring popular musical performances, and TV executives and others with stakes in the medium's advancement were justifiably livid. The NAB's Miller explicitly labeled Petrillo "an economic pirate," a leader with "absolute and dictatorial power over his union," accusing the union chief of antidemocratic practices, a serious claim in the era of intensifying anticommunist sentiments. In his conclusion, Miller stated, "Whether Mr. Petrillo realizes it or not, practically every position which he has taken has defied the immutable tides of technological progress and the right of the American people to enjoy the benefits of that progress. In addition, he has obstructed the normal growth of musical employment" (ibid.).

In testimony two days later at the same House Committee hearing, J. R. Poppele, president of the Television Broadcasters Association, seconded Miller's opinion that it was audiences and musicians themselves who suffered most from the AFM's ban on the televised broadcasting of live musical performances:

The result, while imposing understandable hardships on television broadcasters has not, in itself, deterred the growth of the industry. . . . [T]elevision viewers today have been deprived of the operettas, the musical comedies, the symphony concerts, the first rate film entertainment and multitudes of other forms of entertainment which are naturally integrated with music, and which should normally be expected by the public from this new means of mass communication. In our final analysis, however, it is our thought that the musicians themselves, as well as members of other unions, who normally would be employed for their entertainment value, have suffered the most. (*Weekly Newsletter on Television* 1948: 1).

Despite Poppele's evaluation, the truth is that statistically few U.S. homes actually owned television sets during the immediate postwar years when the AFM music ban was in effect, nor was there yet a sophisticated and expansive programming repertoire to view. The general public did not necessarily miss much at all.

Petrillo knew full well by 1948 that his union was the linchpin in the networks' expanding television operations, and he realized that changes in communications technologies, a gradually growing trend toward industrial synergy across the entertainment sectors, and new cultural performance options required careful evaluation in order to secure the best possible contracts for the union membership. The AFM's obdurate stance may have impeded the industry's progress, yet union was adamant that it would not lose revenue or member remuneration once television was up and running. In the spring of 1948, the AFM's monthly magazine, *International Musician*, directly articulated the union's views on television's growth potential, noting, "Television may prove for the late 40's and 50's what the radio was in the 20's: a big boom. . . . Television may reach the above-average income group, and at the same time hit the mass market. If television does succeed in reaching the quality market, presumably high caliber live shows will be required, at least for some shows over live video" ("Television Outlook" 1948: 7). The tentative nature of the statement, with its qualifying terms "if" and "may," reflects musicians' cautious approach to television at its inception, although it was very quickly evident that their presumptions were accurate, that it was a medium with mass appeal, and that it would rely on musical content performed by union musicians.

Television manufacturing executives had already seen, if briefly, how solid musical presentations could have a positive influence on television purchase patterns. The advertising agencies also promoted televised musical performances in their attempts to motivate consumers to buy new TV sets. These interrelated corporate structures were important in the industrial strategies developed between the conjoined RCA manufacturing arm and the NBC broadcasting network since the late 1930s and between the Du Mont corporation's TV manufacturing and broadcasting branches through the 1940s. Examples of the promotional links between television set sales and musical programming were not rare.

For instance, an advertisement in *Variety* (November 19, 1947, 35) for Du Mont's flagship New York station WABD reflects the network's emphasis on musical performance for attracting viewers, notably almost five months prior to the end of the AFM television ban. Under headline copy reading "The new look in television" is a close-up image of the actor and singer "honey blond, vivacious Sylvie St. Clair," who it is written, "makes her personal appearance on WABD every Wednesday night at 8:15." The advertisement copy also includes what is described as "an unsolicited letter" that reads: "Last night we saw you on television. *This made me decide to buy a television set.* You have been excellent — full of pep — and I thank you very much for the pleasure you gave me. I hope to see you often as soon as I get my television set." Since vocalists were not required to join the AFM, St. Clair was at liberty to sing to recordings on television while unionized musicians waited out the ban. *Variety* later speculated that securing a contract agreement with the AFM would provide the networks and set manufacturers with additional "impetus to receiver set sales. . . . Many people who've been disappointed in the tele shows haven't been activated to buy yet. There's still a margin for stimulus to set-buyers, consequently, and it's expected that improved programming resulting from the AFM pact will supply that stimulus" ("AFM Action to Hypo Set Sale" 1948: 30).

Robert Leiter writes that, in spite of Petrillo's uncompromising posture in negotiations with various entertainment industry factions, "the year 1948 was one in which major decisions were made by the American Federation of Musicians. At the beginning of January disputes were raging with regard to the manufacture of records, the negotiation of radio contracts, the future of frequency modulation, and the performance of live music over television. Each of these difficulties essentially was adjusted by the end of that year" (1953: 164). On March 18, 1948, Petrillo announced the signing of an initial three-year contract with the television networks (with the additional stipulation of trimonthly reviews as the medium grew and developed). The agreement finally allowed music performances to proceed on television while ensuring parity between the television wage scale and that of radio and fair remuneration in the way of residual payouts.

The union's new television pay scale was based on established radio rates, guaranteeing musicians an additional "duplication" wage of $7.50 over radio scale for performances simulcast on radio and television; other aspects of the pay scale included distinctions between local and national network broadcasts. The issue of film/kinescope taping of musical performances for multiple broadcasts was also addressed with the rules of use stipulating that the networks could air the programs only once over either key or affiliated stations. They were not, however, permitted to freely air performances by AFM members at will, and any repeat broadcasts required the union's written authorization ("Television Pay Scales" 1948: 12).

One of the idiosyncratic considerations that emerged from the negotiations involved what television executives termed "tuxedo rates." This nuanced proviso acknowledged the material realities of the transition from radio to television's visual context, offering supplemental wardrobe expenses to musicians due to the fact that "the visual medium will require the AFM boys to dress" ("TV's 'Tuxedo Rates'" 1948: 31). Similar considerations included enhanced compensation for additional makeup and rehearsal time as well as for participation in nonmusical dialogue or visual shtick before the cameras. Such details explicitly highlight television's emphasis on the image and accordingly compensated musicians for aspects of their preparation as *visual* broadcast performers.

As *Variety* reported, at the conclusion of the TV ban many AFM members (as well as those of the Association of Broadcast Unions and Guilds) felt Petrillo had ultimately "surrendered" to the networks with his television deal ("Petrillo's 'I Surrender'" 1948: 27). The crux of the deal hinged on the television performance rights, musicians' wages, and compensation for repeat broadcasting of filmed musical segments, but critics felt that the networks had provided Petrillo with little room to navigate as they pushed for a final resolution to the dispute. Even with his powerful negotiating position, his options had been quickly constrained when the network executives uncharacteristically closed ranks, collaborating as a single industry force unlike the major record labels (and the vastly greater number of vulnerable independent companies) that had tended to negotiate with the AFM autonomously in Petrillo's previous industry showdowns.

With the AFM television performance agreement finally in place, the networks could advance with their programming strategies. The hurdle behind them, the AFM and the networks officially opened the door for professional union musicians to enter the television domain on March 20, 1948, only two days after the AFM TV ban was repealed. The first AFM-sanctioned musical broadcasts featured Eugene Ormandy and the Philadelphia Orchestra appearing on CBS while, within an hour and a half of the CBS show, NBC broadcast a performance by the conductor Arturo Toscanini leading the NBC Symphony Orchestra.

Optimists within the union and elsewhere in the popular music industry surmised that as the medium evolved, "musicians will get more pay on television as more TV sets are sold and advertisers become willing to pay more for telecasting" ("TV's Musical Math" 1949: 40). Even Petrillo eventually admitted that television offered the "only hope" for finding new jobs for musicians, especially once TV's production patterns and viewer practices settled into more consistent patterns[7] ("TV Only Job Hope" 1950: 18).

In retrospect, there are several ways to consider Petrillo's strategies, objectives, and failures during this period. Displaying his antagonistic style and legendary brio, Petrillo may have been forward thinking in his assessment of television's technical development and the increasing trends of convergence among the distinct sectors of the wider entertainment industry. Petrillo's unyielding force, for example, resulted in the first residual payouts to the members of the AFM in 1951 for music in movies that were screened on television.[8] His aggressive responses to the new industrial realities that radically altered the form and trajectory of the recording and broadcast sectors were in many ways appropriate as his corporate adversaries sought to maximize their own power and economic position through collaboration or collusion. Yet his apparent inability to stare down the networks and to have his way with the TV industry may also suggest that his sense of the AFM's power was misplaced and that his authority in such situations was not beyond reproach (even though he retained leadership of the AFM until 1958 and served as head of the AFM Chicago branch until 1963).

Petrillo may also have been blind to the deeper implications of the postwar shifts that were under way throughout the entertainment industry, misreading America's modified leisure preferences and musical tastes. Paul Chevigny explains that Petrillo "came out of an environment in which all music was played live, in which one did not hear music except when produced by an individual or an orchestra. He was never really interested in player pianos, recordings, moving picture soundtracks, broadcasting or any other form of mechanical production. He was interested in work for live musicians" (1993: 24). Indeed, his postwar battles were the most bruising to his reputation as he endeavored to secure a funding pool for live musicians via his transcription funds. Petrillo also failed to adequately gauge the importance and rising popularity of newer music forms — R & B and the ongoing musical activities among the bebop and jazz artists (uncounted numbers of which were not AFM members) as well as the burgeoning Latin music scene — a potentially debilitating oversight.

His adherence to outdated principles, invested in the belief that the previous prosperity would return to the music sector now seems like a grave shortcoming. Like many executives at the major music labels and the editors of several musical journals (such as *Down Beat*), Petrillo maintained faith that the industry was only experiencing a momentary slump before the traditionally successful and lucrative dance bands reclaimed their market dominance in the nation's ballrooms and resorts. They did not.

2

"Hey TV!"

MUSICAL PIONEERS AND PESSIMISTS

The new development of show business—Television—
already is starting to plague the amusement industry.
"NEW FRANKENSTEIN?" 1948: 27

Video Just Possibly Might Aid Musician
DOWN BEAT EDITORIAL HEADLINE, 1949: 10

There was a general sense of disarray at television's inception. Many social and cultural norms were severely knocked off their axis, undermining the accuracy of forecasts or learned speculation. The nation heaved a collective sigh of relief after the war, yet there was also a latent sense of trepidation in the face of so much change. As the previous chapter explains, television emerged within a tangle of interconnected factors (encompassing the economy, labor issues, technology, art and design aesthetics, consumer practices, and audience tastes and behaviors) that influenced its development. With its influential heft, television almost immediately impacted the realm of arts and culture in powerful ways, at times upending established customs. These were strange times indeed.

Within this state of transition and uncertainty, positive and negative discourses each flourished. The postwar entertainment trade press was awash in promises about the great things that television would bring to the arts and to cultural workers, yet there were also voices of dissent urging caution and warning of the potential pitfalls awaiting musicians that acted imprudently. As evidence about television's effects accumulated it became ever more difficult for musicians to know how best to proceed.

Musicians were caught between the dueling sensibilities of opportunity and risk (employing an industrial discourse) or optimism and anxiety (within a psychological discourse); these were among the dominant terminologies that emerged from the ranks of working musicians and from others with stakes in the music industry. Some musicians responded with unbounded enthusiasm, announcing their intentions to immediately join the television ranks, whereas others adopted a more stoic wait-and-see attitude or, more adamantly, they decried television's disruptions in the entertainment industry. The range of responses illustrated the heterogeneity of television's influences and revealed submerged aspects of the relational structure of the music industry to society and everyday life.

In television's early phase, advertising campaigns explicitly addressed the shift from the traditional stage and theater performance contexts to television among young musicians, acknowledging TV's rapidly growing reputation as a potential career builder. For example, in an advertisement for Excelsior accordions appearing in the October 1950 edition of the AFM's union newsletter *International Musician*, the appeal is directly to the reader whose career may eventually — and ideally — lead to television performances. Under large font reading, "Your first big chance on TV . . . make the most of it," the ad focuses on the visual element, proclaiming that Excelsior accordions "have been seen in the hands of America's highest paid artists," suggesting to accordionists that "your big chance on TV may come sooner than you think . . . an opportunity that may well become the turning point of your career. Make the most of it by identifying yourself as an *Excelsior* accordionist." An accompanying image of an accordion player and female singer depicted within the round-cornered frame of a television screen further underlines the association of television, performance, and the instrument on display while the ad copy unambiguously constructs the television as a crucial force of opportunity in the construction of one's professional status.

Through such discursive constructions, television was imagined as either

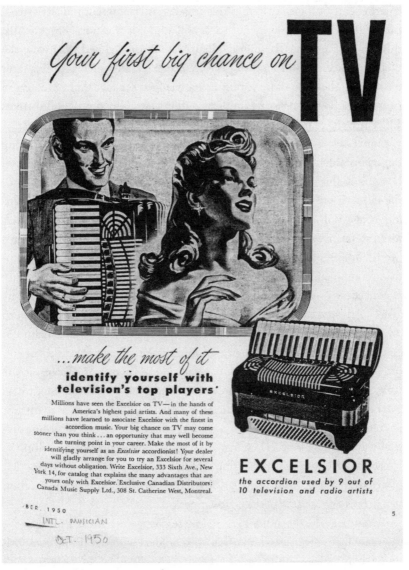

Excelsior accordions. *International Musician*, OCTOBER, 1950.

a goal for musicians as they advanced their careers or a portal to success on a larger scale in the entertainment industry. The optimistic sensibility — exhibited by musicians or corporate executives who found opportunity in such moments of transformation and innovation and that saw the lucrative prospects of reaching a vast, dispersed audience — was widely evident. For them, TV was interpreted as being a boon to the creative and commercial enterprise. It fit logically within the broader entertainment industry structures with which they were already familiar and it was not, subsequently, threatening to them. These individuals were more inclined than were the skeptics to accept the TV networks' promise that television was itself a facet of the arts. They also more readily acknowledged the fact that TV emerged from the radio broadcasting industry with its established program formats and a proven record of success as a commercial and cultural powerhouse.

Conversely, television emerged as a source of threat and anxiety among musicians. Identifying the characteristics of the postwar social subject, Douglas Kellner writes, "Anxiety also becomes a constituent experience for the modern self" (1993: 142). In his view, "One is also anxious concerning recognition and validation of one's identity by others. Further, modernity also involves a process of innovation, of constant turnover and novelty. Modernity signifies the destruction of past forms of life, values, and identities, combined with the production of ever new ones. . . . [O]ne's identity may become out of date, or superfluous, or no longer socially validated" (ibid.). Anxiety was widespread (or it was more often cited than it had been previously), resulting from destabilizing forces including modern technologies, shifting forms of bureaucratic administration, or emergent sites of cultural authority and influence. Musicians, like so many Americans at the time, attempted to read the scene before them and to make sense of new and rapidly evolving social conditions. Meanwhile, TV's potential to disrupt established social rituals or to commodify music and musicians in unforeseen ways heralded radical change and, thus, provoked anxiety within the music sector. Stability is reassuring and in order to reduce the anxiety that comes from uncertainty, musicians strived to redefine their role in relation to patterns or practices in the postwar period.

Teasing out the dynamics between these divergent positions exposes the ways in which musicians (and other stakeholders involved in the composition, recording, and diffusion of popular music) made sense of television's arrival at this particular historical juncture. Within the tensions accompanying early television lie additional lessons about the function and importance of popular music in postwar society and the unique relationship between musical labor and audience leisure. As is generally the case when any new or significant component is introduced into the cultural mix, some trends that are well under way receive an abrupt surge that accelerates the transitional pace. In other instances, social and cultural developments may simply stall, disrupted by the turbulence of these new forces. It is within this context that television's convergence with the attitudes and professional practices of popular musicians is examined.

Music, Labor, and Leisure

Emerging within the unique circumstances of the era, television raised anew the often uneasy relationship between leisure and labor; in a very fundamental way, entertainment also entails work. For TV executives and producers music possessed instrumental value, supplying much needed content for the new medium and, in turn, fulfilling a crucial role in television's corporate financial system. For musicians, their managers, and agents television offered a potential antidote to moribund industrial conditions, presenting an alternative revenue stream and a new promotional apparatus through which artists might acquire leverage in the public eye and in the market.

Though the networks confidently promoted television, the medium's success was by no means guaranteed. Musicians embarked on an unknown path, adjusting their attitudes and practices with no clear sense of what lay before them or what it all might mean. Shortly after the war's end, reports surfaced of musicians testing the waters, tentatively exploring television's presentational possibilities. In an article appearing in the summer of 1948 under the headline "Krupa All Eyes for Video," the music industry trade magazine *Down Beat* observed, "Possibly with an eye for television, Gene Krupa began working up production numbers for his full band during his recent Glen Island Casino engagement" (2). Krupa was surely responding to discussions within the music industry as the networks geared up for full TV programming. The practice of rehearsing new acts at recreational resorts (spread throughout upstate New York's infamous "borscht belt" and across New Jersey and Pennsylvania) was not new, having evolved as a precondition of theater and showroom engagements in New York City. Musicians (as well as comedians and variety show producers) increasingly took their new acts to the resorts for trial runs, honing their performances for potential television bookings.

In several cases previously unknown or struggling artists gained newfound prestige as a direct result of their television appearances. The Kirby Stone Quintette[1] was one of the first beneficiaries of television's new promotional possibilities. After the band's guest appearances on several early television shows, CBS announced the November 8, 1949, debut of *It's Strictly for Laughs*, a thrice-weekly musical variety series (appearing between 7:00

The Kirby Stone Four (Stone is pictured at top). Undated. COURTESY OF PHOTOFEST.

and 7:15 in a then-standard fifteen-minute program slot) featuring music and comedy sketches starring the Stone ensemble. In 1950 the *Down Beat* writer John Wilson cited the Kirby Stone group as "probably the first musical combo to be developed into a name act solely as a result of their work on television" (1950b: 4).

Stone, a trumpeter and valve trombonist of moderate talent, expressed unbridled faith in television. His group was working but it was certainly not a top-billing act and television harbored unknown potentials. Stone's optimism, however, was grounded in his understanding of the corporate entertainment industry and the need to capitalize on all possible opportunities.

As Kay Dickinson explains, most working musicians are not at liberty to wait or squander possible work: "One never knows when the next project or short-term contract will pop up. Performing in these areas means working at one of the more vicious ends of the Western free-market economy; one is a casual worker, rather than a regular employee" (2008: 163).

The benefits of the Stone combo's regular appearances in the New York TV broadcast market were evident after only six months on television, during which the group incorporated novelty songs and visual comedy skits into the act (what *Down Beat*'s Wilson referred to as "jump stuff *a la* Louis Jordan, and pure hokum"). The group experienced rising audience attendance at their local nightclub sessions and enjoyed increased box office revenues, and the TV and club appearances led to more numerous and considerably more lucrative engagements in larger theater venues, eventually landing them a recording contract with MGM. As Stone explained, "We could have knocked around in clubs for 10 years and never have been seen by the number of people who have seen us on television. One night on TV is worth weeks at the Paramount" (Wilson 1950b: 4).

These cases indicate a moment when experienced and much-lauded musicians (such as Krupa) as well as relative up-and-comers (such as the Stone combo) might revel in their professional status as television pioneers and trailblazers. They provide evidence of television's potential as a site of optimism and opportunity, reinforcing the belief among some artists that avoiding television seemed unwise. Some musicians may have expressed early "reservations about the quality of early television and about how it would affect existing entertainment forms, but if television represented the 'future' then (they) wanted to be part of it" (Welch 1999: 102). In spite of its unproven qualities, television symbolized something new and exciting; television was synonymous with notions of modern progress.

Even with this air of optimism and excitement, early television was truly remarkable for its pervasive hit-or-miss approach, creating a parallel anxiety due to doubts associated with the entire enterprise. At the outset, it was impossible to know precisely how audiences might judge and respond to the new visual medium, leaving entertainment executives and artists across all sectors at a disadvantage, unable to accurately forecast television's outcomes and effects. As Samuel Chotzinoff, director of music at NBC, wrote in *Variety* in early 1949, "At this stage in the development of television, we cannot have an impressive record to point to in musical production. When any new medium comes along, it is necessary to feel one's way, to experiment.

In the next few years, we expect to make our quota of mistakes, but we also hope to add materially to the development of music in television."

Executives and network technicians in the TV industry admitted that the construction of a new entertainment option on such a massive scale was fraught with problems as they stumbled forward. The widespread belief (and corporate investors' hope) was that, once the technical and programming glitches were resolved, viewers would flock to the medium and it would draw audiences away from established leisure practices. As it turned out, spectators tuned in despite the technical flaws, watching television by the millions during its developmental phase even as it underwent a difficult growth in full public view.

John Caldwell identifies TV's early foibles as being of consequence to peoples' early perception of television and the artists involved: "Early television was frequently sloppy, at least from a classical perspective that values art for its unity and formal coherence. In many genres, like the comedy variety show, television was formally excessive and heterogeneous. This was due in part to the fact that a programming battle was being waged at the time between several different framing paradigms and aesthetic conditions" (1995: 45)

While the arguments for and against television raged, there was actually a brief sense of relief in some industry quarters as the new television broadcast sector displayed its weaknesses and an apparent inability to establish distinct professional or technical standards. As one Hollywood executive exclaimed in 1949, "The more I see of television during my recent trips east, the less I think the picture business has to worry about its serious inroads. I'm frankly wondering why some of these video programs don't chase people out of the house" (Green 1949: 1). Industry critics questioned the integrity of musicians and TV program producers for creating such "careless," "inept," or "sloppy" fare, stating "too many stars and so-called production impresarios who have been enticed into the medium are treating it more as a sideline for a quick buck instead of trying to vest TV with the type of showmanship perfection it has been striving for" (Rosen 1952: 97).

Industry critics observed that because of television's mediocre quality, audience "fanaticism" for TV was only temporary, falling most sharply among television households that had owned their sets for a year or more. The medium's "novelty factor" was short-lived: "Television, as an entertainment medium, has reached a point where it must compete on strict quality terms with established forms of show biz. . . . If it is to keep people at home, it must henceforth give them better entertainment than they would get in legit and film shows, from radio, etc." ("Tele 'on Own'" 1949: 29).

Musicians were, of course, also witness to television's shortcomings and while some surely believed that *they* could do better onscreen, others were horrified by what they beheld, observing how TV squandered the talents of their peers or, worse, tainted them. In Caldwell's assessment, "Even those generic forms from the period of 'great' television art — like the live anthology drama from New York — flaunted explicit low-tech and anti-style airs as marks of distinction. Volatility, and the sense that television was coming apart at the seams, was instead an aura that reinforced television's obsession with liveness and immediacy. 'The show that you are watching' could, as it were, fall apart at any moment.'" (1995: 48–49). Caldwell is right to note that the medium's limitations were visually inescapable, yet even when they were not, when the production was solid and the performances cohesive, there still often seemed to be a tongue-in-cheek attitude about the shows. The performers or program hosts frequently behaved as if television was a big charade (as on the March 3, 1951, episode of *The Frank Sinatra Show*, featuring special guests Perry Como and Frankie Laine, whose light-hearted banter and off-the-cuff acting indicated a genial relationship with Sinatra). In the able hands of a show host such as Dave Garroway or Ernie Kovacs this effect could be fun and exciting; in other instances where the ironic perspective was either forced or lacking altogether, the outcome was understandably less satisfying. This was especially true of television's many musical variety shows.

Sharp divisions emerged between musicians about how television might aid or erode a career. Among junior artists with fewer years of experience and with a lesser record or reputation, television was greeted with considerable enthusiasm. They simply had less to lose by experimenting in television. Yet well-known musicians with established repertoires and secure industry reputations were often reluctant to cross into television broadcasting, preferring to observe the medium from a distance in order to better understand it.

The popular fan magazine *Modern TV and Radio* reported in 1949, "One vaudevillian who's giving television a wide berth is the greatest of them all; Sophie Tucker. Recently Sophie told me, 'they wouldn't let me be myself in radio either. I'm no ballad singer or missionary, but I am the highest priced

Sophie Tucker with Jimmy Durante. *Colgate Comedy Hour*, NBC, 1950–55.
COURTESY OF PHOTOFEST.

woman in the business, and I'm not going to let television ruin 40 years of building up a professional personality'" ("On and Off the Air" 1949: 6). Though she did appear as a TV guest on occasion, Tucker's response to perceived performance constraints and a need to protect her reputation captures the relatively common belief that the medium's experimental bent and the networks' assertion of artistic control over one's act severely compromised professional integrity.

The trumpeter Ray Anthony, who in 1951 led of one of the nation's top dance bands and whose popular recordings were consistently favored among disk jockeys and jukebox operators, expressed his own apprehensions. Anthony declared his diffidence toward television in an interview appearing under the headline, "Let Others Have Video—I'll Stay in the Ballrooms." He disdained the television producers and program sponsors for the pressures they exerted on musicians, deeming them insensitive to musicians' artistic integrity, and he was also skeptical of the staged production numbers and comedy skits that he regarded as an unsuitable use of his talents.[2]

Although it remains unspoken, Anthony implicitly circumscribes a standard that television plainly failed to meet. He forcefully questioned the impact of the medium on his career, stating, "Television? Not for me. Not me at all. That's for a pioneer and I'm no pioneer. I'm not going to get my feet wet in television until somebody knows exactly where dance bands fit in" (Freeman 1951). Despite the TV industry's calming assurances and paeans to the medium's potential, it was simply impractical to assume that television would benefit everyone. In the performing arts, some will thrive while others inevitably struggle or fail. In this, television was entirely traditional, remaining consistent with the prevailing norms of professional entertainment where talent, industry circumstances, audience tastes, and sheer luck converge.

One did not have to look far to find examples of the difficulty of shifting into television. The popular film and recording star Vaughn Monroe embraced television, hosting the *Camel Caravan* on CBS between October 1950 and July 1951.[3] Monroe admitted that, in preparation for his duties as a video host, he "had to learn how to act a little and also do a buck-and-wing along with his vocalizing, so that he could take part in the show's production numbers" ("TV Can't 'Make' Bands" 1951: 1).

Altering his performance repertoire was considered necessary to reinforce his small-screen profile, thus conforming to television's particular requirements for a visual center and a dominant personality upon which to focus. Monroe's preparation was evidently insufficient, however, and *Metronome*'s review of his television debut was scathing:

> All the negative criticism of TV that we have all heard in the last two years must have been directed against this program. . . . Never has so much ineptness been gathered together and converged on a hapless cathode. Never has so little been made of so little talent. . . . [P]rograms like this make one despair about television, make one feel that the medium is falling fast into a poor imitation of the high school variety show. (February 1951)

In another case, after a much anticipated buildup leading to his first TV foray in February 1952, the veteran bandleader Harry James performed miserably, producing a broadcast debacle that *Down Beat* described as "a 'bomb'" and a "flop" (English 1952: 4).

In his acting manual titled *Auditioning for TV: How to Prepare for Success*

Camel Caravan/The Vaughn Monroe Show. CBS, 1950–51.
COURTESY OF PHOTOFEST.

as a Television Actor, the NBC producer and director Albert McCleery unambiguously articulated the truth of the situation: "If an actor fails — in his
thirty seconds — to project his personality into the room and into the consciousness of the director, he has lost his chance. On camera he would lose
his audience" (Begley and MacCrae 1955: xvii). Even in the face of promise
and optimism expressed by the networks and the prospect of opportunity
extolled by many in the music industry, anxiety and professional paranoia
affected countless musicians who regarded television as a risky proposition
or a threatening force to their careers.

Although TV exposure was quickly accepted as a legitimate means of boosting a musical career, a prominent concern among musicians (and among comedy acts, which were most similarly affected) was television's "appetite" for content — alternately defined as "insatiable," "ravenous," or "voracious" — and its capacity to burn through an artist's repertoire and musical arrangements extremely quickly. Reporting on the situation in relation to comedians, *Variety* identified a looming crisis that also directly affected musicians transitioning to the small screen: "Television in the short span of 18 months has practically gone through what it took radio 25 years to exhaust. . . . Material that had a life-long guarantee in vaude and other show biz media has been drained, leaving the TV cupboard threadbare" (Rosen 1951: 1). As many musicians explained, whereas a series of one-nighters allowed an act to work with a relatively limited repertoire when playing before a new audience each night, television could expend the act's entire song list within a month of steady appearances. Even an extended booking in a hotel or ballroom (which was common among dance bands and singers at the time) usually required an artist to regularly refresh the repertoire, but this would usually be done on the artist's own terms, not according to television production and broadcast schedules.

Television's demands were staggering, and while established acts with a deeper repertoire or wider set of arrangements might be able to accommodate the networks, musicians seeking entry into the new industry were faced with a daunting task. Acknowledging television's content demands, in 1952 the bandleader and arranger Frank DeVol went so far as revising his entire songbook, working from two sets of arrangements, one for the ballroom and one for television presentation (Holly 1952: 9). With television's maturation through the early 1950s, the widespread perception among musicians was that, "after several seasons, a regular viewer would be familiar with virtually every facet of a performer's work, and there would be little incentive to shell out to see him in the flesh. And besides, it is difficult to sell that which has been doled out for free for a number of years" ("Paradox in TV" 1955: 2).

Some artists, such as Eddie Cantor, a former Ziegfeld Follies trouper and vaudeville star, seemed particularly anxious about television's capacity to dilute audience interest or erode an artist's status. As a hedge against overexposure Cantor signed a contract to host the *Colgate Comedy Hour* only once or twice monthly between 1950 and 1954, sharing the host duties with several other top celebrities of the day, including Fred Allen, Jimmy Durante, Donald O'Connor, Dean Martin and Jerry Lewis, Bud Abbott and Lou Costello, and Spike Jones and his City Slickers. This strategy allowed Cantor and his colleagues to develop more material for their program appearances while permitting greater rehearsal time with the new scripts and song lists. The audience, too, was thought to benefit from this arrangement as viewers were exposed to a broader range of comedy styles and personalities. The competing variety program *Toast of the Town*, hosted by the New York entertainment columnist Ed Sullivan, circumvented the hosting dilemma by placing Sullivan in the role of a nonperforming master of ceremonies whose central responsibility was to introduce the acts, engaging in a bit of casual banter before ushering them from the stage following their performances.

Commenting on "music's potentialities in television," Andre Kostelanetz (whose career as a conductor and arranger of light classical music helped to define symphonic "pops" music) refuted the claims that music and musicians were susceptible to the debilitating effects of television's standardized patterns and recurring performances. Kostelanetz believed, perhaps naively, that unlike dramatic or comedy fare, music was amenable to repetition and, thus, was not exposed to the danger of oversaturation; "We are quite willing to listen to the same piece of music time and again. . . . [L]et us not forget that good songs are being written daily — certainly at a greater rate than good dramatic material" (1952).

Despite Kostelanetz's opinion to the contrary, redundancy remained a serious issue among the networks, who acknowledged that, if an artist was promoting a recent hit recording, musical film appearance, or was associated with a popular "signature" song, it was customary that these would be repeated in each TV performance. Further aggravating the situation was the widespread practice of "covering" contemporaneous popular songs; it was entirely common for several versions of a popular song to sit alongside one another on the record sales charts and on jukeboxes of the period. These hit songs were also performed widely on both national TV networks and regional affiliates by celebrity artists and by B-list musical talents, leading to considerable video redundancy.

Television program directors competed for the artists' services on their shows, yet it was not uncommon for a single vocalist, musician, or band to honor several TV booking requests, appearing on various programs across the networks over a two- or three-week period. While acts based in New

York or on the East Coast could more carefully structure their television appearance schedules to avoid overexposure on the small screen, touring musicians arriving in the TV broadcasting hub of New York City from elsewhere often packed several TV appearances into a brief New York sojourn. Peggy Lee, arriving from the West Coast for a booking at New York's Copacabana club in 1951, reportedly included "several television appearances" in her schedule ("Peggy to East" 1951: 5). Television offered alternative performance options, leading many artists to capitalize on their appeal and demand through the practice of "doubling" their appearance schedules.

Doubling refers to artists merging television guest spots with theater and nightclub engagements or radio broadcast appearances—double-booking, essentially—although the term also surfaced within talent management agencies, with *Variety* explaining that at the William Morris agency, "most salesmen in the outfit are now doubling between the various departments and video" ("Wm. Morris Eyes Bands" 1950). Kay Dickinson employs the terms "cross-over performer" or "cross-over artist" and "multitasking" to denote the practice of doubling, positioning it squarely within the dynamics of corporate demand and labor and what she defines as "the *work* of leisure" (2008: 27). Even with the advantage of increased artist and agency revenues or the additional promotional boost, doubling carried inherent problems for musicians. The practice created intense professional pressure and required considerable stamina to meet contractual obligations.

Reports during television's formative years detailed the difficulties encountered by in-demand musicians who attempted to fulfill television contracts within their already hectic schedules. For a select group of elite musical artists who hosted their own TV shows, the effort of sustaining a frenzied performance calendar (including regular recording sessions and radio, theater, or nightclub engagements) was depleting. *Variety* quickly identified doubling as a new stressor among artists ("TV a Fulltime Job" 1949: 1).

Submitting to the burdens of doubling, the intense pace of television production drained Vaughn Monroe during his CBS show *Camel Caravan*. Monroe also performed several "one-nighters" each week and appeared in the occasional western or "singing cowboy" film. In December 1950, Monroe announced that he would cut down on his club and theater performances while also reducing the scale of a major tour, four months in the making, due to "heavy preparation and the rehearsal demands of TV work" ("Vaughn Monroe Refuses Work" 1950: 1). In 1951 it was reported that Monroe had even resorted to employing a "vocal stand-in" to work with the TV cast in the program rehearsals while he was away at a gig and to help ensure that "the strain of the singing bandleader's throat will be brought to a minimum" ("Tired Monroe Has Sub Sing" 1951: 4). Monroe eventually disbanded his traveling orchestra altogether in order to focus more directly on his television career.

Though many working musicians strove to find a professional balance that could accommodate television, some, such as Jo Stafford, were applauded for their impressive stamina and an amazing capacity for doubling. Stafford's resiliency allowed her to merge television performances into her packed agenda, maintaining an active recording and concert appearance schedule (with its attendant rehearsal sessions) while appearing frequently as a TV guest and hosting her own CBS-TV program in the 1954–55 season. She would regularly return from regional engagements or local studio recording sessions with her husband and orchestra leader, Paul Weston, in tow, embarking directly to the TV studio for intense program rehearsals. Known as a "perfectionist," Stafford also employed controversial methods implementing prerecorded music and lip-synching on her program. Though lip-synching intuitively suggests an efficient means of controlling the production process, it also involved a protracted, laborious procedure that "often means a four-hour recording session, with as many as 12 'takes' of a single song before a 15-minute program goes on the air" ("Their Lips Move" 1954: 8–9).

Some nightclub owners and theater managers viewed TV doubling in a positive light, regarding it as means of leveraging additional promotion from the media, assuming that the mention of their establishment might add to its luster and reputation (and, ideally, an increase in attendance and revenues). Other nightclub owners, however, regarded TV doubling as a form of competition that undermined the exclusivity of an artist's appearance, depreciating the noteworthiness of the act's engagement at their venue and detracting from its event status. They looked askance at the practice of TV doubling much as club owners had done prior to television, when musical acts booked overlapping engagements at different local venues or scheduled radio performances while also fulfilling contractual obligations at nightclubs or theaters.

The Latin Quarter's owner Lou Walters took a particularly hard-line approach toward doubling, demanding "that acts kickback a portion of their video salaries to him if it's that important to their career that they appear on video while at his club or shortly beforehand" ("Nitery Ops" 1953: 1). Despite the questionable legality of the kickback scheme, several musicians evidently complied with Walters's demands, perhaps fearing that their failure to do so would result in a ban from the prestigious New York venue.

Nightclub impresarios were not the only ones against music acts doubling their appearances; with heated network and program rivalries, television producers also voiced their scorn for doubling, expressing their opposition to repeat performances across the networks. In July 1954, CBS's Ed Sullivan wielded his formidable industry influence when he forced Vaughn Monroe to abandon an appearance on *The Arthur Murray Party* on NBC that was scheduled for the week following his guest spot on Sullivan's show. According to *Variety*, "Sullivan took the position that he's paying premium fees for top talent and as such deserves some degree of exclusivity. . . . [I]t was merely a problem of maintaining the values of the talent that he purchases" ("Sullivan Stops Vaughn Monroe" 1954: 27). Apart from illuminating industry tactics in an aggressive and at times ruthless corporate environment, Sullivan's heavy-handed but pragmatic position reflects the extent to which musical talent was commodified in the entertainment industry at the time, offering another view onto the deal-making and network enmity that prevailed in television's early years.

When the networks did succeed in launching a performer's career, catapulting a young artist into the upper echelon of celebrity status, the tendency was to exploit the artist by placing the individual in front of the cameras and in the media at virtually every opportunity. It was widely acknowledged that perky young vocalist Kyle MacDonnell had the talent and looks for television when she was suddenly introduced in the 1948 NBC program schedule. Ira Skutch recalls that after only a brief (seven-minute) audition, she appeared on *Disk Magic* "a few times" before being given her own fifteen-minute show, *For Your Pleasure*, performing with the Norman Paris Trio (1990: 60). "A tall, willowy blond, Kyle sang well—not great. But she soon became the first genuine TV star, with her name in the gossip columns, and her picture on magazine covers" (ibid.); *Variety*'s assessment was direct, if somewhat understated, describing MacDonnell as "a nice kid with a good voice" ("For Your Pleasure" 1948).

Recognizing an opportunity, NBC soon assigned MacDonnell to the host duties on *Girl about Town* after which she was dubbed "Miss Television" (appearing in numerous newspaper and magazine articles as well as on the cover of the May 31, 1948, issue of *Life* magazine under the heading "Television Ingénue"). The Du Mont network also made the most out of MacDonnell in 1950, when she appeared four times as a guest on the network's *Cavalcade of Stars* while serving as musical host on *Hold That Camera*. The extensive interest in MacDonnell attests to the fact that her mass exposure did not all occur on the screen, as she was swept up in the emerging media machinery that traffics in hype and hyperbole. Indeed, even after so much attention, MacDonnell's TV career was short-lived and her reputation as a television "star" was largely ended by 1953 (Von Schilling 2003: 102).

The case of Julius La Rosa presents another example where a young artist was overexposed by the networks. Having risen in popularity as a member of Arthur Godfrey's TV "family," the Brooklyn singer was suddenly and unceremoniously fired by Godfrey in 1953 for a variety of ill-defined reasons ("Julius La Rosa" 1953: 1; Stahl 1955; Murray 2001).[4] La Rosa's career was not grievously damaged, however, and he sustained an active touring and performance schedule as well as appearing regularly as a TV guest. In 1955 CBS thrust La Rosa into the network's broadcast schedule with apparent abandon, selecting him to host *TV's Top Tunes* as well as hiring him as the replacement host on *The Perry Como Show* during Como's summer hiatus.

Industry commentators took a dim view of La Rosa's busy summer schedule, specifically isolating the issue of excessive appearances and his limited musical repertoire and narrow guest lists:

> There doesn't seem to be much concern over the fact that these musical shows look very much alike, especially when the same personality, such as La Rosa, is starred. Since current pop hits are being stressed, La Rosa has to repeat tunes on his various shows. Even his guests are coming around the revolving door. Miss Gibbs, for instance, guested on La Rosa's midweek stanza and then showed up Saturday night. At least, however, she changed her material. (*Variety*, July 13, 1955)

Stating his awareness of the network's redundancy problem, the CBS executive and producer Worthington "Tony" Miner admitted, "It is axiomatic that a star holds on to his reputation longer if he is not constantly before the public. . . . A performer may be seen as often as 15 times each year, thereby wearing out his public welcome" ("'Overexposure' Still TV's Biggest Enemy" 1955: 26).

Doorways to Fame and Stairways to the Stars:
Amateur Talent Programs

Even with the many pronouncements about television as a site of innovation, it was not lost on many younger musicians that TV's prime guest appearances were regularly offered to established musicians. The list of program hosts and major musical guests during television's early phase reads like a "who's who" of top recording artists with a similarly deep roster of veteran radio personalities and stars from Broadway or the vaudeville theaters of yore.

While younger musicians regarded television as means to gain a footing in the entertainment industry and to reach a vast audience with relative efficiency, many veteran artists turned to television to revitalize their waning careers. Musical comedians, such as Morey Amsterdam, Eddie Cantor, or Jimmy Durante revived their vaudeville routines for television, turning to the well-worn musical and performance forms for which they were best known, in some cases featuring exhausting vaudeville-style production numbers that left the artists out of breath and visibly perspiring. In an ad appearing in *Variety* in April, 1949, Fred Waring's new weekly CBS television show is promoted not as a novel and inventive addition to the program schedule but, rather, as the culmination of Waring's twenty-year tenure as a bandleader. Television was simply the logical next step in the career trajectory of these musical veterans.

Although they expressed a desire to seek and develop "fresh" new talent, the television networks worked overtime to hire proven artists or (employing a more contemporary discourse) previously branded personalities, who generated wider name recognition among viewing audiences and, importantly, among sponsors. Sponsors favored established name musicians as either show hosts or guests since the corporations could easily discern what they were paying for based on familiarity with the status or genre of the artist concerned. A downside to television's emphasis on hiring established industry veterans and well-known stars, especially on the networks' major musical programs, was that the content on the new medium was indelibly imprinted with cultural articulations of a previous era.

In instances when an established musical celebrity was unavailable or already under contract, sponsors sought to locate and promote another individual whose qualities were perceived as being roughly equivalent. An ex-

Promotion for CBS's *The Fred Waring Show*. VARIETY, APRIL 13, 1949.

ample of this is evident in the 1951 advertisement seeking "a second Dinah Shore for immediate use on a national network radio-TV show . . . a fresh charming, intelligent, capable, young singer on the order of Dinah Shore. She must be able to sing ballads, rhythm tunes and novelty songs as well as being genuinely telegenic. Whichever young lady proves suitable will be given a long term contract and an unusually attractive figure" (*Down Beat*, March 9, 1951, 4).

There were persistent worries among network executives "that earnings from radio might [have to] dwindle before television revenues increased sufficiently to replace it" and, in a related sense, the question was asked, "Were new stars . . . about to kill off the old radio favorites who were still bringing in so much money?" (Weaver 1994: 200). The editors of *Down Beat*, who had proclaimed an initial hopefulness about television's opportunities for young musicians, soon voiced their scorn toward the new industry's low-risk approach to music booking. They criticized what they perceived as an overall lack of originality and progress, posing the question in 1951, "Where are the new singers, new bands, or other musical units discovered on and built up by television?" ("Hey TV" 1951: 10).

Complicating matters in early television was the issue of program expenses. Production budgets were a continual worry for early television producers and their sponsors as they sought engaging content that still cost less than the elaborate dramas and other highly scripted programming that filled out the program schedule. Established musical talent (comprising the industry's stars) did not come cheaply and producers were often forced to make concessions in order to bring the program in on budget. As an antidote to prohibitive costs and the reliance on industry veterans the industry invested energy in a "revival of amateur talent programs. . . .The amateur talent, while satisfying the public demand, is far easier on the bankroll than the average professional variety bill" (Chandler 1950: 33). Most amateur programs were structured around musical performances and while they tended to command a low overhead they also provided an effective alternative to unionized musical talent, a factor that emerged with particular urgency during the AFM's television ban between 1945 and 1948.

Television's amateur talent shows were a carry-over from earlier radio programming, having been well established through the 1930s and 1940s. A juvenile Frank Sinatra was once a contestant (and winner) with the vocal quartet The Hoboken Four on the *Major Bowes' Original Amateur Hour* radio program in the late 1930s, and the Chicago-based *Morris B. Sachs Ama-*

teur Hour radio broadcast provided early hometown exposure to recording stars Frankie Laine and Mel Torme.[5] Even with the end of the AFM ban in 1948 the networks continued to pursue the amateur talent format on the basis of its economic viability and low labor costs, its sponsor-friendly orientation, audience familiarity with the format, and overall viewer approval, as well as offering a proactive means of locating and screen testing new performers.

Among the more acclaimed television amateur talent shows with radio roots were *The Original Amateur Hour, Arthur Godfrey's Talent Scouts, Freddy Martin's "Band of Tomorrow,"* and *The Horace Heidt Show.* Television networks added several key program titles to this list, including *Chance of a Lifetime, Doorway to Fame,* and Paul Whiteman's *TV Teen Club.* While it is difficult to precisely gauge the full nationwide scope of local amateur shows since virtually no original footage remains of the regional productions, press coverage indicates that the genre was widespread and most stations featured some form of amateur programming. Television reviews in daily newspapers and the trade press provide occasional glimpses of the character of amateur programs broadcast on local stations throughout the country, reflecting an extensive array of amateur performances and contestants.[6]

For musical participants — the term "contestants" is also appropriate since most of the amateur programs involved some form of competition and adjudication — televised talent shows constituted a liminal cultural site situated at a juncture between amateur and professional status. While not all singers and musicians appearing on these programs aspired to careers in the entertainment industry, many did and some were already working on a semiprofessional basis with paid engagements in nightclubs and other settings. Those whose performances were deemed superior (and who were rewarded as the "winner" on a given broadcast) were suddenly exposed to an industrial conduit through which efforts toward a professional music career might be channeled. Still other amateur programs featured rawer, less developed kinds of "talent," which at times leaned toward unorthodox musical skills (such as whistlers and spoon or saw players) or visually oriented novelty acts. As *Variety* reported in the spring of 1949, the amateur shows of Arthur Godfrey and Ted Mack were responsible for "bringing back off the shelf a number of old instruments — ukuleles, ebony bone clappers, tenor banjos, and tenor guitars" ("No, Not That!" 1949: 1).

An "amateur" musician is generally understood as someone whose musical interests and pursuits occur outside the structures of the commercial music industry, either as a pastime or casual endeavor. Robert Stebbins provides one of the more thorough analyses of amateurs in which he outlines categories and definitions of amateur labor in several sectors of art, sport, and entertainment. For Stebbins, important distinctions lie between professionals and amateurs but he also makes distinctions between "devotees," "participants," and "dabblers," and, in an age-conscious distinction, between adult "amateurs" and younger "novices" (Stebbins 1992: 38–58). Experience, commitment, and the extent of "seriousness" thus emerge as distinguishing factors that define one's status within an informal but undeniable hierarchy. As Stebbins explains, "amateurs engage part-time in activities that, for other people, constitutes full-time work roles" (ibid.: 41)

In casual conversation the term "amateur" is commonly employed to identify the differences between those with undeveloped musical talent or a want of experience and those for whom music is a professional vocation, performed for pay and comprising a fundamental aspect of how one earns a living; professionals sustain themselves through their music. In some discursive contexts, "amateur" may be deployed negatively, as a pejorative term dismissing one's talent as mere and marginal. It is crucial, however, to differentiate between competitive talent shows and amateur shows since the definitional particulars that set the two categories apart speak to differences of professional possibility and, consequently, labor relations.

Television's early *amateur* shows were generally more inclined to feature older, more mature, and experienced musicians (some of whom may have been paid in prior contexts for their public performances); this cohort is referred to by Stebbins as occupying a "preprofessional" status encompassing amateurs "who intend to join the professional ranks" (ibid.: 46). The *talent* programs generally featured a much higher percentage of adolescent and preadolescent performers (who had never been financially compensated for a performance), as well as a greater number of visually oriented novelty acts. Age figures in such status evaluations: "Amateurs are normally adults although in some fields they may be older teenagers as well. . . . [O]nly adults can be functionally related to professionals" (ibid.: 41), whereas the very young musical performers on these TV shows warrant other designations, which in the entertainment trade press included terms such as "tyro" or "juvenile." These youths might be considered participants with talent but in Stebbins's assessment they are not amateurs in the precise sense of the term.

Mobilizing television's commercial expansion into the American mainstream, the interlocked RCA Victor record label and NBC television network hoped to devise synchronized strategies for locating and promoting new talent from the ranks of amateur musicians. This was not simply a matter of identifying telegenic "fresh faces" but included attempts to capitalize on the vulnerabilities of comparatively malleable amateur musicians who did not have contract experience or the guidance of professional managers or agents. In an internal memorandum sent to several of NBC's top executives in 1949, David Adams outlines a plan to develop a televised "talent hunt" program specifically addressing the coinciding needs at the RCA record label and the NBC television network for "a good new young woman singer of popular songs" (1949a). The criteria for the contest was to narrow the eligible female contestants to "women between the ages of 18 and 25 who are not in the professional entertainment field and are not bound by entertainment contracts" (ibid.). The plan involved dividing the nation into eight "talent regions" and, following a series of local contests with corresponding local television coverage, the regional finals would be conducted over successive weeks "in a program series" with nation-wide semifinal broadcasts from Los Angeles and New York and the finals being aired from New York.

As Adams explains, the winning contestant would receive $2,500 in cash plus the real award, "an NBC radio and television contract" (ibid.). Though it is never explicitly acknowledged, while the program was pitched as entertainment programming for the viewing audience, its instrumental purpose more accurately served the commercial needs and interests of the culture industries. As was the earlier case when networks programmed amateur shows to circumvent AFM restrictions or to keep production costs down, the proposed NBC-RCA initiative was conceived within purely commercial and possibly exploitative contexts, ultimately commodifying the creative talent of young female vocalists.

Adams's proposal was initially supported as a promotional vehicle for NBC television and its affiliates, though it was deemed to be of less value at RCA Victor due to the label's already established mechanisms for locating promising young musical talent. In the end, Adams's superiors (and several regional TV affiliate station managers) vetoed the idea of a nationwide televised talent search contest, judging it as an unlikely means of "uncovering a new and outstanding performer" (Adams 1949b). Adams admitted, "It appears that a more effective method for achieving the latter objective would be a concentrated talent scouting effort among performers who are already professionally engaged" (ibid.). This outcome notwithstanding, similar recruiting efforts were common in the television industry, as indicated in correspondence between the NBC executives Norman Blackburn and Carleton Smith in 1949, in which the men ponder the notion of securing "first call on talent seen on Amateur Hour programs," shortly after *Ted Mack's Original Amateur Hour* landed at NBC from the Du Mont network where it had debuted (Blackburn 1949; Smith 1949a).

Despite Adams's unrealized plan at NBC, discovery was an objective of several of television's early amateur and talent programs. The show *TV Teen Club* featured a discourse of discovery that rested in the personality of the musical veteran Paul Whiteman, whose eye for talent and untested musical teens was renowned. Featuring reasonably talented novices, the ABC show opens with the announcement, "Here's a real club where teenagers are given that all-important first big chance. Discovered by the star-maker who gave you Bing Crosby, Tommy Dorsey, Mildred Bailey and other great stars, Paul Whiteman, is now bringing you teen stars of tomorrow." Whiteman (assisted by his much younger cohost, Nancy Lewis) is portrayed not solely as a professional musician but also as an experienced industry professional whose years as a bandleader provide him with exceptional judgment about musicians' talent potential. The program turns on the isolation of talented and promising teens whose appearance on the shows might provide an incentive to continue their careers in the musical arts. This is consistent with Whiteman's professed intent to improve the conditions under which America's teens learn to appreciate "quality" music.[7]

Whiteman's program shared several key elements with *The Horace Heidt Show* and *Freddy Martin's "Band of Tomorrow,"* most notably in their professed mission to seek young musical talent to fill out their band rosters. While the orchestra leaders were known to be scouting for talented young musicians who might join their organizations their unassailable reputations as established musical professionals actually reinforced and reproduced the subordinate status of the musical contestants. The articulation of the show hosts' professional identities reminds the TV viewers exactly where on the career ladder the musical hopefuls sit within the trajectory of achievement. On most other top amateur programs, the hosts could not claim any remarkable musical talent of their own (perhaps with the exception of Arthur Godfrey's competence with a ukulele); rather, they inhabited the role of show business veterans whose industry knowledge informs their judgment, serving as paragons of experience while gently intoning words of support and encouragement to their hopeful guests.

While TV's industry middlemen sought ways to locate and exploit amateur musicians, outside observers were critical of such initiatives. In 1949, the journalist Paul Denis (alternately adopting the style and tone of serious investigative journalism and scandal reporting in the tabloid fan magazine *Radio Best: The Radio and Television Picture Magazine*) voiced suspicions about the ethics of radio and television "talent opportunity programs," dubbing them a "dubious world of chance." The exposé illuminated the "chicanery" that often accompanied the programs' talent selection methods, drawing attention to ethical lapses in the audition processes, compromised competition oversight, and other questionable propensities. Denis presents an unvarnished assessment of a young musician's slim chance of successfully attaining an audition or of moving from the audition stage to a broadcast opportunity, suggesting grimly that "much of the psychological injury comes from the ludicrous, impossible promises the contests hold out. Doorway to fame, stairway to the stars, opportunity unlimited, and stars of tomorrow are only some of the slogans used. Alas, too often the doorway to fame is nothing but an exit to obscurity" (1949: 47).

Denis explains, "There are many 'talent showcase' programs on radio and television. Since they are not in the form of contests, there are no prizes. Performers appear — without pay — in the hope of attracting attention of future employers. Everybody makes some money out of these programs, that is, everybody except the performers" (ibid.). In his view, the opportunities that evolved from amateur or talent programs primarily benefited the networks or shady industry hacks, reducing the vast majority of amateur musical hopefuls to mere camera fodder.

Ted Mack, host of *The Original Amateur Hour*, defended the process, defining his approach to his talent show as being akin to "a baseball 'farm system.'" In Mack's view, he and other such show hosts "just plain trained people to act at their best in TV" (1951b: 98). Mack is probably more truthful, however, when he employs the corporate industrial terminology of "the new assembly line of supply for video talent," describing the means by which he processes the raw material into a commodified product for public consumption: "Having weathered the rigors of their first big-time appearance, we put them into traveling 'Original Amateur Hour' units. As the fellow says, this is the 'experience' . . . and the change from a trembling beginner to a seasoned trouper is evident in as few as three or four bookings" (ibid.). A month later in an article titled "How to Win!" Mack elaborated on the rigor of the process, noting: "If you pass our audition, you will be seen and heard on radio and television by millions of people. If the radio audience responds well, you go out in a unit and begin the first, real phase of your professional career. And if you're among the three top winners in June, you win a cash scholarship to further your talents" (1951a: 29).

Mack suggests that the ideal method of attaining a preliminary audition is to consult with a "professional teacher" who can best evaluate an amateur's real potential, yet such practical advice is framed within terms more readily associated with fantasy; "Our aim is to help make your dream come true" (ibid.). Misconstruing the material conditions of the commercial market and commodity consumption, Mack writes, "Remember there is always room at the top for you. The law of supply and demand doesn't apply to show business. Entertainment is a commodity that brings people happiness and there can never be an overabundance of happiness in the world" (ibid.: 91). Apart from ignoring the profit-driven motivations of the show and the networks, what is missing in his explanation is that, in joining the program's branded traveling units, an individual must, in fact, sacrifice his or her amateur status.[8] Furthermore, touring in an *Original Amateur Hour* unit also propelled amateur artists into a low-paying professional milieu that generated revenue for the *Original Amateur Hour* enterprise but only marginally remunerated the musicians and did not necessarily position them for full-blown entertainment careers.[9]

For television audiences, amateur and youth talent programs offered a relatively familiar visual experience but they also introduced a new site in which to engage with the narration of American cultural values. The amateur programming genre provided a vehicle that advanced the dominant discourse of "opportunity" and related themes of individual effort and "natural" artistry, promoting the belief that, within an idealized meritocracy, success awaits those who work most intensely or who are endowed with extraordinary talent. Within this perspective, the amateur or talent show is situated within a deeper narrative of American optimism and hope, fairness and justice, and is, thus, much more than just the product of industrial production of commodities. This enters the realm of American myth. The tangible outcomes are apparent, as contestants appear onscreen performing earnestly within the rules and structures of television's amateur/talent genre. Yet the young artists also provide flesh-and-blood evidence that the cultural system is seemingly functioning and that the myth is intact. In this sense, these televised contests reinforce an important ideological element pertaining to aptitude, work, and their respective rewards in a national context where "anything is possible."

As this suggests, the amateur/talent genre also produces discourse, bolstering dominant ideologies while reproducing cultural norms. Affirming the powerful themes of American possibility, Ted Mack writes in soaring terms:

> In show business we are probably more conscious of America's opportunities than in any other business. . . . In show business we have dramatic proof of the realization of America's democratic ideals. . . . The Original Amateur Hour is strictly in the best spirit of the democracy that is all-America. For inspiration take the Polish singer, chased from one refugee camp to another, who learned the true meaning of the torch held high by our Statue of Liberty. The votes of listeners made her a three-time winner. Today she understands why America is called the land of opportunity. (1952: 27)

The "opportunity" referred to by Mack is of a vague and ultimately ideological order, linking the notion of opportunity to principles of freedom and unbounded idealism that are forged in a distinctly American mold. Yet despite Mack's optimistic rhetorical flourish, amateur shows were generally more prone to promote less lofty and more concrete material ambitions among the nation's amateur musical artists of all ages.

For amateur musicians, the real selling point of these programs was the prospect of economic remuneration, of gaining a foothold in the professional music business or, of an even more basic nature, the offer of brief but immediate celebrity and the reward of being seen by a massive viewing audience. Robert Stebbins identifies a category called "conditional preprofessionalism" whereby amateur musical talents express their interest in "becoming professionals in their field, if certain conditions are met" (1992: 46). Television qualifies as part of the entertainment industry's conditional apparatus in its capacity to provide performance context and experience along with its promotional facility in introducing prospective talent to a wider public. Verifying the magnetic draw of an opportunity to grace the small screen, Morley Meredith, a baritone vocalist appearing on the June 25, 1953, episode of *Chance of Lifetime*, states in conversation with the show's host, Dennis James, "I'd like to sing on Broadway and I like television very much too and this has certainly given me an opportunity to be seen by a lot of people throughout the country."

Reinforcing the theme of hopefulness and the sense of excitement that accompanied a televised appearance, TV fan magazines occasionally published profiles featuring prospective young musical talents whose appearances on televised amateur programs briefly bestowed them with a tinge of celebrity allure (Frappollo 1952; "Her Chance of a Lifetime" 1954).[10] *Radio and Television Mirror* explained in 1948 how themes of hope and aspiration constituted an important element of fascination among amateur/talent programs:

> The talent displayed by these unknowns is often amazing, and almost as important are the cheerful persistence and the hopes and dreams that you can hear between the lines of their stories. . . . [T]o be able to see the expression on a young girl's face as she tells a little bit about her background and her ambitions, and to be able to watch her while she sings her song, add to your interest and enjoyment of the show a thousand-fold. ("The Wheel Spins" 1948: 44)

Having bloomed quickly as the new broadcast medium took hold in the national psyche, television's ancillary media added significantly to the circulation of images and narratives pertaining to amateur or talent programs. With feature articles on some of the top amateur programs and their hosts or contestants, fan-oriented magazines helped to reinforce many of the mainstream social perspectives about American television as a medium of optimism and opportunity. These celebrity-obsessed publications amplify public knowledge of the amateur artists that they profile, locating the young musical performers within a media frame that is more commonly reserved for established artists. In such circumstances, the instant celebrity phenomenon challenges conventional notions of artistic labor and practice, effectively altering the lengthy (if romanticized) process of a musician "paying one's dues."

Framing the notions of optimism or opportunity somewhat differently — and, arguably, more realistically — the host of *Chance of a Lifetime*, Dennis James, reminds the audience that the program had, in fact, helped launch several music careers but that there was no accident or luck involved in the procedures by which the program's talent was secured. On the June 25, 1953, broadcast, James embarks on a lengthy monologue stressing the program's diligence and expounding on the authenticity of its mission:

> Just remember, you're giving people a chance of a lifetime that really, truly deserve a chance of a lifetime. Here with this show, this is just a showcase. We think that across this country of ours there's a lot of great talent in

Dennis James, host of *Chance of a Lifetime*. ABC/Du Mont, circa 1950–56.
COURTESY OF PHOTOFEST.

a lot of small cities and a lot of big cities. We feel that not all the talent
you see on the air is the finest talent in the world and we go out searching
with representatives every single week, every single hour, every minute of
every day trying to find that talent and to give them a chance of a lifetime.

In his explanation, James suggests that the labor and investment undertaken
by the program staff mirrors that of the struggling musical talent, producing
a bond that buttresses the authenticity claims of each.

In their introductions and stage banter, the amateur program hosts actively constructed an ideological framework within which performances

were executed, although a 1950 *Variety* review of *The Horace Heidt Show* was critical of Heidt, who, it was thought, "presses the 'opportunity' theme too heavily" ("Horace Heidt Show" 1950: 30). Hosts introduce the amateur contestants and almost invariably guide discussion toward their profession or labor status, family circumstances, and other personal achievements; these brief dialogues very often include mention of the contestants' musical career aspirations and dreams. The narration of subjective histories and personal circumstances functions as a means of introducing each individual and rendering him or her somehow knowable and authentic, someone ostensibly "just like you or me." The audience, it was assumed, welcomed the performance of authenticity embodied by these amateurs, finding pleasure in the earnest articulation of hope. Viewers awaited each performance in anticipation of witnessing a potentially breakthrough moment when "a star is born," eager for the extraordinary or transcendent performance that might launch an unknown into the celebrity stratosphere. The audience members collectively shared a moment of discovery and revelation even as the music and television industry apparatuses embarked on a process of celebrity construction.

The declarations of hope and optimism expressed by most of the show's participants suggest that their television appearances situate them at the boundary between the mundane and the exceptional; this is, for them, a personal event of potentially life-altering magnitude. The repetition among participants of an ideal image of success in show business is clearly measured against the descriptions of their actual vocations: school teacher, student, housewife, salesman, machinist, all of which are described in terms of boredom and monotony. Indeed, in identifying their day jobs and the means by which they generate income and make a living, these musical contestants also remind the viewing audience that they are merely amateurs. After all, if one is employed full-time in some nonmusical capacity, the time allotted to musical pursuits is severely impacted. The sense of upended normalcy of a TV appearance is reinforced in a profile of *The Horace Heidt Show* (published in the mainstream magazine *TV Show*), in which the emphasis is placed on the program's positive impact on a young singer who could finally leave his job as a janitor, or on a harmonica duo whose winning performance and subsequent appearances with the Heidt touring band allowed them to step away from their jobs as truck drivers ("Horace Heidt Trains Talent" 1951: 19).

According to Matthew Stahl (2004), narrative in amateur shows functions as a positioning force, inscribing individuals within a series of social structures and an array of value-laden relations. The amateur musician's goals of success or self-improvement are infused into the preperformance interview, yet these short dialogues with the program host also enunciate a bridge between the realm of obscurity and the potentiality of recognition. Following Stahl's analytical lead, it is clear that the discussions between contestants and hosts are anything but benign, revealing deeper aspects of desire, sincerity, and financial need as well as indicating the submerged elements of professional optimism or anxiety. They are, in a fundamental sense, ideologically oriented within a complex system of hegemonic values and meanings.

As various social values are articulated among eager musical contenders, contradictions and dilemmas in the dominant social order often arise, especially where such critical factors as employment, labor, or class are invoked. In many of these instances, rather than communicating utopian ideals couched in the positive imagery of American promise or the virtues of a meritocratic system, what often resonates most loudly instead is the crisis of class inequality and capitalism's divisive character that produce deep-seated anxieties and fear. John Caldwell also identifies the class-based character of the amateurs' narrative discourses: "*Ted Mack's Original Amateur Hour* made references to the working-class and low-culture origins of its contestants an obligatory ritual. . . . The show repeatedly set up each contestant within a working-class milieu. . . . Having dutifully confessed, each performer was then allowed to act out his or her cultural aspirations" (1995: 34). Seen from this vantage, in gaining entry to the nation's television screens amateur musicians are not celebrating the freedom of American democratic society and the lure of unlimited opportunity so much as they are seeking escape from the struggles of unemployment or the general routines of the working classes, sometimes turning to televised talent contests out of sheer desperation. Television emerges as an implement of salvation in a ruthless and unforgiving class-based social system.

On the January 10, 1950, broadcast of *Ted Mack's Original Amateur Hour*, a contestant is introduced as "a housewife . . . and mother of a twenty-one-month-old boy and she sings popular ballads." In his discussion with the contestant, Mack occupies a paternalistic and patriarchal role, voicing his amazement that a housewife can maintain a home and raise a child while managing to pursue an interest in music. The woman then dedicates the performance to her husband, admitting to Mack the economic difficulties within the family and, with a hint of discomfort, she explains that she is "trying to make good of it. . . . I would appreciate if I could get something from this appearance tonight, such as a job." Later in the same show, a tap-dancing violinist from Detroit appears, explaining to Mack that "a few complications have set in at home. I'm helping to put my younger brother through college and can't make up my mind whether I want to go into a career in show business or not." Mack responds gravely, explaining, "I have to tell you the truth, it's a pretty precarious business," as he signals for her performance to begin. In these instances, the home and the family are not safe and welcoming refuges but sites of economic distress and turmoil. In the minds of these individuals, television and its attendant potential to elevate one's financial or celebrity status offers the opportunity of emancipation from the misery of class oppression.

Reflecting a similar discourse of hardship and anxiety, on the June 6, 1953, broadcast of *Chance of a Lifetime*, contestant Bette Chapel explains that she was formerly affiliated with Dave Garroway's *Garroway at Large* in Chicago but her career had been grievously disrupted by unspecified intervening factors. The *Chance of a Lifetime* slot was her first network appearance since her troubles and she expresses her hope that it will get her back on her feet professionally.[11] After singing "What Is This Thing Called Love?" she is selected by the studio audience as the show's talent winner, compelling host Dennis James to enthusiastically exclaim, "You're back in, kid. It's a thrill seeing you come back into the business." Here, television offers deliverance, presenting the opportunity for Ms. Chapel to reclaim her dignity and to reassert a sense of self-worth as well as possibly recovering her professional livelihood. Significantly, the July 10–16 1953, issue of *TV Guide* features a photo of Chapel with Garroway and other cast members, suggesting that she did rejoin him for at least part of the nine-month run of his new program, *The Dave Garroway Show*, a Friday evening variety program that he hosted along with his morning duties as host of the *Today* show ("Garroway Today" 1953: 14).

While the competitive nature of many amateur and talent shows was a standard feature, the methods of assessment and selecting winners varied. The three most common processes of adjudication involved audience phone-in or mail-in votes, a panel composed of celebrity or expert judges from the music and entertainment industries, or pseudoscientific mechanisms that supposedly measured audience applause. Of the latter scoring method, Paul Whiteman's *TV Teen Club* selected winners with the help of a clocklike mechanism called the "Pops' Talent Tester" that purportedly measured scores. In a similar vein, the scores on *Chance of a Lifetime* were assessed by an "applause-o-meter" that relied on the volume of the theater audience's responses to the performers. The "meter" presented a vague system of measurement and was interpreted with unreliable accuracy by the host Dennis James; on one 1955 broadcast, James obviously misreads the meter and incorrectly calls a tie between two contestants, eliciting audible catcalls and moans from members of the audience in attendance before repeating the "vote."

The prizes for the winning performances also reflected different aspects of the genre, varying according to the age of the contestants and their level of experience. The tyro contestants on *TV Teen Club* were eligible to win a one-hundred-dollar defense bond with the weekly prize consisting of products including a Kelvinator kitchen range, refrigerator, or freezer. On the January 12, 1952, broadcast it was stated that if a new contestant beat the previous five-week winner, the grand prize was a 1952 Nash Rambler Sedan provided by the Nash-Kelvinator Corporation, the show's primary sponsor. Considering the tender ages of the contestants, however, the *TV Teen Club* prizes are peculiar and much more reflective of a parent's material interests. More appropriately, the winners on *Freddy Martin's "Band of Tomorrow,"* all of whom were either high school or college students, were selected by judges—including Stan Kenton—to perform in a thirteen-piece band led by Martin.

The superior musical performances on *Chance of a Lifetime* and the fact that the contestants were often older (with many claiming professional or semiprofessional experience prior to their television debut) required a correspondingly suitable prize. Reflecting the contestants' preprofessional status, the show's formidable award package included "a trip to New York to stay at the glamorous Hotel Roosevelt," an "opportunity" with Universal International Pictures, a "tryout" with Columbia Records, "an engagement at the internationally famous Latin Quarter in the heart of Broadway's Great White Way," and a thousand dollars in cash. For most contestants, of course, the real prize was the opportunity to capitalize on television's broadcast exposure and to leverage one's appearance into wider public and professional engagements. Among the young artists who directly benefited from the program's prize package and TV exposure was the singer Diahann Carroll (then a freshman at New York University), who translated her multiple 1954 *Chance of a Lifetime* victories into an extremely successful and enduring entertainment career.

Not all of the amateur talent programs focused on musical performances per se. CBS TV's *Songs for Sale*, airing between 1950 and 1952 (simulcast on radio during its first season), featured contestants whose song lyrics were judged by professionals in the music and entertainment industry. Originally hosted by Jan Murray as a summer replacement program in 1950, Steve Allen took the helm in the 1951–52 season. The program's musical director was the seemingly ubiquitous Ray Bloch. In advance of its June 30, 1950, debut, CBS explained in a press release that *Songs for Sale* "will feature each week four composers of unpublished songs, plus a panel of four famous songwriters, veterans of Tin Pan Alley, sitting as judges." On the program opener two guest vocalists, Rosemary Clooney and Tony Bennett, performed the new compositions, "alternating them with well known pieces by the four veteran composers." A young Richard Hayes (who had himself emerged victorious on the CBS amateur program *Arthur Godfrey's Talent Scouts* the previous year) subsequently replaced Bennett. Guest artists over the course of the program's duration included Cab Calloway, the jazz trumpeter Dizzy Gillespie, the vocalists Peggy Lee and Johnny Desmond, and the bandleader Guy Lombardo. The revolving panel of judges was also impressive, with representatives from several sectors of the industry; at various times they included the composer and bandleader Duke Ellington, Mitch Miller (a Columbia Records executive), and Sigmund Spaeth (a musicologist and staunch music appreciation advocate who hosted a 1930s radio show and an early musical TV show, both titled *The Tune Detective*).

Songs judged as "most likely to become a hit" were published, and the winning lyricists received a very modest cash prize of two hundred dollars. Yet there was controversy during the program's first season as opportunistic "song-sharks"—professional composers and lyricists—preyed on "amateur cleffers . . . pitching up a get-rich-quick prospectus to their potential customers," who sought an edge in the TV contests ("Song-Sharks" 1951: 1). These "sharks" enticed songwriters by offering to assist in the composition process for a fee, sharing the writing credits, and partaking of a percentage of any rewards should the composition win on the broadcast. The practice was apparently widespread on both radio and television amateur composer programs, although it was declared that "staffers for such shows as 'Songs for Sale,' however, are hep to the operations and throw such entries out of the competition" (ibid.).

After taking over the show's host duties, Allen (a more-than-passable pianist and a prolific songwriter himself) expounded on the music publishing industry and how *Songs for Sale* fit into it, explaining, "I know of no field of profession that is so closed to new talent. . . . Not only does the unknown writer face the almost insurmountable odds in his struggle to get a song published but he also may fall victim to unscrupulous operators" (1952: 18). Allen describes the power and industry influence of "the big firms" with national and international offices, suggesting that the *Songs for Sale* program occupies a role similar to the industry's song pluggers that leverage tunes in the market. The media columnist John Lester lauded *Songs for Sale*, defining it in towering terms and extolling the program for providing

> an important service both to show business and the general public, chiefly for its contributions over more than a year, to the fund of popular music, to which America hums, sings, whistles, works, plays and builds, and from which it draws, even hourly, inspiration and strength. More specifically, it serves America's vast army of amateurs who look to songwriting as a means of that personal expression and recognition for which everyone yearns and all have the God-given right to strive. (CBS press release, February 18, 1952)

The amateur lyricists competing on *Songs for Sale* represented an interesting cross-section of the American social landscape, with earnest songwriting contestants working day jobs as hairdressers, secretaries, educators, business managers, nurses, and other careers further off the beaten path, such as a boxer, undertaker and coffin manufacturer, or cowboy.

At times the contestants seemed to be selected primarily for their unique character and compelling backstory. On the November 17, 1951, show the winner was nine-year-old Marjorie Kurtz, whose composition was conceived, she said, in a dream. Guy Lombardo's music publishing company published Kurtz's winning entry, "Snowflakes," and the Lombardo orchestra recorded and released the track (with vocals by Evelyn Knight) within ten days of the song's broadcast performance on *Songs for Sale*. The disk sold almost 250,000 copies in its first two weeks.[12] Even with the program proving capable of lifting the rare song into the mainstream or of generating interest in an individual's songwriting abilities, Allen offered pragmatic advice to hopeful amateur wordsmiths: "Continue to write songs, but don't put your whole heart and soul into dreaming of the days when you'll be a wealthy composer" (1952: 18).

"Boom" in the Ballroom: KTLA's Remote Broadcasts

Adjusting to the new realities of the entertainment realm, stakeholders in various sectors of the music industry reevaluated their business strategies and plans for the marketing and presentation of popular music. Associates in the Midwest Ballroom Operators Association, for example, expressed the belief at their 1948 convention that television might help to overcome negative attitudes toward ballrooms that in a conservative mindset were often perceived as "dens of iniquity." Association members wanted to add a visual component to the familiar remote ballroom dance band format established in radio, and they further hoped that television would "break down this prejudice by showing ballrooms as they really are" ("Tele Band Remotes" 1948: 45), introducing home viewers to the venues' often ornate interiors and glamorous stage shows. In this context, the incentive among ballroom owners was not simply to polish the reputation of their venues but to promote their businesses and "lure dancers into their establishments" (Emge 1950b: 6).

Down Beat observed that televised ballroom broadcasts could also be quite lucrative for musicians, who stood to earn more than the basic union scale for standard performances because of the new AFM salary stipulations. The union rates explicitly addressed the responsibilities of the orchestras and bandleaders on TV ballroom broadcasts, stating, "The musicians (and the leader) must be able to handle a show, the band must be able to present at least one feature number of visual entertainment value, and be ready to play satisfactory conventional dance music following the TV show" (ibid.).

The remote ballroom broadcasts on the Los Angeles station KTLA-TV garnered particular praise. Originating from several of the area's top venues including the Aragon Ballroom in Ocean Park/Santa Monica, the Santa Monica Ballroom, and the Palladium and the Trianon in Los Angeles, KTLA's ballroom programs (attributed to the ingenuity of Klaus Landsberg, KTLA's general manager)[13] were responsible for increased box office revenues and for elevating the professional status and celebrity profiles of several bandleaders, especially Spade Cooley, Ina Ray Hutton, Harry Owens,[14] Frank DeVol, and Lawrence Welk.

The station itself made news in 1949 when it broadcast the sensational attempted rescue of three-year-old Kathy Fiscus (who plummeted to her death down an uncovered well shaft in nearby San Marino), covering the story with a mobile pickup around the clock for over twenty-four hours, and mesmerizing the Los Angeles area with a steady stream of images from the site of the tragedy. The KTLA historian Mark Williams writes,

> Landsberg realized that telecasts featuring mobile pickups "solved" certain industrial, economic, and programming limitations endemic to local stations, while at the same time capitalizing on opportunities in the burgeoning community for both "entertainment" and "public service" programming. Working to stimulate local interest in KTLA by marrying the topicality of television to that of events within the city, remotes also helped to profile the station as a leading participant in a community medium. (1999: 297)

With its on-the-ground broadcast style, KTLA also helped to define a lively music scene in the greater Los Angeles area, capturing the essence of the ballrooms and, importantly, disseminating musical performances that represented an impressively diverse range of musical styles and cultural referents. Proudly explaining KTLA's commitment to music broadcasting in 1951, Klaus Landsberg stated, "KTLA has gone its own way and gone all the way in pioneering musical presentations in television. KTLA today presents more musical shows than any other station in the country, and all of them are among the top rated shows in the area" (1951: 8). *Down Beat* affirmed Landsberg's evaluation of his station in 1952 with the claim "Hollywood has taken over the reins and is setting the pace in the television industry for the use of bands in TV" (Emge 1952b: 1).

One of the first beneficiaries of KTLA's ballroom broadcasts was Spade Cooley (born Donnell Clyde Cooley), dubbed the "King of Western Swing."[15] Cooley had played fiddle in the 1930s with the influential band The Sons of the Pioneers, where he befriended the future western movie star Roy Rogers, a relationship that also later gave him entrée to the film industry, leading to appearances in several western films. Cooley's broadcasting career began in the early 1940s, when he performed on Gene Autry's radio show *Melody Ranch* in a band led by the country star Jimmy Wakely, and he debuted as a headliner in 1946 with *Spade Cooley Time* on the Los Angeles radio station KFVD. Capitalizing on his popular standing at both the Venice Pier and Santa Monica ballrooms, Cooley was signed as host of KTLA-TV's *Hoffman Hayride* in 1948. *Down Beat* touted the show as the "first remote television broadcast from a dancery" (Holly 1948: 12) with Cooley increasing attendance by one thousand people during his Saturday night broadcasts

Spade Cooley. Undated. COURTESY OF PHOTOFEST.

from the Santa Monica ballroom. According to *Down Beat*, Cooley was the primary catalyst in a wave of televised western music shows originating in the Los Angeles area.[16] When the program moved from the ballroom setting to the KTLA studios (airing as *The Spade Cooley Show*), Cooley's role shifted as well from musician/bandleader to a more conventional role as master of ceremonies and occasional soloist.

Cooley's amiable personality as a host (apparently distinct from his off-screen reputation as an alcoholic brawler who was found guilty of torturing and murdering his wife in 1961) was easily conveyed on television (Kienzle 2003: 3–26). Moreover, his country-infused swing style resonated with the large number of "Dust Bowl migrants" from the Midwestern and Southwestern states who had landed in the Los Angeles area over the previous twenty years in search of employment in the agriculture and defense industries. These hard-tack "hillbillies" were well disposed toward the up-tempo rhythms of the Cooley ensemble, and they converged in droves at the band's ballroom engagements. Citing KTLA's role in his success, Cooley explained, "Television boomed us. . . . [W]e were only moderately successful at the ballroom until the television show caught on" ("Cooley Lauds TV" 1950: 4).

The ballroom broadcast format used by KTLA was also cited as the primary force in the regional success of the Los Angeles bandleader Ina Ray Hutton, of whom *Variety* wrote, "Last summer, Miss Hutton was virtually unknown on the Coast" ("Television Builds Ina Ray Hutton" 1950: 36).[17] The ensemble performed on telecasts from several Los Angeles venues and, citing attendance and nightclub reservation figures, it was noted that "television's power as a talent builder is shown in the skyrocketing Coast career of Ina Ray Hutton." Such was Hutton's success on KTLA that the Los Angeles station KTTV tried to capture some of the excitement with the introduction of *Search for Girls*, featuring Ada Leonard as host, leading her "all-girl" band. After leading a male band during the war years, Hutton's "all-girl" orchestra[18] — or, as girl bands were sometimes indiscreetly termed, "bosom bands" — was assembled specifically for her television program, and *Down Beat* marveled at her sudden revival, noting that prior to her TV show she was "pretty close to the end of her long career as a girl band leader. . . . Today Ina is probably a bigger attraction as a personality than at any time" (Emge 1952b: 7)

Ina Ray Hutton's All-Girl Show offered a mix of staged variety and production numbers featuring band members in various costumes as well as straight-ahead arrangements of popular and standard selections. Surviving footage reveals Hutton's bubbly persona, and she is frequently on the verge of hilarity, giddily leading the proceedings and declaring in one episode, "We still have all the girls and no men allowed," in a manner suggesting a sleepover more than a television program. Even though she was a veteran bandleader and a passable singer and "hoofer," with a professional resume going back to the mid-1930s, Hutton's ample stage and film experience (including several musical shorts in the 1930s with her female band The Melodears) seemed barely up to the demands of television broadcasting. Television obviously tested her abilities, and she was frequently seen looking furtively offstage as if for instruction or support. The show's musical repertoire did not help either, with its hodge-podge of genres (encompassing sophisticated dance band arrangements, barrelhouse boogie-woogie, classical selections, popular standards, and pure novelty pieces) that were often performed with shoddy staging and amateurish enactments. Notwithstanding the various problems concerning staging and content, the show was awarded an Emmy award in 1951 (McGee 2009: 213).

Even with the reputation of a qualified bandleader, Hutton's musical standing was partially compromised by KTLA's production style and an unrelenting emphasis on the orchestra's sexual allure that favored lingering full and half-shots of the female musicians. Whereas the Cooley show was oriented toward a particular working-class audience with rural roots, the Hutton show seemed to target an ideal male viewer whose musical tastes were secondary to the masculine desires fulfilled by the visual exhibition. Commenting on the program, the *Down Beat* writer Hal Holly implicitly confirmed the leering, scopic pleasures derived from an evening spent watching the Hutton show:

> Ina May and her bandmates could be built into one of the biggest attractions in video. And we aren't inferring that they aren't well built right now. Every musician in this band could do the show in a bathing suit. . . . [W]e discovered that Ina Ray, whom we had always regarded as more decorative than useful as a bandleader, actually knows what she's doing with that music in front of her. Not that it matters. We're more curious as to what manner of ingeniously designed engineering device makes that gown she wears stay where it belongs while Ina seems to be testing it to the utmost. (1950: 13)

Holly's colleague Charles Emge employed a similarly gendered perspective in defining Hutton's television appeal: "Videoglers love to watch her as she 'conducts' her all-girl orchestra with her sinuous stick-waving and body-weaving, predicting that she's going to fall out of her tight-fitting gown sooner or later and guessing at her age" (Emge 1952b: 7).

Attesting to Emge and Holly's observations (if not to their analysis), footage of Hutton shows her wearing luxurious, snug evening wear and shimmering show gowns; her female band members are also clad in attractive, though less lavish and revealing stage costumes. The performances invite speculation that Hutton's gowns were deliberately cut tighter than those of her band members or musical guests and that her necklines plunged slightly lower, contributing to the sex appeal of the sprightly blond show host. Perhaps in

Ina Ray Hutton. circa 1948. COURTESY OF PHOTOFEST.

recognition of the orchestra's steamy visual profile, in 1952 the Hutton show aired rather late—between 9:00 and 10:00 P.M.—on Tuesday evenings.

The station KTLA was also a catalyst of the longtime television career of Lawrence Welk, whose regular one-hour show originated on the station on May 11, 1951, with remote broadcasts from the Aragon Ballroom. Welk recalls how Landsberg used the ballroom performances as "a proving ground. If a band showed fan appeal on the Aragon tryout, anything could happen" (Coakley 1958: 221). Of the program's origins, Welk explains that he was initially unaware that his performance contract at the Aragon included KTLA's simultaneous television feed. Upon learning of the arrangement, he was reluctant to sign on for the broadcasts, noting, "We'd been on TV in New York two different nights, and we didn't set fire on the world" (ibid.: 220). Welk later recalled of his KTLA debut, "We received tremendous reaction. In those years I used to say we had more reaction to one television show than we had in all our career in radio" (*KTLA* 1967).

Once again, KTLA's unique remote production format was a factor in establishing the Welk show's broadcast character. By featuring sweeping pans of the attendant audience at the end of each song, a sense of place was established, something that was often lacking in the production styles preferred by New York television producers. Rather than the ersatz night spots portrayed on many New York shows, the KTLA remote broadcasts came from someplace recognizable and, more to the point, actually accessible — someplace *real*. The box office figures at these Los Angeles area ballrooms reflected the added promotional value of broadcasting from their stages, with *Down Beat* commenting that the Welk band "packs them in five nights a week" at the Aragon Ballroom ("Video, Visual Appeal" 1953: 40). As a testament to his appeal and the popularity of the KTLA ballroom format, Lawrence Welk's shows aired nationwide between 1955 and 1982. Although he died in 1992, he can still occasionally be seen leading his "musical family" in packaged specials on the PBS network sixty years after his start at KTLA.

Crisis in the Nightclubs

Even with evidence at KTLA that a well-produced ballroom program could boost a band's profile, increase the venue's box office revenues, and make for an entertaining television show, concerns prevailed in the music industry around TV's economic impact on performance spaces. With steady improvements in network programming and the soaring rate of household TV set sales after 1948, actors, comedians, dancers, and musicians expressed dread at the nation's new "stay-at-home" habits. For them, television's potential to disrupt traditional leisure practices was a source of deep professional anxiety and fear.

Addressing TV's impact on cinema or other performance sites, Philip Auslander explains how "the implication of the cultural discourse surrounding television was that one should watch television *instead* of going to the theatre. The televisual experience is implicitly equated with the live theatrical experience, but is represented as better suited to the postwar, suburban lifestyle: the message is that nothing is lost, and much is gained, by staying home" (1999: 23). Indeed, Sylvester "Pat" Weaver (who joined NBC in 1949 as vice president in charge of television, earning a reputation as one of the medium's most significant architects) described the network's programming strategies as a straightforward attempt to get "more people to spend their entire evening at home with NBC rather than doing what they usually did on many Saturday nights — going to dinner and a stage show or movie, then perhaps a nightclub or a ballroom with a dance band" (1994: 194).

As early as 1947, before home televisions were commonplace, *Variety* reported in detail about the placement of television sets "in small clubs, taverns, etc." in Hollywood "as a serious displacer of other entertainment forms. . . . Others still using a combination of both video and music are regarded as just biding time, waiting to see how tele is received by patrons before shelving talent" ("Coast Tele Sets" 1947: 1). The theme was sustained in 1948 when *Variety* reported further curtailment of live talent bookings at two Hollywood "eateries" that had installed TV sets ("H'wood Eateries" 1948: 1).[19]

In 1948, the *Wall Street Journal* quoted the Paramount Pictures vice president Paul Raibourn, who admitted, "A new purchaser of a television set cuts down 20% to 30% on all other forms of relaxation and amusement for the first few months" ("Television Set Owners" 1948). The new medium's draw soon raised other unforeseen problems; in early 1953 the *New York Times* radio and TV reporter Val Adams (1953) observed an audience trend whereby viewers eagerly sought complimentary tickets to network broadcasts in New York, especially favoring musical variety shows (including *The Ed Sullivan Show*, *Your Show of Shows*, and *Your Hit Parade*). The demand was so intense that people were wait-listed for months and international ticket seekers even expressed a willingness to plan their vacations around ticket availability. This desire to attend TV broadcasts resulted in reduced attendance at radio broadcasts and undermined ticket sales at other venues, including stage shows, music lounges, and showcase clubs.

It must be recognized, of course, that television was but one element within a complex nexus of postwar influences affecting leisure pursuits: changes in family finances and the rise of a credit-based economy, intensified home ownership patterns (with accompanying mortgage responsibilities), increased birthrates and the demands of raising a family, the duress of commuting to and from exurban communities, and numerous other factors could all be cited as significant. Still, faced with the closure of countless drinking establishments, fewer openings of new bars and taverns, and decreased restaurant profits across the country in the late 1940s and early 1950s, the dining and public entertainment industries were concerned by comments such as Raibourn's, pointing to television and the growth of domestic viewing as the likely culprit.[20]

Numerous studies (of questionable statistical rigor) on the topic of television's audience influence emerged in the late 1940s and early 1950s with the data suggesting that within the small but quickly growing proportion of TV households, a shift of significant proportion was under way. These studies (conducted by television network research divisions, consumer and market research agencies, or university research labs such as the Hofstra University Television Research Bureau, founded in 1948) indicated that television viewing commonly exceeded radio listening, reading, and listening to recorded music in the home. The studies also encompassed the realm of public entertainment, attempting to determine how and to what extent television was affecting audience patterns and economic revenues in theaters, bars, taverns, or nightclubs, where musical performances or jukebox systems were typical. With more reliable metrics, a Hofstra survey determined in August 1948 that 42 percent fewer TV families enjoyed "commercial forms of entertainment" (including "dining, dancing, night-clubbing") than did non-TV families ("Telestatus" 1948: 18).

Since television sets were placed in various public establishments in the immediate postwar years, there was spirited discussion about the influence on patrons' habits. A widely held perception, optimistically touted in the early promotional materials of television networks and TV set manufacturers, maintained that television would bring the world to the viewer or in a case of virtual mobilization, the medium might magically "transport" the viewer to other places and spaces. The notion of mobility and transport functioned in reverse as well: referring to the show host Gary Moore, *Television World* quipped, "All his life he had fought against going to cocktail lounges — then one appearance on television and he finds himself in 500 at once" (M. Sullivan 1948: 5). Pertaining to television placement in a bar or tavern environment, the argument was made that watching television was just like being "there" and a proliferation of articles in the late 1940s suggested that a seat at the bar constituted the "best seat in the house," an ideal vantage from which to watch a ball game or prize fight while enjoying drinks and the camaraderie of fellow fans.

People gained new access to television on a daily basis as televisions were installed in public drinking establishments at a rapid pace. Kerry Segrave cites a 1947 *Billboard* study in Chicago that determined that while "only 10-percent of taverns were equipped with a television, about one-third of all sets in the city were in taverns" (2002: 198). By April 1949, it was estimated that "at least 2,500 of New York City's 3,000 bars — roughly 85 percent — have invested in television sets" (Stewart 1949). The bars, grills, and taverns, as well as private clubs and fraternal organizations where TV sets were purchased in the late 1940s, constituted early technological adopters (although it is important to acknowledge the aggressive work of television salesmen and coin machine operators whose persuasive abilities evidently influenced the trend). One often cited joke went so far as to suggest that with television's rapid ascendance and ubiquity, TV trouble-shooting and repairs were a necessary new skill set required of prospective bartenders.

Patrons consequently experienced a sharp upturn in TV-viewing occasions as they moved from place to place, circulating through the city in their usual routines. In the earliest television years there was even a tendency in press advertisements to identify bars and taverns according to whether or not they had installed a TV set, with establishments promoting themselves as uniquely desirable destination spots. As a promotional strategy, public television installation introduced citizens to the medium while normalizing new means of apprehending the world in visual form and in real time.

Anna McCarthy (2001) explains how, in the immediate postwar period, television sets were introduced to public (or "non-domestic") spaces that adhered to their own established codes and patterns, often demarcated by factors such as race, class, or gender.[21] With its public placement, television was fused with the social sites of the neighborhood bar or tavern, a distinct cultural sphere that also often functioned as a central meeting place or an intermediary realm between the home and the workplace. Televisions placed in thousands of small, innocuous drinking houses transformed the character of these spaces, shifting the focus of attention and introducing alternative conversational topics as patrons collectively viewed the onscreen images and commented on performances playing before them. Photographs of taverns in the late 1940s illustrate television's allure, depicting crowded rooms of drinking patrons, heads tilted upward toward the raised television screen. Television was, thus, not simply placed within public establishments that were irrelevant, but it was rapidly integrated into complex and vibrant cultural contexts that involved intricate and sophisticated social rituals. Television landed within localized sites of considerable cultural significance.

Television immediately occupied a mediating role as bar patrons learned to negotiate their social interactions along with their new status as television viewing subjects. Writing in the *New York Herald Tribune* in 1948, Frank Sullivan lamented that television's particular mode of reception stifled traditional bar room chat and social discourse: "I might have been at a wake. No, a wake would have been gayer. . . . Maybe they just felt low at that particular saloon that night. . . . Conversation was dead" (1948). Even the deliberate arrangement of bar stools and folding chairs facing the TV in theater fashion led to an altered barroom setting with a new emphasis on securing seating and competing with other patrons for coveted spots that promised optimal viewing angles (Stewart 1949; "Beer Nursers" 1949). Although there was conflicting testimony about TV's influence on alcohol and beer sales (with TV believed to induce a slight decrease in the pace of consumption), the general consensus was that television was relatively undemanding and, hence, well suited to the disposition of the public tavern.

For whatever merits it held for bar and tavern owners, television directly undermined the status of popular music in these settings. Public TV installation allowed proprietors to circumvent the effort and expense of providing other entertainment options, whether in the form of a small musical act or a jukebox. With unemployment among musicians constituting a pressing issue at the time, any factor that perpetuated depression within the industry was regarded as a threat (a view voiced often and aggressively by the AFM's James C. Petrillo). Rather than an uncomplicated leisure technology transmitting entertainment in the nation's drinking spots, television emerged as a tool for reinforcing an establishment's financial bottom line, sustaining instrumental objectives and facilitating rational cost-cutting practices that ill-served working musicians. Framed in this manner, it is easier to understand why some musicians came to resent television and its expanding social impact in the late 1940s and early 1950s.

Not every drinking establishment was inclined to adopt television and risk disrupting a carefully cultivated atmosphere. *Billboard* reported that genteel social conventions at times weighed against the installation of television sets in cocktail lounges:

> Some of the intimate spots are going on record against video. These intimate spots, cocktail lounges with soft lights and muted music, contend

that their customers come to talk, hold hands, and relax and that tele is "jarring." While other locations are falling all over themselves with signs reading "Baseball Television," "Immediate Seating for Television," etc., the intimate spot owners say they will do a heavy job on the other end of the ticket with announcements and signs saying "No Television." ("Singing Those Tele Blues" 1948: 103)

The upscale cocktail lounge was itself a rather recent development, having emerged as a prominent institution during the war years (Segrave 2002: 166). In defining these social spaces, intimacy is wrapped in a subdued discourse of sophistication and superior tastes, contrasting with the arguably rougher or unrefined nature associated with bars. There is a line implicitly drawn between the working-class sensibilities affiliated with neighborhood bars (ostensibly frequented by sports fans and nondiscriminating *drinkers*) and an effete, bourgeois cultural disposition among the patrons of such "intimate spots." Furthermore, the "muted" musical accompaniment implied in the discussion of the "intimate" lounge setting also subtly hints at a particular aesthetic quality associated with American song "standards" or ballads with lyrics oriented toward themes of love and courtship and light jazz arrangements performed in an understated and unobtrusive style. "Intimate spots" absent of television were conceived as being more accommodating of music and suitable for romantic, mellow affective liaisons of (one might assume) a heterosexual nature.

Television precipitated different problems in musical showcase establishments. The owners of larger nightclubs recognized that TV's rising demand for musicians would lead to a corresponding competition for booking artists, a drain on available musical acts as television siphoned off the top names, and increases in performers' asking fees. In the late 1940s when television was still finding its footing (and its audience), managers and agents negotiated their clients' salaries on a case-by-case basis. Industry experts noted that the salaries paid by the networks generally surpassed those of the lesser performance venues and even exceeded some of the larger or more venerable nightclubs, presenting lucrative new booking opportunities for established musical acts. *Variety* reported that, despite an overall market slump in the general entertainment sector resulting in salary reductions, for many name acts "pay for top talent in television . . . increased anywhere from 250–500% during 1947" ("Video Opening Its Purse Strings" 1947: 27).

As corporate sponsorship stabilized and major advertising agencies committed larger marketing and promotional budgets to television programs through the early 1950s, TV appearance fees climbed further and, for some artists, touring consequently became even less attractive. *Variety* described an almost cutthroat atmosphere in which the major networks jostled for ratings dominance by embarking on a spending splurge in their quest for top talent (Rosen 1953: 1). In one example of the resultant cost hikes, the brassy-voiced Ethel Merman was paid fifty thousand dollars for only two NBC appearances in 1953. These paychecks justifiably thrilled musicians (and their agents and management staff), but the trend was potentially disastrous to the club owners who by this stage couldn't even dream of matching TV salaries. Television's rather sudden and surging demand for musical talent produced a serious crisis in the industry. The deep pockets of the television networks and program sponsors presented a powerful incentive for musicians and their managers to depart from established business patterns associated with the ballrooms, theaters, or nightclubs.

Diverse opinions on the state of affairs inevitably arose. As *Variety* noted in 1951, "Agents believe that the ranks of promising stage and saloon performers, which have been dwindling for some time, can easily be swelled by the influx of talent incubated on television. There is even a belief that talent-testing on television can bring a boom in live entertainment" (M. Kaplan 1951: 2). The positive undercurrent of this perspective suggests that showrooms would benefit from an increase of experienced musical acts that had cut their teeth in television. These television-tested artists often enjoyed greater audience recognition, and they proved capable of filling lounges and clubs due to their new TV profiles.[22] The serious downside for club or theater proprietors was that the artists and their agents could (and did) demand greater remuneration for their club appearances, in the process upending the prevailing economic structure of the music industry's nightclub sector.

Television's long-term contracts with top musical celebrities (especially those hired to host their own programs) further eroded the list of available "A-list" talent on the tour circuits while increasing acts' appearance fees for shows in nightclubs, theaters, or ballrooms. The intensive TV booking binge contributed to declining availability among popular musicians who patrons might venture out to see or for whom they would be reasonably willing to pay a cover charge. The situation became so dire that several Minneapolis venues responded by shifting from mainstream musical entertainment fare to the "blue" market as club owners recast their establishments as exotic bars and strip clubs out of economic necessity. One Minneapolis proprietor explained,

> By showing the finest acts obtainable, TV has spoiled our class of patrons and made them dissatisfied with what we're able to give them — young performers coming up who lack the top-drawer stars' talents, available on the home screens for free. . . . [S]uch stellar acts aren't available to clubs like ours, and if they were, we couldn't afford them because our patrons wouldn't understand our cover charges and higher beverage and food prices which would be essential to meet the payroll. ("TV Hex Ups Sex" 1952: 52)

Even with a rapid increase in musicians' salaries for TV appearances, during the medium's early phase one-night stands or weeklong theater engagements were still an essential facet of the industry. Citing a traditional assumption in the band business, *Variety* stated, "Expensive name combos must range far and wide to maintain earning power" ("Tele's Economy" 1948). Yet the effort of maintaining a professional orchestra, mounting a tour, and traveling from city to city remained substantial. While such tours were indeed lucrative — the "bread and butter" of a musical organization — bandleaders chafed against the extensive costs of taking a full ensemble on the road. Just as TV was emerging in earnest many bandleaders were reducing the size of their orchestras, cutting payroll, and slimming their management retinue in the hopes of remaining fiscally viable (Woods 1948: 193). In some cases television appearances seemed like a far better option for musicians, especially if it meant that the artist or orchestra could sidestep the complexities of touring or if they could maintain a local foothold in the major entertainment hubs of New York, Chicago, or Los Angeles. An extended television booking with an early evening broadcast slot often freed band members to participate in studio recording sessions or other freelance activities during the daytime and to play in the club scene in the late evenings. The ideal arrangement might permit them to "double," alternating between televised performances and regional club or ballroom gigs (and for acts based in Los Angeles or Hollywood, the occasional film appearance).

Tours organized around the band industry's notoriously grueling one-nighters were thought to be particularly exposed to television's impact. Tommy Dorsey was an early and vocal critic of television, grumbling about its deleterious influences on the music industry. Lacking any concrete evidence to support his outlook at such an early stage, Dorsey was convinced that television was already drawing patrons away from his engagements throughout America's heartland as audiences turned to television's "free" entertainment rather than paying for concert tickets.

In 1949, Dorsey mounted a major concert tour that he hoped would top one million dollars in revenue, exceeding his all-time high payoff reached during the war years at the dance bands' peak of popularity. The strategy was primarily motivated by financial self-interest as he attempted to move quickly to "get as much as he can stashed away this year" ("Video Uncertainty" 1949). Dorsey's initiative was also apparently spurred by fears of television's effects and an intensified tour schedule was his response to television's coaxial cable expansion across the nation — something that was still two years off. With television creeping into a growing number of American cities, towns, and villages, Dorsey was certain that it would shrink concert tour revenues in the secondary cities throughout the Midwest, where fans had traditionally clamored for visits by veteran music acts such as his. He took television's development as a personal affront rather than seeing it as the planned growth of a new sector within the entertainment industries.

Dorsey's effusive contempt for the medium was consistent with his generally volatile demeanor and his outbursts about television's encroachment on established public leisure practices were occasionally newsworthy. His outspokenness was particularly pronounced in 1951 — the year the nationwide coaxial cable was actually completed — when, in an expletive-laden interview with *Down Beat*, he exploded in a tirade against television's regional invasion: "That (obscenity) television! Business is pretty good in some places. But in a (obscenity) television area we're dead before we start. As soon as we enter a town and I see those (obscenity) antenna things, I holler murder. People go into debt to buy an (unprintable) TV set and nobody has any dough left. So they stay home" ("That !?*?! Television" 1951: 5) A widespread sentiment in the dance band sector held that, if a top touring orchestra such as Dorsey's was suffering in the regions from television's negative influence, then no one was safe.

Though the precise extent to which television was responsible for box office shortfalls remained unconfirmed, the situation improved slightly for some elite touring musicians by 1953, when television's novelty status began to wear off, leading them to refute Dorsey's dire verdict. Reporting lucrative tour revenues after a four-monthlong series of one-nighters, Spike Jones explained that, whereas television had, in fact, been a problem during his 1952 tour with his manic musical sidekicks The City Slickers, it "no longer exerts any crippling impact as a competitor to touring attractions" ("Spike Jones Revue" 1953: 49). *Variety* noted that the Jones ensemble suffered from television's competition on only one extraordinary occasion, the January 19, 1953, broadcast of the famous "Lucy Goes to the Hospital" episode of *I Love Lucy*, on which Lucille Ball's son, Ricky Jr., is "born." It is worth noting, however, that Spike Jones and his City Slickers had hosted broadcasts of the *Colgate Comedy Hour* and *Four Star Revue* in 1951–52 and the screwball ensemble also made frequent TV guest appearances, undoubtedly promoting the act among viewers and potential concert audiences.

Even as television breathed new life into vaudeville's fading performance traditions and reinvigorated the careers of some musical veterans, it may, finally, have achieved what radio and film did not. By the early 1950s, vaudeville halls were inarguably in their last days and many musicians and comedians begrudgingly acknowledged the end of an era. The *Washington Post* reported in 1953 that the city's venerable Capitol Theater, "vaudeville's last four-a-day stand," was closing its doors due to the difficulties of mounting multiact performances that could sustain box office revenues. Explaining the reasons for shuttering the theater, the *Post* notes, "Even the big name bands, once a huge draw at the house, have fallen off as public magnets in recent years. Another aspect of the supply problem has been reluctance of performers to work 29 shows per week when, through one TV appearance in two weeks, they can earn as much" ("Vaudeville Vanishing" 1953: 19).[23]

Jukeboxes and TV Competition

Among the various players in the music industry to voice their anxiety and alarm, coin machine operators, too, found cause for concern. Jukeboxes had grown as a major purveyor of popular music through the war years, flourishing as an essential component in the promotion of new recordings while playing a valuable cultural role in the consumption and enjoyment of music in public settings.[24] The entertainment trade paper *Billboard* instituted a ratings chart in January 1944 that surveyed the top songs receiving the most spins under the title "Most-Played In Juke Boxes."[25] The coin-operated jukeboxes installed in public establishments were generally leased by coin machine operators who served as intermediaries between machine manufacturers and bar or tavern proprietors. Their income depended on commissions and they were also responsible for overseeing machine maintenance and stocking the units with new disks. Bar owners received a percentage of their machines' take, an arrangement that provided an important incentive to fill the jukeboxes with the latest hits or the most beloved songs with the highest level of popular appeal.

In August 1947, an editorial in *Billboard* contemplated the impact of television installation on the jukebox and music sectors, citing evidence of a 33 percent decrease in jukebox revenue even at this early stage of television's expansion. The editorial ends on an ominous note: "We all know juke boxes are here to stay. Nobody can, at this time, forecast the longevity of television as a jukebox competitor. But we do recognize a serious immediate problem that must be solved right now" ("The Operator and Television" 1947: 112; "Music Biz Eyes TV Future" 1947: 20). The spreading notion of a "problem" among jukebox operators and servicemen was not at all misplaced: television manufacturers were unequivocal in their strategy to press forward with "location tele" as a means of introducing the medium to the public and to generate early television sales until consumer interest and unit retail prices converged, facilitating domestic purchases.

A nonscientific survey in 1947 of Chicago bars and taverns that had adopted television produced inconsistent accounts of TV's influence. Coin operators, bar owners, and jukebox servicemen reported that the greatest drop in jukebox revenues occurred in establishments that had previously been identified as "high play locations" before introducing television; in establishments identified as "low or medium-play spots" (also sometimes described as "marginal locations") the decline was predictably less significant. Furthermore, coin machine operators servicing jukeboxes in smaller establishments such as neighborhood taverns felt television's nip more than those servicing larger lounges, the former smaller sites having installed TV sets at a much faster rate than the latter ("Juke Op" 1947: 110).

There was guarded optimism among some jukebox operators and distributors who contemplated possible forms of collaboration with television manufacturers. Their hope was that, as bar and tavern television ownership grew, jukebox operators might capitalize on their intermediary relationships with both machine manufacturers and proprietors, garnering commissions on new coin-operated TV set leases and developing an alternate revenue stream that might compensate for their losses in jukebox revenue. The initial coin-operated television retail prices were generally in the $1,200–$3,000 range (with the most commonly cited cost being approximately $1,995), prices that many establishment owners considered to be high. Competing manufacturers strove to produce less expensive coin-operated sets for public installation, seeking to bring the retail prices down to—or below—the all-important $1,000 threshold ("TV Set Price" 1947: 104).

Acknowledging the potential business linkage, a trade magazine advertisement for United States Television Manufacturing Corporation in 1947 appealed directly to coin machine operators and jukebox disk jobbers seeking to exploit the emerging bar and tavern market for televisions. Promoting the UST Tavern Tele-Symphonic coin-operated model, the advertisement proclaims, "Television sales are set-ups for men who know the tavern market. Television dealers without your contacts are piling up huge profits. Don't miss out! It's tailor-made for you. Use your contacts to get onto the ground floor of America's fastest-growing industry" (*Billboard*, August 2, 1947: 115).

In an interesting turn, as televisions installed in public establishments displaced the music machines, a minor business emerged around the sale of used and refurbished jukeboxes to domestic households ("Sell Juke Boxes" 1947: 112). Segrave (2002: 152) explains that this practice was a point of serious conflict among jukebox operators; there was considerable peer pressure to maintain strict control over the sale and distribution of the machines (mainly reconditioned units), ensuring that they were never sold directly to public establishments or to individuals (lest they end up in bars, taverns, or other such venues). Local machine operator associations banded together to suppress private jukebox sales, even restricting the sale of parts to individuals for repair or maintenance. The primary concerns were that individually owned machines would cut into jukebox operators' lease commissions and the reputation of the jukebox operators would be tarnished when the machines inevitably fell into disrepair due to lack of maintenance or the erosion of age. Yet with fluctuating jukebox revenues in bars, grills, and taverns and with some outlets dispensing with jukeboxes altogether as television set sales expanded, the sale of used jukeboxes offered a welcome, if unforeseen revenue supplement among struggling coin machine operators, helping them to compensate for destabilized business trends resulting from television installations.

It was not always a simple either-or case pitting jukeboxes against television sets (or coin machine operators against TV dealers). Coin machine manufacturers also attempted to merge the technologies, constructing hybrid units for public installation. The installation of coin-operated musical video machines in settings such as bars and taverns was not entirely without precedent; in 1940 the coin-operated Panoram movie machine that played "jukebox films" (or "Soundies") was produced by the Mills Novelty Company for installation in public establishments. For ten cents the units screened short musical film clips consisting of a broad variety of genres and, as Amy Herzog observes, an often "bizarre" array of visual representations featuring some of the era's most popular musicians (2004: 33).

Although the Panoram offered bar patrons the ability to choose their musical selections, TV's superior programming range and its live broadcasting enabled viewers to enjoy sports, news, educational programs, quiz shows, as well as musical variety shows in real time. Moreover, because of television's immediacy, viewers were treated to contemporaneous song hits performed by the top artists of the day. Since the Panoram clips were produced on film there was a temporal lag that fixed the musical performances in a perpetual past; the Panoram musical shorts were consequently more likely to be out of date. The main difference between the Panoram or Soundie visual recordings and television, thus, lay in the idiosyncrasies distinguishing film and live broadcasting.

Billboard first mentioned the possibility of jukebox-TV units in 1947, noting that regular TV sets in taverns were dominated by the bartenders and failed to offer patrons sufficient freedom in their content selection ("Music Biz" 1947: 20). The manufacture and distribution of coin-operated televisions indicated a desire to integrate the new TV medium with the established coin machine business. Almost immediately, manufacturers sought to extend their markets by producing coin-operated television-jukeboxes that could meet multiple bar room demands.

Among the industry leaders in the manufacture of these hybrid systems was the Videograph Corporation, whose Videograph unit combined television (employing Emerson screens), jukebox, and radio functions. The additional "wall box" feature allowed patrons seated in individual booths to select from television audio, a choice of two radio stations, or jukebox song selections for their listening pleasure while those seated at the bar could watch television on the fifteen-inch screen of the imposing seven-foot tall unit. According to Videograph's president, H. F. Dennison, the integrated features "running simultaneously . . . now offer an operator a chance to double or triple his income from a location where only the juke box has been a source of income to date" ("Coin Machines" 1947: 1).

Tradio, a manufacturer of coin-operated radio sets intended primarily for hotel installation, also entered the field in earnest in 1947, developing a television-radio-jukebox system with a wall box feature similar to that of the

Videograph but offering access to TV audio, an FM station (when the television was not on), the full AM radio spectrum rather than only two stations, and record selections ("Tradio Unveils Video-Sound Set" 1947: 96). Another entrant in the coin-operated television-jukebox business was Speedway Products, headed by Al Bloom, the former secretary of the Automatic Music Operators Association. The experimental prototype for the Speedway unit integrated mechanical components from both an RCA television and a Wurlitzer jukebox ("Video Turns to Coin Biz" 1947: 110).

Although pay-for-play "tavern tele" introduced competition to the jukeboxes, public viewers were soon disinclined to pay for televised entertainment in their local drinking establishments. Realizing that customers were opting for rival bars and taverns that provided free television, many proprietors eventually disabled the coin mechanisms of their units (referred to as "pulling their teeth") or they purchased noncoin TV sets to the detriment of coin machine operators. The trend, turning from coin-operated television sets to "free" TVs with larger screens, was already under way with television set manufacturers drastically increasing production and aggressively promoting household set purchases for domestic viewing.

By mid- to late 1948 (following the formation of the Music Operators of America, founded on January 21, 1948), television developed an even firmer hold on public establishments, further cutting into income derived from jukeboxes and compelling coin machine operators "to demand that bar owners guarantee juke ops a certain weekly income from jukes regardless of times they may be used. . . . [I]n recent months income from jukeboxes in competition with video has dropped sharply" ("Jukes-vs.-Television" 1948: 43). The dominant discourse among coin machine operators was undeniably patterned along the terms of threat, tension, and anxiety, as *Variety* reported in 1949: "Many industry people generally agree there exists now a TV-disk conflict, particularly in taverns, where coin machines and video screens vie for customer favor" ("TV's Disk Effect" 1949: 37).[26]

With television's continued expansion, the image often portrayed by distressed coin machine operators, jukebox maintenance men, and disk jobbers was of a forlorn and ignored jukebox positioned in an obscure corner of a public establishment, while the television, located over the bar or in some privileged position, became the main focal point for after-work and evening imbibers. One coin machine operator explained, "If you can't get the location owner to keep the music machine in a prominent spot, it is up to the operator to let the patrons know that there is a machine in the room. Even if it isn't easy for the patron to see the music machine we must see to it that the patron at least hears the machine. Otherwise they will soon forget to play the machine" ("Tele Still a Headache" 1948: 110). Jukebox design was already vibrant, to the point of being garish, in order to attract attention to the machines. Among the further solutions proposed by anxious coin machine operators was the installation of illuminated signs in taverns to advertise the presence of a jukebox. Machine operators devised collaborative promotional strategies with their local radio stations, merging their song/play lists and developing other gimmicks to advertise hit tunes (Segrave 2002: 205–6). An even more rash response involved the purchase of local televised advertisements promoting jukeboxes. These TV ads aired during broadcast sports events or other high-viewer programming, illustrating the appeals of the machines and otherwise reminding bar patrons and owners that even in the television era, jukeboxes remained an important entertainment option.

In certain circumstances television's encroachment in public establishments was mitigated by other competing factors. After 1949, jukeboxes attained an important role in the industry as RCA Victor began the process of replacing its 78 rpm records with the new 45 rpm vinylite singles. The seven-inch vinyl records emerged as a vital configuration for circulating popular hit songs, reinforcing their importance in jukeboxes. By the early 1950s, several related factors coincided with the overlapping interests of the recording industry, jukebox operators, and proprietors of bars and taverns. For example, some bar and tavern owners saw a renewed incentive in maintaining well-stocked jukeboxes replete with contemporary hit records, especially in establishments frequented by a teenage and student clientele. As the postwar youth culture took hold and teens showed a new aggressive consumerist proclivity, these owners benefited financially.

By stocking the jukeboxes with music that was rarely presented on television but that had high youth appeal (especially uptempo R & B or modern jazz records and, after roughly 1954, rock 'n' roll singles), teen-oriented malt shops as well as bars catering to black patrons emerged as essential sites for the reception of African American musical styles and the emergent youth music, inspiring new taste preferences among teens and fueling new musical consumption practices. Analysts also noticed that when domestic spaces were transformed into "television households" with adults dominating the medium, teens often more eagerly pursued leisure activities outside of the home in their attempts to distance themselves from their parents, revealing yet another factor that elevated the jukebox and the radio in the daily lives of young people.

Though the intense attraction and impact of "ambient television" in U.S. public night spots in the late 1940s was real (McCarthy 2001), it diminished considerably as more television sets were sold to individuals for domestic viewing. Indeed, the next stage of television's evolution harbored potentially worse outcomes for jukebox coin machine operators, although they did not initially register that home viewing could be even more damaging to their livelihood than public TV viewing. At least public TV drew patrons to establishments where a jukebox might be fed coins between or after TV programs.

Instead of debating about jukebox or television supremacy, bar owners and coin machine operators alike soon expressed anxieties about the drift toward individualized or private home TV viewing, expressed in the frequently uttered adage that Henry Ford's Model T automobile took people out of the home in 1908 and TV put them right back into it roughly forty years later. Television's detractors argued that sets located in bars were most responsible for the decrease in live music bookings and the early erosion of jukebox revenue, yet as household set ownership rose sharply between 1948 and 1955, television was blamed for a wide array of public and consumer shifts as well as being cited for declines in public health, morality, and civic engagement.

TV and Record Sales: Amplifying Optimism

With so much change afoot, the recording industry turned to the issue of how television might influence record sales and music consumption patterns. Despite concern that "TV figures sooner or later will exert a fracturing influence upon the sale of platters . . . particularly among the youngsters" (Woods 1949: 173), contradictory reports claimed that "executives of recording companies in New York are finding increasing evidence that television performances are helping sell pop songs on disks" ("Recording Companies" 1950: 41). At this early stage, the divergent arguments amounted to little more than wind in the wires.

Consumer trends were monitored as closely as possible (relying on ever more sophisticated research tools and advertising agency methods) and the findings were published and debated in industry trade magazines such as *Billboard*, *Down Beat*, and *Variety*, whose readers were most invested in the data. *Variety* reported in early 1949 that young record listeners indisputably changed their entertainment habits once they were exposed to television: "What already is occurring in metropolitan centers well-serviced by video transmitters is indication enough.... In most cases they have dropped disks like hot potatoes when a television set moved into their daily lives. And these are the disk buyers of the future. If they get out of the habit of listening to recordings now, it's figured that the industry as it's known today will be a dead duck" (Woods 1949: 173). By August 1949, Ted Wallerstein, president and CEO of Columbia Records, urged calm within the recording sector, arguing that television offered an entirely different leisure experience than did listening to recorded music and was, therefore, not necessarily a threat. At the annual Music Trade Show and Convention, Wallerstein explained,

> There is the fundamental fact that whether it be a motion picture, whether it be radio, whether it be television, none of them interferes with the fundamental thing that the record industry brings to the home — the whole world of music you want, when you want it, and by whom you want it.... [U]ntil some other thing comes along that can supply that, the record industry will be, as it is now, a great industry. ("TV's Disk Effect" 1949: 37)

While Wallerstein's attempts to assuage record industry jitters were commendable and his encouraging predictions of a strong and vital industrial sector proved to be accurate over the long term, early surveys indicated that he was incorrect in his assessment; music listening did, initially, decline within television households (as did other domestic media practices such as reading and radio listening).

The 1951 expansion of the coaxial cable across the nation's Midwest region and into previously isolated sections of the country constituted an important benchmark. Cable expansion offered a new means of introducing musicians to television viewers in the American heartland. One RCA Victor report identified a slight climb in record sales after 1951 (when sales reached almost $285 million), leading the company to announce that "sales are best in television areas and that TV set owners themselves buy more records than non-owners" (Kanaga 1952: 26). L. W. Kanaga, RCA Victor's manager of commercial sales and merchandise division, observed that, after the roughly three years of sales doldrums and consumer confusion (in no small part related to the industry's "battle of the speeds" involving manufacturing and sales of records in 78 rpm, 33 1/3 rpm, and 45 rpm configurations), there were signs of a new market stability and greater consumer confidence.

Sales of home phonograph players also rose, and improved record sales were notable across several genre categories, suggesting that the market reversal was more than a mere anomaly. Commenting on the sales improvements in regions with the highest TV penetration and, more specifically, within TV households, Kanaga explained: "There are several theories as to why this is so. One is that a TV set in the house keeps people home more often, and while they're home their chance of playing records is increased. Another reason might be the fact that, like live musical performances, television 'sells' people on music and makes the recording artists more familiar to them" (1952: 26). Kanaga was certainly onto something important with his speculation that TV could serve as a promotional device, but music industry insiders acknowledged that the networks were under no direct pressure to develop new musical material for onscreen presentation: "Tunes that sell on wax are held to be surefire material for TV shows, and programmers are taking no chances on testing untried tunes. This is especially true of the more expensive shows, where experimentation with new material involves gambling with heavy coin" ("See Video" 1951: 55). Throughout the early 1950s, songwriters and publishers bemoaned the continuance of "an old hat habit" as TV producers advanced cautiously in their song selection and presentation, extending a "play-it-safe policy on new songs" ("TV's Hit-Making Potential" 1954: 41). The musical fare on TV's music and variety shows was dominated by established hits and by "tasteful," familiar songs from the past encompassing "the great American songbook" (beloved "evergreens," "old chestnuts," or what are commonly called "standards") that were proven favorites among bourgeois, middlebrow audiences.

In 1951, *Variety* identified a TV performance by Laurie Anders (on the CBS network's *Ken Murray Show*) that provided a shocking boost for the song "I Like the Wide Open Spaces." After considerable conjecture, here was unmistakable proof that television could function as an effective marketing tool for introducing artists and promoting new songs. Debuting on CBS on January 7, 1950, *The Ken Murray Show*, hosted by the vaudeville comedian Murray (whose TV career began with an appearance on the premiere broadcast of the experimental Chicago station W9XAP on August 27, 1930), provided standard variety fare, featuring a regular cast that included the vocalist Darla Hood and a female dance chorus known as "the Glamourlovelies." On the April 14, 1951, broadcast, Murray introduced a western-themed production number titled "Oh Susanna," which CBS described as "a vignette of lyrical America" in its April 6 press release. The broadcast made an immediate

Ken Murray and Laurie Anders, *The Ken Murray Show*. CBS, circa 1951.
COURTESY OF PHOTOFEST.

impression on viewers, with *Variety* noting, "Video's power to create a pop hit, another facet of the medium's challenge to radio, is due to get its first clear-cut test as a result of the initial excitement stirred by TV on a new tune, 'I Like the Wide Open Spaces'" ("'Wide Open Spaces'" 1951: 46).

Anders, a relatively obscure member of the Glamourlovelies chorus, was a wide-eyed beauty and for this performance she was attired in a semirevealing western-style outfit.[27] Generally unremarkable as a vocalist, she sang the tune with a faux country twang that was characteristic of novelty presentations in the western or "hillbilly" style, playing the role broadly for its humor and excess. Following her TV rendition of "I Like the Wide Open Spaces" (written by the show host, Ken Murray, with Royal Foster and Chas. Wick) she was dubbed the "glamour cowboy" and immediately embarked on a series of TV appearances to reprise the song over the next two weeks, including an appearance on *Arthur Godfrey and His Friends.* The "blonde bombshell" Dagmar also recited the lyrics to the song in her typically flat style on Jerry Lester's *Broadway Open House* on NBC, further associating the tune with the image of empty-headed beauty.

The instant TV exposure contributed to a reported fifty thousand advance customer orders for the as-yet-unrecorded version of the song and spurred inquiries for disk copies from the Hirsch Coin Machine Company, a Washington, D.C., jukebox business. An outpouring of viewer enthusiasm motivated Columbia Records to record and release the single featuring Godfrey and Anders shortly thereafter, rushing "the disk through pressing for early marketing to cash in on the TV plugs" (ibid.). The *Billboard* charts for May 26, 1951, show the Anders-Godfrey recording of "I Like the Wide Open Spaces" in the number 2 spot on the jukebox "Operator's Pick" chart and the number 3 position on the "Disk Jockeys Pick" chart.

The phenomenon of television promoting an untested song and creating an overnight musical celebrity was repeated several more times shortly after Anders's breakthrough. Prior to his on-air dismissal by Arthur Godfrey, *Variety* reported that Julius La Rosa's recording of "Anywhere I Wander" was approaching sales of half a million copies, by far exceeding versions released over the preceding several months by Danny Kaye, Tony Bennett, Fran Warren, and Mel Torme. La Rosa's success with the song was directly attributed to the promotion he received "on a concentrated plugging attack via Arthur Godfrey's CBS-TV shows" ("Godfrey Plugs" 1953: 44).

The promotional power of TV was also realized with the tune "The Ballad of Davy Crockett," introduced on a December 1954 episode of ABC's *Disneyland* program (starring Fess Parker in the lead role as Crockett). The single, recorded by Bill Hayes (whose TV pedigree included regular appearances on *Your Show of Shows*), climbed to the number 1 spot on the *Billboard* charts by February 1955. Parker's subsequent version of the song also reached a top ten position within a month, with yet another version recorded by Tennessee Ernie Ford hitting the *Billboard* top ten the following week. A fourth version, recorded by The Voices of Walter Schumann (under the leadership of Schumann, who also composed TV's *Dragnet* theme song) also entered the *Billboard* charts in April 1955.

Following years of a risk-free approach, television producers and music publishers were ready to buck the trend, "plugging" new compositions on musical variety shows and, in an unusual turn, drama programs. "Let Me Go Lover," recorded by Joan Weber on Columbia records, was performed on a November 1954 broadcast of CBS-TV's *Studio One*. Promoting the single, a Columbia records advertisement trumpeted, "History is made! Thanks to TV's 'Studio One' and its great staff, 500,000 orders in a week. Joan Weber's 'Let Me Go Lover' as featured on the Monday Nov. 15 hour-long show." Later that same month another version of the song recorded by Patti Page was released on the Mercury label with accompanying advertising copy reading, "The sensational overnight song hit from television's 'Studio One' production." The Coral, Decca, and Victor record labels each capitalized on the song's television broadcast, releasing their own versions of "Let Me Go Lover" in short succession. In another example of the emergent practice, Frank Sinatra introduced the Jimmy Van Heusen and Sammy Cahn composition "Love and Marriage" on NBC's September 19, 1955, *Producer's Showcase* "spectacular" featuring Thornton Wilder's play *Our Town* (starring Sinatra with Eva Marie Saint and Paul Newman) ("Van Heusen-Cahn" 1955: 53). The record reached number 5 on the *Billboard* top one hundred chart three weeks later, largely on the strength of Sinatra's televised performance. Dinah Shore's recorded version of "Love and Marriage" hit the charts roughly a month after Sinatra's, benefiting from exposure on her TV show.

Demonstrating an emergent strategy of cross-media marketing—or synergy—in the early 1950s, artists' recording and record release schedules were deliberately synchronized with their television bookings. Record labels shipped the disks to retailers along a timeline that was carefully coordinated with artists' TV appearances. Record retailers, DJs, and jukebox machine operators were also included in the labels' campaigns to maximize market impact. This well-orchestrated marketing approach relied on TV's promotional capacities and its broadening audience base. In the midst of this activity, *Variety* finally acknowledged that television had evolved as a fully accepted force in promoting and marketing music recordings: "While the disk is still the king of Tin Pan Alley, video is now emerging as the top songmaking medium. As the major publishers view tv, there is nothing to equal the impact of a tune getting a visual-aural exposure to several million viewers in one shot. . . . If a song hasn't got it, video will prove that lack also just as fast" ("Gotta Get That Video Plug" 1955: 41).

By 1955 television's centrality within the entertainment sector was beyond question: TV was no longer a mystery and the speculation about its influence within the music sector was laid to rest. The resultant experience with, and exposure to the medium reduced musicians' initial apprehensions and their sense of anxiety abated. Executives, venue managers, agents, promoters, and musicians had a much clearer idea of what television could do; they understood how it functioned as a facet of the culture industries and they recognized the abundant opportunities that TV presented. With the confidence that accompanies stability and familiarity, they went to work, making music in a world with television.

3

Harmonizing Genres

*

Not enough professionals in the business recognize that TV is a
distinct medium with its own artistic and dramatic framework, its
own technical limitations, and a new psychology as far as the
audience is concerned. There are no sure-fire formulas—yet.
WAYNE WIRTH, VICE PRESIDENT AND DIRECTOR OF TELEVISION,
VAN DIVER AND CARLYLE AGENCY, 1948: 12

During television's growth and expansion, music programs
transcended narrow categories and ultimately reflected a broad
range of musical styles and presentational forms. A review of
the main music programs broadcast between 1948 and 1956 encompasses several prominent genre categories, including amateur talent shows, big band "cavalcades" or "revues," DJ and
teen dance shows, "hillbilly"/western musical variety, hit parade
shows, musical quiz shows, and musical variety. In several instances, such as KTLA-TV's famous remote ballroom broadcasts,
individual stations devised their own distinctive presentational
formats involving music. In still other cases, specific broadcast
episodes from the culturally uplifting *Omnibus* series or *Star of
the Family*[1] regularly featured musical artists and performances,

as did the occasional situation comedy.[2] The volume and range of programs featuring musical performances is even greater once regional and local efforts are considered.

Televison hosts and guest artists across these varied program genres can be associated with a correspondingly diverse array of popular music genres such as Broadway show tunes, folk, "hillbilly," jazz, Latin, polka, or rhythm and blues as well as the more mainstream popular music fare (consisting of Tin Pan Alley tunes or "standards" and novelty tunes) that dominated the airwaves, jukeboxes, and record sales as performed by dance bands, female "chirpers" or male "crooners." The generic range is vast, complicating attempts to provide a comprehensive list of each and every televised music program.[3] Following a general analysis of television's music genres I provide a focused discussion of two specific genre types: music programs that replicate the nightclub experience and DJ or teen dance shows.

Musical form, artistic performance, television presentational styles, and modes of audience reception are interconnected elements as Auslander suggests when he writes, "Musical genres and subgenres define the most basic and important sets of conventions and expectations within which musicians and their audiences function" (2004: 10). In this convergent frame, genre is central to an understanding of early television programming and it is well suited to the critical interrogation of the evolution of standards and conventions among musical programs. Yet it is also imperative to note in this context that music genres surely did not mean precisely the same things at television's inception as they do today. The sound and styles of popular music in the immediate postwar period were themselves in formation and in flux, as were the discourses and language through which musical genres were defined in that specific moment. Television executives and programmers were therefore obligated to contend with musical genres in a rather overt manner if they hoped to connect these formal characteristics with appropriate visual traits and, by extension, with audience "collectivities" (Holt 2007: 21).

Analyzing the industrial processes of program conception, technical development, and execution from a historical perspective offers clarity to the multiple factors influencing music programming in television's formative stages. Writing in a 1944 issue of the television journal *Televiser*, Thomas Hutchinson (a one-time NBC-TV program manager, production director with the RKO-Television Corporation, and, later, one of the first television instructors at New York University) comments that "television programming offers a definite challenge to the program builder. . . . [W]e must learn through experience right now just what is good and bad television program material" (1944: 12). Two years later, Hutchinson cited several program formats that could be produced as viable television fare, summarizing his views on programming possibilities: "Just what comprises a good television program is a formula that will probably be heatedly debated for many years to come. The real answer is that probably everything under the sun has its place in a television schedule if it is properly presented. There is nothing hidebound about this new medium. It takes in its stride entertainment from every existing source" (1946: 113). The emphasis on "formula" is instructive because Hutchinson recognized that, as a cultural and industrial apparatus, television would undoubtedly adhere to rational and efficient production processes akin to those already established across the modern media, notably film, radio, and music recording. What such formulas might be and how they would be enacted was less certain, and Hutchinson's comments reflect a query that could be heard throughout the emergent television broadcasting industry.

As these early musings suggest, throughout television's experimental period during the war years and prior to its commercial ascent in 1948, the industry's key decision makers were generally operating without a clear programming rationale, advancing with only the vaguest notions of what "good" television entailed and how to achieve it. More to the point, they were entirely unsure about how to produce television that, whether artistically redeeming or not, might simultaneously conform to consistent production standards, attract audience attention, and generate interest among paying sponsors, thus fulfilling the commercial imperatives of the industry.

Jane Feur explains, "Genre theory has the task both of making . . . divisions and of justifying the classifications once they have been made" (1992: 138). Her valuable insight notwithstanding, it must also be acknowledged that the genre classifications that we assume today were not, in fact, wholly matured in the early stages of television's evolution when formulaic production and programming remained poorly defined. There is an important precondition to the dividing and classifying that Feur addresses; a foundational infrastructure must first progress to the point whereby cultural texts display sufficient coherence upon which to base meaningful genre classifications.

According to John Fiske, "Genre is a cultural practice that attempts to structure some order into the wide range of texts and meanings that circulate in our culture for the convenience of both producers and audiences" (1987: 109). Even as the television industry struggled to establish common and reproducible program traits, executives, producers, and critics all worked to generate a functional discourse through which to understand and analyze the emergent medium and its programming output. Their efforts to build television as an industry and as a cultural force paralleled their desire to "structure some order" by generating a system of standards and a working language through which to define them.

One question underlying this analysis is, if genres exist as a series of cultural texts displaying "certain typical patterns in relation to their artistic limitations and potentialities" (Cawelti 1976: 7), how might we properly address early televised musical presentations during the medium's experimental phase before such patterns, conventions, or standards had been adequately realized as distinct *television* genres? In another sense, if, as John Corner posits, "genre is a principal factor in the directing of audience choice and of audience expectations . . . and in the organizing of subsets of cultural competencies and dispositions appropriate for watching, listening, and reading different kinds of things" (1998: 121), then what production frameworks and terminology are most suitable for explaining television's development of music programming prior to the establishment of systematic norms upon which the relationship between producers, audiences, and programs is founded? In order to respond to these and other questions pertaining to television's musical genres, it is beneficial to first understand the processes that were advanced within the emergent TV industry and to enumerate some of the key decisions taken in collaboration with working musicians.

Television before Genre: Format Definition to Formula Production

The sense among TV's early program developers that "anything is possible" or that "the sky's the limit" was widespread, yet it was tempered by a corporate emphasis on scientific innovation and technical mastery that had precedence over the implementation of program planning. In fact, then as now, technical and aesthetic elements are inextricably linked in the engendering of program conventions and genre patterns since the available technologies inherently influence the mode and product of television programming. Though genre theory overlooks the technical factors that intervene in the enterprise of "making" popular culture texts, it is detrimental to do so.

The technologies of production and the distinct nature of television's technical/aesthetic dynamic emerge as crucial and interlinked factors in the process of program conception, execution, and broadcast. What could be conceived for early television production was strongly linked to what could actually be done, and much of television's early evolution was forged within the vigorous conflicts between technicians and producers who, through either respectful cooperation or more overt struggle, explored what John Cawelti (1976) refers to as the medium's "limitations and potentialities." As this suggests, early television genres and musical programming were connected to early television production technologies and the accompanying contexts within which they were harnessed.

Whereas the science and technology divisions of RCA, for example, received ample funds for the research and development of studio and transmission equipment and the improvement of home receivers after 1926, when the NBC radio network was founded, NBC's Television Program Department was comparatively underfunded and marginalized through the 1930s and early 1940s. According to the television historian Michael Ritchie, television experiments in NBC studio 3H in this period regularly employed musicians but there was little concern for talent or performance content: "For many of the technicians, it didn't matter what happened in front of the cameras, they just needed a warm body or two. Most of the work was designed to test new iconoscope tubes, sometimes ten at a time" (1994: 47). In the mid-1930s NBC also invited advertising men and corporate sponsors to watch their test broadcasts that demonstrated the technical advances of the medium, showing them precisely what it was they were being asked to invest in. In these trial broadcasts, the source of amazement or disappointment was commonly associated with the clarity of the broadcast images rather than the artistic qualities of the musical renditions that were almost always included in the studio tests.

Similar experimentation was under way on the West Coast, where Klaus Landsberg at experimental station W6XYZ (later KTLA-TV) turned knobs and adjusted dials (sometimes consulting with viewers about their reception over the phone while he did so), troubleshooting the technical problems as the broadcast performances unfolded (Kisseloff 1995: 172). For Landsberg, the prospect of interrupting a broadcast and intervening in the audience's viewing experience was inconsequential since the content was deemed subordinate to the task of ensuring a successful transmission. In the nation's TV laboratories and demonstration studios, establishing strong broadcast signals and designing adequate lighting systems, more easily manageable cameras, or improved camera lenses was of greater urgency than providing flawless musical performances or distinct program formats.

Fiske defines formula as "an industrial and economic translation of conventions that is essential to the efficient production of popular cultural commodities and should not be evaluated by aesthetic criteria that dismiss it as mere lack of imagination. Getting the right formula that transforms the right conventions into a popular art form is no easy task" (1987: 110). As this implies, there is a value in observing the manner by which early television producers achieved program consistency and, in doing so, provided the stylistic and structural forms upon which emergent genre classifications were based. Today's pejorative meanings that are often associated with the term "formula production" (cast in typically terse Adornoesque language critical of the culture industries) were not prevalent through television's earliest developmental phases. In an industrial context, establishing standards is a matter of rational corporate efficacy and, thus, a priority objective; for the television networks, formula production was *positive*. Enhanced production efficiency is key to formulaic production practices, linked as it is to various aspects of cost management and profit maximization.

While recurring, identifiable aesthetic and formal features informing genre typification were attained through the formulaic reiterations of television's early production modes, formula production was not the initial factor underlying the emergence of genre patterns. *Format definition* preceded formula production among the network executives and division heads that shaped content and programming schedules. Addressing the formulation of music genres, the genre theorist Fabian Holt explains, "Discourse plays a major role in genre making. A genre category can only be established if the music has a name. The name becomes a point of reference and enables certain forms of communication, control, and specialization into markets, canons, and discourses" (2007: 3). From a contemporary perspective, it is fascinating to observe how television's executives and program developers communicated their ideas and preliminary plans about television music without established genre categories or formulaic models to guide them. Their ability to merge production and performance considerations within a television-specific discourse was fundamental to the overall comprehension of the medium and its content and was, by extension, essential to constructing a cultural understanding of television and its capacity for musical presentational.

Cawelti explains that genre is commonly defined as "the degree to which particular works share common characteristics that may be indicative of important cultural tendencies" (Cawelti 1976: 7). Jason Mittell reflects a related perspective when he cites discourse as a crucial element of genre formation, observing, "the discourses surrounding and running through a given genre are *themselves* constitutive of that generic category; they are the practices that define genres and delimit their meanings, not media texts themselves" (2004a: 13). The general ideas for regular broadcast programs and series were framed in rudimentary terms, yet these first descriptive forays provided the early discursive foundation for more strategic program development, illustrating the ways that the television industry "talked" the medium and its genres into existence and into postwar U.S. culture.

In television's earliest stage there was a notable proclivity toward typifying programs according to their sites of production, granting primacy to the contexts of origin and cultural loci rather than to formal characteristics. With this system of categorization the production processes were a much more central facet of program definition, explicitly encompassing surrounding conditions and related technical considerations in the conceptualization of the varied program types. This definitional tendency prevails in a booklet published by NBC in 1940, erroneously titled *Television's First Year*:[4] "By its very nature, television programs fall naturally into three main divisions . . . those programs which are usually televised outside the studio" (including news, sporting, and special events), "programs originating in the studios" (such as dramas, variety skits, classical or operatic musical performances, juggling acts, or celebrity interviews), and "motion picture films."

A 1940 RCA/NBC press release (dated January 29, 1940) detailing audience survey responses cites elementary rating findings based on evaluations of "live talent, outside special event, and film presentation" with little supplemental itemization of the programs' actual content features. Extending the early emphasis on locational determinants and production contexts, an unattributed NBC memorandum filed in 1942 under the simple title "Program Suggestions"[5] defines various proposed programs including *The World Next Door* as "a studio and film program," *The Garden Adviser* as being "remote from home garden of program's conductor," *Home Is What You Make It* as a broadcast from a "studio simulating living-room and kitchen," *Tiny Tots Variety Hour*, a "studio program in which small children dance, sing, recite, etc.," or *The Western Rancher* based on "film, demonstrations, and exhibits [that] supplement interviews."

At General Electric, a 1945 handbook recounting the production and programming trials of its flagship station WRGB in Schenectady states under the heading "Types of Television Shows" that "teleshows may be divided roughly into two groups — live and film" (Dupuy 1945: 5). While the handbook identifies several experimental program formats, it falls short of articulating a single organizing principal that might indicate a set of standard production formulas or genre conventions — even across programs of a similar nature. In only the rarest of cases do these thumbnail descriptions adopt anything resembling the genre-based terminology associated with contemporary programming. Lacking is any discursive or analytical system of classification that might operate as conceptual shorthand in the industry. This was, in essence, *television before television genre*.

In retrospect, the imprecise nature of format definitions constrained the development of discernible genre standards. The language of genre enables individuals to speak across their differences, facilitating understanding and shared meaning in discussions of core program traits. Prior to the emergence of generally recognizable music broadcasting genre patterns, there were few assurances that what was being communicated in any given context could be consistently reproduced according to a stable system of conventions; there was no tradition or evolved set of standard television practices that served as sufficient exemplars.

Program typology gradually moved beyond spatial designations, showing a tendency to identify the content of the broadcasts, yet in the area of musical programming difficulties remained, as indicated in an NBC document titled *The Artistic Development of Television Programs* by Dr. Herbert Graf, director of opera in television (Graf 1945). Graf, whose previous role was stage director for both the San Francisco Opera Company and New York's Metropolitan Opera Company, displays a vocabulary learned in his prior professional milieu, tentatively introducing music program ideas within loosely delimited parameters and basic categories such as "Opera, Serious and Light." Under the heading "Talent, Known and Unknown," Graf proposes programs including "Meet Our Artists" and "Looking for Our Stars," which are self-explanatory, reflecting a descriptive literalism that was common in early proposals emanating from network Program Development divisions. Under the heading "Folk Music" are brief program descriptions for "Singing America" and "Songs and Dances of the Nations." The latter is thinly summarized as "a series of dramatizations of folk songs and dances of all the nations," with no additional consideration of performance or production requirements. Though Graf's opera background would have adequately prepared him for musical stage productions of considerable scale and sophistication, in the context of television program development he applies only vague and inexact terminology. General Electric's Judy Dupuy offers similar programming and production descriptions in her 1945 handbook, although she exhibits slightly more technical knowledge and deeper television experience in her report on programs within the "Variety and Revue" or "Music and Light Opera" formats (Dupuy 1945).

The broad terminology of early genre definitions also included oblique references to "variety shows," "dance programs," "travelogues," "dramatic programs," or "musical shows" (Shane 1945). These classifications correspond loosely with prevailing entertainment categories common to the Broadway stage and the popular variety shows associated with vaudeville and the urban dance hall as well as cinema. In their employment we can see how previous notions of entertainment and performance presentation influenced the emergent language of television genre classification. Still, in their production and broadcast, early TV's musical programs failed to demonstrate a recognizable cohesiveness from network to network or even from show to show, falling short of the requirements of standardization upon which genre definition is based.

For instance, although variety programs consisting of music, comedy, vaudeville, and minor dramatic scenes were adopted early on as a viable television staple, the conceptualization of "variety" was so broad that there could be no clear agreement on the genre's requisite properties. Variety was conceived as an open format into which almost any performance could be introduced during television's experimental era, as Hutchinson confirmed in 1944: "In variety programs we tried almost anything we could think of. If anyone came along with a new idea, we tried it" (13).

In the absence of presentational norms involving pacing, balance, or composition (not to mention technical factors such as sound and lighting and related elements of overall staging or scripting), the early TV variety shows were generally a muddle. Exacerbating the situation were the deleterious effects of undertrained production staff and performers with little or no television experience, leading to radically uneven structure and quality from show to show. With the hiring of regular celebrity program hosts (a phenomenon that was already noticeable by the 1948 broadcast season) musical variety programs acquired greater structural coherency. (Bud Abbott and Lou Costello, Morey Amsterdam, Milton Berle, Eddie Cantor, Jimmy Durante, Dean Martin and Jerry Lewis, and Ed Sullivan were among the better known and influential forces in this regard.) As staging and technical production formulas were normalized, televised musical variety shows began to exhibit conventional patterns and consistent traits that more readily met the prerequisites of genre classification.

For the networks and local television stations, emergent genre classifications and standard program patterns also informed marketing strategies, facilitating the promotion and advertising of TV shows to viewers. Fiske explains that in the case of modern cultural production, genre functions in the service of multiple interests: "Genre serves the dual needs of a commodity: on the one hand standardization and familiarity, and on the other, product differentiation. But the work of genre is more than economic, it is cultural as well. . . . Genre spells out to the audience the range of pleasures it might expect and thus regulates and activates memory of similar texts and the expectations of this one" (1987: 114). Fiske's emphasis on genre offers an approach for analyzing and defining distinctions between early musical programs. It is in and through musical *and* television genre differences that, for example, *Eddie Condon's Floorshow* stands apart from *The Fred Waring Show*. The two quite different programs of 1948–49 were each hosted by prominent musicians of the day yet their musical orientations and onscreen personae shared little in common. In another example, despite being musical variety programs that each aired on the weekend, *Saturday Night Jamboree*, "TV's first half-hour of Western stars and hillbilly balladeers" (*Saturday Night Jubilee*, 1949), cannot be easily equated with *The Saturday Night Dance Party*, a musical "dance show" (Wile 1951) featuring some of the nation's top orchestras with various novelty and dance acts. Their similarities *and* their differences are forged within characteristics of genre rooted in both television and musical forms.

It was not enough to simply describe these and similar programs as "musical variety" shows since the designation fails to accommodate or describe their unique identifying characteristics in full. At some point the framing of music and performance must be acknowledged, and it is clear that the definition of early televised musical programs also relied on the acknowledgment of *musical* genres since the music performed on the shows was an important factor of TV's program classification. The industry mavens were consequently driven to introduce classificatory mechanisms through which all interested parties, whether corporate advertising executives or ordinary everyday viewers, could comprehend a musical show's main properties.

An indicator of the rate at which genre patterns and industrial production formulas took hold might be found in the expansion of the television industry's annual Emmy Awards, which were inaugurated in 1948 under the auspices of the National Academy of Television Arts and Sciences. In the first year the full list of award categories was limited to Most Outstanding Television Personality, Most Popular Television Program, Best Film Made for Television, Station Award, and Technical Award. In 1949, among several additions were categories for Best Live Show, Best Children's Show, Best Sports Coverage, and Best Public Service, Cultural, or Educational Program. In 1950, however, a broader diversity of genre categories began to emerge as the list expanded with the addition of Best Variety Show, Best Dramatic Show, Best News Program, and Best Games and Audience Participation Show. Best Situation Comedy was introduced in 1952; Best Mystery, Action, or Adventure Program was introduced in 1953; and Best Western or Adventure Series came in 1954.

Indicating the success and genre coherence of musical programming in 1954, the Academy introduced several new award categories at the seventh annual Emmy Awards ceremony, including Best Male Singer, Best Female Singer, and Best Variety Series Including Musical Varieties. The steady accretion of program categories and the more precise definition within which individual programs were positioned offers a pertinent gauge of genre status and consensually accepted categories through this stage of industry growth.

Audiences, Music Programming, and Genre

Genre theorists generally concur with John Corner's view that "genre is a principal factor in the directing of audience choice and of audience expectations (1998: 121). Corner perceptively observes that contemporary television scholars often approach the medium as a unified and universal phenomenon, resulting in a reductive, essentialist perspective. Despite this insight, Corner's critique unintentionally exposes another tendency to assume that the dynamics between TV's genres and its audiences have *always* existed in much the same relational sense as today.

If, as Corner implies, audience knowledge, experience, or prior exposure to television programming are central to the comprehension of genre as a factor in "text-viewer relations," it is logical to assume that the dynamics between producer, text, and audience will have been different in television's earliest period, when the industry was new, when television's content and character were still in formation, and audiences had an undeveloped critical perspective. The public clearly lacked familiarity with television's forms and grammars and, in its nascent phase, rituals of reception had not yet emerged. The network's various public demonstrations and experimental broadcasts initially contributed only a very general understanding of what types of program formulas were best received by viewers. This is not to suggest, however, that the audience was inconsequential or not valued.

Audience members were obviously no clearer on the definition of genre categories than were the network professionals. Viewer correspondence with NBC between 1940 and the mid-1950s reflected a steadily evolving genre-specific awareness and terminology, but it was not spontaneously manifested from the beginning. Viewers in television's early phase usually described either specific musical performance moments (addressing a particular show or presentation) or else they referred to the characteristics of the musical host and guests in rather broad and general terms. Only rarely did they write in a manner that might suggest a commonly shared system of classification. As Karen Lury (1995) reminds us, learning the forms and grammars of television required an educative process, yet until at least the mid-1950s even the corporate producers of television programming were still learning by trial and error what audiences would or would not watch on the small screen, how to package and promote programs successfully, and what to call the program categories that were taking shape.

Throughout the 1940s much effort and money was spent on the strategic assessment of viewer patterns and preferences. In this phase of network information gathering, surveys and other data collection methods were influential in the construction of program categories and they helped to solidify genres across the industry and among the viewing public. With the concurrent rise of professional associations such as the Television Broadcasters Association, numerous industry-centered trade media, and advertising firms working in the industry, the focus on viewing patterns and genre issues was further intensified.

In his assessment of early television broadcasting, John Mundy claims that music-based programs "were catering for what was still regarded within the entertainment business as a largely undifferentiated audience" (1999: 184). While it may be true that the networks were not particularly well attuned to the myriad distinctions among actual or prospective TV viewers in television's earliest phase, this view fundamentally disregards the considerable attention to varied audience sectors within the television and music industries that was documented even prior to the Second World War. With basic genre distinctions such as "race" or "hillbilly" records isolating consumers along racial, social, and regional lines, the music industry clearly demonstrated a capacity to differentiate audiences. Television's relationship with radio broadcasting also contributed to an investment in audience research and program differentiation since radio had, by 1948, developed a keen awareness of its varied listener groups. Because television in the United States was conceived as a commercial medium dependent on sponsors and paid advertising, methods of consumer research were employed early in the project of viewer differentiation (Attallah 1991; Boddy 1990; Mashon 2007).

In the period before regular program schedules were fully realized, NBC deployed program return cards soliciting audience responses about their viewing patterns and preferences, conducting semi-elaborate television rating surveys (such as those administered by NBC's Noran Kersta as early as 1940). Though there was some effort to determine what programs viewers most enjoyed, the selection was sparse and the surveys often stressed the number of viewing hours (in relation to total broadcast hours), the make and model of television in use, and basic demographic features of the viewing household.[6] Concentrated emphasis on audience program preferences emerged more slowly, becoming a standard facet of survey data once a broader range of the public had been exposed to television in some setting.[7]

Countless internal network memos,[8] communiqués between the networks and advertising agencies, and commentary in entertainment trade journals including *Variety*, *Sponsor*, or *Broadcasting-Telecasting* reveal the industry interest in musical tastes and TV genre preferences among music program viewers, also reflecting the gradual distinctions between musical programs themselves (i.e., between program formats, performance and production styles, modes of address, narrative structures, or discursive patterns). Influential television executives at each of the major networks—most notably NBC's Pat Weaver, who moved to the network from the Young and Rubicam agency—were steeped in advertising industry practices and many of the industry's early decision makers claimed extensive radio experience, making them fully aware of diverse audience expectations in regard to both music and broadcast program genres. Journalists and media critics such as John Crosby of the *New York Herald-Tribune* and Jack Gould at the *New York Times* also influenced the public's recognition and acceptance of early

TV genre categories as their commentary intersected with the industry's dominant discourses. The television industry was, therefore, acutely aware that audience tastes were inclined toward at least some degree of heterogeneity.

As a testament to early television's range of music programming, during the 1948 program season viewers could tune in to Arturo Toscanini leading the NBC Symphony in a fine classical concerto, Ed Sullivan introducing popular recording stars or artists from the Metropolitan Opera or Broadway stages on *Toast of the Town*, Eddie Condon leading an ensemble of some of the world's top jazz talent, Morey Amsterdam engaging with his onstage sidekick Art Carney in traditional vaudeville routines replete with novelty tunes (such as his trademark "Yak-a-Puck" song) on the *Morey Amsterdam Show*, or a bevy of young amateurs warbling popular songs of the day on a dozen different shows. Of course it would be incorrect to assume that viewers favored only the programs associated with their specific taste class; indeed, it was widely publicized that Toscanini himself enjoyed many of television's simpler offerings including boxing or wrestling matches and the children's programming that he watched with his grandchildren (Lebrecht 2001: 67; Horowitz 2005: 285).

Age was also an important distinguishing factor as reflected in programming decisions encompassing content and scheduling, with children's and youth programming emerging as early generic designations. Children's shows flourished as a regular component of each major network and most local large-market stations; for instance *Kukla, Fran and Ollie* was created by the puppeteer Burr Tillstrom for the 1939 New York World's Fair, where it was first broadcast on television at the RCA Exhibit. It was later part of the regular broadcast schedule on Chicago station WBKB beginning in 1947, and in 1949 it was adopted as an NBC network program. Another hit children's program, *Howdy Doody*, also first aired on NBC, in 1947.

In the early and mid-1950s, teenagers emerged as a coveted consumer group. The film business was among the first sectors to target the lucrative audience demographic via low-budget, high-energy films that often tilted toward sensationalism and titillation rather than strong coherent narratives. On television, teenage viewers were unambiguously targeted by music programs featuring disk jockeys and robust R & B performances. With the industry strengthening its nationwide broadcast system after the 1951 installation of the transnational coaxial cable, networks and advertising agencies were cognizant of a further set of viewer distinctions based on regional taste differences that were explicitly taken into account in program development. As the music formats evolved and a wider variety of music genres were represented the TV networks were mindful of the differences between northern and southern cultural tendencies, including—but not singularly reducible to—racial views (Classen 2004).

With a growing arsenal of survey data, more precise genre descriptors, and better program definition, the networks forged ahead in the design of innovative and engaging musical shows that would reach receptive audiences. The ongoing adjustments in programming and genre construction were often humorous to behold. In one case, after stumbling through the premier broadcast of NBC's music show *Judge for Yourself* (broadcast August 18, 1953), the popular TV host Fred Allen beseeched the viewing audience, "If you liked the show, tell your friends. If you don't like the show, keep quiet for goodness sake until we get the thing fixed up." His appeal to viewers discloses the "work" of making early television and also very publicly admits to the nature of program metamorphoses, from Program Department conception to a weekly show. More than this, however, Allen's comment is an explicit request for viewers to remain flexible and patient as the producers altered the program formula, tweaking it toward a more accomplished final product that is consistent with the program genre.[9]

Allen's impromptu request is also instructive, for within a historical approach to genre it is important to analyze the ways in which pioneering programs were assembled—how they were linked through a host's banter, the camera work and staging, setting and location, or through the aid of title cards or superimpositions from the opening introduction to the closing announcement of "next week's guests."

Music Genres and Program Structure

John Ellis suggests, "Broadcast TV has developed a distinct aesthetic form. Instead of the single, coherent text that is characteristic of entertainment cinema, broadcast TV offers relatively discrete segments: small sequential unities of images and sounds whose maximum duration seems to be about five minutes" (1994: 112). The ways in which different music programs managed the sequential organization is of crucial relevance to genre analysis of early television programming for it is in the patterned organization of these discrete components that broader resemblances are defined. Musical programs such as *The Perry Como Show*, *The Dinah Shore Show*, or *The Tony*

Martin Show (and other similar shows that appeared concurrently in the period)[10] differed little from one another in a broad sense mainly because of their standardized sequential structures.

Phil Auslander cites the convergence of music and performance genres that stands as an important factor in the construction of a musician's persona: "There are several sets of constraints on the construction of musical performance personae, the most immediate of which are genre constraints. . . . [Genres] are crucially important to performers in constructing their performance personae and to audiences in interpreting and responding to them" (2004: 10). While Auslander is describing musical genre and performance, TV's emergent genre specifications for music-oriented programs are also relevant here. There is notable congruence in the pacing, formal character, mode of address, and each host's general performance demeanor on the Como, Martin, and Shore shows *and* in the strategies through which program sequences were linked within their broadcasts.

Each program featured brief sponsorship announcements and employed a direct mode of audience address and through simple, unassuming scripts, introduced several songs (all within a fifteen-minute broadcast slot). The hosts' amiable characteristics were extended in their occasional repartee with guest artists, most of whose performance styles were consistent with those of the hosts themselves, presenting songs in a reserved, unhurried, and relaxed manner conforming to what Keightley (2008) describes as "easy listening" music associated with "middlebrow" tastes. The term "genericists" can be applied to these particular artists and to others who similarly represent distinct musical styles that are reproduced in a manner that carries over to their TV programs. Keith Negus defines genericists as "those performers who accommodate their musical practice and performance to a specific genre style at a particular time and stay within this. These artists have a repertoire in which all musical pieces fit the particular codes, conventions, and rules of the genre . . . and precisely play everything in such a way" (Negus 1996: 145–46).

Musical accompaniment was also similar across the networks with the offscreen orchestras providing tasteful if conventional arrangements that ensured the centrality of the hosts' singing. The programs were divided into roughly three- to five-minute sequences involving monologues, advertisements, and song performances, reinforcing Ellis's analytical observations about sequential structure. Network producers (and media critics and audiences as well) deemed many of these programs as being remarkable for their

The Dinah Shore Show, NBC, circa 1954–55. COURTESY OF PHOTOFEST.

smooth flow and the capacity to proficiently wed the production process to each host's persona.

Though these programs displayed consistency and an unambiguously mainstream aesthetic, their distinctions are also important from a viewer's perspective. In this context the nuanced details within each program acquire greater significance since the distinguishing traits between each show constitute a necessary requirement for market differentiation. For instance, Dinah Shore was well regarded for conducting herself on camera in an "engaging homey fashion" (Fuller 1951) that appealed to both male and female viewers, yet gender norms of the era positioned her as an endearing *female* singer, underlining important performative similarities with her female peers and differences between her and Como, Martin, or the other male hosts of the day. Shore also had a reputation as a celebrity wife and mother (she was married to the actor George Montgomery, a fact of her identity that she frequently commented on during her program and that was circulated in the pages of fan and family magazines), aligning her with specific social categories and particular cultural values as well as distinguishing her from many

Tony Martin. Circa 1947. COURTESY OF PHOTOFEST.

of the younger, less mature (and arguably less talented) musical upstarts who had hitched their careers to television.[11] She was presented onscreen with a surfeit of good humor and approachability that was largely devoid of the simmering feminine sensuality associated with a peer such as the vocalist Peggy Lee or various other frequent TV guests at the time such as Denise Darcel or Dagmar.

Tony Martin's lush performance style distinguishes him from both Como or Shore; indeed, Martin, more than almost any television singer of his time, maintained the image of the suave nightclub performer, conveying an essence that was explicitly oriented toward a debonair and urbane cultural

Perry Como. Circa 1945–54. COURTESY OF PHOTOFEST.

identity that corresponds with nondomestic realms such as the late-night city scene. Martin displayed a reserved yet potent masculinity that the producers regularly accentuated through various technical methods including subdued lighting and set designs that integrated the host within spaces of refined urban leisure imbued with a hint of the romantic. He looked superb in a tuxedo or dress suit with a tie, yet he often looked even better in a sports blazer with an open collar and wide lapels, adding to his debonair image. His dark, handsome features were emphasized in frequent, lingering close-up shots.

Noting similarities between the Shore and Como programs in 1954, *TV Guide* criticized Martin for his failure "to master the mood of easy informality which has made Dinah one of the medium's top attractions and which, oddly enough, has long been the trademark of Martin himself along the night club circuit" ("The Tony Martin Show" 1954: 23). While his program did not enjoy the same success or longevity as those of either Como or Shore, Martin's frequent guest appearances invigorated numerous musical variety shows.

Como, a classic crooner treasured by NBC executives for his affability was perhaps best suited to the "intimate" nature of television broadcasting and was "a hit" with female viewers. In this regard, Como occupied a middle space between Shore and Martin, not quite feminine but not exactly virile, neither singularly associated with the domestic sphere or with the potentially more exotic domains of the evening nightspots. In the case of Shore and Como in particular, their "relaxed," "casual," and inviting mannerisms are still cited as preferred program conventions that defined the early genre of musical programming.

TV Viewing and Easy Listening

While we might today isolate the carefully calibrated performance styles of the many popular singers and musical artists as elements that reinforce certain dominant values of restraint and conservative decorum or critique musical programs that communicated an idealized image of material wealth and bourgeois taste, it is also pertinent to note that the pop songs performed on such shows were part of a much wider cultural economy of meaning. In his detailed analysis of the musical genre definition "easy listening" Keir Keightley (2008) states, "Easy listening was the dominant form of popular music" throughout North America for roughly twenty years after the Second World War.

This concept is reflected in Murray Schumach's 1947 account of the relationship between music and postwar social attitudes and the displacement of "swing" by "sweet":

> Popular music must reflect the mood of the people. During the war the public worked at accelerated pace and craved excitement. Hot, fast music with blaring trumpets, thundering rhythms, strange harmonies, filled the air. . . . With peace came a sudden change in America's pulsebeat. The new national mood, greatly influenced by returning veterans, called for quiet forms of relaxation. In popular music this meant soothing, singable tunes with sugary, romantic lyrics and no frenzied tempo. (20)

Within this temporal and cultural framework, it is also possible to claim that easy listening was the dominant form of music adopted for early television; certainly Como, Martin, and Shore fit this category, as did many of their contemporaries. With television, however, easy listening music was given an added visual character, in essence providing a series of cues and markers conveying elements of style, comportment, and middlebrow taste that exceeded the limits of a purely aural engagement with the music. In TV's earliest stage, the act of watching did not exactly offer the same "easy" experience as listening.

Keightley explains that in the radio era "easy listening" music constituted a kind of "aural wallpaper," or "a form of background music" that facilitates "unconscious listening" (2008: 317). While this may apply in the context of radio, once television's visual forms were asserted, the sensory demands changed as the viewer was drawn into an altered relationship with the artists, their songs, and their performances. Television's visual character increased the complexity of the overall performance and, as contemporaneous audience letters, critics' news reports, and extant memoranda all indicate, in their regular viewing of popular music programs viewers consciously navigated various social factors such as celebrity identities and image construction as well as aspects such as "performed" sexuality and the communication of sex appeal. These factors were also intrinsic to the construction of the musical genre and with their enhanced interpretive abilities, audiences learned to navigate between the different values that were associated with each artist and their respective shows. Thus, while the music may have tended toward the dominant mainstream "easy listening" genre, the rationale for watching music on TV was not solely rooted in the enjoyment or pleasure of the songs themselves.

It is also pertinent to acknowledge that television's preponderance of show tunes, light Tin Pan Alley compositions, sultry ballads, upbeat novelty songs, or hymns must be measured against the comparatively limited appearance of other musical genres including straight-ahead bebop, hot jazz, traditional/regional blues, unexpurgated rhythm and blues, unvarnished southern gospel, or early rock 'n' roll. These latter musical genres are inarguably identified with African American cultural sensibilities and musical influences, and though occasionally represented, they were a decidedly marginal element of early television broadcasting.

Setting and Genre: TV and the Urban Nightclub

Setting comprised an important aesthetic consideration in early televised music programs, in many cases defining the genre characteristics of the production and performances. Whether simple or elaborate, sets and props were deliberately employed in the construction of ersatz domains to create a sense of place, variably invoking the hectic urban public sphere, the small town

commons, the county fairgrounds, the rural "hinterland," or the more intimate domestic realm of the home. As Lynn Spigel (2008) argues, early television also effectively communicated a modernist aesthetic and associated
middlebrow taste values through evocative set designs and presentational
forms in the postwar era. The modernist aesthetic that she identifies stood in
stark contrast to nostalgic or even regressive elements that were conveyed via
sets or props and costuming as well as through discourse and song selection.
The dialogue and narratives, even in instances where scripts seemed like an
afterthought (if they existed at all), reinforced particular cultural sensibilities with references to distinct social milieux. Announcers, program hosts,
and guest artists each described their programs' ersatz sites as if they were
actually existing places, introducing a series of culturally meaningful venues
that not only helped to position the vignettes but to orient the viewer in relation to these settings.

Some program hosts with deep vaudevillian roots (including such irrepressible entertainers as Morey Amsterdam, Milton Berle, Eddie Cantor,
and Jimmy Durante) and television pioneers with radio broadcasting backgrounds (such as Dave Garroway, Arthur Godfrey, Ernie Kovacs, and Garry
Moore) often toyed with television's spatial domain while making the most
of the medium's "live" character. Reciting scripted lines that articulated a fictional space, they might suddenly veer off-script with a reflexive ad lib, trans-
gressing television's "fourth wall" by overtly exposing the actual conditions
of material production or the broadcast performance space, acknowledging
the fact that they were acting in front of a camera within a constructed environment. In their most irreverent moments, these hosts might walk off
the set altogether, explicitly drawing attention to the constructed nature of
the TV stage set by mingling among the backstage personnel (Garroway,
Kovacs, and Moore were particularly renowned for this). In consciously flexible modes of address, they openly interacted with the television stage and
production crews, the theater's assembled audience, and an unseen domestic
viewing audience. In doing so, they often shifted between spatial discourses
(generally fluctuating between references to "here" and "out there") in order
to accommodate each locus or audience segment, simultaneously speaking
to the physical assembly and those ensconced in their homes or watching TV
at taverns or other public sites.

As the previous chapters have demonstrated, television's ties to existing
media and performance environments were widely discussed at its inception. William Boddy explains that critics in television's developmental phase

isolated the medium's character and content in relation to other more familiar media or performance contexts, noting that for many early commentators, "the medium was a unique synthesis of the immediacy of the live theatrical performance, the space-conquering powers of the radio, and the visual
strategies of the motion picture" (1990: 80). Despite this repeated emphasis
on the influences of the large stage, the film screen, and radio (Spigel 1992;
Marling 1994; Rodman 2010) it is also appropriate to add the urban nightclub setting to this list of television's performative and spatial influences.
Tapes of early television broadcasts reinforce the fact that the nightclub was
a standard setting for musical programs airing between 1948 and 1956.

The nightclub was a pervasive cultural referent in an array of televised
programs, constituting a conventional facet of the new broadcast landscape
that was linked with the music and variety genres. Many shows in TV's first
years were named for the fictional/ersatz nightclubs that they portrayed:
*Bamboo, Café Continental, Café de Paris, Campus Cabana, Chesterfield Sup-
per Club* (later *The Perry Como Show*), *Club Celebrity, Club Ebony, Club Six,
Club Seven, Club 13, Club Nothing, Hit Spot*, and the Liberty Club (portrayed
on *At Liberty Club*). Other ersatz nightclubs included Club Durant (on the
Colgate Comedy Hour with Jimmy Durante), the Gypsy Café (on KTLA-TV's
The Gypsy, starring the vocalist Roberta Linn), the Golden Goose and the
Silver Swan (each on *The Morey Amsterdam Show*), Club Popsicle (*Popsicle
Parade*, featuring Tony Martin), Club Rio (*Flight to Rhythm*), and perhaps
the most widely known television nightclub, the Tropicana (*I Love Lucy*).
The list expands dramatically when regional programs such as *Old Dutch
Revue* (set in the fictitious Old Dutch Tavern, produced by the Cleveland
station WEWS) are factored in. Individual episodes also commonly evoked
the nightclub environment; for instance the March 3, 1951, broadcast of *The
Frank Sinatra Show* featured as guest Frankie Laine performing on a set replicating the famous Copacabana Club in New York. Even when the programs were not set in nightclubs, references to nightclubs were legion with
hosts casually discussing musical artists' actual club engagements or, on ama-
teur/talent programs, promoting future nightclub appearances as part of
the winner's package.

Throughout the 1940s the nightclub possessed an iconic cultural status.
Some clubs were notably dingy, offering tired and even raunchy performances, whereas others (in a hierarchy of quality and taste) were imbued
with the bourgeois ideals of glamour and luxury and the highest levels of
entertainment and artistic excellence. Glamour is not an incidental factor

in this context; television was widely criticized for its lack of glamour, especially in comparison to the glamour associated with the urban night scene, the capacity for photography to visually reinforce the effect of glamour, or the structures of representation and celebrity erected by the Hollywood film industry. The TV networks, aware of television's fundamental shortcoming in this regard, seemed driven to reproduce the basic attributes of glamour.

Their objective was certainly infused with commercial values and the desire to commodify the spatial images of nightclubs and the beautiful, inscrutable creatures that inhabit them, but there was more to it than that. The attempts to reproduce glamour's effect in the new medium was in keeping with the cultural character of the period and "the modernist attention to aesthetic form" that "becomes visible, even most familiar, in the worlds of entertainment and mass culture" (Brown 2009: 8). In one of the more perceptive analyses of early twentieth-century glamour, Judith Brown writes, "Glamour is not just an effect of the entertainment industry; it is also part of a complex aesthetic network that binds high modernism with a range of phenomena. . . . Here is glamour: an experience that moves one out of the material world of demands, responsibilities, and attention to productivity, and into another, more ethereally bound, fleeting, beautiful, and deadly" (ibid.: 1, 5). The aspiration to "move one out of the material world" and to capture and transmit the spirit and affect of the glamorous life was at the core of many of television's nightclub-based programs, although such intentions did not necessarily guarantee flawless results.

The image of nightclubs as spaces of urban leisure and, often, decadence circulated widely. Nightclubs were featured in scores of Hollywood film productions throughout the 1930s, 1940s, and 1950s and celebrity magazines from the period further spread the image of fashionable floor shows attended by finely attired men and women out for a night on the town. Newspaper gossip columnists regularly reported on celebrities from the realms of sports, theater, film, and music as they navigated the nightlife. Radio remote broadcasts from upscale nightclubs and hotel showrooms had, throughout the 1930s and 1940s, also bolstered the nightclub as a symbolic social environment and a desirable leisure destination.[12] Though often cast as a desirable leisure destination and a fashionable cultural environment, nightclubs were also regarded in some quarters as dens of flesh and flash, criticized for being overpriced and gaudy and appealing to the undeveloped tastes of youth or the undiscerning tastes of visiting rubes, tourists, or conventioneers ("Nightclubs" 1947: 109–15).

Attesting to the longstanding tradition of nightclub broadcasts, Vincent Lopez led the first orchestra to ever perform on radio (appearing on station WJZ in November 1921), and he was among the first to broadcast from a major urban hotel: "Lopez and other musicians found that radio gave them free advertising and brought dancers who had heard them on the air to the hotels, cabarets, and night clubs where they played regularly" (Sanjek 1988: 77–78). After a lackluster opening at Chicago's Granada Café in 1927, the Canadian bandleader Guy Lombardo convinced the café proprietors and the owners of radio station WBBM to install a "wire," resulting in a pronounced improvement in club attendance and box office revenue. By 1950, Guy Lombardo was already two decades into his thirty-three-year run at New York's Roosevelt Hotel Grill, a record that included regular radio broadcasts; Lombardo and the Royal Canadians occasionally appeared on television after 1950,[13] reinforcing the orchestra's popularity while enshrining the enduring ritual of televised New Year's Eve broadcasts with his orchestra's classic rendition of "Auld Lang Syne" performed in a plush nightclub or showroom environment.

According to Susan Douglas, artists, broadcasters, and the nightclubs each benefited from these remote radio sessions: "The stations got live music—some of it the finest of the period—and the ambience of a glamorous nightclub, and the hotels got free publicity" (1999: 86). Radio's ethereal, nonvisual nature facilitated a wistful listener disposition as the mediating voice of the program announcer or host provided descriptive cues about the elegant nightclub setting, the well-heeled clientele, and other inviting elements of the broadcast's performance space. Adapted from this established radio format, TV remote broadcasts from nightclub showrooms expanded as a broadcast mainstay and some popular music venues devised innovative strategies to merge their operations with television's particular requirements. Seeking to capitalize on television's emergence and, more precisely, to offset the risk of declining attendance and revenues in the postwar era, several nightclubs and lounges negotiated with television producers to broadcast shows featuring popular artists from their stages. These arrangements were designed to combine the intimacy of the lounge with television's assumed intimacy, creating a symbiotic connection that offered viewers a virtual experience of nightclub entertainment.

Premiering on September 14, 1948, *Club Date* on KTLA-TV offered an hour-long broadcast from the Los Angeles nightclub the Red Feather (featuring the vocalist Frances Wayne, Dwala Graves as piano soloist, and an orchestra led by Dick Peterson), capitalizing on the station's efficient and renowned mobile/remote capabilities. In another instance across the country, New York's Versailles club featured the French chanteuse Edith Piaf with a "pioneering pickup." *Variety* explained that the club sacrificed up to sixty seats and surrendered much of the room's balcony "to cables and other video equipment" (Green 1948: 70), though the Piaf show was deemed mediocre partly due to the club's spatial limitations. A further complication of the Versailles debut broadcast involved the issuance of cards alerting patrons of their imminent broadcast or requesting that they sign a release permitting their image to appear on television. The permissions apparently caused some concern among those who may have been in attendance with "company" other than their spouse.[14]

An internal NBC memorandum (sent by Leonard Goldstein to Ray O'Connell in the summer of 1949) provides another early indication of the network's interests in remote broadcasting from New York's plush showcase nightclub The Latin Quarter. In the memo, Goldstein describes the composition and general quality of the club's house band, the Art Waner Orchestra,[15] offering his recommendation that the network develop a program featuring the group (Goldstein 1949). Later that year, Eddie Meister of the Latin Quarter also conferred with the TV producer Max Liebman (whose NBC program *Admiral Broadway Revue* was then on the air) about broadcasting four shows from the New York club in 1949 before the *Revue* went on the road with remote TV broadcasts from various regional clubs. Drawing on his experience in the New York entertainment market, Lou Walters, the owner of The Latin Quarter — despite being conflicted about the benefits of remote broadcasting in his New York establishment — pitched a remote TV broadcast arrangement for his recent acquisition, the Earl Carroll Theatre-Restaurant in Hollywood ("Package Shows" 1949: 66).

Replicating radio's nightclub format, the Du Mont TV network embarked on several ambitious remote broadcast programs. The network aired the debut broadcast of *Dinner Date* on January 28, 1950, from the upscale Grill Room at New York's Taft Hotel, featuring the Vincent Lopez Orchestra (which had already been engaged at the Taft for almost a decade, building on the successes of its radio broadcasts) with the vocalist Ann Warren. Reviewing the program's premiere, *Variety* proclaimed, "'Dinner Date' looks like one of the first successful entertainment programs to be aired from a remote location. . . . Besides opening up much-needed extra studio space for

Du Mont, the Taft idea also provides some added glamour for hinterland viewers" ("Dinner Date" 1950: 32).

In December 1950, Du Mont announced its intention to produce *Night Life, U.S.A.*, featuring music performances broadcast from up to ten different New York area club locations, partnering with local dance band impresario Frank Bailey. Though the network optimistically boasted that the show would air from 11:00 P.M. to 1:00 A.M. five nights a week, there is no clear evidence that it was ever successfully produced, lending credence to David Weinstein's observation, "Unfortunately, DuMont's early variety programming was not always able to support the lofty claims, and hopes, of the advertising department" (2004: 94).

Over the next six years, venues including the Blue Angel in New York, the Carousel and Chez Paree in Chicago, and Copa City in Miami hosted televised music and variety broadcasts. Copa City went so far as to renovate its facilities in 1949 with the explicit intention of accommodating television remote broadcasts, constructing new "studio" and rehearsal spaces, special TV camera ramps, movable lighting banks, and other amenities to facilitate production. In 1954, Copa City also added additional TV production facilities, allowing for more efficient rehearsals and other backstage considerations ("Miami's Copa City" 1954: 33). The practice of broadcasting from lounges and nightclubs extended even further as talent agencies and record companies gained familiarity with television's unique promotional potentials, having seen what televised performances could do.

In December 1954, General Artists Corporation merged club appearances by singers on the agency's roster with televised music broadcasts, organizing a regional "one-nighter" TV-club circuit in Cleveland, Cincinnati, and Chicago. The approach was intended to boost public familiarity with the artists and to promote new recordings while allowing the partnering nightspots to share the costs for musical performances with local TV stations. The singers also benefited from the arrangement, especially since it was not uncommon in the industry for artists to tap into their advances in order to pay the expenses for promotional jaunts and publicize their new record releases ("Blueprint TV One-Niter 'Circuit,'" 1954: 59).

Club managers facing declining revenues deliberately sought collaborative opportunities with TV broadcasters. Describing the initiatives undertaken by the Latin Quarter and Blue Angel in New York and Copa City in Miami, *Variety* claimed in 1954 that video remote broadcasts, "have also added to their institutional prestige in the hinterlands" ("Top Cafes" 1954: 49). Occasional references to the nation's "hinterlands" reflect an important geographic and cultural dynamic, alluding to the chasm between what urban critics perceived as the trend-setting environs of New York or other larger centers and the cultural vacuum of middle-America. With a propensity for the luxurious and the exotic, dozens of nightclubs in the nation's urban centers unabashedly cloaked themselves in the latent intrigue of the cultural/racial Other or the international cosmopolitan sophisticate, hinting at foreignness, steamy climates, garish fashion, sensual dance and music styles, and looser moral values. While this was somewhat of a norm in larger American cities, the image of hedonistic excess was quite unfamiliar (though not necessarily unwelcome) in the nation's less populated regions. Susan Waggoner explains, "Like an endless costume party, the nightclub era favored anything with a theme. The revues had themes. The menus had themes. Even the clubs themselves had themes. Exotic locales were always popular, and a single night in a single town could take you to Zanzibar, Versailles, Persia, Morocco, or Monte Carlo. . . . Tropical settings were the most enduring of all, and a kind of palm frenzy gripped the era from start to finish" (2001: 35). The nightclub was, thus, seen as an antidote to the routine and mundane existence of mainstream middle-American life; the nightclubs did not constitute solely a destination but an *adventure*. To the extent that it was possible, television producers sought to extend this sense of adventure to TV viewers.

The nightclub setting invited distinct viewer associations and audience expectations, for as John Storey observes, "It is through our preconceptions and prejudices that we organize our approach to a text" (1999: 62). Television broadcasts of musical performances drew on standard characteristics of nightclub style in recognizable — if imperfect — ways, forging explicit connections between the television nightclub and actually existing nightspots in major American cities. In depictions of ersatz nightclub spaces the prevailing image was usually not the dark, smoky, and cramped jazz "joints" of 52nd Street or Harlem but polished dinner clubs or sanitized entertainment establishments designed primarily for the white urban bourgeoisie. A social and aesthetic middle ground between these two race- and class-based domains was presented on the November 29, 1954, broadcast of *The Tony Martin Show*, on which Martin is portrayed seated in a subterranean night spot (replete with faux exposed-brick walls and a revolving ceiling fan) set in New Orleans as he sings Cole Porter's "All of You" (from the play *Silk Stock-*

ings). The ersatz locus — New Orleans — and the staging and lighting imbues the entire episode with the mysterious, seductive undertone that is stereotypically associated with the city and, as Martin sings, the setting is sensually evocative yet tasteful, clearly not a dive, implying a comfortable local lounge.

The locational sensibilities and ideological values constructed through the programs' image and discourse were reinforced through the presentation of what might be defined as *appropriate* musical performances, connoting the unique internal environment of the upscale nightclub. Even in musical performance situations that were marked by high camp or vaudeville mannerisms, such as Jimmy Durante's or Morey Amsterdam's borscht-belt shtick,[16] the chic image of refinement and genteel patronage generally prevailed. In this sense, television's actual and ersatz nightclubs suggested more than simple intimacy or benign entertainment; they communicated complex values associated with the ideals of middle- and upper-class leisure and urban sophistication.

The production logic behind nightclub-oriented TV programs involved a calculated effort to reproduce the feel and affect of contemporaneous evening leisure spots, conveying an allusion to urban glamour. Executive memos circulating in advance of the production of NBC's *Saturday Night Dance Party* in 1951 (the show was scheduled as a 1952 summer replacement for Sid Caesar's powerhouse comedy program *Your Show of Shows*) illustrate this focus and intent. While they initially conceived it as a remote broadcast program from actual New York City nightclubs, network discussions shifted to the idea of a broadcast from an ersatz nightclub constructed in NBC Studio 8-H. In one early memo, the NBC executive George McGarrett describes the show's scenario: "We would stage it with a standard night club setting in 8-H, where we would have ample floor space for night club acts as well as for the actual dancers who would be invited to the Dance Party . . . as well as ample space for tables and chairs to accommodate the 'nightclub guests'" (1951).

In an unsigned and undated copy of a wire transmission to regional network stations (probably sent by McGarrett in 1951), the program pitch for *Saturday Night Dance Party* touts the high caliber of performing singers and orchestras with explicit reference to the nightclub setting: "The entire production will be staged as if coming from an important night club with actual dancers, on camera, and all backgrounds appropriate to night club and floor show flavor." The expression "as if" reflects the deliberate attempt to construct the nightclub's distinctive character while also emphasizing the desire to create a site of significance, aspiring to capture an element of cultural relevance. With the production and financial details ironed out, NBC moved forward with its summer program schedule and the show, hosted by Jerry Lester, aired each Saturday evening at 9:30. Carl Stanton, a network executive, announced the replacement program *Saturday Night Dance Party* to the NBC chief, Pat Weaver, defining the nightclub setting in uplifting terms: "The set will be a lavish night club with all the glitter that Broadway can offer and every seat is ringside. People will be invited to dance, enjoy themselves in the plush décor of NBC's TV Night Club" (1951).

In some cases, however, the attempt to instill an aura of elegance and sophistication went awry, reflecting the industry's concurrent struggle to define the medium and to develop viable music program genres; this is amply evident on a 1950 episode of *Popsicle Parade*, one of early television's more unusual musical offerings.[17] Sponsored by the Popsicle company on CBS, *Popsicle Parade* was apparently intended for a child audience, yet from a contemporary vantage nothing about its performances, musical selection, or set design seems geared toward this preadolescent demographic group.

The program in question opens with the typically suave and self-confident Tony Martin strolling onstage at the ersatz "Tony Martin's Club Popsicle" singing a mambo-inflected version of "Enjoy Yourself (It's Later Than You Think)," written by Herbert Magidson and Carl Sigman and a contemporaneous hit for the Guy Lombardo Orchestra, accompanied by the indomitable Ray Bloch orchestra. While the song and the performance are entirely characteristic of Martin's artistic ouevre, the lyrics seem ill-considered for children (visually portrayed in attendance) with words cautioning against the onslaught of aging, lament about missed opportunity, and regret—even to the extent of entertaining suicidal notions with the line, "Lay down that gun, don't try, my friend, to reach the great beyond." Casually crossing the set while singing, Martin approaches a single table where two young girls sit gripping the sponsor's sweetened ice treat with both hands. Crooning, Martin leans down, making a funny face alongside the giggling girls.

Following his opening number, Martin states to the bleachers of children (intermittently visible at the edge of the set) and to the television viewing audience:

> When the makers of Popsicle told me they were going to give me this space to have our club here on your television and right here tonight it really made me happy. . . . We want you to have a good time, we want you

to dance, we want you to sing. Ray Bloch's going to play some good music for you and then I'm going to sing a couple more songs and then at the end we're going to invite you all to dance. Are you with me?

Martin employs his smooth vocal style to sing the Popsicle theme song and, after a brief filmed commercial announcement featuring Magic Skull rings (which could be attained by mailing in accumulated Popsicle wrappers), he introduces the next number, his 1950 hit "There's No Tomorrow": "Right now I'd like to sing a song for you that you've probably heard around the house for a long time. I'm sure that your mom sings it or your dad sings it. It's an old Italian song. At home we called it 'O Sole Mio.' I've changed the words, I've got a whole new song for you and I hope you like it."[18]

The revised lyrics and ballad arrangement, carried well by the Bloch orchestra, are decidedly not children's fare, however, in that they communicate an unambiguously adult-oriented sense of romantic longing. The fact that the program is set in a fictional nightclub environment with child patrons makes for a performance curiosity. While he sings the lines "There's no tomorrow when love is new / Now is forever when love is true / So kiss me and hold me tight / There's no tomorrow there's just tonight," Martin steps to the table where the aforementioned young girls sit and, bending down toward one girl, he slips a Magic Skull Ring onto her finger as if proposing to her, crooning smoothly all the while.

Across the networks the nightclub concept was sustained by narratives and program announcements accompanied by simple visual effects, establishing a recognizable cultural frame for the music, dance, and comedy performances. The scripted material often constructed a back story for TV's ersatz nightclubs, providing context for the shows' musical presentations. In the case of *Café de Paris*, airing on WABD-TV in 1949, the unusually elaborate back story has the host and singer Sylvie St. Claire inheriting a rundown Paris nightclub. After "hiring" three itinerant street musicians (the Stan Free Trio), St. Claire "secures" a television broadcast contract that allows her to "operate" her small club.

The opening and closing voice-overs of program announcers and the hospitable patter of program hosts also helped to reinforce the spatial character and convivial atmosphere of television's nightclub shows. On the December 24, 1948, episode of *The Morey Amsterdam Show* (on the CBS network) the program opens with an image of couples dancing among the tables of what appears to be a small, dimly lit nightclub. The John Guarnieri Orchestra, barely visible in the rear, plays an up-tempo selection. The announcer Don Russell recites his introduction: "Just a block or two from Times Square, there's a famous little rendezvous where show people, famous personalities, and just plain folks gather nightly. Join the happy gang at the Golden Goose Cafe."

The characterization of the stylish nightclub situated in the heart of the New York entertainment district taps into an established image of well-mannered leisure, glamour, and celebrity, and the notion of an actual nightclub is reproduced through the discursive summoning of actual or known sites such as Times Square, thus diluting the ersatz element of the performance space. After the Amsterdam show moved from CBS to the Du Mont network, the opening sequence of the April 21, 1949, episode features Russell reprising his role as the nightclub MC, again invoking spatial authenticity with the announcement, "Folks, would you kindly hurry back to your tables because it's floor show time here at the Silver Swan, and I'd like you to meet that fellow with the cello, Morey Amsterdam."

Nightclub-based programs ended in a similar manner, with announcers or show hosts thanking viewers for "dropping in" at the club, signing off with the hope that the audience will "come back again next week." Near the end of the October 20, 1950, broadcast of Du Mont's *Hold That Camera*, the host Kyle MacDonnell,[19] seated at a small bistro table in an ersatz club bedecked in an evening gown and elbow-length opera gloves, announces to audience members that there is an empty chair waiting just for them each week. The personalized and direct mode of address enacted by Russell, MacDonnell, and many others effectively aligns the viewer more tightly with the spatial sensibilities of the nightclub as a performance site, downplaying the physical barriers between the viewer's material reality (the home or, perhaps, a public viewing spot) and the imagined "there" of the upscale and exciting urban nightclub. At television's ersatz nightclubs viewers are always welcome and there is always an available table. With a friendly goodbye and a reminder about the next broadcast, the show hosts asserted the program's presence as a destination on the television airwaves.

Lynn Spigel observes, "Television at its most ideal promised to bring audiences not merely an illusion of reality as in the cinema, but a sense of 'being there,' a kind of hyperrealism" (1992: 133):

> Television, it was constantly argued, would be a better approximation of
> live entertainment than any previous form of technological reproduc-

tion. Its ability to broadcast direct to the home would allow people to feel as if they really were at the theater. Television's capacity for transmitting sight as well as sound would give its programs a sense of credibility that radio lacked, while its intimate privatized address would create a more compelling simulation of reality than film ever could. (ibid.: 138)

The phenomena to which Spigel refers were evident in numerous contexts and could be witnessed in such programs as *Club Seven* (airing on ABC between 1949 and 1951) that demonstrated a clear formal attempt to reproduce the experience of presence at a nightclub.

The show opens with an image of a nightclub on a crowded street, while the orchestra led by Bobby Byrne performs a sprightly tune offscreen. The *Club Seven* set depicts a flashing marquee logo emblazoned with the number 7 and a sidewalk advertising board featuring the image of the show's program host, Johnny Thompson. Viewers are presented with the ideal vantage of club patrons who are invited to enter the establishment from the street, and the camera orients the viewer to the club setting as the front door swings open, revealing a dance floor full of swirling couples with the Byrne orchestra situated in the background. The unseen announcer recites the introduction, "Once again we open the magic door in television's brightest nightspot and you're welcome, so won't you come in?" If television was regarded as a "window on the world" by some commentators in the 1940s, the reference to *Club Seven*'s "magic door" functions similarly with the medium serving as a kind of portal through which viewers might pass, if only in a vicarious relationship to the "nightclub" performances before them. The friendly tone of the invitation was, of course, also a standard presentational element of the genre.

As the point of view and mode of address of *Club Seven*'s opening sequence imply, the emphasis is on individual, subjective perspectives and personalized pleasures. In comparison to the large spatial scale associated with film theaters, ballrooms, or Broadway theaters, nightclubs function at a reduced scale that favors proximate contact between the audience and performer. Reflecting this perspective, Dave Rose (longtime musical director for *The Red Skelton Show*) offered the opinion "With television you have it right in your front room. You will be sitting there right beside the musicians, the way it should be" (English 1951a: 4). Musicians and singers in nightclubs appear accessible in ways that those in large theaters or in movies do not, and this sense of proximity and intimacy remains one of the alluring aspects of the standard nightclub or cabaret performance even to this day.

Performances set in the nightclub context generally privileged relaxed, lightly swinging musical arrangements or ballads that were better suited to subtle, finely nuanced physical gestures that could be successfully captured and broadcast to home viewers. Broadcasts of ersatz nightclub and cabaret performances can be contrasted with the exaggerated and often exhausting workouts of such programs as *The Colgate Comedy Hour*, hosted by the wide-eyed Eddie Cantor and the madcap musical comedy of Spike Jones and his ensemble or the elaborate production numbers and musical show tunes that were standard on *The Kate Smith Evening Hour*, as well as on many other musical variety shows. Auslander writes, "Television's intimacy was seen as a function of its immediacy — the close proximity of viewer to event that it enables — and the fact that events from outside are transmitted into the viewer's home" (1999: 16). Nightclub-oriented TV programs airing between 1948 and 1956 displayed considerable consistency and effort in reproducing a sense of intimacy, whether through the artist's performance styles; the tight arrangement of sets, props, and extras; or through technical means including camera cuts and shot positions that privileged mid-shots and close-ups.

The common television staging of musical performances set in nightclubs included closely arranged bistro tables situated around a central floor show area, with well-dressed couples seated mere feet from the artists in a manner that closely resembles an actual nightclub setup. On the aforementioned 1951 broadcast of the *The Frank Sinatra Show*, the joke is constructed around the premise that the guest, Perry Como, and Sinatra are patrons at a Frankie Laine floor show set at the Copacabana club. Rather than occupying a place of celebrity privilege ("ringside" as they call it), the two are seated at the back of the nightclub, behind an obstruction at the worst table in the house (at one point, in an exaggerated gesture Laine pulls out a telescope to see them). As Como and Sinatra gripe about their poor view of the stage, extras are seated at tables immediately adjacent to Laine as he sings "That Lucky Old Sun" (a top hit two years earlier).

Reflecting this type of staging, a 1954 studio photograph of Cleveland station WEWS-TV's *Old Dutch Revue* depicts a small musical ensemble set up in a remote corner of the studio stage with a cumbersome TV camera pointed not at the musicians but at the packed dance floor, where roughly fifteen couples danced. Located immediately behind the dancers are several small tables populated by couples seemingly engaged in intimate con-

Tony Martin. Undated. COURTESY OF PHOTOFEST.

versation. The casual and cozy social atmosphere was further accentuated on many nightclub programs by subtle prop details including beer bottles, glasses of wine or cocktails on the tables (and on some programs, tea cups or Coca-Cola bottles, which might reflect a cautiously temperate attitude, possibly at the sponsor's request).

On many nightclub programs the camera draws behind the seated extras that surround the "floor show" stage, framing them in delicate silhouette with the dance floor and bandstand in the rear. The shot produces a strangely appealing effect suggesting the vantage from a table just behind the front row. Refocusing the lens, the camera slowly zooms into a mid-shot or close-up, passing the extras until the host or musical performers are in sharp relief for the performance. This and other camera practices demonstrate the real work involved in promoting intimacy and viewer engagement while reproducing the essence of the nightclub experience through the manipulation of lighting, visual perspectives, props, and other production techniques.

Whether consisting of hired extras, specially invited guests, or members of the public who applied to attend the live studio broadcasts, the presence of onscreen audience members was crucial to the construction of nightclub *vérité*. Highlighting *Old Dutch Revue*, the magazine *Radio and Television Mirror* unironically referred to the onscreen audience as "customers," describing the show's aesthetics and audience presence in terms that imply an actual and not ersatz environment: "When the patrons are once again seated around the tavern's checkered table-cloths, the stage is filled by a galaxy of guest stars" ("Old Dutch Revue" 1954: 20). Jason Toynbee observes, "Music-making is staged as something performed by musicians for an audience. . . . [T]he theatricality of popular music performance derives from performers conceiving of themselves as performers and audience members thinking that they are members of an audience" (2000: 57). The onscreen audience provides the TV viewer with an identifiable point of reference, helping to concentrate attention on the performance contexts of the ersatz nightclub while buffering what Toynbee identifies as the musical event's "theatricality." In this framework, the production assigns the viewer to his or her audience position, establishing the dominant or preferred vantage from which to best "enjoy" the musical performance on the screen.

Through their visibility, the onscreen studio audiences also ascribe an additional element of authenticity to the televised nightclub space, reproducing an image of nonchalant leisure that loosely matches that of an actual nightclub. This authenticity effect emerged in interesting ways that at times spilled beyond the frame of the television program (validating Spigel's reference to television's "hyperreality"). According to *Radio and Television Mirror*, Cleveland's WEWS-TV received regular calls from viewers seeking the street address of the Old Dutch Tavern portrayed on the station's *Old Dutch Revue*: "Although its gaiety rings so true that, after four years on the air, fans still think it is an actual night spot—at that moment, the tavern is being neatly folded and stacked away against the walls of WEWS' Studio A until the following Monday" ("Old Dutch Revue" 1954: 20).

The portrayal of an audience on the set, however, also harbored its own potential hazards. Reviewing the October 19, 1949, broadcast of *Old Knick Music Hall* on New York's WOR-TV, *Variety* criticized the program's two-hour broadcast marathon and the attempt to integrate an excess of performances, specifically citing the broadcast's floor show "audience":

A nitery provides a natural habitat for an audience that's willing to pay to be entertained. Unlike other café crowds, this customer collection is more than willing to cooperate with the emcee since clientele is accustomed to being asked to perform even when there are no video cameras on hand. However, it's fairly evident that the show's ingredients aren't enough to provide consistent entertainment to either the café customers and the video viewers.

Though the ersatz audience and the TV viewer are linked to the performance through their mutual status as spectators and a shared intimacy, the example of *Old Knick Music Hall* indicates that the bonds may also be forged across less ideal or desirable affective orientations. In this case, they are potentially aligned within a shared sense of ennui rather than enlivened pleasure or mere satisfaction.

In a discussion of television, music, and nightclubs it would be remiss to ignore the Lucille Ball and Desi Arnaz situation comedy *I Love Lucy*, especially since the show employed many of the formulaic conventions associated with other nightclub-oriented broadcasts (further discussion of the program follows in chapter 6). Nightclubs were central in *I Love Lucy*, much as they were in the actual rise of Latin music during the postwar years. Latin orchestras emerged as a refreshing force in the dance band sector, infusing both aesthetic variation and economic vitality into a struggling industry.

For many U.S. citizens, Latin music and dance were inextricably linked through most of the 1940s, and despite a brief postwar slump, there was a major surge in interest in Latin rhythms by the end of the decade, leading to thriving Latin nightclubs in the major New York, Miami, and Los Angeles markets. John Storm Roberts identifies the critical importance of the nightclubs where the Latin music scene was germinated and nurtured, pointing to the 1952 "all-mambo policy" at the Palladium as a catalyst setting off the "great era of the New York mambo" (1999: 129). Media reports of the sensual and athletic dancing in the country's Latin clubs were also increasingly common through the early 1950s, extending a rudimentary awareness of the Latin scene far into the U.S. heartland.

The musical component of *I Love Lucy* hinges on Arnaz's real-life role as a musician and popular bandleader. Indeed, Arnaz's own profession and lifestyle constitutes the referent for his television sitcom role. By the mid- to late 1940s Arnaz was appearing regularly at upper-echelon nightclubs in New York (as leader of the house band at the newly reopened Ciro's and the luxurious Copacabana club) and Miami, performing in a musical style that "was typical of the lusher strata of contemporary nightclub-Latin music" (Roberts 1999: 112). The centrality of the nightclub was accentuated in the premiere episode of *I Love Lucy* on October 15, 1951 ("The Girls Want to Go to a Nightclub"). The episode prominently cites the Copacabana with additional scripted references to the Waldorf Astoria's Starlight Roof club, the latter of which had actually booked Arnaz earlier in his career. The opening banter between Lucy Ricardo (Ball) and her neighbor, Ethel Mertz (Vivian Vance), expresses a frustration with their mundane existence as housewives and their yearning for a night on the town with their husbands:

LUCY: "Ricky hates nightclubs."
ETHEL: "But he works in one. Your life should be just one gay round of nightclubs."
LUCY: "Yeah, that's what I thought when I married a bandleader, but ever since we said 'I do,' there are so many things we don't."
ETHEL: "Well, it was a good idea while it lasted. Gee, it was gonna be the Copacabana."
LUCY (wistfully): "Gee . . . the Copacabana."

The majority of the program's musical production numbers are set in the fictional nightclub the Tropicana, a reference to the prestigious Havana nightspot and a popular Bronx club[20] each with the same name. The club exterior is pictured from time to time in an establishing shot featuring a wide palm-shaped neon sign; the interior set features the conventional television nightclub arrangement with tables situated adjacent to the dance floor. Arnaz, portraying the musician Ricky Ricardo, is leader of the house band and the Tropicana is Ricky's musical base. The club also functions within the show's narrative as an alternative zone to the domestic realm of the home. It is distinguished from the Ricardos' apartment since it is public, yet it is also oriented toward evening leisure activities catering to an ostensibly sophisticated social crowd.

Gustavo Perez Firmat asserts that the Tropicana "is a far more predictable place than the apartment" (1994: 35), suggesting that its status as a rigid, formal, professional space minimizes the potential for spontaneity that is associated with the Ricardo's residence. Firmat implies that, compared to the home space, the nightclub is essentially Arnaz's office or workplace and, although it is said that one *plays* music, for the professional musician the club is primarily a site of *labor*. While the professional practices set in the Tropicana often contrast sharply with the chaotic home scenes, counter to Firmat's view there is much comic pandemonium focused on the nightclub. In each space, however, the cultural or linguistic differences between Ricky and his wife Lucy are always central, providing the pivot upon which the show's humor turns. Firmat is on more solid ground when he notes, "As an extension of Ricky, the club has a 'Cuban' or 'Latin' personality" (1994: 36). The space of the Tropicana thus functions as a crucial signifier of labor, gender, and cultural Otherness, granting the nightclub and its musical scenes added significance in the overall context of the program.

Orchestras were infrequently depicted on television dramas and situation comedies, nor were the house bands commonly featured on programs set in ersatz nightclubs. Unless it was a top orchestra led by a celebrity bandleader, the bands were more often than not relegated to the background. In a reversal of this trend, on *I Love Lucy* Ricky's band is regularly showcased. Ron Rodman explains, "As a bandleader, Arnaz was expected to sing and dance on the program, but the writer and director Jess Oppenheimer decided he should do so only if it furthered the story line. The result was many fine musical numbers featuring Ball and Arnaz, all in some way tied to the plot" (2010: 193).

Bedecked in frilly costumes connoting a Cuban influence that was characteristic of the period, the orchestra is situated much closer to the camera than on most other club-oriented productions, occupying a wider portion of the television screen frame. The bandstand is also situated closely alongside the floorshow "stage," allowing Ricky to visibly interact with the orchestra members between and during musical production numbers. While the ersatz Tropicana includes extras seated as audience patrons at the club, the television viewer clearly apprehends a different, more proximate and intimate image than do the extras. The gaze of the ersatz/onscreen audience is subordinated as the production apparatus (cameras, editing, lighting) supplants their perspectival authority by privileging the vantage of the TV viewing audience.

The orchestra is alternately depicted in rehearsal mode, casually lounging in the Tropicana during breaks in the afternoon practice sessions, and performing "on the stand." The April 21, 1952, episode ("Cuban Pals") encompasses all three of the band's dispositions: at rest, in rehearsal, and in performance. In the musical production numbers set in the club, the musicians are usually seated on a multitiered riser, physically arranged in a manner that was common at the time. The performances by Arnaz, Ball, or their musical guests take place on the showroom floor immediately in front of the band while the cameras focus on the dance or vocal performances from several angles. During the production numbers the band members are invariably visible within the frame, playing in the background while Arnaz conducts from the front of the stage.

I Love Lucy was something of an anomaly on television as nightclub settings gradually fell from favor and their status as a stylistic signifier declined through the late 1950s. The networks no longer constructed the same ornate ersatz nightclubs in their broadcast studios, nor did they broadcast from actual nightclubs to the same extent as they had in the late 1940s or early 1950s. One reason for this may be that audiences had become more familiar with television's presentational style and its genre forms and were consequently less inclined to accept the fabrication of nightclub spaces, regarding the effort as inauthentic and unnecessary. As television evolved viewers more readily accepted the TV studio itself as a legitimate, conventional space from which musical programs were broadcast.

The performance styles and musical forms that crept into the public consciousness and onto the record sales charts by mid-decade also moved away from the primacy of the traditional urban nightclub, producing taste-based fissures between youth and adult audiences. Once the influences of rock 'n' roll were felt, the refined and dignified nightclub environment (and the music associated with it) slowly acquired a reputation as a cultural throwback, aligned with older acts and a decidedly unhip adult clientele. Even as some of the nightclub era's most successful musicians decried the loss of glamour, television eventually turned its back on the nightclubs.

DJ and Teen Dance Programs: Genre and the Youth "Crisis"

Extending a trend that was already under way in the 1930s, media and entertainment corporations in the postwar period aggressively rallied their resources to develop and nurture a responsive youth consumer bloc. Music was inarguably central to youth leisure practices, fueling eager fandom and mass appeal. Teen tastes had helped to propel Benny Goodman's orchestra to the forefront of the dance band sector following his famous Palomar Ballroom remote radio broadcast in 1935 and his subsequent appearances at New York's Paramount Theater (providing a factual base for the November 1, 1951, broadcast of *Your Show of Shows*, featuring Sid Caesar and the cast comically portraying rapt and swooning teen fans at a Goodman show). Frank Sinatra's renowned Paramount Theater concerts in 1942 (appearing with Goodman) and 1944 (the latter provoking what police and the media termed "a riot") and the resultant "mania" of adolescent female "bobby-soxers" solidified Sinatra's status at the top of the entertainment industry's celebrity roster. Each of these cases serve as benchmarks—and precedents—of energized youth enthusiasm for popular music in the pretelevision era. Thus TV presented new conduits through which musical artists, record labels, and advertisers could reach young audience members, introducing an alternative media apparatus for defining youth culture.

Among the TV music program formats developed around an idealized teen viewer was the disk jockey or "platter" show. The genre's genesis was in youth clubs and at teen dances where DJs or jukeboxes provided popular music throughout the 1940s. The concept of the DJ broadcast format implementing prerecorded music was first developed in radio, in part as means of "using musical selection to establish consistent 'core' audiences and as an efficient and cost-effective programming strategy" (Rothenbuhler and McCourt 2002: 371). With radio's transformation and industrial and cultural repositioning in the postwar period there was a proliferation of DJ shows on the AM band that were explicitly directed toward young radio listeners. According to Reebee Garofalo, "It was, ironically, the development of television that opened the door to independent radio (and thus R & B) in the late 1940s by deliberately, if temporarily, sidelining a technological innovation that would have increased the quality of radio transmission measurably—FM broadcasting" (2008: 75).

The status of the radio DJ rose significantly in the same period as television's ascendance. As a matter of industry survival, radio broadcasting was reconceived with popular musical recordings occupying a new, more central role. Stations across the nation developed and refined their pop music broadcasts, emphasizing the spatial primacy of the immediate station territory or urban locale and featuring dynamic on-air DJ "personalities," some of whom emerged as cultural icons in their own right. The cost of spinning records was far less than the expenses associated with hiring studio orchestras or paying for remote location broadcast engagements and, as the recording industry quickly learned, the radio DJ's influence as taste arbiter and song promoter was an essential factor in building stars and selling disks. In an example of deliberate collaboration, the radio broadcast and recording sectors established a new symbiosis with youth at the center of their shared attentions. Social events (dance parties or "sock hops") involving either radio or records evolved in the early 1950s as an essential facet of teen life and the commercial culture industry's awareness of this was reflected in mid-century advertising campaigns depicting teens dancing to spinning 45 rpm disks or huddled around a radio set.

Television producers capitalized on the DJ trend by introducing numerous shows that featured "disk spinners." Horace Newcomb cites *Teen Canteen*, a show mixing variety-style performances accompanied by the spinning of popular recordings, as "the first teen series to appear on television" (2005: 2276). Debuting on the Schenectady station WRGB in 1946, the show transferred to the New York station WPIX in 1948. Also among the first entries in the televised DJ genre was *Disk Magic* (later titled *Musical Merry-Go-Round*), hosted by Jack Kilty on NBC's New York flagship station WNBT in 1947. The show was structured around a series of variety-style performances featuring singers, dancers, and comedians with recorded musical accompaniment. Curiously, Kilty did not actually drop the needle on the records as a professional DJ would; rather, he pretended to do so while the recordings were played from the studio production booth (a practice that, according to contemporaneous reports, resulted in at least one visible miscue). In this case, the DJ was only a program device, a concept character intended to tap into the teen viewing market.

Regional stations were also inclined toward the DJ teen dance genre: the Cleveland station WEWS-TV introduced *Record Shop* in February 1948 and although *Spinning Images* on the Memphis station WMCT in 1949 did not feature an actual disk jockey, the premise did involve a DJ spinning records. The show's unusual format introduced a cartoonist that implemented an "illuminated drawing board which permits artist to work freely and yet remain invisible to cameras and TV audience.... All that is visible to audience is a moving point which leaves a visible line. Cartoons thus created provide 'video' while record is being played" ("Spinning Images" 1949: 63).

In 1950 the radio DJ Soupy Sales (who later attained fame as a children's TV host and comedian) was tapped to host *Soupy's Soda Shop* on the new Cincinnati station WKRC-TV. A Los Angeles station, KNXT, introduced *Peter Potter's Party* in 1950. The program's format featured the popular West Coast DJ Potter promoting hit singles, engaging in casual repartee with his invited guests from the music scene, and introducing the occasional music or dance act. Some critics seemed surprised, however, that the show largely ignored Potter's status as a professional DJ, with *Variety* magazine claiming that Potter's talents and reputation were being wasted. *Picture Platters* also aired in 1950 on KTSL with the host Steve Dunne acting as a disorganized and confused DJ, screening brief film clips that accompanied the music. The

Chicago station WNBQ offered *Record Spotlight* in 1950, a five-minute musical "capsule" hosted three times a week by Howard Miller, a local DJ. In Erie, Pennsylvania, WICU-TV presented one of the oddest admixtures, which featured the DJ Bob Kahle spinning records alongside sewing demonstrations on the hour-long broadcast of *Spins and Needles*.[21]

Teen record shops were commonly represented on the early DJ or platter-oriented programs, and there were dozens of unheralded shows that, while adhering to a standard variety format, were set in ersatz record stores (often constructed with chintzy props) catering exclusively to teenagers. Premiering on January 19, 1949, *Nipper's Record Shop* aired on the CBS station KPIX-TV in San Francisco with Guy Cherney and Mary Milford as hosts, portraying a record shop owner and his "zany" store clerk. The jazz innovator Dizzy Gillespie and a trio headed by a local bassist, Vernon Alley (who had recently returned to the city following tours with the Lionel Hampton and Count Basie orchestras), performed on the show's opening broadcast. *Al Siegel's Song Shop*, debuting on WOR-TV in New Jersey in late 1949, was also set in a record store and featured a youthful "staff" that performed musical hits requested by viewers via telephone call-ins.

The DJ program was regarded as an odd TV genre in early 1950, yet a *Billboard* report from Hollywood identified the successes of several shows in the greater Los Angeles market, especially KLAC-TV's broadcasts featuring the AM radio jock Al Jarvis. The Jarvis show was KLAC's top-rated program at the time, and its favorable advertising revenues led the station to introduce additional DJ programs; DJs also applauded the new TV broadcast format as it provided them with a rather lucrative sidebar to their regular radio duties.[22] Other local stations soon followed KLAC's lead, noting the genre's overall simplicity: the shows were "inexpensive to produce, easy to sell, and perfectly suited for a multiplicity of spot commercials.... With no rehearsal needed, little studio space tied up, and production crews down to a minimum of one cameraman, producer, etc., such airers are about the least expensive type of live programming" ("Coast Jocks Canter" 1950: 15). In a comment that would surely pique the interest (or wrath) of the AFM's James Petrillo, *Billboard* also referred to DJs having "access to 'name' recording talent as gratis guest material" (Bundy 1950: 70).

A well-regarded Los Angeles DJ with radio station KFWB, Peter Potter launched his first late-night DJ show on the Don Lee station KTSL in April 1950. With his second major television foray, *Jukebox Jury*, Potter reinforced the TV DJ's role of taste arbiter. *Jukebox Jury* was a panel program broadcast on ABC from Los Angeles in 1953–54. It featured expert panelists representing various sectors of the entertainment industry, including Touch Connors, Maureen O'Sullivan, and Jane Powell, among others, whose duties involved listening carefully to various new releases by top recording artists of the day (such as Doris Day, Georgia Gibbs, Dean Martin, or Fran Warren). Goaded on by Potter, the panelists were invited to discuss their assessments of each recording, speculating about its audience appeal or market potential and its chances for achieving mainstream success via radio or jukebox play.

Potter's industry reputation as a DJ was well established and his questions to the panelists were frequently framed in stark commercial terms, pressing for comments about each recording's money-making potential, asking, "Would you spend your money on this record?" or "Would you be guilty of putting a nickel or dime in a jukebox so your teenage son could hear it if he wanted to?" Potter's discourse of the commercial "hit" or "miss" record narrowed the options of response, yet the detailed discussions among the panelists often offered insights into social listening practices and general public taste parameters. The panelists were not mere cheerleaders for the artists or industry and their critical comments were at times quite damning, isolating such features as a song's monotony or limited appeal, the weak character of its orchestration, the catchiness — or lack thereof — of the chorus, or the overall quality of the lead vocal.

Music publishers were disenamored by television's "song-judging" programs (which also included Fred Allen's *Judge for Yourself* on NBC), arguing, "a good review of the platter can't help the tune but a bad review could possibly ruin it" ("Too Many A&R Men" 1954: 41). The main point of resistance to the Allen show involved its format featuring unqualified amateur panelists and audience members who judged various "new untried tunes . . . that America will soon be singing." The Potter show was also criticized from the perspective that "the celebs Potter uses as judges are in no position to appraise a disk" (ibid.). The so-called experts or industry insiders comprising the judging panels were, in the publishers' view, only able to offer their personal opinions.

Like their radio counterparts, television station owners and network executives favored DJ shows because of their comparatively minimal overhead and the belief that the teen market represented a vast untapped audience and consumer reservoir. Music industry executives and song publishers, however, adhered to a different agenda, optimistically hoping that TV disk jockeys might function as visual song pluggers, promoting new compositions or announcing artists' record label affiliations. Throughout the 1950s, radio and television DJs were each openly courted by music publishers and industry agents who, through either ethical or illicit means, sought to place their music on radio and TV shows. Well before the radio sector's payola scandal erupted in 1959 ("Gimme, Gimme, Gimme" 1959: 45–48; Garofalo 2008: 153–55), the television DJ emerged as an additional cog in the music promotion apparatus, attaining status as a tastemaker if on a far lesser scale than his — and, indeed, virtually all broadcast DJs were men at this stage — radio counterparts ("TV Disk Jock" 1952: 57).

Teen Platter TV: The Philadelphia Influence

Even with New York's undisputed status as the nation's broadcast center and its deep influence on cultural style and taste or the trend-setting capacities of Los Angeles and the powerful Hollywood film studios, Philadelphia established a reputation as a central source of teen-oriented music and culture at war's end. The city also emerged as an important urban locale in the evolution of the televised DJ platter program. The tightening relationships between radio, television, and disk jockeys were pronounced in Philadelphia, and early TV genre developments there were scrutinized and, gradually, adopted by station managers throughout the country. In May 1945, Philadelphia radio station WPEN debuted its "platter and chatter" show *The 950 Club*, hosted by Joe Grady, who was joined in 1946 by the nineteen-year-old Ed Hurst. Together they regularly visited regional high schools across Pennsylvania and New Jersey, where they played music and held contests featuring product giveaways, meeting their teen audiences in the context of program and station promotions.

In an impressive innovation, *The 950 Club* also invited high school students to congregate at the downtown WPEN radio studio while the show was aired, encouraging the teens to dance to the records selected by Grady and Hurst and to sit in on special studio performances featuring top artists, including Benny Goodman, Vaughn Monroe, Tommy Dorsey, Martha Raye, Noro Morales, Dennis Day, Fran Warren, and Cab Calloway ("Teen-Agers Swarm" 1949: 12–13). The format's party-like atmosphere was immediately successful and, bolstered by its steady teen audience, the program posted the top ratings in the Philadelphia radio market in 1949. Complementing the impressive ratings figures was the suggestion that *The 950 Club* also provided a positive social service, with the trade magazine *Radio Showmanship* stating, "It is a valuable weapon in combating juvenile delinquency" (ibid.), an issue that would soon loom large.

Philadelphia's renown for pioneering teen entertainment was extended with creative initiatives such as the launch of exclusive teen-oriented nightclubs replete with soda bars and featuring musical performances by "name acts," presenting further options for teens to gather in organized and sanctioned settings ("Teenage Nitery Idea" 1949: 66). Underlying the prosocial emphasis of these activities was the dark threat of juvenile delinquency that was perceived as a serious and growing urban menace. Media broadcasting was commonly cited in social debates about how best to engage young people in order to steer them away from illicit or morally unacceptable behavior. In this context, the television DJ genre was tied to broader social issues; framed in relation to a burgeoning youth crisis, the genre did not present music played solely for entertainment but it was part of something more important, something with stakes and greater relevance to the community's overall well-being.

"Youth" was rapidly and widely imagined as a volatile social group and the media lustily pursued any and all incidents of teen irreverence, physical rebellion, or wanton property damage, reporting them as unambiguous symptoms of social decline. Teenagers rather quickly emerged as a frightening social force, "folk devils" with deep symbolic potency, a depiction that was also exploited in a spate of B-list movies produced in the mid- to late 1950s (Betrock 1986; Baker 2005). This, then, was the backdrop against which the televised DJ format emerged.

Some critics derided television's teen-oriented content, suggesting that TV (and the "abomination" of R & B or emergent rock 'n' roll music) was a public scourge capable of corrupting young peoples' values. Notwithstanding negative views, in some circles the televised DJ shows were regarded as a progressive response to youth unrest, presenting a means of engaging teens through musical performance. Facing what many perceived as an alarming teen disaster, some adults sought refuge in the belief that television harbored positive potentials, that it constituted a salvation of sorts.

In a special media profile proclaiming "1949 is Video Year," a banner headline in *Harlem's New York Amsterdam News* announced "Television Cuts Down Juvenile Delinquency: Video Lures Kids Home From Street" (April 2, 1949, 15). Cited in the article is General Electric's vice president W. R. G. Baker, who, sidestepping his obvious corporate interests in promoting television, voiced the altruistic rationale for the installment of TV sets at youth centers and other public venues: "Its magic will help guide the footsteps of our adolescents to these centers of right environment where the picture tube will open up a fascinating new world of entertainment and education" (ibid.). Although Baker's elevated cultural view was consistent with many of television's early advocates, who endeavored to establish educational and cultural programming to appeal to the youth viewer, it was popular culture that was winning teens over. Still, the altruistic theme did not dissipate and several programs explicitly appealed to right-mindedness and healthy social attitudes among teens.

It was in this same period that the famous "symphonic jazz" conductor Paul Whiteman launched one of the nation's first televised teen dance programs from Philadelphia. Responding to emerging reports about restive youth and juvenile delinquency, Whiteman originally sponsored informal Saturday night teen dances that featured a DJ near his Lambertville, New Jersey, farm (Banks 1948: 12; Whiteman 1948; Keegan 1952: 59; DeLong 1983: 283–84). Premiering on the Philadelphia station WFIL-TV (broadcast over the nascent ABC network) in 1949, *TV Teen Club* featured the aging bandleader in the host role (Whiteman was fifty-nine years old when the show debuted), presiding awkwardly over an amateur talent show that also offered young attendees the opportunity to dance to the Whiteman orchestra or to popular records[23] (Clark and Robinson 1976; DeLong 1983; Jackson 1997).

Thomas DeLong recounts that the Whiteman program, "beamed from a National Guard Armory in Philadelphia . . . attracted a massive turnout of young people, who jammed bleachers set up in the arena. Several thousand kids descended on the telecast every Saturday evening. After each actual telecast, which lasted from eight to nine, they danced to the music of a big band for two or more hours" (1983: 289–90). By 1952, the Whiteman show was produced in Studio B at WFIL-TV's new Radio and Television Center for national broadcast on the ABC network. Whiteman was unwavering in his commitment to the concept of the teen "club" as an entertainment option for listless youth, regarding the postwar teenager as being bereft of sound musical judgment and good taste as well as wanting for sites where dancing and pleasurable music could be enjoyed.

As WFIL improved its television broadcasting capabilities, it took a page from the WPEN radio playbook, announcing a new TV program, *Bandstand*, to premier on October 13, 1952. Hosted by former WPEN radio announcer, Bob Horn (with assistance from Lee Stewart) in a seventy-five-minute weekday slot, the show was inauspiciously touted as a "a light touch for afternoon viewing" ("New Shows Are Added" 1952: 19). According to Dick Clark (Clark and Robinson 1976), the program was initially conceived as an inexpensive vehicle for the broadcast of filmed musical shorts from the Snader and Official Film Company collections with which WFIL had been saddled.[24] Horn drew on his industry connections and a genuine awareness of the value of the vast teen market, developing a more substantial show than the station had originally envisioned, including guest appearances by touring artists and prominently featuring Philadelphia students as dancers and occasional interlocutors on the broadcasts.

Horn was also surely cognizant that radio DJs were attaining new renown as celebrity broadcasters (radio personalities such as Alan "Moondog" Freed or Douglas "Jocko" Henderson were just getting established at this stage) and, according to Clark (Clark and Robinson 1976), Horn adopted the perceptive musical tastes of these personality jocks, augmenting his play list of popular tracks and "jitterbug" jazz with more R & B tunes and the emergent rock 'n' roll (mainly recorded on independent labels). This decision was a clear response to the music's increased airplay on local AM radio stations and its obvious appeal among *Bandstand*'s teen audience. By virtue of his position as a radio and television DJ, Horn was also intimately familiar with the particular details of "payola" involving payoffs from record companies for record spins and on-air artist promotion.[25]

Philadelphia was home to an inordinate number of independent record companies, many of which openly paid DJs to spin their disks. The city's radio DJs had proven to be influential in generating consumer buzz for new artists and records, at times creating interest that spilled into the national market. Major record labels, too, were obligated to participate in the payola practice in order to not lose market share to the aggressive independents ("Philly Wide-Open Payola Town" 1952: 37). The television DJ was not, however, an established figure and some in the music industry disregarded the new medium's potential to boost record sales.

The local context for *Bandstand*'s launch is also relevant, for in late 1952 Philadelphia's youth constituency was captivated by the prospect of a "Rhythm Rodeo" featuring a city-wide battle of the bands (open only to musicians under the age of twenty) sponsored by The Philadelphia Inquirer Charities program ("Teen-Age Dance Bands" 1952: 1). Hyped aggressively throughout the preceding several weeks, articles about the forthcoming "rodeo" were regular page-one fare in the *Philadelphia Inquirer*. The event, with Paul Whiteman as master of ceremonies, also featured the Vaughn Monroe band as the professional headliner. The station WFIL-TV broadcast the program on December 5, airing the finale between 11:30 P.M. and 1:00 A.M. ("Melodiers Dance Band" 1952: 13); WFIL-TV was immediately established as a venue for popular music and a supporter of teen-oriented programming in Philadelphia.

With *Bandstand* on the air, WFIL was inundated with teenagers who jostled at the studio doors to gain access to its broadcasts, necessitating enhanced security and various methods of managing the press of youths who wanted to be seen on television and who were eager to dance to their favorite artists and recordings. Acknowledging *Bandstand*'s drawing power, WFIL gave the show an additional half hour of broadcast time in January 1953 and by autumn it was airing Monday through Friday between 2:45 and 5:00 P.M. Further extending the show's reach, on July 22, 1953, WFIL increased its transmission power fourfold to 100 kilowatts, providing "an increase of more than 40 percent in WFIL-TV's service area" ("WFIL-TV Will Increase Power" 1953: 32). Suddenly teens from much farther afield were tuning in to *Bandstand* and, whenever possible, making their way to the station's Market Street studio. While a major draw and an important facet of Philadelphia teen culture, the show also displayed an implicit but undeniable segregationist orientation. Few black youth were seen onscreen and the show's African American performers were kept at a safe distance from the white dancers (Austen 2005: 30; Garofalo 2008: 147; Delmont 2012).

In contrast to the TV shows, high school dances tended to draw primarily from the immediate locale, attracting students from each school along with occasional guests or the rare unwelcome interloper from other schools and other neighborhoods. Moreover, as highly circumscribed public spaces, school dances were exposed to a particular surveillance regime involving teachers, adult chaperones, or hired security. The televised dance programs occurred in an alternative social space, away from the daily routine of school (and for rebellious teens, an atmosphere of subjugation) and they were quickly considered the hottest ticket in town. Upon introducing televised dance parties and teen-oriented music programs in the early 1950s, youths from across Philadelphia — or Chicago, New York, and Washington, where the DJ genre was replicated — streamed toward the local television stations, massing outside the station doors with the intent of gaining entry to the popular after-school shows.

In this instance, the teen dance TV genre acquired a material status as a destination site. The genre was not simply an abstract construct within television's format structure and programming schedule but a new and essential facet of youth's localized social practices. TV's DJ/teen dance genre, it would seem, was merging with a teen lifestyle in a manner that transcended the screen, evolving as a facet of ritualized youth practice. Defying the best hopes of community leaders and TV station managers, the teen DJ and dance genre was construed as a harbinger of unruliness and a source of community concern.

WFIL established in-house standards that aided the station's ability to accommodate the teen attendees and ensure organized and smooth production. Other stations that were developing their own teen DJ programs copied several of the WFIL audience management systems. In order to control the crowds WFIL placed restrictions on the number of people that were admitted to the studio at any given time and a membership program was instated (including individualized member cards) that within the show's first year expanded to over five thousand members. In addition to the membership, "a volunteer committee of 12 teen-agers [was] charged with maintaining order and ruling on proper dress. 'No dungarees, pedal pushers or open sport shirts' is the show's rule" (Harris 1953b: 11).

The TV stations constituted a new nexus where teens from disparate urban neighborhoods converged. They constituted a meeting point where closely defined and fiercely defended turf boundaries gave way, and the emphasis on crowd control and rules of propriety were linked to wider concern about youth and security. Marty Jezer explains, "Gang warfare certainly did mirror international affairs. Young people carved up their cities into little neighborhood-states for security or self-defense. Within each neighborhood a kind of patriotism was strong. . . . [W]hen gangs rumbled, they fought over control of 'turf'" (1982: 240). This played out in particular ways once televised DJ and dance shows became a standard facet of television broadcasting. The DJ genre itself was soon part of a wider discussion about media and youth and, accordingly, it was subject to close scrutiny.

With the defensive apparatuses of the turf structure momentarily suspended during broadcasts, the televised dance parties such as *Bandstand* ideally offered the potential to function as a neutral ground where the city's young citizens could drop their turf-based animosities, congregating to share in the leisure practices affiliated with "their" music. Conversely, when circumstances brought teens from diverse local neighborhoods into one common space, the potential for conflict was drastically elevated. The dance shows presented a site of tension within which opposing groups from different neighborhoods circulated warily, in close proximity and always at risk of shattering a tenuous truce. At times it took little more than a girl dancing with the wrong boy to instigate conflict (and an ill-advised dance could be seen widely, broadcast to teen viewers throughout the region).

Philadelphia encountered several concurrent problems involving youth in 1953, shortly after *Bandstand* debuted and it did not take much for reporters to link the show and the entire DJ/teen dance genre with other problems involving its core constituency. Beginning in the early spring, a rash of newspaper articles reported surging "juvenile crime," "teen-age gangs," "street fights," and a scourge of teen "hot rodders" whose disdain for the law was irrepressible. Philadelphia's police were called to break up fights or to disperse agitated teen throngs, confiscating knives by the score from the young combatants. Teens were simultaneously described in the local media as a "problem," a "terror," and an "invasion." Complicating the situation was the fact that the summer of 1953 was unusually hot and humid and there were numerous newspaper reports about the city's stress and strain of coping with the extreme temperatures. Philadelphia was cast as a heated pressure cooker and the city's agitated youth population was on the verge of boiling over.

WFIL's attempts to manage the crowds of teens that arrived on its doorstep for the *Bandstand* broadcasts during its first year only went so far. Despite station promises that order and proper decorum would prevail, community merchants and homeowners living adjacent to the television station grew wary of the TV dance program that suddenly sprang up in their midst, voicing complaints to civic authorities about the disruption caused by teen audiences inundating their neighborhood. In Philadelphia, and elsewhere, merchants described incidents of theft or harassment by the teen cliques, explaining that their regular adult patrons often felt intimidated by the rambunctious youngsters who massed for the platter and dance TV programs. In some instances it was noted that the more aggressive and volatile teen gangs would linger in the vicinity of local TV stations long after the dance program had ended, drinking and carousing into the evening, creating further fear among adults in the area. In several localized settings (including Washington, D.C., and station WMAL that broadcast *Bandstand Matinee Club* in 1953) the televised DJ genre was increasingly implicated in issues relating to juvenile delinquency.[26]

Interviewed in the *Philadelphia Bulletin* upon *Bandstand*'s first anniversary in 1953, the host Bob Horn acknowledged that his show was a model of sorts, noting that station representatives from as far away as San Francisco had visited the WFIL set "to see what Bandstand was all about" (Harris 1953a: 25).[27] The DJ and platter genre emerged as a distinct, if not dominant, television genre with Philadelphia's *Bandstand* at the forefront of innovation yet the genre's triumph was by no means assured. While several television stations enjoyed clear-cut rewards with their teen-oriented disk jockey shows, their successes never reached that of WFIL's *Bandstand*. For some station owners, the possible financial returns for a DJ show were insufficient to offset the responsibilities and problems associated with managing herds of energetic teen participants in the studios and in the surrounding streets. *Billboard* commented in late 1954 on the genre's limitations: "Altho a selected few radio disk jockeys are making the grade in TV today, the profession as a whole has a long way to go before it masters the new medium. Most of the big name spinners have taken a fling in video during the last five years, but their survival average has been low" ("Disk Jockey Move" 1954: 21). Still, the pursuit of wholesome teen programming involving DJs and teen dancing offered several interesting formal variations (ibid.).

While still at the helm of *Bandstand*, the show host, Bob Horn, launched a late-night program, *TV Danceland*, that premiered on WFIL in May 1954 with special guests including Mitch Miller and Frankie Laine. Airing Friday nights at 11:45, the show was based on the *Bandstand* formula, "with the tempo geared to a higher age group. There are fewer bounce tunes and more slow numbers and waltzes. . . . Program is designed to entertain stay-at-homes as well as participants who write in for station tickets" ("TV Danceland," 1954). As the discourse surrounding the show and the guest artists suggests, *TV Danceland* seems to have represented a bid for a more middle-brow and middle-aged audience that would prefer the "easy listening" musical genre, possibly attempting to retain audience members that had matured out of the teen *Bandstand* demographic. It is possible that Horn himself was moving on, acknowledging the limits of his capacity to connect with the teen audiences and their music (although his alcohol problems and rumored sexual exploitation of young female TV hopefuls were also about to explode in the Philadelphia newspapers, decimating his career).[28]

By 1954 new teen DJ and dance programs debuted throughout the country, airing on local TV stations. In 1954, Chicago station WBKB introduced a two-hour show, *Recordland*, hosted by the vocalist Johnny Desmond, airing on Saturday afternoons. While foregrounding recorded music, the show also featured a regular pianist, Dick Marx, who accompanied Desmond on the occasional tune and guest artists (including the McGuire Sisters). Reflecting the practice initiated on Philadelphia's WPEN *950 Club*, an "assistant," Vince Garrity, also announced high school and college sports scores and other bits of information deemed relevant to a young viewing audience ("Recordland" 1954).

WBKB also introduced a curious offshoot of the televised platter genre in 1955 with *Splatter Party*, a DJ program broadcast live from the swimming pool at the city's Sheraton Hotel. Airing at the relatively late hour of 11:30 P.M., *Splatter Party* merged recorded pop music with athletic handball games, swimming relays, and images of the teen audience cavorting in the pool. *Teen Twirl*, broadcast on Cleveland's WNBK in early 1955, profiled a different high school each week, inviting teens to dance to both recordings and (improbably) a Dixieland house band, competing against one another in dance competitions. Again summoning the notion of teen threat, *Variety* magazine proclaimed, "If this city's juvenile delinquency rate drops to nil at 2 p.m. on Saturday, 'Teen Twirl' can take a vast share of the credit."

With an estimated U.S. teen population (encompassing those between thirteen and nineteen years of age) of sixteen million with access to roughly eight million TV sets, it was determined in early 1955 that "teenagers lack substantial interest in television and are perhaps the worst specific market to reach through the medium" ("Teenagers 'Worst' Market" 1955: 30). A market research agency, Teenage Survey Service, found that teens "listen to radio more than they watch tv principally because of their interest in pop records. 'It follows, therefore . . . that they are more apt to watch tv shows featuring record stars than they would other shows'" ("You're Out of Business" 1955: 1). Despite the survey's conclusion, the NBC executive Sam Fuller expressed the network's doubts about the disk jockey genre in July 1955, noting, "a nationwide disk jockey show, so far as I know, has never paid off." The trend toward DJ/teen dance programs was considerably more widespread in local markets, however, and by 1956 there were an estimated fifty televised disk jockey shows across the country with 60 percent of the shows broadcasting daily and 85 percent of the once-a-week programs airing on Saturday (Bundy 1956: 62).

While Fuller's perspective on a nationally broadcast DJ/teen dance show misgauged the broadcast and music environment, it is also important not to overstate the success of the genre's most renowned and long-lived national show, *American Bandstand* (and subsequent record-and-dance format programs including *Soul Train*, originally hosted by Don Cornelius). *American*

Bandstand's longevity in syndication and the enduring career of the one-time WFIL radio staffer Dick Clark is often misinterpreted as an indication of the vitality of the entire teen-oriented DJ genre. For one thing, despite its start as a DJ-oriented program relying on spinning records, *American Bandstand* thrived on the strength of appearances by top pop music artists (many of them boosted by Clark himself) that lip-synched to their hits; without the revolving door of celebrities the show's survival would have been less certain. The strict disciplinary regime (that included restrictions on appearance, dance style, and language) and what *Life* magazine termed "proper respectability" (Bunzel 1960: 88) associated with the program also ensured a wholesome and aesthetically consistent televised product. This reputation for outward propriety assisted Clark when he was called before a House Legislative Oversight Subcommittee (chaired by Oren Harris of Arkansas) in 1960 to discuss his role in the music broadcasting business and to illuminate the committee about industry pay-for-play practices.

The DJ/teen dance genre, though important from the combined historical perspectives on popular music and television was, in fact, never a clear-cut broadcasting powerhouse and it struggled for a permanent position in national television programming. *American Bandstand*'s endurance is, perhaps, most accurately attributed to Dick Clark's cheerful public persona and his idiosyncratic drive, shrewdness, slipperiness, and unquestionable business acumen as he built the "*AB*" brand and constructed a personal media empire.

4

The Look of Music

*

Music meant nothing to the majority of people
unless it combined a freak stunt.
INTERNATIONAL MUSICIAN, JANUARY 1946, 1

Music by itself isn't enough on tv. If a bandleader wants to succeed
in video, he must become a performer of one sort or another.
"STRIKE UP THE BANDS!" 1954: 16–17

In the context of early commercial television broadcasting, musical performances were unambiguously *for something*, whether that "something" was audience entertainment, sponsor satisfaction, commercial advertising and promotion, an outlet for artistic expression, cultural edification, or some all-encompassing mélange of objectives.[1] While they were capable of identifying the most obvious or egregious shortcomings of their telecasts in general terms, the networks lacked a strong analytical foundation upon which to evaluate performances or to propose solutions for improvement. Akin to genre definition, the processes of performance assessment among audiences and network producers were in an embryonic stage during television's early years.

John Hartley explains how, prior to television's postwar development, audiences were "trained in collective reception," socialized to enjoy their musical or spectacular pleasures in the public sphere and in the company of fellow citizens (1999: 75–77). While he is primarily addressing experimental public TV broadcasts in the late 1930s (in Berlin, London, and New York), he dwells on the notion of experience, noting that television at its inception was positioned alongside media technologies and cultural performances that were widely familiar; experience led to a general understanding of the forms and grammars of the cinema and stage. These performance contexts were part of people's everyday lives (at least in larger urban centers) to such an extent that they attained a ritual status. Karen Lury, too, isolates the experiential as a factor in her claim that it is the accumulation "of viewing experience that informs television viewing in significant ways, ways that are specific to television as an aesthetic and technological form" (1995–96: 115).

Producers and critics agreed that developing the capacity to appraise a televised musical performance involved a learning process. Emphasizing "knowledge built out of familiarity," Lury explains, "the expectations and assumptions generated by the kind of television experienced by the viewer inform their [sic] understanding and appreciation of performance, of the acting and appearing that occurs on the small screen; it frames both feeling and taste" (ibid.). Viewers had first to acquire TV viewing proficiency and interpretation skills, gaining comfort and fluency with television's unique rhythms and presentational grammars in order to knowledgeably critique televised musical performances with authority. This was not only required of the general public but also of early media critics, whose noteworthy commentary appeared in the entertainment industry trade magazines and in urban daily newspapers. They, too, were new to the medium and were, like the audience at large, steadily improving their methods of apprehension, interpretation, assessment, or articulation of televised musical performances.

Compounding the problem at television's outset was the fact that few people actually owned their own TV sets and were, thus, largely unable to watch television performances in their own homes. This understandably constrained the capacity to compare and appraise programming and musical performances across the gradually expanding broadcast spectrum. Even network production staff was at a disadvantage. In a memorandum dated

June 30, 1949, an NBC account executive, Robert Sarnoff — son of David Sarnoff, the network's founder and then-chief of the parent company RCA — sent a list to executive Carleton Smith citing "production personnel who do not now have NBC-owned television receivers in their homes and should have them." Listing eleven staff members who were without home units, Sarnoff notes, "All Producers have sets," but he indicates a critical flaw, pointing out that program directors still lacked home sets. Smith replied within the week, elucidating his support for Sarnoff's initiative and agreeing that the network should certainly supply the directors and producers with sets "as soon as possible," but, as he explained, he awaited the network's revised budget before he could rationalize the additional expense and execute the order (Smith 1949b).

In their efforts to determine the kinds of musical performances that would most fully engage and satisfy viewers, TV broadcast corporations experimented with ways to merge traditional presentational styles with TV's production techniques. The many television industry guidebooks, journals, and production manuals also cited the intrinsic value of musical performance with passages on presentations emphasizing physicality, gesture, "projection" and personality, and other visual traits. In still other circumstances the stress was placed on the technical aspects such as staging and camera work — how a musician's performance might be "lensed" (Appendix). Industry memoranda and media reports indicate that the intricacies of producing coherent and smoothly paced programs with a musical emphasis remained a major challenge well into the 1950s. Television producers were committed to providing performances that were simultaneously proficient and interesting yet uncertainties still prevailed about whether to privilege sound or the image, whether to focus on the music or on the visual performances of the artists before the cameras.

With such questions circulating among musicians and others in the culture industries, television's first sanctioned musical broadcasts following the AFM performance ban were closely scrutinized. The broadcasts were in the classical genre, with concerts presented on the CBS and NBC networks on March 20, 1948, within only days of the AFM's agreement permitting union members to appear on television. The CBS broadcast, featuring the Philadelphia Symphony Orchestra (with the conductor Eugene Ormandy), aired a mere hour and a half ahead of the NBC Symphony Orchestra broadcast (with the maestro Arturo Toscanini conducting). As George Rosen remarked in *Variety*, the effort by CBS to hit the airwaves first was likely a bid to claim bragging rights, but it may also have contributed to "the feeling that the CBS pickup from Philly was a hurried job" (1948: 30).

Cultural critics and press reporters in the emerging television news beat carefully monitored the programs' presentational style, analyzing their overall broadcast aesthetics.[2] Musicians and executives associated with the various sectors of the entertainment industry also chimed in about whether TV's visual character enhanced or diminished the *musical* performances of these titans of American classical conducting. For them, the issues revolved around the broadcasts' fidelity to the actual performance context and the capacity of this upstart medium to serve the musical arts well.

The NBC performance was praised for its dynamic visual presentation featuring tightly choreographed camera cuts with full shots and close-ups of various orchestra sections (and a more distant shot of the stage encompassing the entire orchestra) and frame dissolves that delimited the abruptness that is often associated with sharp camera edits. Throughout the broadcast Toscanini was in sharp focus at the center of the proceedings, shot from both his front and back in a manner illustrating his unwavering intensity on the conductor's stand. The press reviews (and subsequent internal memoranda circulating among NBC executives) were unanimous in the view that maestro Toscanini's performance far surpassed that of Ormandy on CBS.

Toscanini was widely considered one of the more animated orchestra conductors of his era (he was known as an exacting conductor and a man of stormy moods and volatile temperament) and as such he was perceived as a natural fit for television. His program of Wagner compositions was also critically applauded in contrast to Ormandy's selection of Rachmaninoff's First Symphony;[3] Wagner, it was felt, offered a more exciting orchestral experience that was better suited to television. Yet Ormandy's concert was not necessarily less well received than Toscanini's because of his performative shortcomings or a failure on the part of the orchestra but because CBS's camera work failed to achieve the poetic grace of the NBC broadcast. The prevailing critical assessments maintained that the visuals on CBS were "fuzzy" and inadequately coordinated with the orchestra and conductor. Even more damning, however, was the pronouncement that the CBS production was simply "dull," monotonous, and prone to repetition (Rosen 1948).

Critics focused on NBC's technical production and its clever — even artistic — wielding of cameras and employment of innovative editing effects such as superimposed montage sequences. George Rosen's review is worth citing at length:

> The expert camera treatment contributed most toward giving the program historic overtones.... NBC's camera crew achieved the difficult feat of creating a rhythm, always fascinating to watch, in the three-camera play on the orchestra and its celebrated leader. The camera fades were beautifully timed to permit for an almost perfect synchronization with the predominant orchestra sections, suggesting always that the camera crews were working under expert musical guidance. The very movement of the camera seemed to accept the tempo of the orchestra leader to permit for perfect coordination of sight and sound. (ibid.: 30)

In other reviews the "synchronization" between musicians and the cameras was also identified as the most compelling element of the NBC production (Keith 1948; "Toscanini Televised," 1948: 21), suggesting that there was prior technical rehearsal with the orchestra and that those responsible for the broadcast were highly familiar with the musical score.[4] It is also noteworthy that the NBC broadcast was produced in New York's Radio City studio 8-H, a controlled and rationalized environment, whereas the Ormandy performance on CBS was a remote broadcast from the less circumscribed space of the Philadelphia Academy of Music.

Between 1948 and the mid-1950s, several norms for presenting musical performances emerged, including standard camera angles and shot duration (often adopted from earlier film musicals and Soundies). For instance, big bands — with their rows of reeds, brass, and rhythm section — were conventionally shot along a horizontal axis as they played their arranged parts, with medium shots designated for each band section and close-ups for soloists. Other standardized shots included close-ups of harpists (almost always female) depicted through the instrument's strings while they gracefully plucked and pulled, especially at the introduction of a song,[5] close-ups of guitarists fingering their fret boards as they chorded or soloed, or extreme close-ups of the bell of a trumpet as the musician sounded the first notes of a song, with the camera slowly pulling back until the trumpeter was in a mid-shot[6] and, finally, the entire band filled the screen.

Performances by piano players were regularly captured from three distinct angles, fluctuating between a mid-shot or medium long shot from the side (depicting the pianist seated at the keyboard), a mid-shot or medium close-up (framing the pianist head along the full length of the grand piano) and an extreme close-up of the artist's hands on the keys; this latter shot was frequently aided by the reflective surface abutting the keyboard, providing greater visual information. An occasional elaboration featured a bird's-eye view of the pianist's hands although this involved a slightly more complicated camera maneuver.[7]

Shortly after the NBC and CBS symphony broadcasts, the *New York Times* music editor Howard Taubman posed a series of probing questions: "Does seeing musicians scrape and blow and pound and pluck the instruments of their craft help the listener to hear the music any better. Does a close-up of a conductor's gyrations and facial expressions make music more expressive? In short, should conductors be seen?" (1948: 17). His inquiry seems directed at the critical reception and commentary of these initial performance broadcasts that held an almost equal fascination with the musical performances and the production process, reflecting the overall excitement with television itself. While musicians pondered such queries, those in the television industry were even more convinced that establishing a visual performance profile and learning to work within new technical parameters were each crucial if musicians were to succeed in the medium.

Performance Adjustment

Richard Dienst writes, "Television . . . does not simply 'transport' previous forms (theatre, film, radio) but rather translates and recombines them" (1994: 142). Following Dienst, it stands to reason that performance styles and the actual artistic labor involved in making television would necessarily adjust as well. Yet as musicians and other artists quickly realized, it was not always an easy adjustment from radio, film, or the Broadway and nightclub stage to television and the examples of dreadful performances were many. Amateurs, novice entertainers, and veterans alike were often stymied by television's visual demands, and extant footage of early TV broadcasts reveals countless musicians staring wide-eyed at the camera, looking pleadingly offstage for support or guidance, or simply registering their discomfort before the cameras. In such instances, television evidently held the capacity to intimidate and to upend the performance.

Rather than simply stepping into television from other performance realms, actors, comedians, and musicians, were obligated to recast their artistry in specific relation to television's new performance conditions. One wartime journal, *Televiser*, offered informed commentary about the state of television's development across the TV broadcast sector, discussing performance demands along with various technical and aesthetic issues. Between 1944 and 1945, the journal published a series of brief articles under such titles as "Music for Television," "A Radio-Concert Singer Writes of Television," and "Background Music for Television." In the journal's fall 1944 issue, Midge Kline, a studio pianist for the emergent Du Mont TV network[8] focused on several performance themes, describing the shift away from a concentration on audio and music:

> Television has focused the camera on the musician. . . . Not only must the performer be physically attractive, but she should have a friendly, warm personality. . . . However, no matter how glorious the voice, the performer must be telegenic. Many famous radio artists lack television appeal; their appearance disillusions the audience. There is one other qualification for the television singer. She must be a competent actress and "act out" each vocal selection. Costumes and props are utilized with effective results. (1944: 14)

As Kline so clearly points out, the emphasis on musicians' "telegeneity" had not abated since the early 1930s, and in the minds of many musicians their performances seemed destined to a subordinate status.

In a 1945 book introducing television to an unfamiliar public, William Eddy explains how the physical gestures valued on Broadway performance stages were detrimental to TV performances: "This ability to emphasize, or better still, overemphasize . . . becomes a noticeable artificiality before the intimate lens of a television camera. The dramatic student and stage actor would do well to practice restraint in gesture if they wish to prove themselves telegenic" (1945: 274). In their TV acting manual published a full decade later, Martin Begley and Douglas MacCrae reinforce Eddy's early claim that "television does not permit the broad interpretations used on the stage. Television is more intimate" (1955: 20). These authors could easily be referring to countless musical program hosts such as Perry Como of the *Chesterfield Supper Club* and *The Perry Como Show*, whose moniker, "Mr. Casual," perfectly describe his reserved performance demeanor.

The resultant pressure to alter the aesthetics of musical performances remained apparent as television expanded and TV production was refined and standardized. In 1949 Ruth Lee Harrington offered her instruction to vocalists who sought television careers, suggesting performance modifications that eradicated undesirable traits learned in radio. Harrington explains, "Vocalists who hope to make a hit in television will have to acquire a smooth, acceptable stage presence. The mike-clutching technique of radio is out. . . . Facial mannerisms and other unconscious habits, such as weaving and swaying in time to the music, must be eliminated, since they detract from your performance" (1949: 95).

Harrington's comparative analysis is interesting for the way it draws attention to distinctions between radio and TV performances. It was said at the time that radio had eroded skills associated with stagecraft among musicians, a claim that subtly impugned the character of radio performers within a general hierarchy of musical and performance ability. Even though many radio programs were broadcast from theater stages or ballrooms with audiences in attendance, the performances were unseen by the vast majority of listeners. Musicians comprising radio's studio bands were *entirely* unseen by audiences, and it was thought that they, more than the rest, had developed an overly informal approach to performance.

Critics picked up on the visual shortcomings among artists broaching television at its inception, identifying several key problems. Television, it seemed, was highly attuned to the smallest performance details, the camera isolating and then amplifying the simplest offhanded gestures or tics. Even during the first AFM-sanctioned telecast, Eugene Ormandy "was seen to make a surreptitious gesture toward his mouth with his left hand" ("Rival CBS Program" 1948: 46). As playful observers mulled his action, Ormandy expressed his embarrassment: "Mr. Ormandy always sneaks cough drops during a concert . . . but his back usually hides the transaction from the audience. Ormandy had the final word: 'I will never, never do it again'" (ibid.).

In 1948, *Variety* commented on a TV announcer who displayed a habit of "scratching various parts of his anatomy on a recent telecast — something he may have gotten into on radio" ("Nitery Talent and Vaudeo" 1948: 27); the "epidemic" was reconfirmed in 1950 with *Variety* dubbing it "video dermatitis" (Mannheim 1950: 41). This unseemly practice is widely recorded in footage of early televised musical performances with musicians (usually involving orchestra members and members of vocal choruses) who evidently forgot that they were within camera range or who had become accustomed to working beyond public scrutiny in radio or recording studios. Even the image of Louis Armstrong quickly wiping his mouth with his ubiquitous white cloth or unselfconsciously shaking condensation from his horn after a solo was visually accentuated.

The unappealing results of camera close-up shots also emerged as an item of critical ire. One writer took issue with the undesirable aesthetic of close-up camera work, noting, "I have seen the tonsils of several of our most famous singers. And I don't want to mention any names — but if I were (name withheld) I'd certainly have my tonsils taken out" (Mannheim 1950: 41). Andre Kostelanetz implicated television's employment of close-up shots as a negative factor in the broadcast of musical performances, complaining about "too much preoccupation with showing the technicalities of a musical performance. . . . [T]hrough a closeup, now an attractive singer becomes unattractive while singing a high note" (1952).

Traditionally the musical performance begins once an artist is on the bandstand; with television, it begins once the artist steps in front of the camera. With this in mind, the TV host Freddy Martin cautioned his band members to demonstrate care in their onstage interactions when the camera was on them. He requested that they cease idle fidgeting with their instruments or whispering among themselves during televised performances, actions that Martin determined were distracting to viewers (1951: 48). Television consequently warranted new performance sensitivities and a greater self-awareness since the images were being broadcast widely, in real time, with full visual disclosure of every gesture and physical indiscretion.

Another complication emerged as artists struggled to identify their primary audience, uncertain about whether their performances should be pitched toward the assembled theater or studio audience or to the much larger audience of unseen TV viewers. Eddie Cantor was critical of those who played to the house rather than to the camera, explaining that TV performances required a new focus:

> The presence of large, enthusiastic beyond-the-footlights crowds too frequently causes talent to lose sight of the fact that teevee is basically a home entertainment. . . . [S]ome of the current video headliners will eventually be knocked out of the picture because of their favoring the down-fronters at the expense of the home audience. Why should you jeopardize the show for 20,000,000 viewers for the benefit of 1,000 or so in the studio, as too many are doing today? ("Cantor Sees Changes Coming" 1950: 2)

Footage abounds of performers speaking directly to an assembled theater audience or making wry asides to a production crew working just off-camera. While facilitating a certain ad-lib spontaneity steeped in vaudeville traditions, the tendency to play to the house as much or more than to the camera was gradually eradicated from TV broadcasts since it was thought to break an essential contract with TV viewers, who, it was felt, were unduly distanced from the immediate performance context (despite TV's claims for intimacy and proximity).

As Cantor implies, at issue is the question of projection, meaning the capacity of the artist to communicate through the musical performance, connecting with, and somehow affecting the viewer across a spatial divide. He was keenly aware that the camera functions as a mediating technology that should not be ignored or taken for granted. Promising a presentational style that would come across to viewers most effectively, Cantor claimed that his performance was directed toward "one guy—the camera man" (ibid.).

When musicians pitched their performance to the assembled audience they could see and register their impact. Of course, they had no idea how the performance came across to TV viewers, so they were forced to place their trust in the directors and technicians working around them. Building on the lessons from the March 1948 Toscanini and Ormandy orchestra broadcasts, producers attempted to enhance the televised performances by various means, including the employment of rudimentary visual effects (involving the aforementioned fades, image superimposition, split screens, and other imaginative—if basic—editing techniques), camera manipulation, and adjustments to studio and stage lighting. With these methods producers established the formal means of capturing and diffusing musical performances that were uniquely oriented toward the television audience, introducing a distinct television experience.

Singers were carefully tutored in how and where to stand during their performances, and the stage directions invariably had them either fixed in one spot while they sang (referred to as the "park and bark" approach) or strolling nonchalantly among props, pausing deliberately to maximize the effects of lighting and camera framing. Errors and spatial miscues were numerous, with countless examples of performers pausing behind the fronds of a fern, wandering out of microphone range, or stepping into the shadows beyond the spotlight. The emergent production methods also demanded additional rehearsal, yet many musicians claimed that, due to their union's additional salary requirements and other aspects of TV production costs, rehearsal time was kept to a minimum; in interviews, musicians almost always complained that they needed more time to nail the performance. With time and practice, however, producers resolved some of these staging problems that were endemic to early TV broadcasts.

In an article on the popular program *Cavalcade of Bands*, *Down Beat* provided insightful tips from the show's associate producer, Henri Gine, indicating the state of TV production and musical performance in this period.[9] Offering his views on performance preparation, Gine cautioned musicians on such subtle details as their wardrobe selection, noting, "If you're a musician making your first video appearance, *don't* polish your horn; *don't* wear a tie clasp; *don't* wear a gold watchband if you're doing a solo, and *do* wear a solid color tie" (Niccoli 1951b: 4). The admonition is relevant; as early TV broadcasts reveal, when the cameras caught the glare of buffed metal objects the image often flared, obscuring the shot of a soloist or horn section.

The *Down Beat* article is also interesting for the detail with which it delineates the criteria for the successful broadcast of big band performances, including such factors as song selection and arrangements. This included discouraging ballads unless they were "rhythm ballads" and suggesting songs with "jump and verve" or novelty pieces with a pronounced visual component. Affirming the logic of several orchestra leaders, Gine offers his meticulous suggestions for executing an effective performance before the studio camera: "Musicians must keep their eyes on the leader at all times, and when a soloist goes up to do his stint, he must have memorized it, because if he looks at the music he appears to the viewers to be asleep. . . . And finally, the boys of the aggregation must never, *never* look bored or lackadaisical" (ibid.).

Frank DeVol also recognized that television required special attention, and he accordingly revised his entire repertoire, creating a secondary book of arrangements for his band's TV performances ("DeVol Finds Dramatics" 1952: 6). He displayed a studied attention to the state of television production at the time noting, for instance, that the standard distance of the microphone from the singer in a television context necessitates different performance considerations and alternate musical arrangements so as not to overpower the vocals. DeVol also described how, by deviating from the orchestra's characteristic unison playing and instead emphasizing soloists, his TV arrangements were easier for cameramen to follow, presenting more interesting or engaging visuals for television viewers. If, by 1954, Tommy Dorsey could realistically claim that "a name band must have four different books — one for hotel engagements, one for theaters, one for one-night stands, and one for the South" ("Strike Up the Bands!" 1954: 16), then it was surely also true, as Frank DeVol demonstrated, that television warranted an additional set of arrangements.

Performance and Production: Musicking and Televising

Addressing the varied activities surrounding any musical performance, Christopher Small introduces the term "musicking":

> To music is to take part, in any capacity, in a musical performance, whether by performing, by listening, by rehearsing or practicing, by providing material for performance (what is called composition), or by dancing. We might at times even extend its meaning to what the person is doing who takes the tickets at the door or the hefty men who shift the piano and drums or the roadies who set up the instruments and carry out the sound checks or the cleaners who clean up after everyone else has gone. (1998: 9)

In Small's conception, "musicking" is a verb encompassing a set of overlapping and mutually reliant activities. Music is relational, linking a series of practices and, hence, the individuals involved in these practices. The concept of musicking is most provocative for the way it extends the traditional associations between performance and other music-making practices such as composition, rehearsal, presentation, and listening, encompassing an array of interconnected factors and forces.

Although Small doesn't dwell much on technological innovation, it is appropriate to identify the rise of new technological possibilities and innovations that influence musical performance, for in their emergence new dimensions of musicking also come into play. Widening the scope in the context of early television broadcasting, the various detailed elements of video production, staging, programming, promotions, and the narrativization among program hosts or promotional spokesmen might all be reasonably situated within Small's definition of "musicking." These elements not only give shape and life to a televised musical performance; they also suffuse each performance with an assortment of social meanings forged within discourse and conjunctional relationships.

Small explains that the individuals who conduct ancillary duties of every type "are all contributing to the nature of the event that is the musical performance" (ibid.: 9). Affirming this holistic approach in specific relation to television broadcasting and performance, Gilbert Seldes noted in 1950, "The style of television acting (it could be called the level of self-presentation) is determined by a unique capacity of the entire system, from camera through the control room to the receiver in the home: the capacity to transmit and deliver a completely rounded human character. This is the source of its special power, this is what it must exploit to become totally successful" (185). In his observation, Seldes displaces the centrality of the performance itself, focusing instead on the linked practices of broadcasting and television studio production and reception contexts that converge to enable the diffusion of the musician's performance.

In spite of its analytical value, Small's concept imposes an arbitrary primacy on the musical event. His approach devalues other driving forces that merge within the endeavor of "musicking" and that may, under specific conditions, actually surpass the musical event. While musicians quoted in early music and entertainment magazines refer to the vital significance of their performances (including rehearsal, touring, recording, and other factors in the life of a professional musician), among television executives, directors, and others on the television side of the industry (encompassing set designers, stage managers, lighting technicians, and cameramen) the dominant purpose of *their* enterprise was the production of top-quality television programs and, ultimately, the generation of sponsor-driven network profits. For them, it was not actually *musicking* that constituted the primary task or paramount objective, but *televising*.

Whereas the musician or singer is intent on delivering a successful or affective performance (based on a prior professionally determined sense of what constitutes a good — or bad — performance), TV directors are working with a separate purpose; their efforts are concerned with uniting a succession of distinct performances, creating what they conceive of as a cohesive and satisfying whole. The musical instance constitutes but one component of a larger and arguably more complex process. The distinction between musicking and televising creates a rather significant schism between *artistes* across the performing arts, the program producers (whose work focuses on having shows come off without a hitch), and the network executives (who adhere more explicitly to business aspects of financial exigency and economic pragmatism).

The practices of televising immediately presented a disruption in the entertainment sector by altering the dynamics of musical performance in relation to prevailing modes of production and diffusion, transforming the general cultural landscape within which musical performance occurred. According to Phil Auslander, "In addition to dominating the economics of performance, the televisual shapes the conditions under which performance is now perceived" (2000: 6). Not only did musicians carefully modify their performance aesthetics and stagecraft skills toward television's production modes but those who were most popular in the medium were very quickly identified as *television* performers. Whereas in television's very earliest stages professional musicians were introduced with announcements about their live venue engagements or current hit recordings, in short order it was the live performance venues and record labels that integrated statements touting artists' broadcast appearances, including banners reading "as seen on television."

The disparities between musicking and televising in TV's nascent period were also exhibited in bicoastal broadcasting traits. Although the New York network shows frequently emphasized highly staged, visually elaborate musical productions broadcast from either large retrofitted theaters or smaller studios equipped with an assortment of sets and props (exemplifying the processes of televising), the remote ballroom broadcasts on the Los Angeles station KTLA offered an alternative method for music broadcasting that was more in line with the precepts of musicking. The KTLA ballroom broadcasts, spearheaded by the general manager, Klaus Landsberg, skillfully captured the spontaneity of the musical performances and observers were most impressed with the station's manner of displaying the artists in a highly naturalized format — "as they are" — without significant alterations to their standard presentational style.

In New York, NBC and Du Mont were especially successful in their deployment of remote broadcasting units and, while they also aired shows from some of the city's prestigious public venues, their remote work (focusing on sports, news, or public events, and occasional "vox populi" or "man-on-the-street" encounters) did not include musical performances to nearly the same extent as KTLA. Reflecting on the different methods of broadcasting popular music, Landsberg was convinced that his station's broadcasts were more true to the performances, communicating an authenticity that he believed was missing in programs originating on the East Coast. Landsberg explained in the station's early days that he perceived East Coast productions as being invasive, accusing the major networks of overproducing their programs and displaying a tendency "of interpreting the music for the audience. . . . [T]he true enjoyment of music can easily be distorted by production numbers" (1951: 8).

Tony Mottola in an advertisement for Gibson Guitars, *Metronome*, January 1949.

In Landsberg's view, KTLA's ballroom broadcasts simply transmitted the musical performances to the southern California viewers in a raw and arguably more honest form that lent them a unique and compelling vérité. Recalling his start at KTLA in 1951, Lawrence Welk admitted his preference for the organic character of the station's production process compared to the elaborately staged studio productions that had come to dominate the airwaves: "It was an unusual television show because we had no rehearsals. They just moved in with several cameras and shot as we went through our paces at a regular dance" (KTLA 1967). Notwithstanding his insinuation that his performance was not altered or affected by the cameras, it is evident in successive program episodes that his TV skills improved and that he integrated the logic of televising with his musical responsibilities; over the years his on-screen banter flowed more naturally, his interaction with the cameras was smoother, and he projected a much more confident presence at the helm. Welk, it would seem, grasped the fundamental aspects of both musicking and televising, merging them on his show.

Even with Landsberg's well-known obsession with television's technical end, KTLA's ballroom broadcasts ultimately provided a more balanced combination of musicking and televising. Landsberg's critical estimation of the East Coast networks is valid; the musical performances associated with many early New York TV shows were, in fact, often prone to excess. Blunt and literal in their presentation with sophisticated set designs and costuming forged in the Broadway stage tradition (and recognizable from the aesthetics of Soundies or Snader and Official film music clips), the network productions often overworked the basic thematic elements of a song's lyrics in the attempt to overdetermine the performances' connotations. *Your Hit Parade* carried the production practices involving complex staging to extremes, especially when a song recurred on the "hit parade" over successive broadcasts, necessitating different visual skits with each weekly reprise (and causing some hilarity among the cast, whose unscripted giggles at times overtly registered the silliness of their overstated performances). The visual exaggeration of these productions, while not without entertainment value, frequently overwhelmed the musical performances.

Even after the early successes with remote broadcasting, the bandleader Claude Thornhill remained skeptical that television could ever give music its due. As he explained in 1950, "This television thing has me puzzled, and, frankly, I'm not enthusiastic about the idea of these TV broadcasts of bands from ballrooms, such as we encountered — walked into, you might say, when

The Fred Waring Show. CBS, April 18, 1950. COURTESY OF PHOTOFEST.

we came into the Palladium" (Emge 1950c: 4). Contributing to Thornhill's consternation was the realization that, as the host of the show, he was called upon to perform double duty from the bandstand, both leading the orchestra and acting as the television host for the home viewing audience, functioning at the junction between musicking and televising. As a piano player, Thornhill's mobility was sharply restricted, and he contributed less to the visual component of the televised performance than did other bandleaders such as Ina Ray Hutton, Fred Waring, Lawrence Welk, or Paul Whiteman, who hovered at the front of the band and in front of the camera; they were better able to serve as MCs for their programs. Thornhill also admitted to being plagued by the interventions of television producers who attempted to introduce comedy skits that they hoped might augment his orchestra's performance, a concern that further intervened in the process of musicking.

The focus on televising regularly produced tensions among TV producers and the music celebrities they contracted for broadcast appearances. In an example of the conflict between musicking and televising, the bandleader Fred Waring wrestled with CBS executives for direct input in the production and performances on his program throughout the late 1940s and early 1950s, seeking to assert greater autonomy and control over the show's musical performances. Waring was well known in the music industry for his close attention to both business and performance details and for having an intensely hands-on — even strict — approach to all aspects of his orchestra and extended "Glee Club" vocal ensemble, running the operation as a corporation and as a musical unit.

Irrespective of his extensive experience in the music industry, Waring was confounded by television's particular organizational structures and production methods as he admitted in a 1952 CBS press release: "On entering television with a full hour show, none of us realized the problem with which we were to become involved. Not only were we required to prepare 60-minutes of entertainment each week . . . we were burdened with major crises involving sets, choreography, costuming, and other time consuming projects with which we were quite unfamiliar" ("Fred Waring to Present" 1952). Waring's widow Virginia recalls additional difficulties encountered by the venerable bandleader: "Fred's thirty-year battle with stagehands, radio engineers, advertising agencies, and sponsors to uphold his artistic standards was multiplied twofold in the new medium. Television programs are produced by a team of people. . . . Fred's passion for changing things for the better and his need for flexibility in programming would be seriously hampered by these 'production by committee' methods" (V. Waring 1997: 232).

In developing his program, it was Waring's expressed opinion that television should conform to the demands and character of musical performance — not the other way around — suggesting a logic that is consistent with the primacy of musicking. It was the practice of televising, however, that created the major barriers to Waring's musical project. Even though he had been centrally involved in NBC's historic TV broadcasts from the 1939 New York World's Fair (making him far more experienced with the unique practices of televising than most of his musical peers), he had developed a somewhat cynical attitude toward television. Responding to the tensions he confronted, Waring proclaimed, "Television is villainous. An hour on television is tougher than thirty 15-minute radio shows" ("Fred Waring to Present" 1952) adding the lament, "The entertainer is at the mercy of the technician" (V. Waring 1997: 232).[10]

Criticizing the corporate structure and management practices of the networks, Waring cited his veteran status in the music business and the value of his experience and know-how in comparison to the relative upstarts at network television (and, surely, the advertising agencies): "The youngsters who are brought in fresh out of college with *no* experience and are trusted with responsibilities where they have authority over veterans of show business is a terrible thing. It belittles the artist" (ibid.: 232). To his credit, Waring was not beyond admitting that, in the specific contexts of television production (or televising) he had much to learn and he proved to be as critical of his own programs as anyone. He eventually convinced CBS brass to share production responsibilities and, embarking on what he and the network agreed was a process of experimentation, Waring and the production staff, including the director, camera men, lighting crew, and sound crews — and his own, hand-picked codirector, Bob Banner — established a collaborative relationship, constructing a signature program that reflected the performance and entertainment standards for which the band was known.

The positive effects of the *work* on the Waring show were evident, as *Variety* acknowledged during the program's second season: "This show remains as one of the pace-setters of the video air-lanes. . . . [It is] still hallmarked by that inventiveness in staging and attentiveness to the smallest details which has made this 60-minute presentation a standard for superlative production" ("Fred Waring Show" 1950: 31). This joint effort positioned the longtime bandleader precisely at the nexus where musicking and televising unite, although in 1954 Waring acknowledged his "self-imposed misfortune" of serving as musical director and program director, a dual role of which he proclaimed, "To any orchestra leader who asks the advisability of this double trouble, I'd suggest he avoid it" (70).

After nearly a decade of trying to establish equilibrium between the logics of musicking and televising, network programs still often lacked perfect balance in the views of many critics. *Time* magazine's commentary on the state of televised music near the end of 1955 reflected that the ongoing problems resulting from incompatibilities between musicians and television producers, between musicking and televising, had yet to be satisfactorily resolved:

TV seems to be demonstrating that music should be heard and not seen. In emphasizing video at the expense of audio on musical shows, TV men often sacrifice good sound, and sometimes good music, without managing to get good TV. The televiewer who closes his eyes and listens can hear how crude, sloppy and badly balanced most TV is. Opening his eyes he can see how overbaked and tasteless the images that go with music can be. Last week's musical shows ranged from a brand-new opera to the singing of vintage popular songs. Most were calculated to make a music lover run to his radio or record player. ("Radio and Television" 1955: 91).

Tradition, Nostalgia, and Familiarity

At the outset, network TV producers sought to manifest their own unique performance codes that were, if not explicitly original, at least distinct enough to be noticeable. For television to truly stand as a significant entrant in the entertainment industries it was necessary to define its discreet qualities, differentiating the medium from other previous entertainment options. Although television's early musical performances fluctuated between moments of modern creative expression and a pronounced reliance on longstanding presentational norms the networks progressively "reimagined many traditional forms of popular culture," adapting them "to their particular needs and strengths" (Murray 2005: 42).

The lingering influences of established performance modes resulted in musical performances that explicitly foregrounded tradition (in both the selected music and the performance aesthetics), especially on early musical variety shows. The trend was not isolated to television, as the *New York Times* reported in October 1947. Citing a "revolution in Tin Pan Alley" the *Times* explained, "popular music has come around full circle and is now, in effect, somewhere in the Twenties. . . . [R]ight now many of the songs that are soothing the public's ears and nerves are revivals, right off the stockroom shelves" (Schumach 1947: 20).

The notion of "the past" permeated many early televised musical performances, yet the temporal logic was constructed in idealized terms summoning the effects of nostalgia and audience recognition simultaneously. Complementing the appeal to a familiar and idealized past were the pervading discourses of "better days," "simpler times," and a celebration of the basic pleasures of carefree reminiscence (not to mention the possibility of better music) that were intended to diffuse comforting cultural values. None of this was particularly new in musical theater, having evolved as a common characteristic of the Broadway stage, yet the tendency acquired new meaning in the domain of television broadcasting, an emergent industry that was ostensibly modern, progressive, and forward-looking. For the more astute critics of the period, the conflicting presentational standards that mingled traditional performance forms with a more modernist aesthetic logic began to look like a rather overt paradox.

Denise Mann argues that televised musical variety programs structured around nostalgia and historical performance traditions selectively adopted traits from the past, excluding many pertinent cultural elements. As Mann explains, variety show performances in particular constituted "'simulations' of popular culture traditions from the past": "Many of these fragments of past performances emerged out of ethnic theater — leisure practices which took place in communities defined by ethnic, class and gender specificities; however, once these forms were transposed to television, they were stripped of any previous associations with the community. These nostalgic images from the past appeared on early television variety shows in an abstracted, fragmented form" (1992: 46–47). Mann's interpretation implies that it was obviously not *really* the past that flickered into view on the TV screen but a hybrid construct of "the past" with history providing a loose representational framework instead of a rigid structure. Because the past on television was discursively framed and mobilized through an array of representational approaches (with signifying objects including props and set design, costuming, and, of course, song selection) it was also prone to manipulation and methods of accentuation that ultimately articulated contemporaneous notions of "the past" as well tapping into a more thoroughly modern affect.

Not everything of the past was deemed appropriate for staged performance; the war years (encompassing both the first and second world wars) were rarely represented in an explicit or detailed manner on early musical variety shows in spite of their influence in relation to social life and cultural creativity. The networks dared not risk raising negative connotations associated with war that might stain the spirit of optimism and bonhomie radiating from the screen. Still, patriotic announcements were abundant and the appearance of enlisted men in uniform (especially on amateur/talent shows or occasional recruitment programs sponsored by the American military, including *Guide Right* on the Du Mont network between 1952 and 1954) was not uncommon, reflecting the U.S. military involvement in Korea between 1950 and 1953 as well as the ever-ready stance against the "red threat" of communism and the Soviet regime.

Focusing on television's role in the dissemination of modern aesthetics and accompanying middlebrow taste, Lynn Spigel explains, "Quite paradoxically, it was television's oldest and most populist form — vaudeville — that turned out to be the ideal showcase for modern art" (2008: 44). She lists several prominent TV musical and comedy variety shows, noting that they "provided a stage for the popular presentation of modern art movements, from abstract expressionism to Beat poetry to modern dance" (ibid.). Extant footage and the occasional production notes or executive memoranda bear this out, yet the modernist sensibilities to which she points stand out starkly against the palate of the past that was also in high circulation in the musical variety show genre. Indeed, representations of modernism and timeworn tradition were often juxtaposed, at times within the same variety shows. This duality indicates an interesting characteristic of the immediate postwar moment, and of television in particular, as society simultaneously looked backward and forward, attempting to interpret and communicate the *geist* of the cultural condition in and through the new broadcast medium. Musical performance was intrinsic to this process.

In introducing musical segments, the nostalgic discourse most favored by program hosts included statements like "Let's take a stroll down memory lane" or "Now, performing an old favorite from days gone by," and similar expressions that framed the performances in relation to a particular temporal moment.[11] This ubiquitous discursive strategy reinforces Karen Lury's emphasis on experience and familiarity, for as she makes clear, while accumulated experience from exposure to television programs is significant, "it is also, in part, a social and emotional experience, weathered and fitted into the individual psyche" (1995–96: 116–17). Television's early musical performances were, therefore, situated within a broader collective social experience and tapped into the vivid facets of recall and memory that help to shape modern meaning among individual viewers and the collective audience.

Such typical elements of recall and memory were summoned in the musical performances on the May 13, 1948, broadcast of *The Swift Show*. The program opens with the hosts Lanny Ross and Sandra Gahle recalling happy times while leafing through a photo album that, with the album's intrinsic status as a material record and an image archive of the past, evokes the accumulation of personal reminiscences. This prop device is well suited to the program's theme involving the portrayal of forty years of popular song in America, with the vocalists basing their performances of Tin Pan Alley tunes ("A Bird in a Gilded Cage," "My Wild Irish Rose") and popular songs ("Body and Soul") within the contexts of reminiscence, recall, and general familiarity. Each decade between the turn of the century and the 1940s is granted special attention in the show, providing an organizational logic to the program's narrative and contributing coherence that is associated with the evolving musical eras of the early twentieth century. Having reached the music of the 1940s, the program winds down with what host Ross terms "a prediction" about life in the 1950s (then only two years away). This leads to a performance by the guest vocalist Patti Page who inexplicably sings "You Turned the Tables on Me," a 1936 composition by Louis Alter and Sidney Mitchell and popularized by the Benny Goodman orchestra featuring the vocalist Helen Ward.

In August 1948, the ABC network introduced a program called *Gay Nineties Revue* that was unambiguously based on the theatrical forms of the late nineteenth- and early twentieth-century music hall, replete with the master of ceremonies Joe Howard, a seventy-nine-year-old vaudeville veteran, sporting a costume associated with the traditional vaudeville stage, including a top hat, tails, and a cane. Describing the show's premier broadcast, *Television World* commented that, while the program "is no great credit to New York city's newest station" WJZTV, Howard "is one of the marvels of show business. . . . He is one of the old timers to whom a song is more than words and notes" (Fox 1948: 12). Opening a broadcast in December 1948 with the tune "Whistle Your Troubles Away," Howard turns and addresses the camera and assembled theater audience directly, demonstrating a veteran's theatrical demeanor and invoking an aura of familiarity associated with the spirit of a musical past: "When you come here on Friday nights, you're going to see a lot of our song pluggers and actors from the different theaters — Hammerstein, Fourteenth Street, the London, the Bowery — and you'll see a lot of people that you've seen on the stage and you'll be glad to say hello to them." Tin Pan Alley songs and other musical genres affiliated with vaudeville and music hall shows abounded on *Gay Nineties Revue*, with the cast costumed in garb representative of the turn of the century. The musical renditions displayed a range of fading styles, including the close harmonies of a barbershop quartet that was reminiscent of black and white acappella groups that were exceedingly popular during the "gay nineties" but in decline by mid-century.

Such trends toward performed nostalgia and reminiscence did not suddenly disappear in the mid-1950s even with the rise of rock 'n' roll. For example, on one 1954 episode of *The Frankie Laine Show*, the cohost Connie Haines sings the 1938 Johnny Mercer and Harry Warren composition "Jeepers Creepers," a Tin Pan Alley classic that had previously been recorded by Louis Armstrong, the Paul Whiteman Orchestra, and the Mills Brothers, among others. Later in the program, introducing Frankie Laine before he sings the 1938 Herb Magidson and Allie Wrubel tune, "Music, Maestro, Please," Haines comments, "And now you folks who were out on the town during the gay thirties may remember this next song. The restaurant that boasted of a dance orchestra, the side street, the little club, and the depression-haunted ballroom all played this melancholy torch song, and now Frankie sings it for us." The contradictory references to "the gay thirties" and the "depression-haunted ballroom" notwithstanding, the discursive appeal attempts to anchor the performance in a historical context that is at once memorable and reassuring, imbuing the performance with an aura of consensually agreed-upon value. In this manner, the show's producers implicitly acknowledge a social contract of a unique nature, bonding audiences and performers. The troubles of the past were offset by positive elements, including good music and easy entertainment, factors that television also combined to ease the strains of modern living in postwar America.

Program executives determined early on that televised performances stood the greatest chance for success if they were organized in a manner that made the most sense to audiences by remaining consistent with the dominant aesthetics of the day. This may partially account for the prevalence of song "standards" encompassing tunes from the still-evolving "great American songbook," compositions by Tin Pan Alley songsmiths, Broadway musical selections, and popular music that was recorded and distributed to the general market. Song standards, known and loved by a generation of music audiences who came of age in the 1930s and early 1940s, had an instrumental utility for television broadcasters, providing a point of recognition within which early television viewers could comfortably cohere.

According to Keightley, "Melodic, easily whistled, nostalgic music that is used to accompany everyday activities is equally populist music. This 'music for everyone' can express a democratic impulse that must be acknowledged as valuable" (2008: 330). Standards were widely adopted in television, with the major distinction being TV's methods of recontextualizing recognized songs through variations in staging, costumes, and other performance details that inflected songs toward a distinct historical period or social environment.

Song "standards" were introduced in several ways. For example, in her premiere program broadcast on the Los Angeles station KTLA in 1951, Ina Ray Hutton introduces "Basin St. Blues," a song written by Spencer Williams in 1926 that was featured on countless early television shows. Hutton describes the song as "a popular tune, a standard really," identifying it on one hand as "music for everyone," while on the other hand distinguishing its esteemed status in contrast to the other less familiar or less revered numbers in the program's repertoire. Moreover, as Hutton's all-girl orchestra — bedecked in shimmering evening gowns — illustrates, television could easily dress up the well-known song standards in visual form, giving them renewed vigor through an array of performance presentations. Television's performance contexts constituted the "new" that was grafted onto the reliable and trusted musical elements of the "old."

Keightley offers the perspective that, by the late 1940s and early 1950s, the song standard had acquired symbolic meaning that merged specific compositions with adult, bourgeois cultural values: "The standard offers a point of articulation of age, taste, and social power. . . . [S]tandards clearly stand for the cultural esteem attributed to the taste of a culturally and economically dominant formation" (2001: 31; Keightley 2008). As this suggests, the audience most devoted to the song standard also comprised a desirable viewing segment for networks and their program sponsors, embodying "an adult listening formation distinguished by class as well as by age" (Keightley 2001: 8) and displaying an ostensibly more refined cultural taste. The familiar and well-known character of song standards that permeated early TV broadcasts carried an aura of quality and enduring value that, while easily adaptable to the ideals of television as a cultural medium, were also highly functional within the commercial exigencies of advertisers and corporate networks.

Squares and Cats

Familiarity was of utmost important to television's programming development since so much rested on the medium's capacity to display qualities that were pleasantly reassuring yet still fresh. Rick Altman reminds us that merging music and visual presentation in commercial contexts has long depended on a degree of familiarity: "From the very beginning of film music, efforts were made to balance the twin requirements of novelty and familiarity. Like turn-of-the-century bandleaders and orchestra conductors, film musicians made ample use of old favorites. . . . [T]hese songs worked so well because they were the repository of cultural memory that exhibitors knew they could bank on" (2007: 217). For audience members, the familiarity factor conveyed "an experience of recognition and return that fulfills an anchoring function" (ibid.: 222). Taking into account the television industry's pronounced economic imperative, Jane Feur explains how TV reproduced this established reliance on things familiar, suggesting, "from television's point of view, unlimited originality of programming would be a disaster, because it could not assure the delivery of the weekly audience" (1992: 144).

While television was new, its performances could not be too novel, too demanding, or otherwise offbeat at the risk of alienating viewers, especially in the medium's formative stages when winning new audiences was most critical. It was, to considerable extent, familiarity and professional experience that led to the hiring of reliable TV pitchmen (such as Dennis James, a ubiquitous show host across the early TV spectrum), prominent radio celebrities, and stage comedians. The networks were reluctant to program performances that might exceed conventional tastes or that were deemed to be somehow deficient in commercial appeal, limiting music and cultural expression, and denying performances of music associated with a modernist avant-garde aesthetic.

Though there was a distinct likelihood that something impressively *good* might cross the screen, occasionally something jarringly original emerged in a musical performance. As an exceptional example of an impressive *and* relatively unfamiliar performance, on February 24, 1952, the Du Mont program *Stage Entrance* (hosted by Earl Wilson) featured an unexpurgated and incendiary bebop performance of Tadd Dameron's composition "Hot House" performed by Dizzy Gillespie and Charlie Parker (who each accepted *Down Beat* music awards from Leonard Feather on the program), accompanied by Dick Hyman on piano, Sandy Block on bass, and the drummer Charlie Smith. Despite the fact that the program format and camera work did not break from the standard forms of 1950s presentation, the musical content and Gillespie and Parker's riveting performance were decidedly unconventional for television. This was a performance that broke sharply from the past, catapulting television music into the postwar present.

Lawrence Welk constitutes an interesting case; he was a musician with popular appeal but a limited track record in the market. He fell into television quite by accident, yet he was able to succeed in the new medium, building his status as a television pioneer into a symbol of integrity, reliability, and longevity. His TV performances on KTLA were, in effect, a model of midcentury conventionality. Welk's early programs open with a shot of the crowded Aragon ballroom and the logo *Lawrence Welk and His Champagne Music* (reflecting Welk's intent to brand the orchestra and distinguish his sound) briefly superimposed over the live image. The camera then shifts to Welk and the orchestra while bubbles (emanating from an onstage machine) slowly waft across the screen, again in a superimposition.

The first Welk broadcasts reproduced several of the formal characteristics that had proven successful with earlier KTLA ballroom sessions featuring Spade Cooley. The buzz of the audience is audible as the master of ceremonies introduces Welk, conveying a palpable sense of anticipation among those present in the ballroom. In another tilt toward the Cooley show and what was still a relatively uncommon practice for adult-oriented television at the time, many in the ballroom audience danced in front of the TV cameras while the orchestra performed in its decidedly low-key (and in comparison to his KTLA colleague Ina Ray Hutton, entirely asexual) style.

Lauded for his "caring" demeanor and the "friendly and welcoming" disposition of the band, Welk was an immediate hit on television with an estimated 1.5 million regional viewers tuning in by early 1953 ("Video, Visual Appeal" 1953: 40). Even with his newfound acclaim, many musicians and music or TV critics frequently dismissed Welk as a "square" for his conventional musical style and his ostensibly out-of-date traits; it was widely held among musicians that Welk represented music's past. Expressing a sarcastic attitude toward Welk's "sweet" song arrangements and subdued personality, *Down Beat* reluctantly acknowledged that the Aragon's weekly box office revenues were reaching record highs and throngs of viewers were tuning in: "Whether we like it or not, it could well be that Welk has touched off a TV trend" (English 1951b: 4). Welk explained his obligation to "give people music they understand . . . steady and simple," readily admitting, "even though the 'cats' may think we're corny, I'd even like to have simpler music, even less complicated arrangements" (Freeman 1953: 6).[12]

Welk's reference to "cats" is multiply inflected, revealing important details about his approach to music and performativity. In one sense Welk might be articulating the generational dissonance that prevailed in the period. His penchant for popular songs and standards from the 1930s and 1940s and the accompanying performance style positioned him within an older set of aesthetic values that were challenged by young talented artists who felt that their creativity was contained within the rigid, machine-like structure of the dance bands. Fundamentally, his utterance diminishes those whose music Welk thinks little of, disparaging tastes and performance styles associated with bebop and progressive jazz and the cultural and musical domain of black artists (few of whom ever performed in the Welk orchestras).

For Welk, bebop and improvised jazz were incompatible with the notion of professionalism and a controlled or disciplined performance regimen to which he firmly adhered and that were the foundation of his television success. Welk's opinion also converges with Scott DeVeaux's description of the "jam session as a symbol of alienation . . . not simply a form of escape but an act of defiance" (1997: 205). DeVeaux explains that the improvised performances of the jam session exist beyond the dominant values of popular taste, peripheral to market concerns and "carefully set aside from the monetary economy" (ibid.: 204). Such performances would logically be at odds with Welk's values as both a businessman and a musician. If Welk's music was commercially viable in the ballroom and on television, then the jam sessions and club dates populated by free-wheeling improvisers—"cats"—were deemed illegitimate, marginal, and inconsequential.

Welk clearly regarded the experimentation that was typical of jam sessions as a barely tolerable annoyance (if not an outright waste of time) even though the jam sessions were regarded as an important training ground, "an integral part of an aspiring musician's musical education (ibid.: 212), or a rite of passage among "serious" jazz musicians. For jazz purists and "serious" artists, the Welk band was beyond redemption. Lewis Erenberg echoes DeVeaux's perspective, noting that the music Welk implicitly associates with "cats" is characteristic of a "style of defiance" adopted by "bohemian intellectuals" (1998: 232), a cohort encompassing progressive black jazz musicians and the poets and bongo players comprising the early "beat generation." This angle of race and culture incorporates a geocultural sensibility that differentiates between performance styles at the Aragon Ballroom in Santa Monica, where Welk held court, and the small jazz clubs lining Central Avenue that formed the core of the Los Angeles jazz scene and the heart of the city's African American and white hipster communities.

Welk's disdain for "cats" might also register as a statement about his own origins in North Dakota, a state that is ideologically rooted in "the American heartland." Victoria Johnson addresses the ideological and hegemonic meanings of a heartland identity within which Welk was situated: "The squareness of the Midwest is idealized in different historical moments, as the site of 'authentic' culture . . . At root, this aspect of the Heartland myth plugs into the long-standing debate over cultural populism and cultural elitism wherein 'square' is associated with the 'common,' 'ordinary' person pitted against the 'elitist' snob" (2008: 17). Here, the "authenticity" instilled in the concept of the American heartland is at odds with the concept of "authenticity" associated with cats, the jam session, and the urban jazz scene.

Johnson draws out further distinctions whereby the nation (or the national culture) is "populated by squares in the middle steeled against hipster elites from either coast" (ibid.). Discursively minimized in the music industry trade journals *Down Beat* or *Metronome*, Welk is the embodiment of Midwestern/heartland values and the antihip aesthetics of an older artist, and he openly embraced this identity throughout his performance career. This was, for many TV viewers and fans, a substantial part of his performance allure. Regardless of the curt invectives lobbed at Welk, television producers believed that he projected just the right elements for television, tapping into the populist mainstream desires of "middle America." The smooth and evenly paced performances characterizing Welk's remote TV broadcasts and his later shows from the TV studio served as an industry model and were frequently reproduced in subsequent orchestra-based programs in the early 1950s, including that of Welk's one-time mentor, Guy Lombardo.

Location, Persona, and Performance

An awareness of musical artists, their performance styles, and their song repertoires was of consummate importance in negotiations between the networks, early corporate sponsors, and Madison Avenue advertising agencies. In much the same way that the familiar and accepted qualities of song standards represented a desirable option for musical programming, the celebrity artist's performance style and identity also conveyed known values and qualities. Hiring established artists seemed an obvious choice for broadcast networks for, as Phil Auslander asserts, "Part of the audience's pleasure in pop music comes from experiencing and consuming the personae of favorite artists in all their many forms and this experience is inseparable from the experience of the music itself and of the artists as musicians" (2004: 9). Entertainment veterans and musical celebrities embodied known qualities of performance style and persona and they carried added representational weight in the cultural realm, existing within a complex economy of value and meaning.

For instance, Dinah Shore, the pianist Liberace, or the guitar and vocal act Les Paul and Mary Ford were each well known for their reserved and intimate performance style, which television executives and program sponsors regarded as being highly accessible to viewers. Yet their broadcast performances were also constructed in a particular way, benefiting from the symbolic values associated with the home and not those of such alternative public sites as the nightclub, cabaret, or theater. *The Liberace Show* premiered on February 3, 1952, on the Los Angeles station KLAC with broadcasts from the Music Hall in Beverly Hills.[13] A local success, the program was picked up as a summer replacement for the Shore show on NBC, where it was produced for syndication.

The pianist's renowned familial loyalty included hiring his brother George as musical director, and the series transferred its discursive focus to the home and the joys of family (with frequent references to his mother and his younger brother between songs), making it an appropriate replacement for Shore. *The Liberace Show* was, significantly, set in what appeared to be a well-appointed home piano salon; in some episodes the window curtains behind Liberace were "open," revealing a bucolic backdrop hinting at suburban space and middle-class comforts (as on the show's special Thanksgiving episode airing November 19, 1954, which featured a performance of "Turkey in the Straw").

Darden Pyron explains that the domestic theme was intrinsic to Liberace's TV persona and to his audience appeal:

> If his ideal was playing to a happy family circle gathered around the family piano, his intimacy with the camera and with the television audience underlined his familial-like affection for the viewer. . . . He reified the theme with a close, domestic setting and, still more important, he included real family. Thus, if he ritualized his performance, he also ritualized family and domesticity into his program. . . . Liberace persuaded viewers that he was a member of their domestic circle. He also constructed a mythical television family around the real-life Liberaces. (2000: 146–47)

Liberace very quickly grasped that the link between the domestic and television realms was forged within a sense of intimacy that could be extended through his performances. He constructed his television identity accordingly, casting his repertoire and performances in a method that transferred

Les Paul and Mary Ford. Circa 1954–55. COURTESY OF PHOTOFEST.

easily from the ersatz domestic locus of his show to the audience's home spaces; in an explicit example of his conscious attention to the notions of "home," Liberace performs a rollicking boogie-woogie version of the 1951 Rosemary Clooney hit "Come On-a My House" on the aforementioned Thanksgiving broadcast of 1954. Even though he is today often associated with glitzy costumes, an undeniably queer performance aesthetic, and the theater spaces of Las Vegas, his earlier flamboyance emerged primarily through his piano playing. His 1950s TV image was much more reserved, reflecting the mannerisms of a plain, dutiful — and closeted — mother's son.

In the case of the *Les Paul and Mary Ford Show* (airing in 1954–55), the domestic sphere was presented as a defining cultural space that informed the artists' creative and relational identities despite their professional activities during their commercial heyday. Their status as a married couple was foregrounded on their TV program; stages and theaters that comprised a rather significant factor in their lives were downgraded or even eradicated as a facet of the musical couple's profile. The program characteristically opened with Paul and Ford welcoming TV viewers into their living room, back patio, or kitchen, where they perform their hit songs while Ford conducts mundane domestic chores such as arranging flowers, toying with the toaster, feeding their pet bird, or making sandwiches for lunch. In some televised performances, Paul's renown as a technical wizard and an inveterate electronics tinkerer was also emphasized, focusing attention on the masculine domain of the home workshop. It was here that Paul developed the unique multilayered sound characterizing the couple's music, often represented on the show as a single electronic curiosity known as "the Les Paulverizer."[14] Steve Waksman explains that the couple's actual New Jersey home, built in 1953 was, in fact, designed to accommodate Paul's obsessive technical interests and his desire to extend the recording studio or workshop into almost every room in the home (1999: 64). In Waksman's assessment of the show's domestic orientation, "Les and Mary would play from one home to another, publicly transmitting a version of domestic life predicated upon the incorporation of electric technologies into the comfortable privacy of middle-class homes" (ibid.: 61).

Prior to an artist's appearance on the TV screen, an executive decision maker or, more likely, a committee would evaluate the musicians' symbolic resonance, assessing whether or not they were worthy enough to appear on television. We can see how the idiosyncrasies and personae of certain top TV musical talents were desirable in industrial terms: Spike Jones and his musical agglomeration could promise madcap musical fun; Eddie Cantor could deliver tireless Broadway style song-and-dance performances with unflagging energy and humor; Tony Martin could be relied upon to express a warm, lush romantic mood; Dinah Shore was perky and welcoming, a pleasant and inoffensive songstress whose character was informal, bright, and cheerful. With repeat viewing, TV audiences gained ever-greater familiarity with these artists' types, coming to appreciate them through their appearances in the domestic sphere.

In ideal terms, artists might, through their regular TV appearances, become the equivalent of "friends," trusted and reliable assets in the average

TV viewer's daily life. Some television analysts of the period even went so far as to suggest that these program hosts were almost like "one of the family" and that the TV set itself was obligated to sustain its "congenial" character if it was to remain at the center of viewers' home life. For all of its positive attributes, however, familiarity can also have a taming effect that can temper a performer's impact, draining him or her of the desirable elements of spontaneity, innovation, or surprise that were much valued in early live television. TV viewers could, and inevitably did, demonstrate a blasé attitude toward the repetitive and forced performances of many top musical program hosts.

Within the specific historical conditions of postwar American consumer society, TV show hosts were required to "exude an honesty or 'naturalness' that would engender trust in the audience" (Murray 2001: 187), displaying a "natural, genuine, or authentic performance style" (ibid.: 196). In his 1948 television guidebook *Understanding Television*, Orrin Dunlap extolled the virtues of the songstress Kyle MacDonnell, "television's first new star," isolating her capacity to communicate in an effortless and authentic manner: "She was natural in every gesture; her cheerful smile, her songs, and her action were of 'living-room quality.' She appeared on the television screen as naturally and graciously as if she had joined the family circle. Naturalness, intimacy, and friendliness are her halos of success. She is telegenic!" (68–69). There was always a chance, of course, that the desired "naturalness" and easy familiarity for which an artist was initially hired might ultimately be corroded by television production and the medium's commercial character. Further complicating the equation is the possibility that tying a popular musical artist to sponsorship duties where they were expected to promote and extol the virtues of their sponsors' products, could effectively blemish the artist's carefully honed persona, devaluing his or her own professional identity.

Promotional materials and correspondence among network executives and between the networks and program sponsors divulge the extent to which audience familiarity and celebrity persona were discussed in endeavors to link products or corporate entities with the most suitable program formats and musical performance styles. In 1950, NBC launched its first prominent daytime program (airing between 4:00 and 5:00 P.M.) hosted by the renowned singer and popular entertainer Kate Smith. In the network's promotions (sent to affiliated stations and to prospective sponsors), Smith's ample vocal and performance talents—referred to as "her skilled showmanship"—and her song repertoire are certainly acknowledged but they are secondary to her likely appeal to female viewers and her long and impressive record of fund-raising (especially her role in helping to sell over $500 million in War Bonds during the Second World War and raising $400 million for the Red Cross in peace time). Smith's primary credentials are ultimately based on her marketing performance and the familiar role as "one of America's greatest and most believable salesmen . . . appearing for the first time on the greatest demonstration selling medium in history—television" ("Showletter" 1950). It is evident that the industry evaluation of Smith's success was predicated not on her musical performances but on her sales performance.

In another example, internal correspondence between the NBC executives George McGarrett and John Dodge in 1955 addresses the upcoming season of *The Perry Como Show* that was sponsored by the Armour meat company. McGarrett is assured of Como's value to the sponsor, explaining, "In Perry we have a warm, genial personality whose casual approach . . . has garnered for him tremendous loyalty among viewers. . . . We have no aspirations to change his manner, his delivery, his personality, his singing, etc., so that our first foundation for Perry is Perry the man as we know him today" (1955). As with Kate Smith, it was Como's established persona and public credibility, fused within his famous performance traits, that were coveted by the sponsor and the network. It was deemed unwise to tamper with his performance mannerisms lest he falter in his capacity to connect with viewers/consumers.

The networks and advertisers openly celebrated these show hosts' "natural" performance talents and innate approachability, yet, as Auslander cautions, "We must be suspicious of any supposition that musicians are simply 'being themselves' on stage" (2004: 6). Such cautionary advice is especially valid when considering the expense and human energy involved in selecting and presenting musical artists within overtly commercial broadcast contexts. A television persona is a construct and the production process is absolutely intrinsic to an artist such as Como's success, establishing a general tone and presentational mode that was relaxed and accommodating. Elaborating on the phenomenon of persona construction (or the transformation of a musical artist into a "television personality"), Auslander explains,

> Musicians' costumes, make-up, and general appearance, along with any sets, lighting, props (including musical instruments), and visual effects they may use, usually express their personae, which remain continuous

throughout a performance and across their performances, not the individual characters they may portray from song to song. . . . [T]he performers are not the sole authors of the personae they perform in these many contexts: producers, managers, agents, publicists, and the entire machinery of the music industry collaborate with artists, and sometimes coerce them, in the construction and performance of their personae. (2004: 9)

Kay Dickinson, too, underscores the folly of attributing underlying essentialist qualities to performers, noting the "fabricated" nature of the musician's self that is "a result of the corporate work undergone on it in order to create profit" (2008: 176). Understood within this framework, Como's TV persona was not an innate, unprocessed attribute but the outcome of commercial demands and focused labor.

Writing in *Down Beat* in 1951 (when Como's show aired on CBS), Ria Niccoli identifies the deliberate process of constructing Como's casual persona and extending his TV and music reputation: "Perhaps the most outstanding thing about a Perry Como rehearsal is the amazing absence of any rushing, screaming, production-hysterics or similar allied TV occupational hazards. Everybody walks, talks, and acts as if he were attending a well-bred tea party . . ." (1951d: 4). Affirming the produced character of the Como show, *Down Beat's* Radio and TV critic Jack Mabley also cites the evolution of Como's television performance style and the special attention to production and the carefully nurtured Como effect: "Perry almost relaxed himself right out of the business. He blew lines right and left, and the production was horrible. I had a feeling that a great deal of planning and rehearsal went into achieving the casual atmosphere of the 1955 Como" (1955: 46).

Poor Production and Weak Performances

Industry hubris and promotional overkill were to be expected as the networks developed their program schedules in the late 1940s and early 1950s, yet after so much advance hype there was a widespread sense of disappointment with the overall results. TV executives could not realistically disregard the fact that after years of buildup their broadcasts were often a disgrace, falling far short of the established standards in other entertainment media where popular songs were performed. Abysmal scripts, awkward staging, clumsy technical production, and inept performances plagued early programs. Regardless of where the blame might lie, there was general consensus among musicians and media critics alike that weak TV performances appeared amateurish and unprofessional.

As an unproven medium, television was granted initial latitude among musicians (and viewers) as the industry went through its developmental phase but it was difficult to ignore the fact that performances were often excessive, exaggerated, and inauthentic or, conversely, musicians appeared unanimated, oddly disconnected from their performance, and detached from the viewing audience. Taking the barrage of deflating commentary to heart, the TV networks continued to experiment and improve the situation by alleviating technical or production weaknesses and instituting performance quality standards.

As an example of these early flaws, between roughly 1947 and 1949 it was not unheard of for program hosts and guests to huddle around several microphones, visibly reading from their printed scripts in a manner that was typical of radio. Script reading even continued into the early 1950s in a few rare cases, such as the Chicago-based broadcast of the ABC morning variety show *Don McNeill's Breakfast Club* (later titled *Don McNeill's TV Club*), but this mainly occurred when programs were simulcast on radio and television. Without scripts, hosts frequently stammered through ad-libbed lines, revealing their lack of preparedness. Orchestra members had an advantage since it was acceptable to place sheet music arrangements on a music stand, although vocalists — such as the singing chorus on the McNeill show — occasionally still relied on their lyric sheets as they performed, obscuring their faces from the camera in the process.[15]

Poor musical performances were often the result of new and complicated production processes and the fact that even the technicians were learning on the job, as John Caldwell indicates: "In addition to the sense that stations and producers were desperately struggling to find successful *performance formats* for the new visually defined medium, early television also showed off its *technical limitations*" (1995: 46). Production problems included such rookie errors as capturing the overhead boom microphone in the picture frame or inadvertently catching stage personnel on camera as they scurried across the back of the set, diverting attention from the performance. In at least one instance the program stage director was visible at the edge of the screen, script in hand and equipped with headphones, completely oblivious to the fact that he was well within camera range. Television directors and technicians could not deny their inexperience as they exercised a trial-and-error approach to production. In a lukewarm review of a new youth-oriented amateur program, *Stars of Tomorrow*, airing on the Los Angeles station KTTV in March, 1950, *Variety* acknowledged the effects of technical inexperience and television's brief production history, noting, "If the KTTV mike could talk back to the 'stars of tomorrow,' it would most likely say, 'we're all in the same boat, kids, we're starting out too.'"

Presentational problems frequently undermined the musical performances in particular, and the press did not excuse them for their failings. In a *Variety* review of the June 3, 1948, broadcast of *The Don Lee Music Hall* on the Los Angeles station KTLA it was stated that the show "certainly rates A for effort," yet the artists "were constantly too distant from the telecamera so that their features were either indistinct or too blurred." A generally positive review of the CBS premiere broadcast of Ed Sullivan's *Toast of the Town* on June 20, 1948, emphasized the broadcast's production weaknesses, referring to the trouble Roland Gillett, the director, had "with one of his cameras, which kept going out of focus." The show's struggles continued through much of its first season, as a review of the September 19, 1948, broadcast indicates: "Any act with more than one person was too often out of camera range and the lack of advance preparation completely ruined the Louis Jordan orch's performance. With no apparent instructions on where to stand, Jordan was out of mike range throughout his two numbers."[16]

Stagecraft and performance ability were also points of contention. *Variety* offered a negative assessment of the musical performances on Eddie Condon's NBC musical program *Floor Show* in September 1948: "On the vocal and feminine side there is Liza Morrow. She is well-known and can sing a song, but like so many of the other girls, Miss Morrow will have to learn what to do with her arms if she's going to linger in front of the cameras." The harsh critical reception of substandard stagecraft remains unmistakable in the *Variety* review of the January 19, 1949, broadcast of *The Arthur Godfrey Show* on CBS:

> Bill Williams is a potentially promising singer, although he doesn't know how to move in front of the lens . . . Janette Davis cannot move either, handles herself poorly, and although she boasts a fair enough voice she needs plenty of coaching for the camera. All of which means that Lawrence stands still. Miss Davis stands still. The quartet stands still. The orchestra sits down and so does Godfrey. There's no animation in the

show. Besides, something or somebody has got to stand off those slow ballads with which the vocals persist. It's all too much radio. Which may be all right for AM but this is TV — and a full hour.

A general cynicism consequently emerged as TV viewers and media critics weighed in with their opinions about weak performances by top musical artists.

As a partial defense of their flawed programs, many TV producers unfairly accused the musicians themselves, assuming that musicians should be, by their very nature, well prepared for their TV performances since they rehearsed regularly for their nontelevision performances in various public contexts. Insufficient rehearsal time and lack of advance instructions about TV staging rose as a prominent issue among musicians who were accused of weak performances. With scripted comedy skits, minor dramatic sequences, and other dialogic exchanges placing additional burden on musicians, TV programs often seriously neglected rehearsal time specifically dedicated to the performance of musical numbers. Kay Dickinson explores precisely such issues in her analysis of failed musical performances in cinema. As she explains, the failures were (and often still are) primarily focused on the aesthetic shortcomings of the individual or the specific performance yet rarely is the critical emphasis placed on the industrial processes of labor that also impact the final outcomes. "Failed film-music collaborations" are, in her view, the product of aesthetic *and* work-related factors (2008: 22). Sometimes decisions that influence the aesthetic outcome of a broadcast are based on corporate or production considerations. As surviving industrial memoranda indicate, these considerations are frequently monetary in nature, harboring a corporate rationale that contains the musical performances within a larger ideology of enhanced efficiency or increased cost-effectiveness.

Defending musicians with the comment "They are deserving of better treatment and so is the listener," Harry Sosnik (a popular band leader and musical director of several successful 1950s TV series) explained, "The quality of music heard in the home over TV today is disgraceful — mind you through no fault of musicians, arrangers or conductors. The people in charge are so busy with the picture that the listeners' ears are insulted" (1951: 29). The typical proposals for remedying such broadcast failings included greater rehearsal time, more space for larger orchestras, more technical attention to the musical arrangements and artists' performance styles, drama courses for musicians, and over the long term, greater experience in the medium. Until

Peggy Lee recording "He's a Tramp." Circa 1955. COURTESY OF PHOTOFEST.

these problems were rectified, however, the negative reviews continued to mount.

Without assured flow or consistency broadcasts were characteristically uneven and the differing onscreen talents between musicians were starkly illustrated. Every so often it seemed that a single broadcast encompassed all of television's performance strengths and weaknesses. This occurred on the May 23, 1954, broadcast of *The Colgate Comedy Hour* (hosted by Bud Abbott and Lou Costello) featuring guests Hoagy Carmichael, Peggy Lee, and the orchestra of Eddie Sauter and Bill Finegan. The artists each represent a different musical style and their individual approaches to television are similarly distinct. In this broadcast episode, Carmichael delivers a warm but generally uneventful performance that is mildly affected by poor sound quality, exacerbating his vocal limitations but not compromising his wonderful way with a song.

Up next, Lee's performance is sublime. Lee first offers a sultry, mesmerizing version of the ballad "Johnny Guitar," bedecked in a Spanish-style dress and hooded shawl that bestows an almost angelic image as she strolls lazily across a set appropriately designed to evoke a southwestern frontier at sundown. In her next song, however, her demeanor is radically transformed by the hot mambo arrangement of the Rodgers and Hart standard "Bewitched, Bothered and Bewildered," with a sophisticated jazz guitar (probably played by her husband, Dave Barbour) soloing briskly beneath the song's uptempo rhythm.[17] Her delicate gestures and wistful look perfectly match the beautiful orchestral accompaniment with its Latin influence and the brilliant staging and appropriately diffused lighting enhance the entire performance.

Changes in the "formal and textual economies of style" and the "new presentational burdens of television" (Caldwell 1995: 45) compelled musical performers to more carefully consider the distinctions between a concert performance and a performance for television. Lee stands out as a popular vocalist whose agreeable, subtly sexual personality projected well on the screen but to her infinite benefit, she also evidently worked hard to improve her performance technique and, thus, reinforce her television presence. In fact, Lee's stagecraft was unusually well documented in the music and entertainment press.

Her first major television program was on May 9, 1946 (on television's first hour-long musical variety show, NBC's *Hour Glass*)[18]; it garnered a positive review, but there was a two-year lag between this appearance and her next TV performance. In March 1948, *Down Beat* noted Lee's superior stagecraft during a three-week stand at Ciro's nightclub in Los Angeles (appearing with her husband and his quartet) despite her minimal experience as a singer with a small combo. Part of the amazement lay in the fact that since parting ways with the Benny Goodman orchestra, with whom she had toured and recorded between 1941 and 1947, Lee's trajectory seemed primarily oriented toward a recording career. The review states, "Filmdom know-it-alls were stunned by her professional showmanship" ("Peggy Astounds Ciroites" 1948: 9).

In August 1948 Lee appeared on Ed Sullivan's *Toast of the Town*, receiving a favorable review in *Variety* with comments on her ballad-heavy repertoire and her camera-friendly looks, especially in close-up shots. The next September, the *Down Beat* writer Jack Egan reported on Lee's progress as a performer, writing that several years prior "she was lost when she stood on the stage — didn't know what to do except sing" (1948: 16). As Egan observes, "Peggy's charm, poise, personality, and general approach . . . show the training of a trouper who's brushed up on some of the finer points of showmanship" (ibid.).

Four and a half years later, in January 1953, *Down Beat* again featured Lee in a story about her impressive and continuing growth as a performer. Here it is revealed that her development through the late 1940s and early 1950s—precisely coinciding with her step into television—was guided by Mel Ferrer (a talented Broadway and Hollywood film actor and producer at the La Jolla Playhouse), who, apart from telling her that she was "fat" and needed to slim down, "taught her how to project her personality in the manner of musical comedy singers—but without losing any basic musicianship."[19] Ferrer instructed Lee on how to manage interstitial chat and song segues onstage and how to enact "small but dramatic gestures with her hands" ("Peggy Lee's Progress" 1953: 7), something that she clearly perfected.[20]

After Lee's enthralling performance, the real problems with *The Colgate Comedy Hour* episode emerge when the Sauter-Finegan band takes the stage.[21] The band was mainly a studio unit, but in 1954 it set out on an extended tour even though the dance band sector was terminally weak; the tour was a financial failure from which the orchestra never fully recovered. Their 1954 NBC-TV appearance offers possible insights onto why the tour failed. As the Sauter-Finegan performance segment indicates, even with stage direction and other professional pointers, stage experience was often not enough on its own to surmount TV's performance idiosyncrasies and complexities.

Their segment starts with a close-up of a man opening a large invitation card reading, "You are cordially invited to attend the annual Midtown Department Store employee's reception and dance. Music by the Sauter-Finegan Orchestra. New Directions in Music." Serving as an introduction to the performance, the invitation is an oddly bland framing device since a company party is not a particularly noteworthy event. The opening image dissolves and the curtain rises on the full orchestra positioned on an unevenly lit stage. There is, however, a huge liquid stain on the floor in front of the bandstand that is highly visible and distracting, suggesting that some sort of mishap had occurred prior to airtime (after a sponsor announcement, the extent of the stain was noticeably diminished).

The band stumbles immediately with a miscue when it begins playing the opening number just as Bill Finegan steps forward to introduce the act to the TV audience: "You know there's been a lot of confusion about this band . . . ." The orchestra lurches to an awkward halt (except for the audible sound of shuffling and bumping from the stand) as Finegan offers a hackneyed, meandering introduction to the first song, one of the band's popular compositions, "Midnight Sleigh Ride" (an unusual choice considering that the program was broadcast in May). Though the song arrangement is moderately creative, demonstrating Sauter and Finegan's combined talents, the performance itself is remarkably lackluster and the bandleaders are unengaging, exuding nervousness, discomfort, and an entirely amateur mien. The lighting array also produces an odd and distracting back shadow, and the camera is restless, roaming across the bandstand without any apparent motivation. In one instance Eddie Sauter, lightly striking a small triangle, is caught in a close-up with a curiously perplexed look on his face before the camera shifts to another section of the orchestra. With such clumsy production, the obvious deficiencies in "telegeneity," and the lack of a captivating performance dynamic, the Sauter-Finegan Orchestra segment seriously undermines the program's overall quality.

Sauter-Finegan was never regarded as a top performing act and its television limitations were consequently of minor relevence. Conversely, because expectations had been so high, *The Frank Sinatra Show*, airing on CBS in 1951–52 received special attention for its performance shortcomings. Sinatra was already recognized as a brilliant performer, able to work a midsize room or a large theater with equal panache, and he expressed optimism as he embarked on his TV show, declaring, "Almost anything can be done in television—or at least tried" (Sinatra 1951: 11). Television, however, was something unknown to him, and Sinatra admitted to feeling out of place and overwhelmed by the rapid pace of the production process (frequently expressing his preference for film acting compared to the challenges posed by live TV). Feeling the sting of the critics' lash, Sinatra blamed his pitiable television performances on inadequate studio conditions and the sorry state of production: "From a purely technical point of view, we have discovered that television, as it is today, is unequipped in the matter of studios, theaters, and stages. There's seldom enough room, not only for the actors, but also to jockey the cameras into position so that the director can get the shots he wants" (ibid.: 19).

Sinatra's complaints correspond with Simon Frith's view that, "Stress is therefore associated with fears that instruments and equipment won't work properly, that rehearsals were inadequate, that one might be too tired or ill to keep up. . . . The basic point is that for the musician, the highest stress factors are those that impinge directly upon the performance" (1996: 53). While Sinatra was undoubtedly more familiar with the cameras than were many of his musical peers, owing to his experience in Hollywood films and his early exposure as a regular TV guest, he ultimately failed to overcome the particularities of live television. With his performance inadequacies on full display, Sinatra increasingly confronted television as an adversary and his much-anticipated program did not survive past its first year.

Without indicating Sinatra by name, *Variety*'s TV critic, George Rosen reprimanded the networks and the artists themselves for what he perceived as a "lack of integrity with which many TV performers are approaching the medium." According to Rosen, the 1952 television schedule was marred by "sloppy, careless production and performance on some of the top-budgeted programs. . . . [T]oo many stars and so-called impresarios who have been enticed into the medium are treating it more as a sideline for a quick buck instead of trying to vest TV with the type of showmanship perfection it has been striving for" (1952: 97). Many of these very same criticisms were leveled directly at Sinatra.

Noting Sinatra's patchy TV performances, the editor of *Metronome*, George Simon, reserved his most fierce condemnation for the vocalist's air of imperviousness and for his grossly inept comedy routines, citing the host himself as the program's main liability: "Concentration on the warm, human Sinatra had never been a part of his big-time CBS show. . . . As a solo comedian he has proved nothing. His often contrived, smart-alecky routines have murdered nobody except Sinatra himself, because by stepping so far out of the 'boy-next-door' character and into 'the-guy-in-Lindy's' role, he has negated much of the good that took years to create" (1952). Extant program tapes depict Sinatra awkwardly muddling through mildly comic and self-deprecating monologues, often placing his own lean physique at the core of the jest. Sinatra also adopted an odd distinctive gesture, mugging for the camera and delivering his punch lines with a shrug of his shoulders, incorporating a juvenile "va-va-voom" expression that seemed intended to add extra zing in putting the jokes over. It was all a sad display for a singer of Sinatra's status.

On the January 1, 1952, episode of the Sinatra show (featuring the celebrity impersonator George DeWitt, the Three Stooges comedy trio, and musical guests Yvonne DeCarlo and Louis Armstrong), Sinatra seems particularly baffled, especially in the face of the Stooges' nonstop, screwball antics. With up to eight people crowding the frame in one particular scene (set in Sinatra's ersatz chic bachelor apartment on New Year's eve), the stage is in total disarray with extras, guests, and Sinatra all packed together within the set's close confines. As the skit unravels, cues are missed (at one point Sinatra delivers his line and turns to open a door *before* the buzzer sounds), a prop is accidentally knocked from its perch, and the Stooges' randomly spray fluids from a seltzer bottle around the set. The stage blocking is dreadful and it is obvious that the Stooges are improvising to such a high degree in their inimitable style that Sinatra has trouble following them, unsure of where to stand and when to recite his lines.

Seeking to reestablish some order after the Stooges' pandemonium, Sinatra quips, "Everything on this show is planned." This, in turn, leads to a self-reflexive metacommentary on the show's production and subsequent chaos, employing ironic jibes about the program and the performances in a manner that was common on television in this early period. When Sinatra disingenuously asks DeCarlo what she would like to sing, she responds, "Anything you want, as long as it's something we rehearsed." DeCarlo's comment toys with notions of formal preparation and free-form improvisation, acknowledging that the performances seem to be nudging the show to the verge of dissolution. These metastatements and brief asides, akin to theater and vaudeville norms, present an interesting aspect of live television by providing the viewers with a glimpse of the relationship between performance and production. The audience is made explicitly aware that anything can happen at any time and that rehearsal and advance preparation do not guarantee that the show will proceed without incident.

Regardless of whether or not the lines were scripted or spontaneous, Sinatra's timing is atrocious and he struggles with the comedy material, stammering, looking off camera, and running his hand through his hair nervously, all the components of what critics at the time regarded as aspects of a "bad" performance. These varied tics offer an example of what Karen Lury terms "corpsing . . . the forgetting of lines, giggling inappropriately or in other ways 'breaking the frame' of the performance" (1995: 127), often when the host and guests engage in spontaneous high jinks. Corpsing, however, also reveals the human element of the performance by exposing the artist's fallibility. Lury explains that corpsing "let[s] the viewer in," engendering "a moment where the television performer reveals his or herself as truly live, uncontrolled and expressive. . . . [I]t suggests that form of direct communication, the existence of a real bond between the performer and viewer, which television seems to promise, yet which it can rarely deliver" (ibid.: 127). Though this aspect of performative authenticity seems, on the surface, to be an acceptable byproduct of Sinatra's comic presentation, contemporaneous critical opinions did not necessarily see it that way.

The pattern of the New Year's Eve show shifts sharply away from raw comedy when Louis Armstrong arrives to perform his first number. Following a brief dialogue with Sinatra, Armstrong nods offstage to the orchestra (led by a longtime Sinatra collaborator, Axel Stordahl), raising his horn to his lips and, after a short introductory horn passage, he sings the opening phrases of "I'm Confessin' (That I Love You)," a song first introduced by Fats Waller in 1929 and recorded a year later by Rudy Vallee and Armstrong himself. Armstrong's vocal phrasing is languid and playful, the orchestra accompaniment subdued and elegant, and Sinatra can be heard offscreen at one point scat singing in unison, eliciting a broad smile from Armstrong.

Later in the program, Armstrong returns to join Sinatra for a duet and as the two professionals banter, there is a clear sense of *simpatico*, a mutual admiration that is palpable in their interaction. For this number, Sinatra invites Armstrong to "sit down, Louis, I want to sing for you, daddy"; seated on the piano bench alongside Sinatra (a potential affront to the racial sensibilities of southern television audiences at the time), Armstrong picks up his horn as they embark on a sweet and stylish rendition of "Lonesome Man Blues." The two casually exchange lyrical verses and the occasional ad-lib line, harmonizing on the chorus and generally turning in a musical performance that is simultaneously convivial, engaging, and refined. Perhaps owing to the song's bluesy composition or to Armstrong's influence, Sinatra modifies his phrasing and bends the notes liberally, demonstrating a spontaneity and improvisational flare that contradicts the stiffness and tension of his previous comedy routines. Alongside Armstrong, Sinatra seems unassailable; his musical strengths are at the forefront, exposing the deep well of talent that the network and the program sponsor surely hoped to tap into in the first place.

Carrying a show was a huge responsibility and the tales of established musical celebrities of Sinatra's stature who felt drained by television's demanding schedule—or frustrated by its inability to deliver flawless musical performances—were legion. Indeed, despite his success in Hollywood (including an Academy Award in 1953 for Best Supporting Actor in *From Here to Eternity*), well-received television guest appearances, and at least one exceptional musical "spectacular" (the brilliantly produced *Max Liebman Presents Fanfare: Songs for Young Lovers*, broadcast November 7, 1954), Sinatra did not venture into television again as a program host until 1957.

By the mid-1950s, television's potentials, while not exhaustively tested, were at least well enough known that more strictly defined technical practices and performance styles took hold, providing the base from which stable broadcast conventions evolved. Similarly, with television's professionalization, the dictates of producers and stage managers (as well as sponsors and talent agencies) increasingly delimited the productions, necessitating greater compliance among musicians who were new to the medium. An overall focus on the production process streamlined and improved the general quality of musical performances.

Though controversial, the implementation of prerecorded vocal tracks was also occasionally adopted as a means of ensuring vocal quality during live broadcasts or to free singers to partake in the physically demanding production numbers. While show hosts such as Betty Hutton or Jo Stafford accepted dubbing as a rational means of production control and efficiency, others including Perry Como, Bob Crosby, Eddie Fisher, Jane Froman, Tony Martin, and Dinah Shore explicitly eschewed the practice on the grounds that it was unethical *and* placed them at risk of a technical glitch that might expose the performance ruse. In Shore's evaluation, "Pre-recording destroys the warm intimacy of TV as a medium, forcing a singer to concentrate so hard on synchronizing the lips with sound tracks, tape or acetate disc that spontaneity goes out the window . . . On TV you're offering your whole personality—and you can't record that" ("Their Lips Move" 1954: 8–9). For Shore, the live television performance was closely aligned with authenticity, sincerity, and identity, and she was savvy enough to understand that these are her best attributes, precisely what her program sponsors and fans value most.

As stage managers, sound engineers, and cameramen gained experience and improved their skills, performances were increasingly subjected to the controlling apparatus of the production process. The intense pressures on a singer or musician to deliver a single "knock-out" performance that would override various constraints or failings gradually diminished within a technically improved production regime.

Funny Hats, Novelty Tunes, and the Crisis of Musical Integrity

According to Neal Gabler, television's mid-century ascent is best understood as the culmination of a long phase of cultural change, what he terms a "revolution": "In the end, after all the imprecations had rung down around it, entertainment was less about morality or even aesthetics than about power—the power to replace the old cultural order with a new one, the power to replace the sublime with 'fun'" (1998: 21). Gabler explains, "Entertainment itself was the cosmology that had governed American life with increasing vigor since at least the turn of the century. That meant the new consciousness was a function not of television or even images but of entertainment" (ibid.: 56). Many cultural observers in the immediate postwar period agreed that television alone should not be accused of inflicting damage on the popular music sector.

The element of transition was noticeable in the critical discourses pertaining to popular music and performance. In 1947 the *New York Times* invoked the concept of "revolution," blaming record labels, publishing houses, and the Hollywood film industry for the shift from "hot" jazz toward well-liked but lightweight and inconsequential song arrangements (Schumach 1947). The industry trade paper *Down Beat* regularly castigated music artist agencies and managers in the immediate postwar period for sanctioning poor "presentation" and for urging orchestras to adopt play lists of "syrupy" or banal dance music that the critics believed was a simple commercial gambit catering to the lowest common denominator of public taste.

A further belief maintained that the music industry's postwar misfortunes could be traced to aesthetic deficiencies and performance weaknesses. Critics in the music industry demanded improved staging and closer attention to visual innovation in order to boost the "entertainment" quotient of musical performances. Musical acts of the late 1940s and early 1950s were pressured to incorporate "novelty" or comedic elements into their stage shows, fulfilling Gabler's notion of a wider inclination toward "fun." Ballroom managers also aggressively courted orchestras with strong visual appeal and they, too, encouraged acts to implement onstage antics that might stimulate audience interest and, thus, generate superior revenues.

In a 1947 editorial column titled "Showmanship, New Talent Needed Now," *Down Beat* sounded an alarm, explicitly identifying performance shortcomings among musical acts. The magazine states that dance bands "were neglecting showmanship," suggesting, "after 10 years the public was deciding that it wanted a little more for its $1.50 than the privilege of hearing a few star side-men and a brass section blowing its lungs out" ("Showmanship, New Talent" 1947: 10). Referring to one novel approach, the column favorably cites Xavier Cugat's performances at the Capitol Theater in New York City as a positive response to the entertainment crisis. Since it was still relatively common in 1947 for musical ensembles to perform several shows daily, appearing in large urban theaters between film screenings, Cugat imaginatively integrated the large screen into the performance.

Working with previously filmed material and an obviously well-rehearsed script, Cugat took the stage only to be interrupted by his own image enlarged on the theater screen behind him. Feigning surprise, Cugat engaged in deliberately casual banter and witty repartee with his filmed likeness, adopting the dual roles of interrogator and respondent with a comic twist before gradually segueing into the band's opening number. Acknowledging that Cugat's professional status and his comparatively privileged access to film producers exceeded those of most of his contemporaries, *Down Beat* upbraided musicians and bandleaders for their failure to revise their performance strategies, concluding, "There are devices possible to present magic in a less boring fashion on stage" (ibid.). As Cugat's unique example implies, performance innovation in the late 1940s was at least partially tied to the addition of humorous visual practices, reinforcing the sense that musical presentation was insufficient on its own.

With industry trends toward a more pronounced visual performance mode, music industry insiders carefully monitored television's growing demands of musical performers. Under the headline "Novelty Needed If Bands Want Video Contracts," *Down Beat*'s editors distinguished between "good listening" and "good watching," suggesting that musicians "get out the paper hats and props, boys. No big rush. Just keep it in mind. When musicians do get into television, they're going to find themselves faced with a demand for visual presentations" ("Novelty Needed" 1948: 10). The famed bandleader Paul Whiteman, musical director at ABC-TV at the network's inception, was equally explicit in his belief that "new techniques of musical presentation will have to be developed" ("Scott Adapting Quintet" 1948: 20). Always an advocate of musical excellence, as a new ABC spokesman Whiteman was also comfortable pressing musicians to accommodate television's visual requirements, urging the employment of "camera tricks, comedy, and novelty bands" (ibid).

After 1948, there was a surfeit of articles and commentary about artists deliberately revising their acts, developing what was known in the industry as "funny hats routines." Some musicians went so far as forming entirely new musical agglomerations with a prominent visual orientation, integrating novelty tunes into their repertoires and initiating what was termed "a bit of business" via comic props, costumes, and scripted mayhem.[22] This trend can be seen in Gene Krupa's preparations for television performances at the Glen Island Casino in 1948. Krupa's onstage flamboyance and his energetic drumming style had elevated him as a celebrity member of the Benny Goodman orchestra of the 1930s and as a successful leader of his own unit through the 1940s. In rehearsals, Krupa and his band members reportedly

Gene Krupa. *METRONOME*, SEPTEMBER 1948.

sported "tams, horn-rimmed glasses and exaggerated gestures for their travesty on the new idiom of modern jazz" in the group's performance of "Bop
Boogie Woogie" ("Krupa All Eyes" 1948: 2). A photograph of Krupa appearing in *Metronome* the following September verifies the description, revealing Krupa's visual abandon with the drum master sporting a contrived faux
bebop look. A brief description of a one-night performance at Chicago's
Melody Mill club in late autumn, 1948, indicates that Krupa continued
to incorporate "a little be bop burlesque with berets and smoked glasses"
("Will Funny Hats Be Savior?" 1948: 3).

The most perceptive and autonomous bandleaders realized that success
on television involved more than simply transferring a preexisting performance style or format to the new medium; they needed to reconceive and
update their entire act, usually including some sort of novelty. Like Krupa,
countless working musicians began testing out novelty tunes and comedy
sketches with the unambiguous hope that they might boost their chances
for television exposure.

The thrust toward humorous visual performances intensified as artists responded to the shifting industry expectations. Reviewing a 1949 broadcast
of *Adventures in Jazz, Variety* noted that, in a case of broadminded program-

ming, the program emphasized "bebop" music featuring the Charlie Ventura orchestra and George Shearing performing legitimate bop-infused arrangements. Yet the program also featured a performance by Guy Lombardo and the Royal Canadians, an act renowned for its "sweet" sound with no affiliation with the bebop genre. Like Krupa before him, Lombardo parodied the sartorial style stereotypically associated with bebop and the 52nd Street jazz scene where the phenomenon was centered, appearing "disguised as a bopster" in a thin attempt at comedy.

With the falling fortunes of larger dance band ensembles, many of the more inspired musical improvisers and top-notch soloists found satisfaction and acclaim in smaller ensembles, where they were unfettered by the near machine-like precision of the large band format and where they could shine on a more individualistic platform. Aesthetically, bebop stood as the new idiom of jazz artistry, distinct from the commercial fare of the big band that was comparatively devoid of spontaneity. According to Krin Gabbard, the break from the dance bands and the swing genre articulated values aligning bebop with "the other avant-garde movements of the twentieth century" (1996: 124). Many younger up-and-coming musicians gravitated toward bebop and "modern" jazz that was successful in the small clubs of Manhattan and Harlem. For them, the dance bands were regarded as occasionally interesting remnants of a previous era. Countless small combos formed and groups appeared in amalgamations with fluctuating personnel, "gigging" in intimate spaces (such as the legendary basement clubs that lined New York's 52nd Street) rather than in the grand ballrooms or casinos of the past. Reflecting the spirit of the times, bebop "removed familiar signposts, seemed unstable and filled with urgency and restlessness" (Erenberg 1998: 229).

That bebop and modern jazz artists were specifically selected for mockery is worth analyzing. Progressive jazz musicians were commonly criticized within conservative and traditional music circles for their cerebral, technical approaches to music and, in a performative mode, for their apparent exertion as they played their instruments and labored for their art (the image of a soloist's facial contortions or physical writhing was, for more straight-laced musicians, unnecessary or even grotesque). According to Bernard Gendron, bebop musicians, "were reprimanded for their preoccupation with showmanship, their undignified publicity stunts, their mannerisms and their argot" (1993: 150). Yet television producers generally valued such dynamic visual characteristics. Although bebop musicians (and, to a lesser extent, "authentic" jazz artists) were consistently marginalized on television, images associated with them and their milieu were widely appropriated. Their style as much as their musicianship identified them as Other both within jazz circles and in wider society and in the hands of would-be comedians, the surfaces of the mostly black bebop artists were exploited, subverted, and re-presented for television's majority white viewership.

The musical mockery emerged in often troubling ways as musicians such as Krupa and Lombardo or comedians including Milton Berle and Sid Caesar offered tasteless caricatures of the bebop look and sound. The racial overtones of the onscreen jibes were exemplary of television's treatment of bebop, though some hosts such as Steve Allen were unfailingly enthusiastic, maintaining affinities with bebop, modern, and cool jazz musicians and the black artists that excelled in these idioms. In their comic turns, white TV performers attempted to pervert the symbolic value of "cool" or hipness at-tributed to black musicians and the bebop subculture, in the process dimin-ishing the subversive potentials of adventurous or *risky* music by amplifying them in a burlesque form and making them more palatable for a nonurban white audience. These comic performances extended the repertoire of white devaluation of black cultural expression while, whether consciously or not, employing television as a tool in a regressive agenda.

Musicians' attempts at visual humor and slapstick routines were con-spicuously aligned with performance practices of the vaudeville tradition. In February 1947, *Variety* speculated that television could potentially con-tribute to the revitalization of Tin Pan Alley and songs forged in the earlier vaudeville style, citing the medium's penchant for vocalists to fill space. It was reported that music publishers were anticipating being called upon to contribute songs that, as in the vaudeville tradition, accented "simple melo-dies and 'story' lyrics and the sort of material that permitted, or even de-manded, they go in for histrionic byplay," leading to an emphasis on "actable ballads" and "novelty tunes suitable to more 'sight' consumption" ("Video's Vaude Song-Styling" 1947: 41).

Upcoming artists and hopeful amateurs were encouraged to develop and perfect the visual elements of their stage act, as Ruth Lee Harrington sug-gested in her 1949 treatise *Your Opportunities in Television*, when she fore-cast that top ratings and viewer appeal would "undoubtedly be reserved for those who can inject some novelty or humor into their musical repertoire" (91). *Down Beat* reinforced these sentiments in the same period, noting that vaudeville constituted an ideal "training ground for the development of television talent. . . . All of this is good news for musicians. Vaudeville acts performing in television must have music — live music — whether they sing, dance, or even if they're acrobats" ("Thank TV for Vaude Revival" 1949: 10). Musicians were not expected only to provide backup accompaniment for comedy acts, however, but were drawn into the midst of the vaudeville-inspired high jinks.

The vaudeville influences preferred by television producers were those that carried on the best practices associated with such sites as Tony Pastor's Theater at 14th Street in mid- to late nineteenth-century New York City. Rather than the explicitly bawdy humor common to the era, Pastor promoted generally well-mannered performance fare that catered to a vast mixed-class audience. Musical variety and vaudeville in this strain were expected to be visually engaging, agreeable to all, and offensive to none, yet they were also enjoyed for their apparent spontaneity, traits that were consistent with the performance modes of live television broadcasting.

Vaudeville-inflected performances gained prominence as television executives sought experienced and adaptable entertainers — song-and-dance men (and a few women) — who could be relied upon to carry an evening's broadcast proceedings efficiently and with a degree of mirth. As Susan Murray explains, "Eventually commentators assumed that the stage comic . . . would be best suited to television work. This was primarily because of the trained comedian's ability to maintain the intensive schedule of television, his or her penchant for improvisation in live work, and, of course, the broadcast experience that many had acquired on radio" (2005: 41). Such was vaudeville's aesthetic appeal and perceived viability for television variety programming that when the ABC network debuted on August 11, 1948, with a broadcast from the New York station WJZ-TV, the new network aired what *Variety* described as "a lavish four-hour inaugural that brought back live talent to B'way's Palace Theatre for a spectacular one-night stand." The trade journal declared the event a success, noting that the show "played like a traditional Palace bill . . . the type that exemplifies the highest standards of variety" ("Nostalgic Palace Vaude Bill" 1948). The opening broadcast featured reputable and familiar talent, presenting a host of established vaudeville acts, "all of whom played the Palace in its heyday," ending with a musical finale led by bandleader (and the network's musical director) Paul Whiteman (ibid.).

Several vaudeville-trained comedians with actual music skills — including the program hosts Morey Amsterdam (cello), Jack Benny (violin), Eddie Cantor (vocals), Jimmy Durante (piano), and Sid Caesar (saxophone) — were tapped to host their own TV shows, where they occasionally employed their auxiliary musical talents; others, such as Henny Youngman (violin) or Victor Borge (piano), appeared regularly as variety show guests. Spike Jones (with his band, the City Slickers, an ensemble of highly skilled musicians) was tapped as host of *The Colgate Comedy Hour* in 1951. Based on their notoriously loopy stage act (and their zany traveling shows, "The Musical Depreciation Revue" or "Musical Insanities of 1954"), they offered a prime example of the comic farce and props-based performances that were steeped in the vaudeville aesthetic. Though meeting with mixed responses among African American audiences and critics, the broad facial mugging of prominent black musical artists such as Louis Armstrong, Cab Calloway, Lionel Hampton, or Louis Jordan also reflected vaudeville's penchant for minstrelsy and physical humor, satisfying TV broadcasters' desire for "entertaining" visual content.

Additional evidence of the major networks' commitment to embracing vaudeville and novelty in televised musical performances is found in a 1949 memorandum sent by NBC's Robert Wade to the NBC executive Carleton Smith. In the exchange, Wade explains the pressing need for NBC to provide more space and improved facilities for the prop-making department in acknowledgment of the medium's prominent and growing visual demands: "Practically every musical or variety program, because of the visual nature of television, now requires an increasing number of so-called trick props or 'gimmicks'" (Wade 1949). This indicates an additional dimension of the networks' investment in reproducing the vaudeville stage. The networks did not just mobilize the spirit of vaudeville at the level of performances but extended vaudeville's aesthetic legacy through the construction of an entire representational apparatus including sets, props, and costumes.

With comedy and humor encroaching on the bandstand and stage during television performances, the issue of musical integrity was increasingly broached in the music press. William Kaufman and Robert Colodzin enunciated the need for new performance sensibilities in their 1950 manual *Your Career in Television*, where they describe the ideal presentational forms for popular music, foregrounding the "combination of telegenic personalities, addition of a dash of 'visualizing' . . . and utilization of camera flexibility" (28). Musicians evidently took such suggestions quite seriously, with some reorganizing their entire act as a means of conforming to TV. *Down Beat* reported in 1951 that the bandleader Freddy Martin, host of *Band of Tomorrow* and a frequent guest on shows including *Cavalcade of Bands*, had accumulated "a large and special supply of songs written exclusively for presentation

Morey Amsterdam with Milton Delugg (accordion) and his band with host Wayne Howell. *Broadway Open House*, NBC, 1950. COURTESY OF PHOTOFEST.

Caesar's Hour, featuring the Benny Goodman Orchestra. NBC, November 3, 1954. COURTESY OF PHOTOFEST.

on television." Martin explained, "They are not dance tunes, but production numbers containing story line, humor, integration, and movement" (Niccoli 1951c: 5).

When Frank DeVol announced that he, too, had an entire new set of arrangements for future television appearances, he admitted to enrolling in a "course in dramatics" in order to "develop musical products that are marketable in television" (Holly 1952: 9). Photographs of the DeVol unit's televised performances (on the Los Angeles station KTTV, remote from the Lido ballroom in Long Beach) portray the band playing in a serious and restrained manner as well as depicting them mugging for the cameras, leading *Down Beat* to comment that "TV turns musicians into schizophrenics" ("DeVol Finds Dramatics an Aid" 1952: 6).

Commenting in late 1948 that the comic trend "probably won't be greeted by superhipsters and brow-furrowed music critics with much hat-waving — funny or otherwise" ("Will Funny Hats Be Savior?" 1948: 3), *Down Beat* asserted its industry influence over aesthetic judgment and good taste. Ironically, despite its earlier call for greater innovation involving visual histrionics and perhaps "a bit of business" on the bandstand, such practices apparently tipped too far on television and were soon a major point of derision for the magazine's editors and writing staff. The harsh assessment of TV's funny hats routines emerged in numerous contexts. In 1949, *Down Beat* disdainfully reported on the broadcast performance of the Ike Carpenter band that was developing its new visual act: "The band, not long ago known for its sincere approach to jazz, soon will find itself wrapped, stamped, and delivered into the funny hats class if its course isn't drastically altered. Carpenter is a genuine guy and a good musician, but his present musical tack will carry him into watery commercialism for sure unless checked pronto" ("Ike Heading Down" 1949: 3). The phrase "watery commercialism" is perhaps telling of the attitudes within the music industry at the time; though musicians had been compelled to comply with commercial corporate directives in the culture industries for decades, television's arrival created new demands and concessions. Musicians sought assurance that the networks' economic imperative would not overwhelm the quality of their musical performances or otherwise compromise their reputations.

Television's attempts to accommodate both high and low culture fare, exacerbated by the fixation on visual display, often produced strange juxtapositions, with "legitimate" musicians being booked on variety shows between animal acts and plate spinners. Ultimately, the trend reproduced a system of ideological value upon which hierarchical relations in the music sector were founded, demarcating the line between serious musical performance and sheer novelty. As Simon Frith argues in the contexts of professional musical presentation, "Performance inevitably comes to feel like a compromise, a compromise which is blamed on the audience. But musicians are also, in my experience, surprisingly quick to accuse each other of 'prostituting' themselves, whether by following the whims of an employer, an audience, or a market" (1996: 54). The stakes attached to distinctions between legitimacy and what is today called "selling out" were significant, especially in terms of cultural capital, professional status, and personal attitudes within the distinct contexts of musical artistry. The pressure to add "corn," "novelty," or "a bit of business" to televised musical performances created the grounds for conflict and dispute about musical integrity. The result was a change in the relational status between those musicians perceived as maintaining integrity (the "serious artists") and those regarded as commercial hacks who stooped so low as to wear funny hats.

"Funny hats" was quickly adopted as a formal discourse in the music business to discuss visually excessive musical performances and slapstick comedy routines that, after 1948, were regularly oriented toward television. For example, the bandleader Fred Nagel was disparaged in *Down Beat* in December 1948 for embarking on a new stage act replete with "straw hats, firemen's hats, all kinds of hats," as well as employing fake beards and false noses in comedy skits intended to boost his band's visual profile for television. Nagel's turn toward "gags" and "gimmicks" and his willingness to adopt "what many dance band and jazz musicians scornfully call a funny hat routine" marred his reputation among his peers, leading *Down Beat* to comment that Nagel was not a "name" bandleader and was not, by implication, anyone to be taken seriously ("Will Funny Hats Be Savior?" 1948: 3).

The discourse of "funny hats" persisted: in June 1949 it was reported, "Lionel Hampton is preparing for the Era of Funny Hats" when the agile percussionist and vibraphone virtuoso overtly reoriented his act for television broadcast appearances ("Look Out!" 1949: 2). In 1950, Freddy Martin stated that, among the young amateurs to be auditioned on his new TV show *Band of Tomorrow*, "versatility and *telegenity* (!) will count as much as musical ability," with the addition of funny hats and other performance trappings such as "monologs, tumbling, card tricks — anything that can be projected over television" ("'Band of Tomorrow'" 1950: 6). Though Martin later recanted, the damage was done, and his comments were derisively repeated in several subsequent instances.[23]

With so much importance placed on TV's performance element, executives in the broadcasting and music industries depended on musicians to offer aesthetic concessions and make compromises, often pressing them to modify their performance styles as the television sector developed. Extant corporate memoranda suggest that inflexible musical artists — those with either a reluctance or inability to accommodate the television industry's particular visual demands and the call for funny hats — were at times criticized and more harshly judged by network executives than were those deemed to be appropriately compliant. The willingness among some musicians to acquiesce to network authority and relinquish their performance autonomy was regarded by TV's chiefs as a positive attribute, demonstrating what Frith identifies as a desirable "collaborative potential" and a sign of "professionalism" (1996: 60). Simply stated, TV production processes demanded revised attitudes and alternative methods of preparation, rehearsal, and performance for musicians seeking opportunities in the new medium. Those who resisted might be commended by their fellow musicians for holding to a certain standard of performance quality and musical integrity, but they might also find fewer performance options on television.

Although TV's executive and production cadre emphasized the visual aspect, not all musicians felt compelled to fully integrate the skits and jokes of the funny hat set. Some of television's most successful musical program hosts never strayed far from a straightforward performance style, generating strong viewer loyalties without embellished mannerisms or excessive visual humor. With only the occasional digression toward comedy skits and over-the-top visual humor, show hosts such as Perry Como, Eddie Fisher, Frankie Laine, Tony Martin, Dinah Shore, and Jo Stafford won accolades for their comparatively reserved performances. Their production and performance styles distinguished them from their peers who were associated with the stalwart theatrical traditions of Broadway's Great White Way or broad vaudeville histrionics. Not that that these artists were without a sense of humor, but they usually avoided cavorting before the camera, instead plumbing the subtle nuances of gesture whether it was via a slight smirk, a gentle snapping of the fingers, or a light kick of the heel on the upbeat.

Emphasizing the "relaxed" presentational style featured on Como's fifteen-minute, thrice-weekly CBS program in 1951, *Down Beat* described the broadcast as featuring "strictly music. No acts, no dramatics" (Niccoli 1951d: 4). Como explained the differences between his half-hour and fifteen-minute programs noting that the former exacted added unwanted pressures for comedy turns and novelty numbers: "When I had a half hour show I died a thousand deaths. A half hour show calls for funny hats and I'm not funny" (Como 1953: 3). The "sweet" or "easy" song selections and "casual," "relaxed" TV performances with which Como, Shore, and many other singers are associated still stand as the pinnacle of television's so-called Golden Age.

Framed within contexts of authenticity, musical sincerity, good taste, and seriousness some musicians openly espoused a preference for performance styles that reflected their artistic integrity. For them, the new industry conditions contributed to a resolute stance that musical principles should not—indeed, *must* not—be sacrificed for television's image needs. It was their view that an ill-considered foray into television with its intense demand for novelty might undo years of hard work, damaging their reputations with their fans and undermining their status within the profession. Television presented another front in the battle between art and commercialism, and musicians who committed themselves to the music could not be accused of surrendering their values—of selling out—and they watched in awe as television's trend toward novelty tunes and comedy skits accelerated.

Some musicians, such as Ray Anthony, Bing Crosby, and Guy Lombardo, actually earned respect among their peers—if not necessarily among their accountants—for initially rebuffing the lure of the television networks. They were suspicious of offers of broadcast exposure and lucrative contracts that were accompanied by expectations of acquiescence to the medium's visual demands.[24] Resistant musicians argued that audiences deserved better than the novelty and comedy promoted on television. Acknowledging the difficulty of finding a suitable performance balance, *Down Beat*'s editors warned that the only thing worse than an "absolute lack of enthusiasm on a bandstand" is the opposite, "a form of manic hyperaction for which there is no apparent motivation, accompanied by foolish grins, sometimes half-apologetic, bad jokes, and worse costumes" ("Not Every Man" 1951: 10).

Artists attempted to establish such a balance, navigating between novelty and legitimate musical performances, advancing with the belief that the two were not mutually exclusive. It was reported in early 1949 that the Chubby Jackson orchestra, with "an eye cocked on television prospects," was also adopting a "funny hats" routine that included "a 13-piece crew with an additional three men to work on novelties. The latter are actors who'll hold dummy horns and work on special effects and do lines with Chubby between numbers." Jackson attempted to "keep the musical standards at the highest," with the bandleader admitting in a fascinating statement, "I have two idols . . . Charlie Chaplin and Charlie Parker" ("Chubby Rehearses" 1949: 1). Without explicitly commenting on issues of artistic integrity, it is clear that Jackson attempted to find a middle way through a tangle, seeking an acceptable balance whereby the visual antics on the bandstand might provoke humor without detracting too much from the ensemble's genuine musicality.

Jackson's strategy of incorporating trained comedians into his act is unique for the lengths to which it goes toward maintaining the integrity of his band and protecting his musicians from the taint of television's thrust toward funny hats. The band members, of course, were not expected to sit idly by as the comedy ensued but were predictably drawn into the antics between numbers. Yet Jackson tried to ensure that his band members remained musicians first and foremost while guaranteeing that the funny hats routines and other novelty pieces were placed firmly in the hands of comedy professionals who could execute the humorous passages with professional aplomb. Announcing the launch of the Kirby Stone Quintette program, *It's Strictly for Laughs*, in a November 1949 press release, CBS enunciated the symmetry between authentic musicianship and humor, defining the forthcoming show as featuring music "with a sense of humor but without the usual funny hats, checkered suits and seltzer bottle-in-the-face technique" ("Television News from CBS" 1949).

The bandleader Harry Ranch, whose stage show and repertoire regularly featured novelty tunes and visual comedy skits, articulated his frustration as musical acts pushed ever further toward the comic realm. He very much wanted to maintain his band's musical integrity by framing the humor in a predominantly musical context, stating in 1951, "Scratch a musician, even the serious ones, and you find a comic. What I wanted was good musicians first of all, but they had to have a strong flair for comedy" (Freeman 1951: 13). Ranch perceived that his accent on "serious" musicianship with the occasional novelty tune was being challenged by the television industry's emphasis on bold comic humor. He complained, "Most of the time there's no real comedy and no music either. The funny hats boys have ruined it for those of us trying to lay down good music with a sense of humor thrown in" (ibid.).

Many musicians embarking on television careers articulated what Frith describes as "the threat of the ultimate embarrassment: the performance that doesn't work" (1996: 214). The consensus was that a weak or stumbling performance in front of a nightclub or theater audience was unfortunate but not necessarily devastating; a lame, contrived, or embarrassing performance broadcast live to an unseen audience of millions was potential career suicide. The negative effect was exacerbated with the gradual rise of a knowledgeable press whose concise television reviews and critical commentary were printed in daily newspapers, music magazines, and TV journals, extending the potential range of damage as the word of embarrassing performances circulated into the public realm.

Embarrassment surfaced on several occasions as a definite cause of concern within musical circles. Under an editorial headline in 1951 reading "Not Every Man a Comedian," the editors of *Down Beat* remarked that the televised skits and comedy gags executed by musicians might deliver short-term audience attention and adequate remuneration, but the accompanying potential for broadcast errors and performance missteps remained high. As the column claims, with the increasing emphasis on comedy, "the audience is embarrassed by the evident embarrassment of the musician" ("Not Every Man" 1951: 10).

These two, coterminous embarrassments — that of the audience and that of the musician — are not, however, of precisely the same nature. The audience may feel something resembling embarrassment for the musician who ineptly executes a funny hats routine, but the musician is actually experiencing an embarrassment that borders on humiliation or shame. Shame acknowledges a deeper transgression involving the acknowledgment of a proper ethical stance that has been subverted. For the "serious" musician faced with the demand for a humorous TV performance, the abandonment of what he or she knows is right may push the individual beyond mere embarrassment into the realm of disgrace and, accordingly guilt.[25]

The pianist Stan Freeman offers a case in point. Freeman was, at age seventeen, "the youngest faculty member at the Julius Hartt School of Music in Hartford, CT" (Simon 1950: 30). His experience among top musicians included stints in the Glenn Miller and Tex Beneke orchestras, preparing him well as a professional performer. Yet on television he was aware that the entire performance hung on his ability to project an easygoing character, get out a few gag lines, and otherwise demonstrate his musical talent with panache. Exuding confidence in his musical talents and his ability to execute his repertoire with aptitude and good taste, he nonetheless expressed doubts about his nonmusical comedy skills. For him, the desire to avoid humiliation — at the very least — became an objective as he took his first steps in the new medium.

Kay Dickinson's critique of the industrial appropriation and exploitation of musical labor is relevant here as she describes the issue of "mismatches" or failed film-music collaborations: "Mismatches disclose more fully ... how musicians, like film stars, balance upon the knife edge between autonomy (they are seen as the primary site of what is produced in their names) and becoming commodities (selling out, compromising, essentially becoming something that is traded, rather than 'just themselves')" (2008: 177). Freeman voiced his frustration in surrendering to the TV director's request for something humorous to accompany the broadcast of his solo performances, stating, "Even though I'm doing it myself, I don't think it's a good thing ... as a musician, I won't play badly. If I can play well and surround that with comedy I don't feel that I'm compromising as a musician" (Wilson 1950a: 4).

In another interview, Freeman distinguishes between his roles as a musician and as a TV entertainer, explaining that his appearances on NBC's *Candlelight Revue* required a performative lift that he then included as a standard element of his nightclub repertoire (Simon 1950: 31). Yet his descriptions of his situation — an attempted justification, really — harbor a latent begrudging attitude toward television, with Freeman hinting at a forced compliance and his sense of shame. His plaint understates the fact that new performance standards encompassing novelty numbers and visual slapstick were institutionally defined by broadcasters and imposed upon mid-range talent such as he. While he was apparently well paid for his performances, as hired labor he was also required do the bidding of his employer, risking embarrassment and shame.

The anguish in trying to plot a course between serious musicianship and television comedy led to Freeman's further lament, "It's too bad that you can't sit in front of a TV set and listen to good pianists such as Lennie Tristano or George Shearing instead of people who play with their feet like Sonny Kendis or Vincent Lopez" (Wilson 1950a: 4). Many musicians described this conundrum as they contemplated the extent to which they would participate in production numbers and perform in funny hats routines and, thus, risk public embarrassment. Even though Freeman stated, "I still don't plan to lose my integrity" (Simon 1950: 31), a photograph of him seated at his piano with a sad-eyed hound at his elbow, reveals that, for all his desire to maintain a professional profile as a serious musician, his act had already gone to the dogs, succumbing to television's unrelenting order for humorous or visually enhanced performances.

5

Music in a "Sepia" Tone

*

Early television programming spanned multiple forms and genres and featured performances by a broad cultural cross-section that always encompassed African American artists in some capacity. It is a common (and accurate) assertion, however, that black actors were generally underrepresented in early television and when portrayed they were often relegated to secondary positions, cast in diminished roles as support players, or portrayed in subservient roles as domestics or menial laborers, mainly in broadcast drama or situation comedies. The controversies associated with the televised version of *Amos 'n' Andy*, airing on CBS television between 1951 and 1953 (Ely 1991; MacDonald 1992; Hilmes 1997; Bogle 2001; Doherty 2003; Pondillo 2005), and, to a lesser extent, Beulah, on ABC between 1950 and 1953 (Bogle 2001; Pondillo 2005), helped to focus the critical debates about race and representation on early television. These programs remain of crucial relevance in the contemporary study of race and TV broadcast history, yet they also often obscure other important facets of black representation in television's nascent phase.

A distinction is in order here; while black actors surely fared poorly in dramatic roles and on the early situation comedies, surviving television program tapes and contemporaneous press reports reinforce the fact that black musicians were regular and prominent participants in early television. There are significant differences between the status of actors seeking roles in dramatic presentations and that of musicians seeking access to the many variety shows and music-oriented productions; in the latter case, the process involved a different set of priorities. Early TV had the power to deepen and reinforce prevailing stereotypical representations of black artists, but it did not do so in a singular or uniform manner. The representational structures, framing, narrative forms, and genre formats each constitute an influential factor in the character and content of early television programs and performances.

This is to say that it is impossible to draw simple equivalence between, for example, a top dramatic actress on the scale of Hattie McDaniel performing as a domestic on a scripted program such as Beulah and Louis Armstrong appearing as himself in a loosely organized skit alongside Frank Sinatra on *The Frank Sinatra Show* or the comedy team Bud Abbott and Lou Costello on *The Colgate Comedy Hour*. While McDaniel was heralded for her excellent thespian talents and her professionalism, the role itself must be taken into account within the contexts of history, as must Armstrong's endearing television persona. McDaniel's artistry was, in her early 1950s TV role, interpreted through her performance as the reliable house servant, a timeworn role that was standard in literary novels and stage and movie scripts. Indeed, McDaniel's enduring reputation is based on her amazing stagecraft and the capacity to elevate any role through her dignified and thoroughly expert enactment.

Armstrong's was, on the surface, a more literal performance of artistic subjectivity, and he was often typecast as a musician or a bandleader. This naturalistic component, which was not dissimilar from the scripted material that Sinatra worked within on his 1950–52 show, offers a testament to Armstrong's powerful persona, suggesting that his outsized personality and celebrity status were, by the 1950s, difficult to contain within a script. Krin Gabbard (1996) analyzes the ways that Armstrong negotiated the institutional forces of a racist society and the corporate forces of the entertainment industry as well as navigating the realm of public opinion.

As Gabbard explains, Armstrong was always performing in some capacity (even if it meant inhabiting the role of Louis Armstrong, musical luminary and star of stage and screen) every time he raised his trumpet to his lips or opened his mouth to sing. Yet his TV roles, like his film roles during this period of his career, usually involved some element of self-representation, performing a version of the musical artist named Louis Armstrong.[1] His performances were interpreted differently by black and white audiences as well as between younger and older black musicians, and while he may have come across as obsequious or as a conformist to his critics, he was also regarded as a wily and talented showman who was in control of his career and the definition of his public persona.

Black musicians on early television were exceptional in many ways; they were generally depicted as being debonair and beautiful and, framed within television's staged opulence, they were also often quite far removed from the everyday realities of most citizens, either black or white. Many musical performances were set in opulent showrooms or other realms of elite privilege (although such settings were almost exclusively oriented toward white patronage, except on programs featuring all-black casts). Broadcast into the homes of the majority white TV-viewing audience, black musicians were also safely accessible and eminently consumable, especially when surrounded by lavish stage sets or other signs of affluent sophistication. Black musicians were presented in sharp contrast to the subservient role of the female domestic or the male servant on TV's drama or comedy programs or to the representation of subordinate working-class laborers. They were often portrayed in a constructed environment that conveyed elite privilege, performing while surrounded by the trappings of a bourgeois lifestyle.

The prevailing expectations through the 1930s, 1940s, and early 1950s maintained that an actor would inhabit a scripted role and, in character, articulate values and sensibilities associated with his or her race and culture. Few scripts, of course, were actually created by black writers, and black directors infrequently helmed programs, with only a few doing so in regional markets or on independent TV stations. Racial stereotypes and disrespectful portrayals of blacks were written and directed primarily by whites, most of whom were disinclined to correct the erroneous content. Musicians, however, were held to slightly different standards of representational responsibility. They were expected to perform their selections ably and with finesse, perhaps engaging in brief repartee with a show's host and, occasionally, joining in the scripted dialogue. In the case of televised music, black artistry was actively sought and, for the most part, presented respectfully to television audiences.[2]

Television, of course, inherited many of the practices established in radio broadcasting and as a cultural institution it also reproduced elements of corporate institutional authority, manifesting them in program content and hiring patterns. Issues of race and racism that had surfaced throughout the 1920s and 1930s continued well into the television era, at times following a rather straight trajectory, at other times displaying historically inflected idiosyncrasies. It is therefore helpful to revisit corporate radio broadcasting in the period prior to television's emergence as a commercially viable medium in order to discern how race and musical performances were approached from an institutional perspective and how the networks' institutional practices gradually adhered to television. While NBC figures prominently in this discussion it is safe to assume that many of the phenomena ascribed to NBC in the 1920s–1950s also pertain to the other networks as they developed their own television broadcast capabilities and their corporate racial policies.

Black Music and Early Broadcasting: NBC before TV

In a letter addressed to "R.C. of America" in 1926, NBC's first year of operation, Mrs. Charles F. Reid, a self-described "ardent radio fan" from Baltimore, Maryland wrote about her experience while tuned in to a featured performance by a popular singer of the day, Wendall Hall:[3]

> Tonight, having a number here to hear the Victor Concert which we enjoyed, we were very much humiliated by having Mr. Hall refer to our race (Colored) as Darkey, after I had just told them of his exceptional ability as a broadcasting artist. . . . This word Darkey is considered a slander to us, which I do not think is sanctioned by you. An explanation will be much appreciated to show those present that such is not to be expected in the future from station W.J.L.

The letter offers an indication of early radio listeners' critical reception skills and agency, displaying a willingness to act on their own behalf to challenge or reprimand the broadcast networks for perceived breaches in good taste and propriety. The writer's respectful tone notwithstanding, the letter also identifies a serious issue that would hound the broadcast networks for the next several decades as executives struggled to devise consistent policies on racial representation in radio and, later, television broadcasting.

Despite David Sarnoff's noble claims about the educational, artistic, and cultural virtues of radio broadcasting, NBC and the other network broadcasters were inured by years of social conditioning, producing the grounds for racial insensitivity and, at times, outright bigotry in radio content. Underscoring this were the blackface exploits expounded by minstrel and vaudeville acts. Many early radio entertainers introduced minstrel skits to the airwaves, extending conventional blackface performances that depicted woeful or blissfully ignorant southern blacks and a host of other stereotypical identities. Freeman Gosden and Charles Correll, for example, first broadcast their successful creation *Amos 'n' Andy* on the Chicago radio station WMAQ in 1926, airing nationally on NBC in 1929. Although the program appealed to white and black audiences alike, it was not unvaryingly accepted (numerous black organizations and irate listeners expressed their opposition to its stereotypical characters), spurring heated debates about the dilemmas of racial representation and listening pleasures in American broadcasting (Ely 1991).

As radio broadcasting developed through the 1920s, traditional vaudeville was in sharp decline, and by the decade's end most of the major theaters were combining vaudeville with feature film presentations. Faced with declining professional prospects, many vaudevillians took their acts to the radio airwaves, giving them a new performance venue and huge audiences. The radio historian Susan Smulyan relates how comedians and performers arriving in radio from the vaudeville stage "lacked experience with the restrictions imposed on home entertainment." According to Smulyan, "Broadcasters worried that while theater audiences might be willing to listen to vulgarity and ethnic humor in vaudeville houses, radio listeners would not want such subjects, language, or performing styles in their living rooms" (1994: 120). Vaudeville's success had long relied on tweaking the norms of social propriety, a custom described by Robert Snyder as "an old practice in nineteenth-century show business—that of establishing a show's claim to refinement before going beyond the boundaries of acceptability" (2000: 132).

In the early 1930s, a rush of Jewish comics and singers converged on the airwaves, bringing with them repertoires featuring broad and often racy skits, many of which centered on urban culture and Jewish identity. Irish comedians and singers, too, were prominent and like their Jewish counterparts their broadcast humor frequently turned "blue," inflected by years of fulfilling the expectations of vaudeville patrons and working for the broad laughs of the urban audience. Program monitors for NBC maintained special vigilance over artists whose backgrounds in vaudeville influenced their irreverent content and lent them what some regarded as an aggressive style of delivery.

The radio networks were at this stage still defining themselves as corporate entities and their executives wrestled with programming issues in their effort to balance engaging content with the dominant values of social acceptability. With network radio gradually penetrating the American heartland, some regional radio managers grew concerned that the raw urban (and ethnic) character of many of its rising broadcast stars might offend, confuse, or otherwise fail to appeal to rural audiences who had rather different cultural backgrounds and social mores. Broadcasters also recognized vast regional differences in the parameters of social tolerance relating to race. The networks remained especially cautious in dealing with the prevailing racial predispositions of their southern white listeners who were perceived as being less accommodating of sympathetic renderings of black characters or who defended the discriminatory lyrics of "coon songs" and the potent presentation of blackface minstrelsy. As radio program managers learned, fulfilling the divergent tastes and demands of America's vastly heterogeneous population was virtually impossible.

The early intent of NBC to sanitize its broadcast content is apparent in numerous internal corporate memoranda from the early and mid-1930s, suggesting that the network executives were conscious of the potential negative impact of airing offensive or objectionable material. For instance, in a 1932 memo sent by John F. Royal, NBC's vice president of programming, to Bertha Brainard in the network's Program Department, Royal explains, "It is imperative that from this date on no remarks of questionable nature be permitted in our continuities. . . . [R]adio got its great start by giving clean, wholesome entertainment . . . and we must stop material in bad taste."

Royal was undoubtedly referring to radio broadcasts of vaudeville-style comedy routines and musical numbers; prior to his career at NBC, Royal had himself occupied a managerial role in the Keith-Albee vaudeville theater chain (Gilbert 1940; Bergreen 1980), offering him a keen insider's perspective on the aesthetics and conventions of vaudeville performance, including minstrel skits and blackface acts. A "radio man" with NBC since 1929 (when he became manager of the Cleveland station WTAM), Royal was appointed vice president in charge of programs at NBC in 1930, whereupon it fell to him to monitor scripts and broadcasts, appraising content and ensuring that general standards of propriety were maintained. In his role as program monitor, Royal articulated the still-evolving distinctions between public and private reception that radio broadcasting enabled and, further, he was instrumental in delineating NBC's early broadcast profile for millions of American home listeners. The network's interpretation of good taste and what was "acceptable" radio fare for domestic reception in the 1930s, it seemed, was to be defined for the public by John F. Royal and employees in the Program Department.

Although there was ample concern about bawdy or lewd sexual humor, NBC's Program Department was also explicitly cautious in its musical programming, remaining mindful of the language and discourses of race, ethnicity, and religion, recognizing that offhanded comments or distasteful song selection could summon the indignation of a large audience bloc. While vaudevillian humor was prone toward risqué jokes and thinly concealed sexual double entendre or toward mirthful narratives about the faults and foibles of Jewish or Irish social relations, it was minstrel skits or song lyrics that most regularly provoked angry responses from black listeners.

The often tactless racial lyrics of Tin Pan Alley and the more insidious "coon song" genre, popular since the late nineteenth century, had survived into the 1930s, emerging as common fare on early radio broadcasts. The "southern songs" (such as "Darktown Strutters Ball," "Mississippi Mud," "My Old Kentucky Home," "Kentucky Baby," "My Curly Headed Baby," or "Way Down upon the Swanee River") and much of the Stephen Foster songbook were deemed the most pernicious as they regularly deployed a host of racial stereotypes, articulated the basic tenets of racial discrimination, and employed explicitly derogatory language referring to black folks in altogether unsavory terms.

In 1934, the network published the NBC *Program Policies and Working Manual* inscribing the basic presentational guidelines for scripts and broadcast content, including the network's stance on lyrical transgressions and racial insensitivity in popular songs. The manual was intended to establish a standard approach to continuity issues in the Program Department and throughout the network, yet there was a notable element of insensitivity in the manner in which the Program Department conducted its own business. Commenting on the network's content and continuity acceptance in 1935, John Royal revealed his own propensity toward racial bigotry even as he attempted to assert the network's new formal policy: "We should eliminate the word 'nigger' wherever possible. Of course, these darkies put a lot of pressure on us and they are sometimes too exacting, and there are certain songs where the word 'nigger' must be used. However, it is wise to cut it out as much as possible" (Royal 1935).

By 1938, NBC reiterated its internal guidelines, distributing a general memorandum to its employees governing racial language and bigoted discourse, particularly relating to the broadcast of popular music: "Please let this serve as a reminder that songs containing the words 'nigger,' darky,' and 'coon,' etc. in the title and lyrics should not be programmed. These always bring complaining letters from negro listeners and if this can be explained to sponsors or program builders they surely will see the wisdom of not including anything on programs which may be offensive to any peoples" ("NBC to Employees" 1938). As this rationale for content monitoring suggests, it was not the commitment to respectful representation of the black citizenry that motivated the network's policy but the dedication to protecting sponsors' interests by circumventing inappropriate content that might stain their corporate or product image. As newspaper reports, internal memoranda, and documented testimony relates, this justification was to dominate at NBC through the 1940s and into the 1950s as television broadcasting evolved.

Race and NBC's "Blue Pencil Specialists"

While the nation recovered from its involvement in the Second World War, there was an intense focus on domestic issues with efforts across various social sectors to repair the tears in the social fabric and to adjust to new cultural realities. The media historian J. Fred MacDonald positions television's emergence within this vital transitional phase in American society: "The politics of postwar America also encouraged many to envision a bright, bias-free future in television. The new medium emerged in the midst of a liberal, reform-minded period in history" (1992: 5). With the Truman administration's progressive racial initiatives resonating powerfully throughout the country, vestiges of federal policy could be discerned in the practices and discourses of the major corporate broadcasters as well.[4]

Thomas Doherty offers perspective pertaining to African Americans on early television: "Within the context of the time, television was a sympathetic, even breakthrough medium for African Americans. Its salutary role in the realignment of American racial attitudes began long before Rosa Parks refused a backseat bus ride in Montgomery, Alabama in 1954.... Like the rhythm and blues beckoning from the radio dial, the siren call of African American culture enticed television" (2003: 71). Doherty's positive emphasis does not align precisely with the many critical readings of early television but this is not to suggest that he is missing the point. Television did present myriad new possibilities for the public portrayal of black subjectivity and despite the realities of racial exclusion or outright misrepresentation, black talent and artistry was also broadcast widely to an unprecedented nation-wide viewing audience. There were, as Doherty asserts, countless new performance opportunities for black actors, dancers, and musicians on the new visual broadcast medium.

With increasing frequency influential organizations such as the NAACP, the National Urban League, and a growing number of locally active groups representing black interests (such as the New York–based Negro Actors Guild or the Coordinating Council for Negro Performers, the latter of which was formed in 1951) raised methodical and vocal opposition to demeaning portrayals of blacks on radio and early television broadcasts. Advocating "Negro" dignity and demanding respectful portrayals of the race, black leaders sustained their criticism of the networks, haranguing NBC (and the other networks), as one internal memorandum suggested, "for a long period of time" about stereotyping in radio drama or the broadcast of songs with objectionable lyrics.

As television programming evolved, the "Negro" press watched developments extremely closely, proving to be adept observers. Press columnists and reporters for such papers as the *New York Amsterdam News*, the *Chicago Defender*, or the *Pittsburgh Courier* celebrated momentous performances by black entertainers and congratulated the networks for respectful depictions of the African American community or, conversely, publicly reprimanded them for repeating the worst transgressions of the radio years.

African American journalists also campaigned publicly for fair and equal treatment within the broadcasting industries, with newspaper columnists emerging in the 1940s and 1950s as influential spokespeople who leveraged their access to public relations executives in the broadcast industry. In his analysis of black performance in American film musicals Arthur Knight (2002) identifies a long and strong tradition of localized press coverage of film actors and musicians, describing a dialogical dynamic whereby artist performances, culture industry trends, and labor issues in the entertainment sector were positioned in relation to the values and interests of the African American community. This pattern of reporting extended to artists appearing on early television.

Serving as a community conscience, Harlem's newspaper of record, the

New York Amsterdam News, reported concerns in June 1948 that the NBC radio program *National Minstrels* might reproduce the racial degradations associated with traditional minstrel performances.[5] The show's producers (the Gale advertising agency) defended the production and its potential audience appeal, stressing that with an all-black cast and careful script oversight, "National Minstrels will be a radio show that they will be proud to associate themselves with," although the reporter suggests with no apparent irony, "The network has no fear that Southern stations will refuse to air the show. The minstrel is 'a natural' to please whites" (Garlington 1948: 14). The minstrel show was also a facet of early television,[6] with national network broadcasts occasionally featuring minstrel vignettes—such as those aired on the October 8, 1950, and October 28, 1951, CBS broadcasts of the *Fred Waring Show*[7]—with regional programs in the South and West maintaining the tradition. Among the latter were the 1948 broadcast of *Mississippi Minstrels* on KTSL-TV in Hollywood, *Dixie Show Boat* on KTLA Los Angeles in 1950 (picked up in September 1950 by the New York station WPIX),[8] and *McMahon's Minstrels* in 1950 and Tiny Stowe's *All Star Minstrels* in 1951, each on the Los Angeles station KTTV.

Of particular interest in the case of *National Minstrels*, however, is the fact that the bandleader Lucky Millinder, the show's host and musical director, was granted special oversight of the program's content, occupying a position as "the person who will check the script or throw out anything he believes to be offensive to Negroes" (ibid.). Millinder's role, referred to colloquially as "Script Policeman," officially falls under the title "Continuity Acceptance," a designation that acquired considerable importance as the networks honed their policies of racial representation in the early 1950s.

The Continuity Acceptance Radio/Television Department at NBC was guided by what were considered to be basic standards of "common sense" and "good taste" as defined in various network manuals and internal memoranda. The department's stated mission was "based on the belief that, by maintaining high program standards, we are in a better position to fulfill our responsibility to serve the public, and at the same time—to build a better advertising medium for ethical advertisers" (*NBC and You* 1948: 30). Continuity Acceptance executives and employees were charged with the responsibility "to negotiate all changes in script material with either the agency for the sponsor of the program in cases of sponsored programs, or pertinent NBC personnel responsible in cases of sustaining material" (ibid.: 31). The work involved evaluating radio and television scripts prior to production, monitoring broadcasts for general appropriateness, ensuring consistency in the application of content standards, and responding to audience complaints about questionable or offensive performances.

The network further defined Continuity Acceptance as "a form of public relations. Its purpose — to create harmony between the advertiser and the radio listener and good will for NBC" (ibid.). Despite this idealistic description, however, Continuity Acceptance was also an apparatus intended to protect the network and its sponsors from audience complaints, organized protests, or law suits; advancing the causes of civil rights and improved race relations were secondary considerations. Doherty explains,

> More stringent than the regulatory authority of the fcc, however, was the dictatorship of the customers eyeballing the goods. As an advertiser-supported medium in embryonic development, television was exquisitely sensitive to viewer protests and product boycotts. Casting the widest possible demographic net possible, the networks strived for '100% acceptability' and assiduously avoided offending any group of potential viewer-buyers, no matter how small in number or eccentric in outlook. (2003: 61)

Referring to himself at one point as a "blue pencil specialist," NBC's Continuity Acceptance manager, Stockton Helffrich, described his work as simple "editing," a process that encompassed the evaluation of programs and, when deemed necessary, the excision of questionable aspects from programs — "blue penciling" — prior to their airing in the attempt at "improvement" for broadcasting "to a family or a home audience" (1950a).[9] In a rather fundamental sense, the blue-pencil work of the Continuity Acceptance department involved censorship and, as Helffrich's reference to the general primacy of domestic reception implies, the editing instinct was initially informed by an underlying set of assumptions about middlebrow sensibilities and an ideological alignment with white middle-class values.

There are numerous examples of the kind and scope of the blue-pencil work at NBC with the rise of television. Correspondence among network executives indicates that the Continuity Acceptance department regularly convened in response to lapses in judgment among the programmers' ranks or when they were called upon to address TV viewer complaints and objections from regional station managers (who were often among the most vocal critics of network broadcasting emanating from the larger urban centers); many of the issues the department dealt with involved music broadcasts. In early 1950, a series of memoranda circulated between Helffrich, Jack Hein, and a longtime programming employee, Edna Turner, pertaining to the January 31 broadcast of *The Old Gold Amateur Hour*, hosted by Ted Mack. Amateur programs proved to be among the most integrated of television fare in the medium's nascent phase, presenting the prospect of a large black viewing audience (and providing a career springboard for promising black talent). At issue in this instance was the broadcast performance by a white amateur contestant, "a farmer from upstate New York," whose rendition of "Without a Song" included a lyrical reference to "darky's" [*sic*].

In his message, Helffrich explains that NBC was taking a hard-line approach to derogatory language and racial "epithets," noting his dismay that the lyrical passage had aired at all since the production notes for *The Original Amateur Hour* clearly indicated that the lyrical phrase "darky's born" should have been substituted with the more neutral phrase, "man's born." Indeed, the program's extant production notes further instruct that another song, "Shine," performed on the same broadcast be similarly amended, excising the term "colored boy." Apprising his fellow executive Hein of the situation and reminding him of the network's "policy on racial considerations," Helffrich states, "You probably don't know that around epithets descriptive of various races and creeds we have had considerable to-do. We carefully delete words like 'mick' or 'kike' or 'coon'" (1950b). The exchange between Helffrich and his colleagues acknowledges a serious concern among the broadcast network's executives, reminding them that nothing less than NBC's public reputation was at stake and protecting it required carefully defined ethical standards and rigorously monitored program content.

In another example of the Continuity Acceptance manager's responsibilities, Helffrich received several letters and memos following Lena Horne's February 1951 appearance on the network's broadcast of *The Colgate Comedy Hour* with its host, Eddie Cantor. Horne was already an established veteran of nightclub and showroom stages and her musical performances were renowned for their energy and enthusiasm. Furthermore, her physical beauty was widely acknowledged, making her an ideal candidate for television's unique visual demands. The *New York Amsterdam News* had enthusiastically reported Horne's January 1951 appearance as "guest hostess" with Sid Caesar and Imogene Coca on NBC's *Your Show of Shows*, a privilege that was granted only to celebrities with sufficient name recognition and proven television experience (Garlington 1951: 23). The paper was equally excited about her forthcoming appearance with Cantor.

Her appearance on *Your Show of Shows* was marked by an initial display of stage jitters and, as Gavin explains, the nervousness that logically accompanies a performance in front of an estimated fifteen million viewers: "Horne was terrified. A photographer snapped her just before air-time, biting her nails as she stared at her script. Coca remembered Horne shaking as she waited to greet the studio audience. TV cameras — and much of America — would scrutinize her every move, and she had just one chance to make good" (2009: 231). There is a submerged sense that Horne's performance carried with it the burden of representation and that her success could be construed as a success enjoyed by all the nation's black citizens and a reflection of their shared achievement; a faltering performance would be their collective failure. The stakes were indeed high, but reviews and commentary afterward declared her performance a stirring triumph.

For his part, despite a persistent "willingness to sing and dance in black-face" (Pondillo 2005), Eddie Cantor was a staunch supporter of American civil rights and could be counted among early television hosts on the national networks (including Steve Allen, Milton Berle, Dave Garroway, Arthur Godfrey, Dennis James, Ted Mack, and Ed Sullivan) who could claim a consistent record of vocally defending the hiring of black artists on their shows. The entertainment trade journal *Variety* noted that Horne's guest turn on *The Colgate Comedy Hour* would coincide with Brotherhood Week and "besides singing, Miss Horne will join Cantor in a pitch on racial and religious understanding" ("Lena on Cantor's TV" 1951). This socially progressive element to the broadcast and her strong rendition of the songs "Where or When" and "'Deed I Do" notwithstanding, Horne's performance received criticism not only for the bold "U-shaped" plunge of her gown's décolletage but also for the robust character of the musical performance. One reviewer commented, "With a gown cut so low that it was probably a good thing she didn't bend over for her bows, she demonstrated that TV is just as much her métier for that uniquely sexy singing as films or niteries" (Gavin 2009: 231).

The NBC network was surely sensitive to viewer complaints about female attire, since the competing network CBS was at the time confronting its own public relations fiasco involving TV Faye Emerson, a TV talk show personality whose dresses instigated something akin to a moral panic. Although Emerson's low-cut décolletage generated considerable consternation, she herself was relatively demure in her style and presentation. Her television role was mainly restricted to interviews and casual chat rather than full-bodied song and dance numbers such as Horne's. Moreover, Emerson was white and, thus, framed within a rather different social system of meanings related to sexuality, allure, and display.

In the view of the assistant general manager at the Philadelphia station WPTZ-TV, Horne's "action and her style of delivery made her performance border dangerously on the obscene" (Tooke 1951). This perspective strays toward a racialized interpretation of Horne's performance, raising stereotypes of the sexualized body of the vivacious black female entertainer. A less ambiguous complaint from a North Carolina attorney reprimanded the network for broadcasting Horne's "immodest display" (which he described as an "outrageous affrontery" unsuitable for his home) while channeling his indignation toward a distinctly racial issue: "This Horne woman may be a good singer but if I am not misinformed she is a woman that married a white man and we still have a large number of states that make such a marriage a crime" (Brown 1951).

Placing the impact and importance of such letters in perspective, Thomas Doherty writes,

> If formal ratings were doubted or discounted, more tangible reactions from viewers were read as scripture. Letter writers, telegram senders, telephone callers, and other unscientific samplings kept the ears of the station managers close to the ground. The general rule of thumb was that for every person who took the trouble to call or write, ten people felt the same impulse. . . . Facing a deluge of vituperative letters — actually facing a trickle — television executives tended to crumble and fold. (2003: 63)

Assessing the broadcast after receiving letters from several more station managers who had professed discomfort with Horne's appearance and were forced to fend off their own viewer complaints, Helffrich (1951) cited NBC's Continuity Acceptance criteria and the requirement for consistently applied standards. He explained that the primary responsibility ultimately fell with the show's director, noting that aesthetic precautions should have been more carefully followed: "I understand now that the daring of the gown, and the excessive cleavage, were noted at the dress [rehearsal]. Some of the shadows accenting Miss Horne's interesting bosom were eliminated by increased lighting, but on the actual show said higher lighting wasn't used *and* Miss Horne added a bit more oomph to her rendition than used at the dress."

As this example of a relatively minor continuity crisis indicates, television created an entirely new set of issues with which to contend within the domain of race and representation. Yet, in maintaining professional standards, the entire broadcasting industry was also obligated to alter or redesign content and programming to accommodate the political and cultural transitions in postwar America, not least of which included race and gender. In this sense, NBC sought to maintain its solid standing as a well-intentioned and socially responsible institution even as it strived to engage new audiences, expand its profits, and reinforce its overall financial status.

Sepia Revues and All-Black Productions

In television's earliest stages, segregated programming was common, leading to the occasional production of what were termed "sepia" revues — musical variety programs comprised of all-black casts — most of which were associated with regional stations and that were, in several cases, extensions of previously established live revues or radio programs. In 1945, for instance, Judy Dupuy cited the sepia revues *Sepia Tones* and *Ebony Escapades* on General Electric's experimental Schenectady TV station W2XB (later WGRB), noting within the language and tenor of the times, "The camera is particularly favorable to Negro performers, catching and projecting their natural rhythm" (1945: 16). In the nation's urban centers, several all-black revues aired between 1949 and the mid-1950s, including *Happy Pappy* on Chicago's WENR-TV, *Sepia* on WFMB-TV in Indianapolis, *Adams' Alley* on the Los Angeles station KLAC, and several other all-black shows airing in the Midwest, Washington, D.C., and the San Francisco/Oakland markets. *Variety* noted in early 1950 that "in recent months as many as 10 all-Negro tele shows have hit the air and one originated in the south" ("Negro Talent Coming Into Own" 1950: 30).

The St. Louis station WAVE-TV featured an all-black revue in 1949, titled *Club Ebony*, which aired on Sunday evenings between 8:30–9:00 p.m.[10] Starring the Odell Baker Quintet (with bandleader Baker acting as a nightclub waiter and program mc) and accompanied by the female blues vocalist Edmona, the male baritone Dabney, and a novelty musical act, the Gutter Pipers, the premier broadcast of *Club Ebony* featured as guest artist Lionel Hampton, who doubled his booking schedule, performing on the TV program and onstage later that evening at the St. Louis nightspot The National. *Club Caravan*, erroneously touted as "the first all-Negro television show in America" (Garlington 1949b: 24), began broadcasts in the spring of 1949 on Newark's WATV, airing each Thursday 9–9:30 P.M. Hosted by Bill Cook and with music by the Grady Hodge orchestra, *Club Caravan* featured vocal groups including The Heatherstones, The Orioles, and The Ravens and solo artists such as Dinah Washington and Milt Bruckner.

S. W. Garlington, cultural reporter for the *New York Amsterdam News*, described the program as "interesting," but he questioned the format, asking, "Why Negroes only? Ed Sullivan and others with TV shows have Negroes on their shows, so why should Bill practice something that looks like jim crow in reverse?" (ibid.). His query challenges station and network executives' lack of commitment to black cultural forms, engaging the issue of onscreen race mixing and cultural miscegenation that was, in the view of bigoted viewers, deemed unacceptable. For a growing number of black culture critics, the "sepia" musical variety shows reflected the timorous character of TV broadcasters who were unwilling or afraid to challenge the tastes and values of a small-minded constituency of white viewers.

In September 1949 CBS launched an hour-long sepia program, *Uptown Jubilee*. The program attracted prominent musical names, and its September 20 broadcast included as guest artists Juanita Hall, Louis Armstrong, and Harry Belafonte, among others, with music provided by the Don Redman orchestra. A popular Harlem celebrity, Willie Bryant, served as the show's host, legitimizing the production for many of New York's black viewers. Bryant was a recognized name, having previously hosted an all-black NBC radio variety program, *Night Life*, in the mid-1940s, and he was closely affiliated with the Apollo Theater on 125 Street in the heart of Harlem, where he often served as master of ceremonies. By the early 1950s, the *New York Amsterdam News* was referring to Bryant as "the unofficial mayor of Harlem," an honorary designation that acknowledged his local heft.

Variety gave *Uptown Jubilee* a favorable review, describing the program as "entertaining," "well paced," and "frequently imaginative," yet it lamented that it was programmed against Milton Berle's new show, *Texaco Star Theatre*, which premiered on September 19, 1949. Displaying an attitude that preceded the practice of strategically competitive programming, the *Variety* report reads, "Whether it's politic to fight one variety show with another remains to be seen. It's unfortunate to the majority of listeners that two high-caliber shows should be opposite each other. . . . CBS has a good vaudeo show—it's just unfortunate that outside influences will determine its network tenure" ("Uptown Jubilee" 1949: 32). In October, the show's name was changed to *Sugar Hill Times*, maintaining the same format as its original incarnation. Initially scheduled for a full hour, it was soon reduced to a half-hour program, a shift undoubtedly influenced by the difficulties of competing against TV's top-rated host, "Mr. Television" (MacDonald 1992: 20).

Like its predecessor, *Sugar Hill Times* featured an impressive talent roster with musical performances by Thelma Carpenter, The Orioles, and Belafonte, although as MacDonald suggests, "These were all competent acts, but none was considered top-rank at the time" (ibid.). With its reduced air time and a scheduling shift (airing every second Thursday at 8:30 P.M., pitting the show against another ratings force, musical quiz show *Stop the Music!*), *Sugar Hill Times* appeared only twice more before cancellation, to the disappointment of Harlem's black TV viewers.

Several "sepia" programs were also produced in Los Angeles during this period. As he had on *Club Ebony* in Indianapolis, Lionel Hampton participated as the main attraction at the launch of KLAC's *Adams' Alley* on September 5, 1949. Hampton performed with six members of his band, reportedly playing for union scale, a move that reflected the program's reliance on major national talent who would perform at base salary out of good will, boosting the program without straining its financial resources. Hosted by Los Angeles DJ Joe Adams, the program adopted a musical variety format featuring what *Down Beat* described as "modern jazz and music for the people" (Emge 1949: 9). *Adams' Alley* also included a seventeen-piece vocal chorus that performed a full gospel number each week as well as singing popular tunes such as "Smoke Gets in Your Eyes."

In 1951, it was announced that the Los Angeles station KTLA was broadcasting "an all-Negro and all female show," *The Cats and a Fiddle*,[11] which was surely a television first while fitting comfortably alongside the station's other progressive musical programs. The promotions for the half-hour broadcast (airing Monday evenings) stated that the film and nightclub veteran Vivian Dandridge (sister of Dorothy Dandridge) would serve as the show's host, introducing "a six-piece combo, girls and female guests" (Garlington 1951: 23) that replicated KTLA-TV's all-girl show featuring the Ina Ray Hutton band. As the jazz trumpeter Clora Bryant recalls, the show, featuring the Hollywood Sepia Tones, of which she was a member, aired only six times in 1951. It was folded due to an inability to secure sponsorship (Tucker 2000: 322; Bryant et al. 1998: 361–62).

There was hope and, ultimately, disenchantment accompanying the 1953 debut of *11:30 Club Mantan* (later titled *11:30 Revue*) on New York's WOR-TV. Announced with much fanfare, the program starred the film and stage veteran Mantan Moreland, with musical performances by Slim Gaillard and the Claude Hopkins ensemble, and several accompanying comedy and dance acts. The "sepia" revue was expected to generate interest among black viewers but WOR-TV woefully misgauged its audience while failing to enforce certain performance standards involving the program host, Moreland. Even after considerable promotional buildup and enthusiastic public anticipation, the *11:30 Revue* received scathing reviews following its premiere broadcast, owing primarily to Moreland's "antiquated buffoonery and clowning" (Webb 1953d: 25).

Alvin Webb, an arts and culture reporter, described how Moreland had inexcusably resorted to the "use of stereotyped dialect that may have earned him quite a few bucks as an eye-rolling, cigar-puffing buffoon in the movie industry, but which certainly will not win many Negro TV viewers over to his side, slowed down the pace of the maiden effort" (ibid.). Despite the show's pluses, including Slim Gaillard's fine performance and the smooth performances by "an interracial four-piece combo with Claude Hopkins at the helm" (ibid.), Moreland's atrocious performance sealed the show's fate. Indeed, Moreland was fired after the first broadcast for ostensibly deviating from the "straight-written script . . . and delivering his lines in the ancient, hackneyed, outdated, 'darkey-comic' format" (ibid.) and no further installments of the program were ever broadcast.

As the Moreland episode indicates, network initiatives to introduce "tasteful" and "respectful" musical variety shows exclusively featuring black program hosts and musical artists were not always sufficient to appease or please black commentators; the critics did not blithely accept just anything. One further instance where the networks' well-intentioned efforts received critical rejection arose in 1953 around the CBS network program *Omnibus*. The March 1953 broadcast of *Omnibus* featured George Gershwin's jazz opera *135th Street*, considered an obscure Gershwin work, with an accomplished all-black cast that included Etta Warren, Lorenzo "Larry" Fuller, Jimmy Rushing, and Warren Coleman along with a fifteen-member dance troupe. Initial interest in the program was partially influenced by the popularity and comparatively highbrow status associated with *Omnibus* and its patrician host, Alistair Cooke. Still, reviewers took issue with the production portraying what was described as a Harlem "dive atmosphere of a basement café during the prohibition days of 1920."

Dismissing the broadcast in a review published in Harlem's *New York Amsterdam News*, one reporter identified the surfeit of stereotypes on display as the presentation's main flaw: "The participants are gin-happy, care-free Negroes with plenty of hip-shaking rhythm in their bodies and no morals in their souls, dance and shoot dice on a full time basis" (Sellers 1953: 13). By the mid-1950s, with the rise of organized civil rights activism across the nation and a more liberal approach to television broadcasting at the networks, "sepia" or "all-black" music programs gradually lost favor and were phased out.

The Issue of Black Musical Program Hosts

Black musical celebrities were commonly featured as invited musical guests on the many musical variety programs in early television. Between 1948 and 1955, the list of television guest artists discussed in papers that primarily served the black community reads like a veritable who's who of classical, jazz, and popular music.[12] In what was fairly typical coverage at the time, the *Chicago Defender* offered a New Year's summary of African Americans who had performed on television, identifying the programs that had favorably presented them as being either "liberal" or "democratic" (Roy 1954).

Guest appearances by black musicians were so highly valued within the major U.S. cities that they often attained event status among the nation's black journalists and audiences. Announcing the August 27, 1949, lineup for the first anniversary broadcast of Eddie Condon's NBC program, *Floor Show*, the Harlem-based writer S. W. Garlington touted the stellar musical roster that included Billie Holiday, Louis Armstrong, and Earl "Fatha" Hines. The show's format was structured around a dramatic narrative with Holiday portraying the famed blues singer Bessie Smith, while Armstrong's performance included him telling a hep children's tale titled "Louis and the Three Bears" (Garlington 1949c: 20).

Although black musicians emerged as a staple on the many early musical variety shows and amateur programs throughout television's formative years, few black artists were ever hired as program hosts. Significantly, even though the broadcast was a one-off presentation during television's experimental stage, the entertainment industry veteran Ethel Waters was featured as a trial host on NBC-TV in 1939. According to Donald Bogle (2001) this technically situates the multifaceted Waters as the first African American to host any television show. Still, the absence of black program hosts on national network programs between 1948 and 1955 cannot be easily squared with the discourse of tolerance, good will, and opportunity expounded among TV network executives who possessed the authority to enact change. Nor is it comprehensible considering the record industry successes and commercial popularity of numerous black musicians in the postwar period.

The paucity of black program hosts on the networks might be conceived as a case of authority denied, for the program host exists as an authoritative figure, directing the proceedings and controlling the program discourse — MC may stand for "master of ceremonies" but it can also be interpreted as "man in charge." This authority was almost exclusively extended to white individuals. The black guest musician, conversely, conforms to a secondary or subordinate position within a racially stratified hierarchy. The guest musician, for all his or her talent and artistry, still serves as a hired hand, accompanying the white host in a supportive role. Such power relations and assigned positions in the new broadcast medium reflect longstanding historical patterns, reinforcing traditional boundaries of authority while diminishing the sense of achievement and possibility among black artists. Thus, even as television evolved as a new and influential cultural institution, it initially failed to alter the established structures of power and authority and maintained prevailing inequities by delimiting the contours of black representation.

There were also some unexpected outcomes with television's inception. *Variety* explained that while all musicians should anticipate upheaval, black musicians were the most likely to be negatively affected by the major TV networks' narrow, racially prejudiced booking patterns. Yet in a curious twist some black acts were well compensated for their ability to fill a growing void in the nightclub sector as television drew away top white talent ("Paradox in TV 'Brush'" 1955: 2). In this regard, television's early biases exacerbated an already existing multitiered salary scale, maintaining industry disparities between black and white musicians, yet the conditions also offered new opportunities among black musicians whose access to nightclubs had previously been constrained.

Some musicians, such as the percussionist and vibraphonist extraordinaire Lionel Hampton, were unambiguous and vocal about their desire to host a regularly scheduled, nationally syndicated program, but the goal eluded him. Like her contemporary Hampton, the vocalist Thelma Carpenter expressed her desire to enhance her profile in television in 1950, citing her television experience that began when the industry was "still so green at the game" ("Pretty Thelma Hoping" 1950: 22). Carpenter had moved through the ranks of several prominent dance orchestras, getting her start with Teddy Wilson in 1939, eventually touring and recording with several of the top bands of the day, including those of Coleman Hawkins, Count Basie, and Duke Ellington. Carpenter was also a regular featured vocalist (1945–46) on Eddie Cantor's *It's Time to Smile* radio show on NBC; as this trajectory suggests, by the end of the 1940s, she was an established veteran of stage and studio with credibility among the nation's broadcast networks.

In a revealing statement, however, Carpenter acknowledged how race and television aesthetics converged, requiring attention and, ultimately, negotiation: "This year . . . I'm going to put up an all-out fight to get a real chance in front of the television cameras. The make-up boys don't even have to worry about toning me down for the cameras, because anyone can see, I'm already brown" (ibid.). This statement, uttered without apparent irony, points to a range of rarely discussed issues confronting black artists: first, the very act of gaining access to the medium involved considerable effort and a degree of strategy and while this is also true for white artists, the stakes and strategies differed across racial lines. Second is the issue of the politics of complexion and the different attitudes toward light- and dark-skinned blacks that Carpenter identifies. Her comment about her complexion articulates a submerged discourse of color politics that positions the comparatively lighter-skinned Carpenter higher in the ranks than her darker-skinned peers. Finally, in the event that a black artist did make it to the screen, various standard production practices (such as lighting or makeup) were generally oriented toward the presentation of whites and were, thus, often ill suited to the portrayal of black performing bodies. Despite her upbeat approach, eagerness, and positive intentions, Carpenter was never awarded her own program and her television prospects did not noticeably improve.

One of the early favorites among New York's black cultural reporters was the musical mainstay Bob Howard (known as "the piano jive bomber") who performed regularly in and around the city throughout the 1940s and early 1950s, occasionally touring in Canada, the United Kingdom, and continental Europe. A stage veteran, Howard had appeared on Broadway in the role of "Pooch" in the 1944 production *Early to Bed* (featuring music by Fats Waller); he appeared in several Soundies musical film shorts and also recorded for Decca in this period as well, releasing titles such as "I'm Painting the Town Red (to Hide a Heart That's Blue)" backed with "I Never Saw a Better Night" (by Bob Howard and His Orchestra) and "Sweet Emalina, My Gal" backed with "On Revival Day" (by Bob Howard and His Boys).

Howard's start in broadcasting came on the independent radio station

Bob Howard. Circa 1950s. COURTESY OF PHOTOFEST.

WHN, where he hosted his own musical program in 1945, and by 1948 he was appearing on CBS radio, hosting a quarter-hour prime-time quiz show, *Sing It Again*, airing on Saturday evenings. His CBS contract facilitated his move into television as the network expanded, where he debuted as host in July 1948, appearing each weeknight in fifteen-minute slots (the show was slightly jostled in the schedule between 1948 and 1950, although it never aired later than the desirable 7:00 slot at CBS).

The CBS television show provided a new visual forum through which Howard extended his reputation as an energetic piano player and effortless raconteur. Notably, although the program lacked a single underwriting sponsor, records show that its advertising base encompassed an A-list of American corporations including Trans World Airlines, Chevrolet and Dodge automobile manufacturers, Esso, Polaroid, Chase and Sanborn Coffee, and almost two-dozen other companies. Sponsor satisfaction with Howard's hosting duties was impressively high, as indicated by letters addressed to him from various corporate sponsors and advertising representatives at Madison Avenue agencies. Sponsors were plainly proud to be associated with the jovial and talented musician in his television endeavor.[13]

As the TV program's sole artist, Howard dominated the proceedings as he had with his radio show, handling both the entertainment and commercial announcements without assistance. With the show's premiere, CBS distributed a press release (cited widely and quoted verbatim in magazines and newspapers at the time) describing the show's creative process, explaining how Howard eschewed rehearsals and prebroadcast planning (with the exception of the network's standard song clearance process) in favor of an informal ad-lib approach that was evidently valued by sponsors and viewers alike. The fifteen-minute broadcast generally included three advertising messages per show with each costing between three hundred and four hundred dollars, generating up to six thousand dollars per week for the network in an era when television was still operating at a deficit. In 1949, *Sponsor* magazine lauded Howard's program, citing his solo effort as a model of economic efficiency that maintained low overhead for the station ("TV Costs" 1949: 58).

Howard's repertoire encompassed novelty and Tin Pan Alley numbers and various blues songs performed in a raucous style (described in newspaper or magazine articles and press releases as being "unorthodox," "unique," "rollicking," "effervescent," or "bouncy"), merging elements of the traditional music hall, the corner pub, and a Harlem rent party. Working from a weekly song list of roughly twenty selections for his daily quarter-hour broadcasts, Howard divided the songs into three general categories — "standards," "pops," and "special material" — to ensure variety, as well as frequently accommodating listener requests that were mailed into the station each week. Indicating his local popularity and profile, enterprising songwriters and music publishers appealed directly to Howard via mail, entreating him to consider their songs for his repertoire, describing in letters their familiarity with the program and his particular musical strengths with "jive," blues numbers, or ballads.

Renowned for his spontaneity (at times improvising lyrics to add a timely or locally relevant inflection), Howard displayed a tendency to deviate from a song to tell a joke or, as one report observed, making the most of the new visual medium with performative flourishes such as lighting a cigar with one hand while continuing to play with the other (Garlington 1949a: 24). Extant production notes reveal an additional feature of the program, the occasional sing-along segment (structured to accommodate viewers' home vocalizing), with songs including such chestnuts as "Baby Face," "I'm Looking over a Four Leaf Clover," "I've Been Working on the Railroad," "Margie," "Tea for Two," and "Till We Meet Again."

In spring 1949, Howard's CBS program was referred to as "the oldest Negro TV show" ("TV High Spots" 1949: 15), but this accolade was trumped in September 1950 when the network announced that Howard "has made nearly 600 consecutive WCBS-TV appearances, something of a record for any TV artist" and that the musical quiz show *Sing It Again*, hosted by Howard on CBS radio, was due to be simulcast on the television network. Despite these network promotions, however, Howard's tenure at CBS ended soon after for undisclosed reasons, and the pianist quickly resurfaced on New York's WOR-TV in February 1951 (where in March 1951 it was announced that he had made eight hundred televised appearances). Howard's show on WOR-TV maintained the same basic program format as it had at CBS, with the new contract demanding a much more rigorous schedule, broadcasting twice daily (at 1:30 P.M. and again at 7:15 P.M.) five days a week.

Among the contemporaneous African American musicians hosting their own musical program on local television were The Southernaires, a gospel vocal quartet that was awarded its own TV show on New York's WJZ-TV. Debuting in the summer of 1948, the group was appropriately slotted on Sundays at 2:30–3:00, but the program did not survive to the end of the year. More successful, however, was Amanda Randolph. Although often overshadowed by her contemporary Hazel Scott, Randolph was the first black female musician to host her own TV show in the postwar era. *Amanda* debuted in 1948 on Du Mont's New York station, WABD; the fledgling television network showed an early willingness to work with black artists prior to the rise of the civil rights movement despite the misgivings of some executives in the broadcasting industry. According to David Weinstein, "Dumont was especially willing to take risks in order to establish the new medium. The upstart network had no history in broadcasting . . . and no preconceptions about popular entertainment" (2004: 186). Another possible motivation for the Du Mont network's willingness to feature black musicians more prominently could lie in the fact that their artist salaries were generally lower than those of their white counterparts and the network was notoriously pressed for both sponsorship revenue and program content. In this assessment, black musicians simply represented a more cost-effective option.

With a long career performing religious and secular music, Randolph's evolution led her from the church to burlesque and vaudeville houses as well as accompanying silent films, playing nightclub engagements, and performing on radio broadcasts. In describing her transition from the church to popular/secular settings, Randolph explained how "it took a little time to get out of the decorous hymn way of playing. But for eight dollars a week, what could they expect — Hazel Scott?" (Garlington 1949d: 17). She acknowledged that while her musical reorientation was driven by economic circumstance, it was also an advantage as television emerged as a new and untested performance environment. Randolph's career was ultimately prone to adjustment and accommodation with television presenting another new situation within which she could display her professional flexibility and her musical talents.

Prior to hosting her own TV show, Randolph had been cast as "Aunt Martha," a musically inclined family maid, on the CBS-TV program *The Laytons* (enacting a character akin to that of Lillian Randolph in the radio, film, and television versions of *The Great Gildersleeve* or Ethel Waters on the popular show *Beulah*). After her sixteen-week turn on *The Laytons*, Du Mont contracted Randolph to help pioneer its daytime programming schedule, where she was first scheduled in the noon-to-12:15 slot, later airing between 10:45 and 11:00 A.M. The *New York Amsterdam News* reporter S. W. Garlington describes *Amanda* as a solo format quite similar to that of *The Bob Howard Show*, with Randolph personally handling the advertising announcements: "Amanda Randolph is herself, chatting, playing the piano, singing a song, giving encouragement — and urging the ladies to go right on working" (1949d: 17).

Despite her musical bonafides, however, Randolph was frequently subject to production decisions that were not particularly flattering and that diverted attention from her musical talents. According to the monthly newsletter, *Television Opportunities*, "On Amanda Randolph's program *Amanda* broadcast daily on WABD, Patsy, N.Y. restauranteur [*sic*], makes his pizza pies in rhythm to music. By the time a musical selection is finished ye pie expert hath pounded the dough, rolled it, applied the tomato paste and cheese, and ovenised it. Amanda plays the piano as the pie taketh shape" (Levey

1949). Another difference between the Randolph and Howard programs is that Randolph also regularly interviewed guests (described as "young people with promising talents and just plain people who, in their own quiet ways are leading interesting and generous lives"), with a particular emphasis on "Harlem residents." The interactive aspect may have introduced an interesting community element to her show, but it also shifted the emphasis away from the music.

After the demise of her eponymous program roughly a year later, Randolph returned to a series of secondary, stereotype roles, appearing (uncredited) as the housekeeper in the acclaimed 1950 Joseph Mankiewicz film *No Way Out* (featuring Sidney Poitier) and as Sapphire's mother on CBS's *The Amos 'n' Andy Show* between 1951 and 1953. In 1953 Randolph was cast in the title role on *Beulah*, succeeding Ethel Waters, Hattie McDaniel, and Louise Beavers (suggesting an unfortunate interchangeability of the black female lead), and in 1955 she again followed Louise Beavers, this time playing the maid Louise on the ABC comedy series *Make Room for Daddy* (starring Danny Thomas), where she appeared for almost a decade.

In February 1950, Randolph's acknowledged professional rival Hazel Scott had her program *The Hazel Scott Show* debut on WABD, airing in the New York market on Wednesday evenings in the 7:45–8:00 slot. As a child, Scott was recognized as a piano prodigy and musical virtuoso. As she developed her skills she acquired a reputation for her unique capacity to "swing the classics," demonstrating real talent across the genres. With a busy nightclub schedule (which, early in her career, included New York's famous Cafe Society, with its nondiscriminatory door policy), Scott was regarded as something of a Harlem institution, a status reinforced by her marriage to the local pastor, activist, and celebrity politician Adam Clayton Powell Jr.[14] Bogle explains, "She represented half of a new kind of Negro couple: educated, cultured, political, outspoken; a modern woman who didn't brook fools easily" (2001: 16). Scott was regularly featured in the entertainment and society columns of the *New York Amsterdam News*, with the arts and culture reporters commonly touting her Hollywood movie roles and discussing her guest appearances on TV programs such as Jackie Gleason's *Cavalcade of Stars*, which was broadcast on the Du Mont network.

In April 1950, *Variety* reviewed the Scott show, approving of its overall structure and musical quality while identifying the host's personal charisma as a major attribute. When so many films and radio broadcasts were casting black actors in relatively submissive or docile roles, as threatening figures, or

Hazel Scott. Circa 1940s. COURTESY OF PHOTOFEST.

in a range of other racial stereotypes, Scott was presented as a sophisticated lady, an urban and urbane exemplar of style and refinement: "Most engaging element in the air is the Scott personality, which is dignified yet relaxed and versatile enough to switch from a reverential spiritual . . . to a sultry torch tune. . . . Setting is a modern room off a penthouse terrace, which provides a vivid opening and closing as the camera pans across the skyline" ("Hazel Scott Show" 1950). The show's success on New York's WABD convinced Du Mont's executives to broadcast it to the entire network, and in June 1950 it began airing three nights weekly, between 7:45 and 8:00.

Even with the positive reception among viewers and sponsors that a renewed Du Mont contract might imply, Scott's identification in the in-famous anticommunist publication *Red Channels: The Report of Communist Influence in Radio and Television* (1950) — Lena Horne and Paul Robeson were other celebrated black singers "listed" in the publication — placed her on the defensive, and her professional career was seriously undermined by the accusations of socialist sympathies.[15] Scott's repudiation of the allegations and her vociferous protest were for naught as Du Mont responded to sponsor anxiety by canceling *The Hazel Scott Show* in late September 1950 rather than confronting the tempest associated with the host. Indeed, over its last months the program actually aired without a sponsor, and Du Mont made little effort to seek new sponsorship or to support Scott through her crisis. In retrospect, the network's denial that the *Red Channels* incident caused the show's cancellation seems disingenuous. According to Bogle,

> The fate of Scott's show indicated even at this early stage that television would flee from any signs of controversy, especially political controversy. But the demise of the *Hazel Scott Show* also indicated something else. Hazel Scott had carried her off-screen image — that of a political/social firebrand — to the little screen. African American viewers watching her were aware of her past and what she might represent for the future, especially during the rise of the civil rights era. (2001: 18)

Several months after Hazel Scott disappeared from the Du Mont program schedule, the *New York Amsterdam News* announced that the pianist Reginald Beane and his trio had signed on as musical accompanists for WABD's *Once upon a Tune*, a musical comedy series ("Reginald Beane Trio" 1950: 26). The Beane trio was a biracial ensemble, featuring the white bass player George Mele alongside the black vibraphonist Tyree Glenn and Beane, but, perhaps more to the point after the Scott affair, the group was comparatively apolitical and, hence, uncontroversial. Beane's musical abilities and experience were also beyond reproach; he had established himself professionally when he accompanied Ethel Waters in 1938, and appearing on Broadway in several productions during the war years before returning to the Waters act. In 1948, Beane had a role as Wesley, the pianist in the Hollywood film *Time of Your Life* (starring James Cagney), and he occasionally appeared on televised dramas, mainly typecast in musical roles.

In 1951, another talented black piano player, Lorenzo "Larry" Fuller, signed a thirteen-week contract with WABD to host the program *Man about Music*, premiering on September 27, airing in a fifteen-minute slot at

10:30 P.M. each Thursday. Fuller brought extensive musical credentials to his Du Mont program, having previously performed with the Kansas City and Yale University symphony orchestras as well as performing as a lead in several successful Broadway musical productions. Along with his television responsibilities, Fuller was also a radio DJ, hosting a daily program on WLIB radio. Fuller's combination of musical and acting skills made him valuable to television producers who coveted artists with extensive stage experience for their Broadway style musical productions.

The vocalist Billy Daniels also signed a thirteen-week contract (with ABC) in 1952 to host a program that was broadcast each Sunday evening. The Daniels program, "the first black show to be broadcast nationally by a single sponsor, the Vitamin Corporation of America for its Rubitol B-complex vitamins" (MacDonald 1992: 20), had an unprecedented reach for a show hosted by a black artist as ABC affiliate stations carried it in some of the largest U.S. markets, including Boston, New York, Philadelphia, Chicago, Denver, Los Angeles, and San Francisco (ibid.: 19). Daniels's biggest hit (and his signature song) was his rendition of the Harold Arlen/Johnny Mercer composition "That Old Black Magic"; so closely was he associated with the song that promotions for an appearance at New York's Copacabana club at the time described him as "that old black magic man." Each fifteen-minute broadcast segment opened with the (possibly self-referential) theme song smoothly crooned by the charismatic Daniels, "That old black magic has me in its spell, that old black magic that you weave so well."

While celebrating the achievements of African American musicians and the few local TV program hosts in broadcasting in the early 1950s, cultural watchdogs continued to question why none of the top celebrities with nationwide recognition and deep experience had been tapped to host a network variety show. Reviews of performances by such demonstrative individuals as Cab Calloway and Lionel Hampton regularly referred to the fact that these artists were already well acquainted with the processes of television production, having made many guest appearances. As musical and television veterans, their entertainment acumen prepared them well for the medium.

Describing a televised appearance by Lionel Hampton in March 1951, S. W. Garlington wrote, "Lionel Hampton's revue over WABD-TV (Channel 5) last Thursday night on the 'Cavalcade of Bands' show proved to be one of the highlights of the week's TV offerings. Not only was Hampton dynamite, but every one of the youngsters in the show were 'on the ball'"

Lionel Hampton. Circa 1940s. COURTESY OF PHOTOFEST.

(1950a: 19). Roughly a month later, Garlington covered Hampton's performance at the New York nightspot Bop City, pausing to reflect on the racial incongruities at play:

> I could not help but think of the fact that if he were white, then he would have a big spot (a commercial spot) on either radio or TV not just as a guest, but as the regular, featured artist. Hamp (and Co.) is the best musical aggregation in the biz. Why hasn't he a commercial spot on radio or TV? Is it because of jim crow on the radio, or because these people (Negroes especially) interested in the Hamp are too stingy to buy time on the air and sponsor the Hamp. What do you think? (1950b: 19)

If Garlington gently raised the matter of television's exclusion of black celebrity music hosts in the pages of the *New York Amsterdam News*, his successor Alvin "Chick" Webb, who became the paper's culture columnist in 1953, was less reticent in his critique.[16] He lashed out at the television industry in several ways, but he reserved special wrath for the networks' refusal to provide program vehicles for the top black music talents. Referring to the need for a "TV Branch Rickey" (a reference to Wesley Branch Rickey, the owner of the Brooklyn Dodgers, who integrated major league baseball when Jackie Robinson first donned the team's uniform in 1947), Webb expressed the belief that "a terrific bonanza awaits the TV company that will hire a Negro performer of the stripe of Sammy Davis Jr., or Timmie Rogers to star in a big-time variety comedy show. . . . Negro Americans await the coming of a genuine television Messiah who will make the channels of this great industry a real sounding board for a democracy that can work" (1953a: 28).

Webb's reference to Branch Rickey was timely; in January 1953, NBC announced that Jackie Robinson would lead the WNBC-WNBT Music Foundation, a new nonprofit agency, as the director of community activities. With funds administered by NBC, the foundation's stated goals were to "provide record players and records of all the major labels and speeds . . . to all organizations that require them," concentrating on facilities serving "the poor, the elderly, or the infirm" ("Jackie Robinson to Direct" 1953; "New NBC Music Foundation" 1953: 3).

Michael Omi and Howard Winant explain how, in the postwar era, African Americans intensified their political analyses and honed their cultural critique, expanding "the concerns of politics to the social, to the terrain of everyday life" (1994: 96). Television and popular music were clearly situated within the vernacular realm of the everyday, but each was critical to what Omi and Winant refer to as "the great transformation" within racial politics. They suggest that such transition required "an ideological or cultural intervention, the politicization of black identity, the rearticulation of black collective subjectivity. It was this change which would eventually place radical objectives on the agenda of racial minority movements" (ibid.: 98). Webb's critical expression and sharp rebukes of the broadcasting industry and the major television networks in the *New York Amsterdam News* were exemplary of this transformative moment.

Like others working in virtually every cultural sector at the time, Webb called for direct confrontation with the broadcast and entertainment industries, expressing sensibilities associated with the emergent civil rights movement. By mid-1953 not only was he openly critical of the racially exclusionary programming policies of the major networks but he also derided the "passive resistance" methods of the Negro Actors Guild and the Council of Negro Performers, which he believed were weak and ineffective in their dealings with the TV broadcasters. Advocating "militant action" against both the television and theater sectors (1953b: 25) Webb repeatedly encouraged readers to call or write letters directly to the television stations, networks, and program sponsors, demanding the desegregation of the small screen, culminating in threats of a massive Negro boycott if the situation was not improved.

Defying any notion of a univocal response to blacks on television, other voices took a softer stance on the situation. Webb's aggressive approach was offset by a January 1954 article in the *Chicago Defender* that displayed a much more conciliatory tone. Citing a list of black musical and thespian talents who had appeared on television through 1953, the reporter Rob Roy acknowledged, "There is no question but that the latter artists handled themselves spectacularly. It is also a known fact that any one of the artists would have been a hit on his own show" (1954). Rather than confronting the broadcasting institution and attacking the executive decisions that maintain black musicians' secondary status, however, Roy praised the democratic principles and liberal attitudes of a handful of white program hosts. The *Defender* seemed comparatively content to celebrate programming that offered black artists "the crumbs," whereas Webb (like the Coordinating Council for Negro Performers) forcefully called for the equitable dispensation of industry "plums."

Among members of the black press at the time there was a common acceptance that CBS — not NBC — was the more progressive broadcast corporation when it came to race relations. As it was doing in the technical and programming realms, NBC aggressively sought to vanquish its industry competitors (especially CBS) by revising its race policies and embarking on an initiative to establish closer working relations with the nation's black communities. To achieve its goals, NBC hired Joseph V. Baker, a public relations expert from Philadelphia, seeking his assistance in navigating the potential pitfalls of black representation in radio and early television and ensuring greater interaction between NBC's executives and America's increasingly influential black leadership.

Baker was regularly called upon to evaluate potentially offensive scripts and to assist in responses to outraged, bigoted TV viewers, essentially bearing the burden of representation for the entire NBC network. Among Baker's main achievements during his 1950–54 tenure at NBC was the "Integration without Identification" policy, advocating the assignment of dramatic roles to blacks. His agency also served as "blue pencil specialists," specifically vetting song lyrics and other script content for derogatory or racially insensitive language and he was a constant presence in discussions involving network hiring practices for technicians and other production positions (Forman 2007). The other networks were aware of NBC's progressive initiatives involving the Baker agency as they, too, attempted to integrate their programming schedules and workforce.

There was a hint of progress in mid-1953 when it was announced that Sammy Davis Jr., having hit his stride as a multitalented performer with the Will Mastin Trio, had signed a television contract with ABC to host his own program (Webb 1953c: 26). Davis and the Mastin Trio were the first black act to perform at the Copacabana in 1952 (at Frank Sinatra's recommendation), following the club's desegregation, and they accumulated a ream of TV credits by 1954, appearing frequently on such top-rated shows as *The Colgate Comedy Hour* and *The Ed Sullivan Show*. But by April 1954, the network had still done nothing to produce a vehicle showcasing Davis's talents, and Webb expressed his doubts about ABC's commitment to developing a show around Davis despite assurances from ABC's vice president of programming and talent, Robert Weitman, who denied rumors that southern advertisers and affiliate stations were resistant to the notion of airing a show hosted by a black man.

As Weitman explained, the Davis show was actually planned with an "all-Negro" cast, which would not be deemed as reprehensible to southerners as would a program featuring a mixed cast (Webb 1954: 24). Rather than assuaging the critics' complaints about ABC's compliance with southern racial tenets as his comments were intended, Weitman's stated rationale seemed instead to confirm critics' fears of network concessions to both southern viewers and nervous sponsors. Weitman had obviously caved to the pressure of so-called southern sensibilities.

In 1954 Davis was seriously injured and lost his left eye in an automobile accident, surely complicating the ABC deal. Despite its seriousness the incident did not hamper his recording or nightclub career, and upon his recovery Davis returned to an active roster of club, theater, and film dates as well as appearing as a guest on various television variety shows in preparation for a career as a solo artist. Mirroring the ABC-Davis negotiations, it was also announced in 1954 that NBC had an expressed interest in developing a program around the handsome and versatile singer Harry Belafonte following excellent reviews of his appearance on Ed Sullivan's *Toast of the Town* the previous March. This program stalled as well.

Near the end of 1955, with no noticeable movement from the networks on either the Davis or the Belafonte program, Webb again decried the networks' failure to embrace black program hosts:

> The same blank wall of frustration applies to other Negroes, including Lena Horne Dorothy Dandridge, Billy Eckstine, Duke Ellington, Ethel Waters, Marian Anderson, Pearl Bailey, and Harry Belafonte. Television will throw them a bone from time to time, but the meat, a program of their own, remains hidden away in the deep freeze of intolerance. . . . Since the Lord has gifted certain humans with rare artistic abilities the viewing public is being cheated of many hours of enjoyment until such a time as these personalities are starred in the regular lineups, not in the role of pinch hitters. (1955: 18)

The Belafonte show never did air, and though Davis's ABC venture failed to materialize, he did finally host his own variety show on NBC in January 1966, over a decade after reaching his prime as an artist.

Musicians, Miscegenation, and "Southern Sensibilities"

Whereas gaining access to the television airwaves constituted an ordeal for top black musicians, staying on the air was a trial of another kind. Even with their widespread presence on the small screen, black singers and musicians mainly performed among white artists for a majority white studio and viewing audience. Television was shifting away from the public viewing contexts associated with bars and taverns by the early 1950s, evolving as a domestic medium that privileged middle-class status and white cultural values. In this regard, Herman Gray's emphasis on the issues of labor, performance, and spectatorship are well considered: "In the televisual world of the early 1950s, the social and cultural rules of race relations between blacks and whites were explicit: black otherness was required for white subjectivity; blacks and whites occupied separate and unequal worlds; black labor was always in the service of white domesticity" (1995: 74–75). As this implies, black bodies on television were, ultimately, subjugated bodies, objectified and commodified within the TV networks' industrial contexts for the viewing consumption of a predominantly white mass audience.

The caustic attitudes of southern whites, operating according to traditionally sanctioned systems or illegal — but generally accepted — racist practices, remained a matter of concern for the New York networks and their sponsors. The divide between North and South was often rendered most palpable through the cultural forms of the arts and entertainment sectors, where the friction of difference and disdain generated the most heat. The geocultural influences of urban life in broadcast centers such as New York, Chicago, or Los Angeles greatly impacted the content and character of television programming, contrasting sharply with local and regional attitudes and practices. These were, after all, large cities that were prone to greater degrees of racial intermingling if not yet full integration. But in many instances, the networks seemed willing to compromise black artists and audiences simply to avoid confrontation with white supremacists in the South: "Despite the argument that the specter of the 'white Southern market' was actually a myth, to the entertainment industry it was a reality. TV executives and advertisers feared alienating the white consumer in the South" (MacDonald 1992: 20).

Throughout radio's development, NBC and CBS in particular had become highly cognizant of the complexities of "southern sensibilities," fielding complaints from southern white racist viewers while attempting to minimize offensive and potentially damaging broadcasts. The networks were caught in a bind, attempting to tap into the increasing wealth of the nation's black consumer bloc, estimated by *Sponsor* at roughly fifteen million people ("The Forgotten 15,000,000" 1949a; 1949b; 1952), without alienating the larger and more lucrative white base. Though postwar liberal attitudes had contributed to real progress in social policy and civic practices, racist tendencies did not magically disappear with television's emergence.

On the contrary, the new visual medium provided a new site of consternation in the South (Torres 2003; Classen 2004), although it warrants stating that the South had not remotely cornered the market on racial intolerance and bigotry in this period. Whereas "black and tan" nightclubs or speakeasies[17] of the 1920s and 1930s presented a space "in which whites and African-Americans mingled in ways that were effectively forbidden under more conventional circumstances" (Gabbard 1996: 64), television was no speakeasy and race mixing was a highly tendentious subject, especially in the South.

Such concern was evident in 1950 when Lloyd T. Binford, the city of Memphis's appointed chief censor, weighed in on the unique challenges presented by television to his appointed duties. Memphis was then one of the nation's top ten black media markets (with a black constituency totaling roughly 45 percent of the city's overall population), and Binford's authority to dictate the city's film options was reinforced by his close ties to the powerful political machine of E. H. Crump, who dominated the local political sphere from roughly 1910 until his death in 1954. Renowned for banning Hollywood films that either depicted blacks in a favorable light or portrayed white and black characters on an equal social basis, Binford wielded substantial influence throughout the South, where other local censors watched his decisions carefully, often following his lead. Despite his reputation, Binford's local bans in Memphis were not as deleterious as they might seem on the surface; films that were censored in Memphis, Tennessee, were commonly screened just five miles away in West Memphis, Arkansas, a factor that actually drew film patrons — and public revenue — away from Memphis proper.

Binford's core responsibilities rested with cinematic fare and his censorious decisions were tested by Hollywood's emergent tendency toward more liberal script content and more respectful representation of African Americans, including narratives that featured white and black characters portrayed as cooperating equals. Arthur Knight writes, "By the fifties, race film was an eviscerated, untenable category and the few works that did hew to the category were musical 'revues' that tacked together recycled single-story shorts" (2002: 232). As the network television broadcasts originating in New York or Chicago began to reach Memphis via kinescope or regional cable, Binford turned his attention to television, pledging his commitment to scrapping TV programs that contravened the South's racist authoritative principles while acknowledging that, because television was a domestic medium, his influence was severely restricted. His efforts, however, were certain to impact musical programs most harshly since they, more than situation comedies or dramatic series, were prone to feature black and white artists on the same stage on relatively equal footings. Regardless of his critical statements about television's onscreen racial miscegenation, Binford also admitted that he had never actually seen a television show and was, thus, basing his official pronouncements on mere hearsay (McMillan 1950: 25).

Another case involving southern white anxiety and TV's onscreen miscegenation occurred in 1952 when the Georgia governor Herman Talmadge declared, "Several network programs violate the spirit of the south's segregation laws" ("Webs Brush Off Talmadge Beef" 1952: 1). Acknowledging that television had evolved primarily as a domestic medium, Talmadge held that the programming content was "just about equivalent to visiting somebody in his home" (ibid.: 20). While domestic entertainment and the accompanying discourse of the home theater (Spigel 1992) may have been valid for TV set manufacturers' advertising campaigns or for network promotions as each sought to entice consumers, its meaning was much more insidious and spiteful in the contexts of southern racial hostility.[18]

Describing the dilemma facing southern censors and other opponents of television miscegeny, Thomas Doherty writes,

> From a Confederate point of view, violations of Jim Crow custom on television were far more insidious than in motion pictures . . . to preview shows telecast live was impossible and to stop the network feed and not telecast shows already sold to sponsors meant bankruptcy. Trapped by technology and commerce, station managers in the Deep South telecast images of interracial amity they would never have countenanced in their hometown newspapers or at the local Bijou. (2003: 72–73).

For many southern whites, the medium's domestic character collided with prevailing racial views about the production of televised entertainment; blacks were not welcomed in the home of white set owners via the TV screen except under very specific conditions that ensured depictions of a perceived innate inferiority.

While the televising of black actors and musicians was generally deemed to be acceptable, white supremacists demanded assurance that they would be cast in either "all-Negro" productions or in subservient roles and that they never performed alongside whites, as Talmadge phrased it, "on a purely equal social basis." In this formulation, performances by the biracial Reginald Beane Trio or an integrated unit such as the Benny Goodman orchestra, appearances by Lena Horne or the Will Mastin Trio with Eddie Cantor on *The Colgate Comedy Hour*,[19] or Frank Sinatra and Louis Armstrong seated side by side on a piano bench on Sinatra's show would be unacceptable to those harboring a "Confederate point of view." Evidence of the intense resistance to programs with liberal portrayals of race relations originating in New York can be discerned in a searing letter to NBC in 1952 from an incensed Memphis, Tennessee, television viewer who voiced his support for Governor Talmadge's pronouncement against broadcast miscegenation:

> Down here in Memphis, Tenn., we are limited to your outlet. We can't turn to Columbia or American for a change of programme and have to take what you offer. Can't we have one program without a bunch of niggers? I like negroes and have employed as many of them as most people but I do not care to have them in my home, as guest and to be a participant with *white* people. I really think it is insulting to try and stuff the negroes down our throat in order to commerciaise [*sic*] your soap or some other product.... We sure will be glad when we can get Columbia or any other programme that isn't of a *nigger* origin! (Warfield 1952).

Talmadge explained how the production conventions of network television represented "a complete abolition of segregation customs" upheld by the South and, wielding the most threatening weapon he could muster, he hinted at the possibility of an organized boycott of the networks and their program sponsors ("Webs Brush Off Talmadge Beef" 1952: 1). Although the Du Mont network was not extensively available to viewers in the South at this point and was, thus, less vulnerable to such intimidation tactics, the other major networks took the threat of southern boycotts or other forms of retribution against sponsors seriously, despite their corporate disavowals.

Indeed, as Steven Classen explains, new regional TV stations (such WJTV and WBLT-TV, which both began broadcasting in Jackson, Mississippi, in 1953), were "aligned at their conception with white supremacist and segregationist interests, as newborns WJTV and WLBT complemented an already intimidating white power bloc including prominent white business leaders, bankers, politicians, clergy, and police departments determined to thwart integrationist or 'black freedom' advances in the fifties" (2004: 1–2). The stations functioned locally as extensions of white authority, and the screen itself emerged as a segregated site that was, like any other public space in the South, prone to close surveillance and careful policing of racial mixing, constituting what Classen describes as a "strategic battleground" (ibid.). These affiliated stations were largely unable to override the major network broadcasts originating from the studios in New York, Los Angeles or Chicago, thus usurping their "informational and representational control" (ibid.: 33).

Among many racially intolerant TV critics, the popular quartet the Mariners constituted the zenith of onscreen race mixing and as a result the group rapidly became the focus of white supremacists' indignation. The group, consisting of two African American vocalists (Nat Dickerson and Jim Lewis) and two white vocalists (Martin Karl and Tom Lockard), met in 1943 during their wartime stint in the U.S. Coast Guard. After winning several radio talent shows, they were recruited by Arthur Godfrey and CBS, where they resided throughout television's nascent phase. Godfrey's unwavering support of the group frequently won him plaudits from the black press and other cultural organizations and, when called to respond, he did not hesitate to discuss his liberal hiring practices and progressive approach to race in postwar America. The celebrity profile magazine *Radio and Television Mirror* cited an incident in Washington, D.C., involving a scheduled performance at Constitution Hall, run by the conservative Daughters of the American Revolution,[20] which demonstrated Godfrey's commitment and loyalty to the group: "The Godfrey gang was booked for a benefit at Constitution Hall, which is operated by the D.A.R. When the D.A.R. objected to the Mariners appearing on their stage, Arthur withdrew the show and booked it at the Armory. On the occasion when Governor Herman Talmadge of Georgia attacked Godfrey for having Negroes in the quartet, Godfrey answered that he was sorry for a man with such a stupid bias" (Merwin 1953: 96).

The members of the Mariners were not themselves overtly invested in addressing the group's racial composition, preferring to discuss their music and careers primarily in a professional context, yet the themes of race and liberty repeatedly emerged in the popular media's coverage. In an artist profile published in 1953, *Radio and Television Mirror* presented the quartet as a unified amalgamation of dedicated, strong-willed musicians, "rugged individuals" who, in true American fashion, adhere to a democratic management principle: "When a decision must be made we vote. Majority rules" (ibid.). Adopting a rational liberal discourse of particular resonance in the early stages of the campaign for civil rights, the article ends with the statement "The Mariners live, as they sing, in harmony" (ibid.).

Two years later, the magazine published another feature story on the quartet, again citing their rugged individualism, free-thinking subjectivity, and shared leadership as the foundation for the group's success and longevity. In this profile, published under the title "All the Brothers Are Valiant" (an apt reference to the 1923 film about seafaring siblings, *All the Brothers Were Valiant*, that was remade and released in 1953), the camera is invited into each of the men's homes, replete with photographs of wives and children and discussion of their artistic trajectory, family life, and community involvement (Cohen 1955). The warm humanity and social equality of the members is emphasized and, with this depiction of backstage domesticity and casual informality the Mariners received a form of standard celebrity treatment that was the norm of popular fan magazines at the time, personalizing the artists by portraying their everyday lives while simultaneously exalting them as celebrities. Such coverage of black musicians was still quite rare in mainstream fan media, making this particular story more interesting, yet it came shortly after the 1954 *Brown v. Topeka Board of Education* Supreme Court ruling and the dawn of the organized civil rights movement.

In the 1955 article, race is again cast as an implicit subtext yet it breaks the surface in the coverage of Jim Lewis. Lewis was the group's only college graduate, the Mariners' founder, and in its early days he served as the group's manager in charge of business and bookings. He was in 1955 also national vice president of the American Federation of Television and Radio Artists (AFTRA), a relatively powerful organization with clout in the entertainment sector. In this capacity, Lewis's efforts to expand the options for black artists unambiguously emerges: "I have been doing my best to get Negroes a better break in radio and TV. . . . The resistance is all concentrated in the industry, from the top to the bottom. It's not the public at all, so far as I can see. . . . My success has been small, but I keep trying" (Cohen 1955: 70). Lewis's stated mission with AFTRA was significant, especially when considered in the context of prejudicial hiring practices and other forms of discrimination impacting black actors and musicians. Reinforcing Lewis's concerns, a survey released in March 1955 by the New York NAACP branch vice president, Odell Clark, indicated, "The number of Negro musicians employed by the networks is practically nil. . . . We found one or two who are employed regularly, but outside of guest appearances by some of the bigger names, a Negro musician hasn't much chance of regular employment on the networks" (Altbush 1955: 3).

Though a later entry, it is worth citing Nat "King" Cole's problems during his television foray as host of his own program. Cole was a major recording and touring star, with numerous television guest appearances between 1949 and 1956. In 1955 CBS announced that it had signed a contract with Cole for a "minimum of 10 guest shots on an exclusive basis" on major programs. The network was believed to be "experimenting with formats with possibility that he'll eventually have his own spot" in the CBS program schedule ("Nat (King) Cole's TV Guest Shot" 1955: 27). Despite CBS's interest, Cole emerged on the NBC network in 1956 where he encountered a different set of issues than lesser-known artists or others who sought to host their own television vehicles.

Premiering on November 5 with much initial fanfare, the Cole show debuted without a sponsor, and many NBC affiliate stations (especially in the South) balked at picking up the program. The southern issue was not insignificant in Cole's case; the previous April, Cole had been viciously attacked — onstage, in mid-performance, in front of an all-white audience — in Birmingham, Alabama, by members of the White Citizens Council (the majority of the audience was deeply embarrassed, apologizing to Cole). The incident confirmed that while Cole's refined musical style and his suave persona might be admired in many regions of the country, it was not going to win over hardened white supremacists.

Cole was renowned for his warmth and elegance and, with Perry Como as a model, his fifteen-minute musical program settled on a straightforward production approach without excessive flourish or "funny hats." The show was "as simple as could be" (Epstein 1999: 270), and Cole projected wonderfully on the small screen, but the show was continually in a financial bind, failing to secure permanent sponsor support. Lack of sponsor support meant that there was "nothing to work with but the 'talent' and the camera — small budget, little rehearsal time, and no technical or writing staff" (ibid.: 272). Cole carried the program on the strength of his talent and charm, accompanied by an impressive roster of top musical guests, many of whom were his personal friends (who, in the show's second season, appeared on the show for union scale as a sign of friendship and support and a means of keeping the budget down).

The network's sincere effort to keep the program on the air (as Epstein indicates, at one point the show was costing NBC an estimated $18,000 a week) proved fruitless without a firm sponsor commitment, and the show was dropped in December 1957. Many speculated that the inability to secure a regular sponsor was race-related, with nervous corporations unwilling to risk alienating white viewers (especially those in rural areas or the South) or to associate their brands with a black artist. Though frustrated and fatigued by the ordeal, Cole expressed his gratitude to NBC, placing the bulk of the blame on timid advertising agencies and corporate sponsors rather than the network itself: "The network supported this show from the beginning. . . . From Mr. Sarnoff on down, they tried to sell it to agencies. They could have dropped it after thirteen weeks. . . . Madison Avenue is afraid of the dark" (Watson 1998: 33; Epstein 1999: 276).

As the examples and profiles presented here suggest, the portrayal and presence of black musicians on television were never singular or homogeneous in nature but were, rather, affected by many of the same complex forces that buffeted society more widely. Describing a much later moment in time, Herman Gray locates television's "representations of blackness . . . at the intersection of social and cultural discourses within African American communities and the dominant culture . . . the popular discourses and commercial media landscapes across which these constructions of blackness circulate help shape their meanings (and counter-meanings) for differently situated publics" (1995: 36). This observation was no less true in the late 1940s and 1950s, when television rapidly expanded, permeating the cultural realm. The television broadcasting enterprise, like society more generally, was deeply implicated in the circumscription of race and identity and as a result, it constituted another locus in the struggle for equal rights and justice. Black musicians and the black press were, each in their own way, highly engaged in liberating the airwaves and challenging the attitudes and practices of this nascent sector of the entertainment and culture industries.

6

Maracas, Congas, and Castanets

*

Latino (and Hispanic) musicians fared somewhat better than did their African American counterparts in terms of accessing the major network program schedules and hosting their own shows. Latino musicians and lively orchestras performed in numerous contexts across the television spectrum, introducing U.S. viewers to new musical genres and alternative cultural aesthetics in the postwar period. With the decline of the traditional dance bands in the immediate postwar period, Latin rumba bands emerged with particular vigor, combining Latin American rhythmic patterns with the conventional section playing of the U.S. dance bands, infusing percolating bongos, claves, congas, maracas, and timbales to the more familiar jazz band styles. The nation's "hotter" swing bands, too, increasingly adopted Latin musical motifs, with artists such as Duke Ellington, Woody Herman, and Stan Kenton inviting Cuban and Puerto Rican horn players or percussionists to join them in concert and recording sessions (Gottlieb 1947: 10). The result was a vibrant musical hybrid that stood as a basis of cultural interaction and dialogue.

Among early television's more prominent Latin musical acts were the orchestras of Xavier Cugat, Machito (Francisco

Grillo), Esy Morales, the trumpet virtuoso Rafael Mendez, and the band-leader and sit-com star Desi Arnaz, although a vast array of both famous and lesser-known Latin artists also appeared regularly on regional broadcast stations, particularly those across Texas and the Southwest region. In addition to music performed *by* Latino artists, there was also a substantial volume of Latin or Latin-influenced compositions that were performed by non-Latin talent, drawing from and extending the influences of postwar popular musical trends associated with the rumba (or rhumba as it is was also spelled), mambo, or the subsequent cha-cha-cha.[1]

Latinos were certainly not the only cultural group to receive special attention on television for their musical and cultural expression. Hawaiian "hapa haole" music, for instance, emphasized "the music of Hawaii plus the music of the faraway mainland 'Hit Parade'" (Owens 1970: 2).[2] The conductor and composer Harry Owens and his Royal Hawaiians, an orchestra comprised of native Hawaiian and off-island/Caucasian "haole" musicians (including Owens), were featured on radio broadcasts from Hawaii on the NBC, CBS, and Mutual networks in the late 1930s, eventually appearing on the Los Angeles television station KTLA in 1949 (Owens 1970; Williams 1998). Arthur Godfrey also featured a Hawaiian artist, the female vocalist Haleloke, who was a regular member of Godfrey's multicultural musical "family" (Cohen 1954).

German, Polish, and Scandinavian polka musicians (usually accordionists) were also featured prominently on television's music shows, especially those programs emanating from the American Midwest (such as *It's Polka Time*, hosted by Bob Lewandowski on the Chicago station WHFC or Cleveland's Johnny Vandal Orchestra, seen every Sunday on WEWS-TV from 1949 to 1961) as well as appearing prominently on the nation's amateur programs. Such was the interest in polka music that in 1954 at the height of the Latin mambo craze, *Variety* reported on the phenomenon under the headline "Polka Biz Jumping Like Mambo" (Brown 1954: 41). In other instances, national cultural identities were communicated in and through musical performance as in the case of professional artists such as Edith Piaf, Maurice Chevalier, or Denise Darcel, whose TV appearances extended conventional notions of Frenchness.

While the numerous cultural heritages and their accompanying musical genres contributed to early television's polyglot nature, Latin music was nonetheless unique. The scope of its cultural influence was impressive as it was integrated across music-oriented programs, emerging in countless performance contexts. Latin music attained intense popularity among U.S. musicians and the public alike, and its influence was most fully felt in precisely the same period that television emerged as a commercial medium. As the U.S. navigated the nation's changing cultural character through the war and in the postwar era, striving to accommodate the rapidly rising Hispanic and Latino population, so, too, did the television networks strategize to incorporate these artists into their program schedules, further amplifying the cultural influences that were already circulating through other leisure and entertainment sites.

Television, Latinos, and the Global Perspective

In a characteristically bombastic pronouncement on television's promise in 1939, RCA's David Sarnoff forecast that "television will finally bring to the people in their homes, for the first time in history, a complete means of instantaneous participation in the sights and sounds of the entire world" (1939: 428). A year later, NBC, lauded the network's accomplishments in a promotional publication titled *Television's First Year* (1940). Pictured on the cover of the document is a burnished wooden television console featuring an airplane on the TV screen; the accompanying text offers several references to the capacity of the new medium to capture images and transport them to the viewers' screens "across the skyways of the world." In another, slightly later example of this global ideal, a 1946 book by Thomas Hutchinson was published under the title *Here Is Television: Your Window to the World*.

As these examples indicate, even in this very early period before television was fully viable from either a technological or commercial standpoint, the concept of a global medium was firmly entrenched. Despite the promissory exclamations of Sarnoff and other top TV network executives or commentators that television could contribute to better relations among nations, it was entirely clear that the dominant view was from a U.S. vantage, that the "window to the world" was neither transparent or bidirectional and the vantage upon foreign cultures and marginal peoples privileged the domestic spaces of North America. It was also evident that, in the context of commercial broadcasting, the "world" constituted a vast resource base and a deep reserve of audiovisual content that, in its exoticism or its simple foreignness, provided rich broadcasting potential.

Television, like the entertainment sector more broadly, benefited during its developmental stage from increased human traffic and the patterns of global migration that brought international cultures to New York and other major U.S. urban hubs. Nightclubs, concert halls, radio and recording studios, and other performance venues all presented artists from diverse cultural backgrounds whose musical repertoires reflected their national or ethnic origins. As television evolved and the burgeoning industry hungered for quality broadcast material, musical performances by Latino musicians were especially valued by TV producers for their verve and their unique *difference* in relation to standard North American popular fare.

It is generally true that Latin American actors were seldom hired in early television programming, particularly dramatic or dialogue-driven productions where accented or poor English skills were regarded as a deficit. When they were cast in TV programs, Latino characters were often portrayed in negative or stereotypical fashion. Dramas for TV frequently took their lead from the film industry, where Latin men inordinately portrayed criminals, such as thieves or murderers, predatory lotharios, subordinate lackeys and ineffectual buffoons, or lazy ne'er-do-wells, and the women were commonly portrayed as hypersexualized sirens. Latin American *musicians* were highly visible on early TV, either typecast or appearing as guest artists on literally hundreds of music and variety programs where dialogue was not required. There were numerous programs broadcast on national and regional TV outlets after the war that were unambiguously Latin-themed. Among these were *Let's Rhumba* (a Latin dance instructional program) airing on NBC in 1946–47; the Du Mont network's *Flight to Rhythm*; *Bamboo* on WCBS-TV; KTLA's *Latin Cruise*; *Spanish Varieties* on San Antonio's KEYL-TV; *Rhumba Club* (another dance instruction program) on the Milwaukee station WTMJ-TV; *Pan American Casino* from the Baltimore station WAAM-TV; and *En Busca de Estrellas* (a Spanish-language amateur talent program) broadcast on the Los Angeles station KLAC-TV.

Photos in a 1951 NBC manual, *Operation Backstage: Staging Services Handbook of the NBC Television Network Operations Department*, offer a view of the set of WNBC's *Latins in Manhattan*, and in 1952 *Variety* published a review of *The Latin Show*, a program broadcast on WOR-TV in New York that featured the ten-piece La Playa Orchestra directed by Rene Touzet and that was coproduced by the influential Latin recording label Tico Records. One Los Angeles–based music program, *Chico Swingtime*, offered consistent bilingual fare targeting Hispanic immigrants and second-generation Mexican Americans with popular tunes sung in both English and Spanish.

Reaching a predominantly Spanish-speaking viewer market was a complication for the television industry and its sponsors in part because the industry was largely clueless about the audience composition. In Oscar Gandy's assessment,

> When the US advertising industry made its early attempts at organizing an approach to [the Latino] market, it was confused about the nature of Latino ethnic identity. The industry appeared to be genuinely confused about how to characterize this population. Clearly, the Hispanic market was defined by more than language and national origin, but confusions about the place of race, culture, and class often led the industry to fall back upon traditional stereotypes. Considerations of economic efficiency led the industry to construct the Latino market as a single, homogeneous entity. (1998: 125)

Reflecting Gandy's observations, in 1951 *Sponsor* offered a seriously reductive and stereotypical profile of "Juan Lopez," a Spanish-speaking composite — a Latin everyman — from the Southwest region, whose attributes were categorized as being definitive of the average Latin-American consumer. Citing an estimated Spanish-speaking market of between three and four million people, *Sponsor* encouraged broadcasters (especially radio broadcasters), corporate manufacturers, and their advertising agencies to pursue this "overripe" but elusive population, traversing the "virgin territory" by playing various forms of Latin music as well as airing appealing soap operas and news programming ("How to Win with Juan" 1951).

For Latin musicians, television was a vital factor that helped to sustain them professionally, ensuring that they were seen and heard by millions of people across the country, reaching eager Latin American audiences as well as the much larger U.S. audience sector that would otherwise have had little or no access to Latin music. Latin music consequently evolved as a standard facet of early television and the many musical forms and genres (including Spanish flamenco, Mexican borderland corridos, boleros or mariachi compositions, Brazilian samba, Cuban and Puerto Rican rumba, conga, *son*, mambo, and cha-cha-cha) were virtually unavoidable in television's formative years.

Through continual portrayal as foreigners whose energetic, seductive, and winsome performances were staged for the primary benefit of U.S. TV audiences, Latin musicians were effectively located outside the symbolic boundaries of the domestic nation. In television's nascent phase, there was only a minimal attempt to convey greater knowledge or awareness about the cultural character and social realities of foreign peoples, although elements of their traditional folkways were frequently staged for television viewers. They were more succinctly on display, presented as if in a living museum. The correlative idea might be the folkloric festival complete with songs, dances, and curious cultural traits of various nations, or the World's Fair that provided a global showcase for the simultaneous display of traditional cultures and consumer commodities associated with modernity and futuristic progress.

Extending many of the themes and practices first realized in Hollywood cinema, Mexican and South American actors and musicians were recruited and welcomed on U.S. television screens within the political idealism of global good will, but they were not necessarily welcomed into U.S. viewers' homes in a physical, nonvirtual sense. To borrow a term from David Morley (2000), Latinos were accommodated as "mediated strangers" who are met but never fully known. From this perspective, even though their images, their songs and dances, their elaborate costumes, and their cultural mannerisms filtered into millions of American houses via television, Latin musicians on early television were themselves never "home" in any direct sense.

The American Culture Industries and "Good Neighbors" to the South

Television's "launch" at the 1939 New York World's Fair stands as a crucial moment in the medium's development, beaming its content to roughly 2,000 set owners and an estimated audience of up to 8,000 viewers in the greater New York area by the end of the year ("RCA and NBC Present Television" 1940), rising to roughly 3,000 household sets and an additional 150 public televisions with an audience of approximately 15,000 people by April 1940 (*Television's First Year*, 1940).[3] Steeped in the rhetoric of international harmony and understanding—mixed with a technological determinist perspective and a heaping dose of commercial can-do marketing—the World's Fair presented a context for the articulation of U.S. corporate values and the expression of a particular image of global relations. As George Black (1988) explains, the fair also offered President Franklin Delano Roosevelt the opportunity to reinforce his "vision of a world of Good Neighbors," a reference to the Good Neighbor policy between the United States and Latin America that he had outlined at his 1933 inauguration.[4] Its noble discourse of friendship and mutual respect aside, the Good Neighbor policy was also part of a strategy intended to uphold the themes and protocols of pan-American defense against looming European forces and, in a secondary objective, to enhance cultural exchange with Mexico and Central and South America. As history reveals, the policy also provided a motivation and rationale for U.S. corporate, economic, political, and cultural intervention in the southern tier that continues to this day.

In its earliest formation, television emerged within a particular historical juncture as the world's nations girded for war on a transcontinental scale. The U.S. urgently sought to establish a more closely aligned economic and military front and to gain assurances of hemispheric accord by fostering good will in the Americas. This is to say that television evolved in a period of remarkably strained political and cultural relations, when the constructs of a nationally defined "us" and a foreign or ideological "them" were widely resonant and under revision. The discourses of cross-cultural dialogue and international cooperation that were so often expressed among television's early advocates during the war years were in many instances imbued with an accompanying sense of necessity as the United States entered a period of conflict and uncertainty.

During the early stages of the Second World War, prior to the official U.S. entry into the fray, President Roosevelt promulgated versions of the Good Neighbor policy with a degree of urgency, what Shari Roberts describes as "an attempt to maintain hemispheric unity in the face of foreign invasion" (1993: 5). As Roberts explains, the Good Neighbor policy was eventually inscribed into the Office of War Information guidelines for the U.S. film industry, providing a catalyst for portrayals of continental alliances and North American — South American unity and the depiction of convergent interests and general support between the United States and foreign nations. The endeavor resulted in a surge of films with South American (and Canadian) themes and settings and was responsible for the rising profile of artists including the Brazilian star Carmen Miranda. Miranda's performative and sartorial excesses are exemplary, as they signify a dynamic Latin American type: beautiful and slightly wacky, accessibly feminine rather than aggressively masculine, exotic but danger-free, and through music and dance, able to dilute, subvert, or ignore the heated political elements that were also characteristic of the nations "south-of-the-border." Miranda and other similar Latin types, while still displaying a certain stereotypical hot bloodedness, presented an alternative to the corrupt, dictatorial *caudillos* or "strong man" leaders, many of whom ascended to power through military coups or sham elections.

These strategic efforts to merge political policy and cinema established a precedent of sorts, especially since the film industry influenced several of television's presentational aesthetics, providing performance and content cues that were taken up and recontextualized in the emergent broadcasting medium. The titans of the TV broadcasting industry, led by General David Sarnoff at RCA/NBC (who during the Second World War attained the rank of brigadier general and served as a communications consultant answering directly to General Dwight Eisenhower) and CBS's William Paley (who also served directly under Eisenhower as deputy chief of psychological warfare) were not blind to television's value as a propaganda tool on the domestic front, nor were they beyond approving program proposals that included themes of international cooperation and American might. Finally, the networks actively sought content that might also appeal more broadly, reaching new audiences and, consequently, new markets.

For instance, as early as 1943, the NBC president, John F. Royal, received an internal memo addressing the company's strategy to identify and exploit talent from South America, Mexico, Cuba, and Central America, requesting that he "consider the possibilities of bringing some outstanding artists to America for use on short-wave and by telescription so that all of the Latin American countries might enjoy the great artists of the southern hemisphere" (Bate 1943). In this example, NBC executives were thinking expansively, conceiving of their market on an international scale and reflecting similarities with American economic policy at the time.

While Latin America constituted an important realm in political contexts, through the 1940s and early 1950s corporate executives within the U.S. music industry were also focusing their interests on the continent. Those in the music industry had witnessed the opportunities and good business sense (especially exercised by smaller independently owned record labels) of recording music by American blacks and rural whites through the late 1920s and 1930s, resulting in lucrative successes with artists in the "hillbilly" and "race" categories. For many in the corporate music industry, Latin American music was similarly conceived as a primary resource "ripe" and ready for extraction, refinement, and distribution for sale and consumption in both South American and U.S. markets. Not only did Latin music provide an appealing novelty for North American listeners, it was also eagerly received among the growing Latin American immigrant population.

In 1940 the National Association of Broadcasters (NAB), in concert with NBC, CBS, the National Independent Broadcasters (NIB), and the Independent Radio Network Affiliates (IRNA) and other radio broadcasting organizations created Broadcast Music Incorporated (BMI), a performing rights organization. Broadcast Music Incorporated was intended to provide an alternative to the American Society of Composers and Publishers' (ASCAP) and to the increased licensing fees for the airing of ASCAP-registered compositions. It immediately introduced competition to the licensing field (Sanjek and Sanjek 1991). Frustrated by ASCAP's monopoly dominance, financial overreaching and extortionist user fees, and sheer arrogance, the upstart BMI organization facilitated music licensing for composers who had traditionally been excluded from joining the ASCAP roster. An objective of the move was to offer a new outlet for country music and folk songwriters, black composers, and international composers, including those of Latin American heritage who were previously marginalized by ASCAP. In the ensuing "ASCAP versus radio music war" (ibid.: 78), the NAB's member stations openly challenged ASCAP by boycotting all compositions affiliated with the ASCAP catalog and drawing solely from the emergent and rapidly expanding BMI roster. As Reebee Garofalo writes,

> For about ten months in 1941, no ASCAP music was heard on the radio. In its stead, authentic regional styles, supplemented by melodies in the public domain, were broadcast to a national audience via mainstream outlets. As the broadcasters had predicted, there was no public protest. There were, however, a few key acquisitions by BMI that contributed immeasurably to the success of the boycott. Ralph Peer, who had moved into the international market, offered a catalogue of Latin popular music. (2005: 55)

Ralph Peer, owner of Southern Music Publishing and a former employee of Victor Records in the label's "race" and "hillbilly" sectors through the 1920s, was BMI's man on the ground in South America.[5] Peer's primary responsibility involved negotiating with South American licensing organizations and lobbying government policy makers and other officials to enable BMI to license international compositions. Through the war years, Peer helped BMI to expand its relationships with performing rights organizations throughout the South American continent and in Mexico and Cuba, allowing BMI to gain an upper hand on ASCAP in the Latin music sector.[6] One senior BMI executive put an altruistic gloss on the organization's Latin initiative in February 1946, describing "a campaign carried on by BMI in cooperation with governmental departments interested in the 'Good Neighbor' policy," noting that the approach had facilitated several Latin American "popular music hits" and contributed to U.S. public interest in the music from South America.

Consistent with the objectives of the Good Neighbor policy, in the fall of 1945, the U.S. State Department (in close consultation with the NAB, BMI, and ASCAP) established a cultural committee "to develop an interest in this country in the music of South and Central America and other cultural aspects of those regions" (Ryan 1945). As documents from the period illustrate, U.S. cultural corporations, with the assistance of the federal government, embarked on a campaign to establish footholds throughout South America, identifying business opportunities, seeking potential collaborators, nurturing governmental support, and discovering new artistic talent.

Though affiliated in the State Department's initiative, ASCAP and BMI were anything but cooperative. Sensing opportunity and the potentials of expanding cultural ties with South America through the mid-to-late 1940s, the rabidly hostile U.S. organizations engaged in a heated competition to dominate the South America and Cuban music markets. ASCAP and BMI each sought to establish monopoly ties with the controlling Latin American copyright agencies and broadcasters and each sought assistance and mediation from the U.S. State Department, the Attorney General's Office, and the embassies of various Latin American nations. Citing a "world cartel in violation of the anti trust laws of the United States," BMI appealed directly to the U.S. attorney general, Tom C. Clark, requesting that he address ASCAP's aggressive postwar entry into the South American market, where BMI was already an established presence, explaining that ASCAP was deliberately undermining BMI's existing relationships with foreign licensing organizations. The NAB, logically, sided with BMI on the issue, convinced by the smaller organization's arguments following a flurry of correspondence from BMI's Sydney Kaye, a former CBS lawyer and copyright authority who was elected as BMI's "operating head and attorney" (Sanjek and Sanjek 1991).

Using language very similar to that employed by BMI, the NAB president, Justin Miller, implored the U.S. assistant attorney general, Wendell Berge, to take stern measures in curtailing ASCAP's status as "an international cartel" and to "insure compliance by ASCAP with the anti-trust laws of the United States" (1946). The aggressive pursuit of new music licensing opportunities in South America by ASCAP and BMI, however, also helped to facilitate the introduction of Latin music to American audiences and, through increased exposure, U.S. audiences gradually developed a familiarity and taste for it.

The underlying themes of hemispheric good will and the accompanying effort to locate, record, and distribute Latin music in the U.S. continued to resonate in the entertainment industry throughout television's early years. For instance, in 1951 NBC TV was approached about initiating a Latin American series consisting of thirteen half-hour shows, "each dealing with a different Latin American country." The format was intended "to provide an entertaining and informational program about the country. It is proposed that we arrange to have the outstanding entertainers of the country appear on this show — in many cases these entertainers will be well known to American audiences. In some cases it will be necessary to import these entertainers from the respective countries" (Taylor 1951). The TV series proposal emphasized musical performances as well as brief dramatic vignettes portraying key moments of each nation's history, yet the production was ultimately reductive in its framing, relying on costumes, dance, and other spectacular features to communicate the character of the Latin American cultures. Such reductionism corresponds with Ana Lopez's criticism of Latin American representation in U.S. media: "It is not surprising that the boundaries of the Latin American community have been closely associated with music, dance, and their performance and representation as stylistic markers of (imagined) national essences. . . . In fact, we could argue that in addition to being 'narrated' — a fictional or enunciated construct — the nation (and some more so than others) is also insistently sung and danced" (1997: 310).

In many instances, the national distinctions and localized cultural traditions among musicians from Mexico and Central and South America were explicitly enunciated but they were just as often diminished or conflated. Latinos were all too commonly cast as a homogeneous "them" who were on-screen to perform for an idealized "us" that, in the skewed views of sponsors and television executives, was primarily comprised of middle-class, urban, white consumers. Television, it would seem, was inclined to air a rather conventional image of Latin American culture, reproducing primary motifs and performance genres that could be easily traced back to folkloric festivals and to cinematic renditions of South American leisure.

It was also suggested in the 1951 program proposal that, along with the musical performances, the episodes might include one-minute filmed interviews with top government representatives or, ideally, presidents from throughout South America. Absent was any acknowledgment of, or reference to a dilemma in presenting aggressive military strong men who were then in power in Argentina, Bolivia, Colombia, Paraguay, Peru, and Venezuela. As this suggests, while executives in the U.S. culture industries associated Latin music of the period with the symbolic construction of national identity, the rhythms and musical instrumentation were also erroneously perceived as being *merely* entertainment, detached from other aspects of cultural life and, ultimately, apolitical.

A further contemporaneous expression of this perspective is evident in the April 21, 1952, *Time* cover story reporting the "nearly bloodless" coup led by Cuba's Fulgencio Batista and describing "exuberant Havana" as "one of the world's fabled fleshpots. The whole world dances to its sexy rumbas and mambos" ("Cuba" 1952: 38). The lived realities of corrupt nondemocratic rule and authoritarian repression, not to mention other pertinent issues relating to class and racial inequalities, were easily subsumed by the music as the image of a carefree existence and perennial carnival was isolated and diffused through U.S. media organs.

Mobility, Cultural Imagery, and the Televised Latin

With increased international travel after the war years and through the 1950s (whether as a facet of business, tourism, or immigration) perspectives on the world were shifting and television's status as a "window on the world" gradually changed. The expression "window on the world" implies that distant places and peoples are situated on the other side of the screen for the stationary viewer. Yet evolving discourses of mobility, travel, and cultural exploration were also employed with networks and TV set manufacturers each promising viewers a virtual tour of the world and its cultures; viewers might take a trip without leaving the comfort of their own homes.

Expanding on Anne Friedberg's concept of the "mobilized and virtual gaze" (1993), Anna McCarthy refers to "virtual mobility" and television's "promise of a viewing experience in which the gaze substitutes for the physical exploration of space" (2001: 73–74). This concept accommodates a production logic that draws other spaces and places toward the home, constructing the ideal perspective in ways that establish an ideologically informed dynamic between the privileged viewing subject and the televised object of the gaze. Whereas McCarthy's analysis focuses on the potentialities of commercial merchandizing and commodity consumption, the presentation of disparate locales (even in ersatz forms) and varied cultures in televised musical performances also orients viewers in relation to different geographies—and geographies of difference—producing another context for consumption. Images associated with particular places around the world are presented for sight consumption to be sure, but they also tap into an alternative system of curiosity, desire, and enticement that is entirely seductive. With the rise of new commercial tourist options and enhanced emphases on automobiles and national travel in the postwar era, the world was both accessible and eminently consumable in new ways. Postwar consumers were confronted with a barrage of advertising and promotional materials inviting them to explore the world and its cultures; television's demonstrative visual traits fit into this apparatus quite easily.

According to Joshua Meyrowitz, technological mediation permits individuals to "travel through or 'inhabit' electronic settings and landscapes that are no longer fully defined by the walls of a house, neighborhood blocks or other physical boundaries.... [S]trangers become partial neighbors in a '19-inch neighborhood' of shared mass-mediated communications and mass-produced products" (1990: 129). No doubt for many viewers the concept was ideal, for while they may have enjoyed the televised spectacle of other cultures *and* cultural Others, many viewers also welcomed the mediated nature of the contact. Lynn Spigel explains, "Numerous commentators extolled the virtues of television's antiseptic spaces, showing how the medium would allow people to travel from their homes while remaining untouched by the actual social contexts to which they imaginatively ventured" (2001: 35). David Morley and Kevin Robins comment on the phenomenon in slightly different terms: "If, in days of old, explorers and anthropologists set off on long journeys into the unknown to bring us back written accounts of the strange customs of exotic Others in distant places, today we are all ethnographers to the extent that all kinds of Others are exposed to our gaze ... in the form of electronic representation on the television screens in our own living rooms" (1995: 130). As immigration patterns registered ever-rising numbers of global citizens, including Hispanics and Latinos from numerous countries (displaying a wide variety of national, regional, and local distinctions) who settled in U.S. urban locales, television mitigated a majority white population's direct contact with the hordes by filtering the "undesirable" cultural factors and relieving the duress of actual travel in unfamiliar milieus. This was, in effect, a new form of armchair anthropology or virtual tourism.

Musical performances, Broadway plays, and films had established the practice of constructing elaborate visual and narrative travelogues since the dawn of Tin Pan Alley in the late nineteenth century. Ethan Mordden (1983) employs the term "pastiche numbers" to describe the manner in which late nineteenth-century music hall productions portrayed ethnic themes, juxtaposing identifiable aspects of diverse national cultures through variety shows and song and comedy sketches (often evoking racial and ethnic stereotypes) to create a dynamic mélange of contrasting customs and traditions.

The presentations of the American music hall helped to inscribe an image of modern America at the turn of the century, a nation open to the world and the diverse cultural influences of its peoples yet prone toward cultural assimilation within the powerful discourse of the "melting pot." Moreover, as access to various public spaces such as the vaudeville and music halls was gradually democratized, the audiences for these "pastiche numbers" also increasingly reflected at least a trace of the cultural or ethnic hybridity portrayed onstage. The pastiche numbers offered a cultural parade for the audience's enjoyment, but with elaborate staging and increasingly sophisticated production, these performances also invited the audience on a conceptual journey via song, dance, and costumed splendor.

Mordden suggests that by the time the musical comedy had settled into the more standardized modes of the Broadway theater institution in the early twentieth century, the pastiche number was in decline, either entirely absent from stage productions or sadly prone toward inanity. Citing productions such as *The Lady of the Slipper* in 1912 and the 1914 production *Chin-Chin*, Mordden notes the proclivity toward improbable characters or story lines and musical numbers encumbered with an absurd mix of cultural and musical motifs (1983). It was generally in musical numbers that the sonic patterns and rhythmic signifiers of other lands and peoples were most explicitly motivated and despite its decline on Broadway and in other theater productions, "the pastiche number lived on in other venues, other media" (Keightley 1998). This included such films as the 1930 musical film *King of Jazz*, starring Paul Whiteman and his Orchestra, which "ends with a remarkable ethnic pastiche which purports to tell the story of the creation of jazz" (ibid.).

Television, of course, drew from both Broadway and cinema to some extent, and in its evolution TV producers (many of whom had transitioned into the new broadcast sector from the theater) frequently adopted the pastiche model, portraying the collision of national or ethnic cultures and implying exotic foreign locales, carrying the audience into elaborately conceived environments of worldly Otherness. It was not uncommon in television's early years for musical variety shows especially to present a series of production numbers, each referencing a different country and culture, as was the case with the January 1950 debut of *Cavalcade of Bands* on the Du Mont network. The premiere show moves through musical themes and aesthetic motifs that in succession represent Manhattan (with the accompanying "Manhattan Square Dance"), a nondescript Caribbean island (featuring the rumba hit "Babalu"), and Paris ("La Vie en Rose," performed with a set image of the Eiffel Tower in the background). Americans apparently *liked* to see images of the exotic, if only in highly stylized and ersatz representations, and television presented a new entertainment medium through which to fulfill this perceived audience desire. In a new way, the notion of being "carried away" by a performance or the expression "to be moved" by a song or production number also suggested a metaphorical movement or a shift in a television viewer's affective disposition.

Televised musical performances adopted many previously established presentational forms. For instance, song lyrics summoning distant Latin American encounters were certainly nothing new by the late 1940s; in 1920 Irving Berlin wrote "I'll See You in C-U-B-A," evoking a tourist's desire for the pleasure, otherness, and escape from domestic restrictions offered by the exotic Caribbean isle:

Not so far from here
There's a very lively atmosphere
Ev'rybody's going there this year
And there's a reason
The season opened last July
Ever since the U.S.A. went dry

Ev'rybody's going there and I'm going, too
I'm on my way to
Cuba there's where I'm going
Cuba there's where I'll stay

Owing much to the title of the 1940 hit recording "Down Argentina Way" (written by Harry Warren and Mack Gordon and recorded by Bob Crosby and his Orchestra) and the 1941 film of the same title, it was common in television's early stage for program hosts to refer to imaginary musical journeys to Latin America in which the viewer was invited to take a musical trip "down Panama way," "down Havana way," or "down Rio way." The expression refers to the pseudo–Latin American themes of the composition while connoting cultural exploration and ethnographic contact with "good neighbors" to the south, further implying the allure of Argentina and, by extension, the entire Latin American culture.

The Guy Lombardo band (and the Kay Kyser and Freddy Martin orchestras) also offered a novelty number with a Latin American twist, releasing the hit "Managua, Nicaragua" (by Irving Fields and Albert Gamse) in 1946–47:

> Managua, Nicaragua, is a beautiful town,
> You buy a hacienda for a few pesos down. . . .
> Managua, Nicaragua, what a wonderful spot!
> There's coffee and bananas and a temp'rature hot,
> So take a trip and on a ship go sailing away
> Across the agua to Managua, Nicaragua. Ole!

This particular passage is typical of the time with a primary emphasis on tropical heat and the accompanying notion of affordable escape, indicative of an emergent tourist market. The lyrics identifying culturally appropriate items do not explicitly reference U.S. trade policies involving agricultural imports from Central America, but this can be discerned in the references to Nicaraguan produce as coveted facets of the evolving American culinary regime. Central and South America were at this point increasingly perceived as sites of U.S. consumption and the resources, both natural and cultural, were considered ripe for exploitation. Additionally, the occasional sprinkling of Tin Pan Alley lyrics with snatches of Spanish ostensibly imbued the songs with an element of authenticity, although the terms and phrases were rudimentary, introducing little more than a general tourist's familiarity with the language.

The emphasis on foreign travel and multiple hybrid cultural inflections in early television productions inspired the idea of a vast geocultural realm and with it, images of the exotic, erotic, romantic, and precarious world of other cultures "down" in the deep mysterious lands of Latin America or the Caribbean. Still, while calling forth the image of an exotic elsewhere, cartographic references such as "down South America way" also have a distancing effect that reinforces the geographic and cultural otherness of Latino musical performers on numerous musical variety programs on early U.S. television. Although bringing television audiences closer to Latin America through its music and dance was presented as a desirable objective, it seems that maintaining a certain distance was also important.

According to Keightley (1996), the premise of musical journeys and aural adventures became common in the postwar period, in part through the promises of the "hi-fi" stereo after 1948 and the subsequent promotion of audio authenticity or "fidelity." There was a notable trend in advertising and promotions for both television and the hi-fi stereo to foreground the themes of virtual travel and the capacity of these new domestic media to transport the viewer or listener away from the humdrum elements of everyday existence (Spigel 1992; Keightley 1996). Audiences in the postwar era demonstrated a desire for more direct contact with other places and other cultures. Seeking escape, alternative experiences, or a jolt of unbridled exoticism, non-Latino U.S. audiences eagerly pursued a host of options that harbored traces of cultural Otherness or that promised a degree of adventure. Travel agencies certainly had a role in producing and promoting images of exotic adventure in this period, but so too did a savvy entrepreneur like Walt Disney as he developed the extravagant concept of Disney Land with its constructed globalism in the early 1950s.

Keightley explains that in the 1950s, "the search for the exotic and the authentic went hand in hand. An interest in the 'truly different' might be described as a search for the 'authentic exotic,' whether avoiding tourist traps when traveling or listening to 'local' music from world cultures" (1998: 2). The entertainment industry wasted little time in capitalizing on such postwar consumer desires for "the authentic exotic." Recording and television executives aggressively responded by searching for South American talent that could be introduced to the U.S. market, allowing them to present "authentic" representatives of Latin culture. The television programs featuring Latin American or Spanish musical performances are, thus, situated within a global/local nexus (Robins 1991) whereby localized Latin traits are diffused globally through the media, rendering them "international" (and potentially exotic) in the process, even as they are relocalized (and deexoticized) upon their reception within the homes of U.S. viewers.

The codes of exotic Otherness were often written into televised musical texts in a manner that relied on some fundamental essence of a specific place, identifiable perhaps by explicit mention, such as when a TV program host or bandleader described a performance with reference to Barcelona, Havana, or Rio de Janeiro, or when a song's title and lyrics alluded to a national region, inflecting it with a distinct cultural perspective (evident in two 1946 recordings: Frank Sinatra's "The Coffee Song," with its references to Brazil, or the aforementioned "Managua, Nicaragua"). Keightley explains how, in the postwar years and throughout the 1950s, Latin music rose "as a kind of lingua franca of exoticism" (1998). This was achieved through the widespread circulation of music and images in the film, television, and recording industries, as well as through the promotional apparatus of the travel and tourist industries.

The Latino artists on television screens were also often portrayed as spectacular yet decontextualized commodity objects, made to traipse across a theater or network studio stage, and placed in front of the cameras to enact their exotic, primal, and virile musical culture for unseen but receptive audiences throughout the U.S. In early television productions, the motif of musical Otherness was often embedded within the sound of the conga drum or the rattle of maracas or castanets, accompanied by stage sets constructed as Mexican or Spanish dwellings—elaborate villas, adobe "casitas," or Caribbean-style thatched huts—and featuring props such as fake palm trees or wild cacti.

In early television musical performances it is no simple, evenly aligned process of exoticization that is on display, for Mexicans and Latinos of Central and South America were also represented as residing within what might be defined as a *spectral* realm where mystery and mysticism converge. This spectral quality, when strongest, is also deeply inscribed by the mystery associated with the racial Otherness of either the native "indio" and hybrid "mestizo" identities or by the Latino "mulatto" inheritors of African traditions. The spectral or mystical quality was frequently depicted in early television through a combination of stage sets, costumes, or dance numbers that drew heavily on stereotypical images of primitive or tribal rites. These elements, in unison with musical accompaniment, function to motivate concepts associated with a Latin Otherness, reinforcing the archetypal alignments of exoticism and the potent possibilities of erotic allure of faraway places and deep, mysterious traditions.

Reflecting the notion of a virtual vacation adventure, KTLA in Los Angeles aired *Latin Cruise* in the autumn of 1949. Produced by the station's architect Klaus Landsberg, the program offered a showcase for Latin music, featuring as host and bandleader Bobby Ramos, accompanied by the singer Lita Baron, the male vocalist Ardo, and a small dance troupe. The half-hour broadcast was set on the ersatz cruise ship *Amigo* with a floorshow that drifted into Latin cultural waters. Debuting concurrently with KTLA's program was *Tropic Holiday*, airing on the New York station WNBT in the late-night slot at 11:15 on Friday evenings. With music by the accomplished Esy

Morales orchestra, the show featured its host Sandy Bickert portraying a sailor whose reminiscences of his South American exploits provided the narrative structure for the music and dance performances.

The "torrid exhibition of singing and dancing" by a "crack contingent of Latino talent" on *Tropic Holiday* was well received in the pages of *Variety*, and the entertainment trade magazine also cited the program's later air time: "There's a good reason, however, to keep this show out of the reach of kids. The Latin performers go native and the entertainment, aside from being topnotch in its genre, is hot as a chili pepper. But there shouldn't be any moralistic squawks as long as the audience is confined to adults" ("Tropic Holiday" 1949: 28). Such associations of Latin culture with an open and explicit sexuality were frequently revealed in commentary of the time, reproducing the defining features of cultural difference in the U.S. context and extending stereotypical images of the hot-blooded, passionate, and emotional Latin identity.

The Esy Morales unit also provided musical accompaniment on *Bamboo* that debuted in early 1950 on WCBS, New York. Imitating the narrative theme of *Tropic Holiday*, the premise of *Bamboo* involved its host Al Thaler portraying "a rum-soaked, sun-helmeted traveler sitting in a native saloon and reminiscing about the esoteric, erotic dances and music of the hot climes" ("Bamboo" 1950: 37). The program emphasized multiple cultural tropes "embracing Latin America, Africa, Java, Bali, and all the lands where the bamboo grows" (ibid.), but the musical genres clearly cleaved toward the English and Spanish Caribbean, with performances by Abbey Lee and Haitian drummers and dancers from the much-lauded African American choreographer Katherine Dunham's studio performing a "provocative rhumba."

There was much visual and narrative labor involved in the construction of simulated foreign locales and the creation of a whiff of the exotic in early television broadcasting. The processes of communicating the concept of the journey and of transporting the viewer to another geocultural dimension were often quite detailed. Exemplary of this labor is the Du Mont program *Flight to Rhythm*, which aired between March and September 1949. Though it was short-lived, the program remains relevant as an instance of early television portrayals of South American and Latin musical cultures. *Flight to Rhythm* conforms to the earlier cinematic trend of linking narratives to exotic locales with the music occupying a central role in signifying the geocultural context and location while attempting to maintain a reality effect — the "authentic exotic" — throughout the program.

Flight to Rhythm opened weekly with an extreme close-up of a conga drum being beaten "savagely," with an introduction featuring a brief filmed vignette of the host, Ralph Statley (performing the role of Club Rio bartender, "Nick"), and the regular musical cast members Delora Bueno and Miguelito Valdes on an airport tarmac boarding a plane, the "flight to rhythm" of the show's title.[7] The invitation to watch the program is framed in the context of a touristic journey, a trip with a specified musical and cultural route as the voice-over intones: "Via the drum, the accents of the maracas, listen, it's the rhythm of Rio calling. So come along with us as we fly the melody airlines to Miami, and then past Mexico, Costa Rica, over the equator and the jungles of the Amazon and then . . . Rio." Reinforcing the voice-over and anchoring the concept of a Brazilian location, the set includes a glimpse out the ersatz Club Rio's window onto the city's famous topography, including an image of the iconic Corcovado Mountain topped with the familiar statue of Christ the Redeemer. The depiction of knowable landmarks and locales or the citation of place names signifies an actually existing Latin American environment as the Du Mont network's production strategies strived to establish the representational links that aligned the program with the authentic local culture of Rio de Janeiro.

As the imaginary itinerary suggests, the show was set in a virtual Rio but it sampled from across Latin American cultures, with Miami located as a cultural bridge or portal city connecting the United States and South America. Once at "Club Rio," the stage set where the action unfolds, the show's musical performances were impressively inclusive, with lyrics sung in English, Portuguese, and Spanish. Although the music was often Brazilian in origin, when it was not errors in attribution occasionally occurred in the classification of musical genres and their national origins. Despite an effort to highlight the nations of South America and to represent an encompassing musical pan-Americanism, the show often essentialized the Latin character through musical misidentification. In some instances the rhythmic and musical traits were incorrectly attributed, claiming, for example, that distinctly Mexican or Spanish musical motifs are from Peru or elsewhere in the continent; these errors marred the program's explicit attempt to achieve place-based authenticity. Such flaws notwithstanding, the performances on *Flight to Rhythm* were accompanied by a generally competent orchestra featuring Spanish guitar, congas, gourd shakers, and maracas to propel the Latin rhythms, augmented by the occasional blaring trumpet or dynamic piano flourish that are also often associated with the most robust Latin music of the period.

Nationalist tendencies loomed large on *Flight to Rhythm*, as depicted on the May 15 episode. On this broadcast, the opening musical number features Delora Bueno singing the Brazilian national anthem. With the music soaring, the image of Bueno dissolves, revealing the Brazilian flag; these two images are then merged, portraying Bueno completing the anthem with the country's flag superimposed over her before the camera pulls back for a group shot encompassing the show's entire cast. Later, referencing Brazil in a different context, the program host Ralph Statley engages in a light comedic skit with Valdes, exclaiming, "I wanted to get into the Carnival, Mardi Gras spirit," as he nonchalantly assembles a series of fruits. The ensuing "funny hats" routine perpetrated by Statley and Valdes includes a predictable and sophomoric stab at humor with each sporting a Carmen Miranda–like fruit hat that tapped into a stereotype that, by 1949, was already tired and overworked. The comedy routine segues into a musical performance by Valdes who, defying his legitimate vocal talent, sings a medley of Latin numbers (including "Tico Tico") in a deliberately camp fashion that more closely resembles a spoof than a sincere musical rendition. Valdes was a respectable singer and a fine purveyor of the Cuban *son* and the rumba musical forms, but on *Flight to Rhythm* his talents were often wasted as he was drawn into feeble vignettes with the comically challenged Statley.

Near the end of this broadcast, Statley steps forward to perform the novelty number "The Coffee Song" (composed by Bob Hilliard and Dick Miles), with lyrics extolling the virtues of one of Brazil's major agricultural exports, citing the abundance of coffee in the region while equating coffee's roasted scent with a lady's fine perfume. The episode ends with the show's cast presenting Bueno with a floral bouquet and a letter from the Du Mont network reading, "to Delora Bueno. The Du Mont television network is happy to congratulate you for being named Good Neighbor of the Year by the Pan-American Union." With this, the orchestra embarks on a samba rhythm and the cast links up in a conga line, snaking among balloons, streamers, and a seasonally appropriate May pole.

Another episode of *Flight to Rhythm* (date unknown) dedicated to Peru also exhibits a prominent nationalist orientation, opening with the Peruvian national anthem and an image of the nation's flag. The show's musical numbers feature the song "Baile de Bola Bola," sung in Spanish, and "The Girl Who Came from Peru," sung in English. At one point, Bueno says to her co-star Valdes, "You know, Miguelito, these Spanish numbers are so beautiful. Sometimes people ask for us to do these numbers in English but sometimes it just doesn't mean the same thing. Now why don't we show the listeners what we mean," and the two vocalists demonstrate their linguistic fluency, performing the next tune in both languages.

The geocultural locus of the musical "journey" is radically and inexplicably shifted, however, as Valdes returns to the screen to sing "Babalu," a Latin American hit when he recorded it in Cuba in 1939 (earning him the monicker "Mr. Babalu"); Valdes reprised the song in the 1945 production *Pan-Americana* (directed by John Auer), a film that provides a template of sorts for *Flight to Rhythm*. In this performance, Valdes delves into his cultural heritage, invoking the Orisha deities Shango and Babalu Aiye that are central to the Cuban Yoruba religion and Santeria practices, genuflecting to a large tribal mask and primitive statue (which may or may not be of Cuban origin). As the band plays an elegant and well-structured Cuban *son*, the program's dance team, Alicia and Roberto, circles around the statue in a manner connoting ancient tribal rites. In the production number's finale Valdes bows respectfully in a prayerful mode and the sequence ends with a close-up of the statue.

Just prior to the episode's closing credits, Valdes is presented with an award by Alianza Inter-Americana, an association that is "organized to work for more sincere union among the countries of this hemisphere," presenting the singer with a citation "for fostering good will and understanding between the Americas through your music." The episode, with its ungainly blend of exotic mysticism and contemporary cultural politics offers a pertinent example of the complexities of representing the Latin "Other" in U.S. broadcasts.

As this indicates, the array of television's representational images in musical performance addresses dominant and prevailing ideas within the U.S. mainstream about the people and cultures of the Spanish-speaking Caribbean, Mexico, and Central and South America. Television's performance aesthetics and staging methods adopted traces of national and ethnic characteristics, casting them semiotically as signs of deeper or more far-reaching cultural traits. Class also stands out as an important line of demarcation, for musical performances were often aligned along an axis of economic and cultural differences, portraying wealthy urban sophistication or comparatively impoverished rural imagery in a manner that foregrounds conceptions of class and status.

For instance, musical presentations that strongly summoned Mexican imagery often portrayed class distinctions in interesting ways. Some musical performances, usually boleros and Latin-tinged ballads, were set within up-scale villas reflecting refined cultural tastes and class attainment. The visual staging suggests the country's colonial past with its Spanish influences and it was not uncommon to hear elements of flamenco mixed into the osten-sibly Mexican musical performances. In these cases, there was often a his-torical aspect to the production with the set design referencing an imagined and idealized Mexican past from the mid-to-late 1800s more than modern Mexico. Female singers were predominant in these particular performance contexts, strolling the stage as they sang tender love songs in either Spanish or English. The European colonialist flourishes were pronounced, revealing that in the minds of the television producers, Mexico's cultural and musical identity remained indebted to its Spanish heritage.

In contrast, performances also commonly portrayed small rural commu-nities of either Mexico or the U.S. Southwestern region with stage sets de-picting primitive adobe houses with extras lounging lazily, attired in pon-chos, sandals, and sombreros. Much as the conga drum and percolating percussion came to represent a Spanish Caribbean or Afro-Cuban identity in early television musical productions, the sharp attack of the trumpet and the omnipresence of the mariachi band emerged as an important cultural signifier of Mexican location and identity. In performances of this nature, the music was frequently inclined to merge Mexican motifs (mainly through the trumpet arrangements) with U.S. country music, creating a hybrid musi-cal style that is still audible along parts of the U.S.–Mexican border.

Leo Carrillo's Dude Ranch, broadcast on the Los Angeles station KCOP in the early 1950s, exemplifies the cultural convergence of Mexico and America. Carrillo was an established stage and Hollywood film character actor who was most famous for his role as "Pancho," the ever-present Mexi-can sidekick on the popular TV western *The Cisco Kid*, which aired between 1950 and 1956. Carrillo's program prominently featured western-style music performed by the adept house band, The Plainsmen, augmented by various guest singers who performed in a range of musical styles usually, though not exclusively, singing in English. Referencing the iconic, even stereotypical, image of Mexicanness that Carrillo embodied, the show opened each week with a title card featuring the image of a sombrero emblazoned with the pro-gram's name.

Carrillo was not a singer himself, and his role as program host was gen-erally limited, moving the show along, introducing guests, and providing the context for the musical numbers. As the Plainsmen end their opening number on a 1951 broadcast, Carrillo comments, "They were playing an old Spanish tune with American words." Carrillo's emphasis on American—not English—words was consistent with the pronounced U.S. patriotism he exuded: in fact, Carrillo regularly emphasized three dominant themes on his program: American patriotism, the sanctity of motherhood, and Christian values. In this episode, he states "We do welcome every good American to this ranch at anytime and we have a ten-foot fence to keep you in, not out and I always greet the different nationalities because I think they make great Americans—all of 'em." Carrillo's effusive patriotism and his concurrent pride in his Mexican heritage were not without their hitches, however. After telling a drunken-Mexican joke in a 1951 episode, he ad-libs, "I always like to listen to their little accent and that sort of thing because I was raised with them and they have a great heart and they're wonderful people." In this instance (with his peculiar distinctions between "us" and "them") it seems that Carrillo is expressing an identity position that, to borrow Gustavo Pérez Firmat's (1994) relational construct, tilts toward the American side of the hyphen between "Mexican" and "American."

On early television programs involving Latin music and cultural themes, the idealized notions of the past (imagined through performance vignettes with primitive overtones) were, at times, comingled with progressive ideals of the present, yet neither dimension fully permits the Latino identity to emerge on its own terms. Rather, early television producers colonized the representation of Latinos, providing a cultural space that was, through music, dance, and costuming, highly circumscribed. Television in effect constituted a territory or a reservation where Latino identities might be witnessed but where they were also isolated, contained, or safely bracketed from the moral and aesthetic values of the dominant social mainstream.

Desi Arnaz, Ricky Ricardo, and America's Most Recognized Latin Orchestra

With its debut on October 15, 1951, *I Love Lucy* emerged as a regular site of cultural collision in television's early programming. The themes of racial, ethnic, and class difference were written as a standard component of the show's weekly antics, woven into the half-hour episodes along with popular and Latin songs sung in both English and Spanish. Starring the comedian Lucille Ball and her husband, Cuban-born Desi Arnaz (who met in 1940 on the set of the RKO musical *Too Many Girls*, directed by George

Abbott), the program was an immediate success, airing for nine seasons. As the show evolved and Lucy and Desi became established TV celebrities (appearing as featured guests on numerous television shows and in the pages of television gossip magazines) their popularity was circulated back into the program's scripts. As I explain in chapter 3, the plots of many episodes depict Desi's real-life role as a musician and actor as well as making frequent references to his audience appeal as a bandleader. Arnaz's television character consequently evolved as a hybrid amalgamation of his various career exploits (with an added hint of his widely documented backstage infidelities and sexual peccadilloes).

Arnaz's actual musical trajectory began in 1936 when he joined the Siboney Septet performing rumba numbers at the Roney Plaza Hotel in Miami between sets by the headline acts. He later joined Xavier Cugat's Orchestra, singing with the esteemed Spanish leader's band in the famous Starlight Roof room at New York's Waldorf Astoria Hotel. In 1937, Arnaz assembled his own band (with Cugat's assistance and mentorship), performing a vague, poorly executed approximation of the rumba with a band decked out in preposterous "rumba shirt" costumes (Arnaz 1976). Stumbling at the outset and desperate to succeed, Arnaz drew on his memory of the rum-fuelled conga lines he had witnessed during Cuban carnival celebrations as a child, pulling out his conga drum and instructing the band to follow him in a stylized group dance (ibid.). The conga evolved as an iconic element of the Arnaz persona, popping up repeatedly in publicity photographs and in movie posters such as that of the 1949 release *Holiday in Havana* (directed by Jean Yarbrough and costarring Mary Hatcher), in which Arnaz is typecast as a conga-playing Cuban bandleader.

Gustavo Pérez Firmat describes how Arnaz's identification with the conga as an instrument, a musical genre, and a dance was established as early as 1937 when he is said to have led the first conga line on American soil, in a Miami Beach nightclub. Firmat explains that the conga "was ideal for big production numbers. It was a group dance, it was simple to do, and it had the requisite foreign, festive air to it" (1994: 54). The dance phenomenon was clearly established in the United States by 1939, when actress Claudette Colbert was famously portrayed leading a conga line of tuxedo-clad elites in a scene from the movie *Midnight* (directed by Mitchel Leisen), with the movie's Latin orchestra performing onscreen in the background. Between 1940 and 1942 the Xavier Cugat Orchestra, featuring the vocalist Miguelito Valdes (who had replaced Arnaz) and (in the early phase of their careers) the

Latin musical icons Machito and Tito Rodriguez, also recorded a track, "Me Gusta la Conga."

With the popularity of his conga line act, Arnaz was awarded the nickname "The King of the Conga," distinguishing him from other musical "royalty" in the swing, rumba, and mambo genres. The conga is more than just a carnival dance; it is also a drum with cultural roots in the Afro-Cuban musical traditions that, by the late 1940s, were growing in prominence throughout North America. Citing the African origins of the conga and the instrument's subversive potentials, Winthrop Sargeant explained in 1947, "The big conga drum, which occasionally makes its appearance during the carnival, reverts to the status of an illegal instrument. It has been outlawed except during fiestas for a good reason: the conga drum has been used as a jungle telegraph, roaring out secret messages from town to town in the Cuban hinterland and from neighborhood to neighborhood in Havana" (1947: 151–52).[8] Sargeant explicitly links the conga and the accompanying staple of Cuban music, the maracas, guiros, and bongos, with cultural primitivism, negatively articulating the story of "Cuba's tin pan alley" toward "bullets and marijuana," "prostitution" and venereal disease (defined in the song "Penicilina" or "Penicillin"), and suggesting that the "homicidal musical limbo of Havana" floats between the "heaven of international success, money, New York nightclubs and Hollywood fame" and "the underworld of African Cuba" (ibid.: 151). Arnaz is clearly associated with the former realm of the upscale Cuban elite, tapping into the African root of the conga primarily when it served the image of exoticism and mysterious allure.

With no particular talent as a drummer — a "congero" in the Afro-Cuban parlance — Arnaz tended to implement the conga drum as a basic prop, throwing it over his shoulder to indicate the Cubanness of his musical performances. Indeed, in several episodes of *I Love Lucy*, Arnaz's trademark song "Babalu" (the Miguelito Valdes hit that Arnaz adopted as his own signature song) was performed with great exuberance, with the camera employing full shots that display Arnaz's energetic dancing and earnest conga pounding, accompanied by tightly framed facial close-ups that illustrate his passion. For instance, he incorporates the conga drum into his performance of "Babalu" on the November 19, 1951, broadcast of *I Love Lucy* ("The Audition"). While singing the tune with its haunting invocation of the Orisha deities, Arnaz loosens his shirt collar and jacket in preparation for the song's strenuous finale. He ends his performance bathed in a single spotlight, pounding frenetically on a huge conga drum slung around his shoulder, re-

Desi Arnaz, *I Love Lucy*. "The Audition," CBS, November 19, 1951.
COURTESY OF PHOTOFEST.

prising his energized performance histrionics from *Too Many Girls*. Through
the force and power of the drum and the conga routine associated with his
youth, Arnaz established a formula that communicated his Cuban heritage
and carried him through his variegated career in music, film, and television.

The basic narrative device linking Arnaz's musical career with an onscreen persona had previously been established in *Too Many Girls* and his
starring role in the 1946 B-film *Cuban Pete* (directed by Jean Yarbrough) and
Holiday in Havana from 1949. While his lead roles in these minor pictures
offered tangible career returns (further promoting his musical ambitions
and reinforcing his legitimacy in Hollywood), there were more oblique ad-
vantages to be accrued from Hollywood's development of films with Latin
themes. Roberts describes how American audiences were exposed to an
ever-expanding assortment of Latin cultural influences, gradually naturaliz-
ing the Latino presence in the United States: "However mixed the film industry's motives in turning to Latin material, the 1940s film musicals both
reflected and augmented Latin music's popularity in hybrid forms that
made it more acceptable to American audiences and more quickly absorbed

into American styles. They were, in fact, part of the process whereby Latin-originated rhythms were becoming a part of the structure of U.S. music" (Roberts 1999: 108). Arnaz was, by the late 1940s, one of the direct beneficiaries of the nation's rising curiosity and engagement with Latin musical forms and he displayed a shrewd capacity to exploit the entertainment sector's steady investment in Latin culture. Branching out from his regular nightclub engagements into broadcast media in the late 1940s, Arnaz replaced the dynamic Latin-influenced Stan Kenton orchestra as the house band for radio broadcasts of *The Bob Hope Show*, a position that extended his professional contacts and name recognition. When Lucille Ball sought to shift her popular CBS radio program *My Favorite Husband* to television in 1950, she remained adamant that the program would cross to video with her real husband appearing in the lead male role.

While "ethnic" characters proliferated on such early TV comedy programs as *Amos 'n' Andy* (African Americans), *Duffy's Tavern* and *The Life of Reilly* (Irish Americans), *The Goldbergs* (Jewish Americans), *Life with Luigi* (Italian Americans), or *I Remember Mama* (Norwegian Americans), Hispanics and Latinos were not prominently featured on family-oriented situation comedies. They were far more frequently featured in the contexts of music and dance performances, where they constituted an indisputable asset to TV. This narrow representational frame functioned in at least two ways: it effectively positioned Latin Americans at the margins of social dialogue and the associated dimensions of rational civic discourse (exacerbated by the pervasive linguistic gulf existing between Spanish and English speakers). It also helped to solidify the association of Latinos with the erotic domain of music and dance, transforming them into objects of sensual display and consumption according to the entertainment industry's logic of commodified leisure.

Network executives from CBS who wanted Ball for the television show were hesitant to sign a television contract that included Arnaz, whose comedic talents were marginal and whose fractured English was thought to be distracting at best, at worst untenable for the new medium. With his limited English-language skills, Arnaz was an unlikely candidate to costar in a new television show, especially at the medium's inception, yet as a *musical* presence he was deemed to be recuperative within an acceptable cultural category and an appropriate social vocation. The network executives ultimately conceded, and Lucy had her husband.

Ball and Arnaz developed their initial TV concept involving a bickering but loving couple in 1950, embarking on a nationwide vaudeville-style music and comedy tour to "test" their material with the public, perfecting many of the show's first-season routines while on the road (Andrews 1976; Arnaz 1976). Some of these routines also found their way onto television prior to the debut of *I Love Lucy*. In 1950, Ball and Arnaz were guests on *The Ed Wynn Show* on an episode that introduced many of the linguistic and musical conventions that became hallmarks of *I Love Lucy*. Opening with a skit featuring Arnaz unleashing a torrent of Spanish at Wynn and toying with the sexual innuendo structured around the stereotype of the Latin lover, Wynn explains to the viewing audience, "People know Desi as a singer," offering a segue into Arnaz's version of "The Straw Hat Song" (a tune that was introduced on the eighth episode of *I Love Lucy*, airing on December 3, 1951).

Later, responding to Wynn's request for "Babalu . . . that song that made you famous," Ball brings Arnaz his large conga drum, presenting Wynn with a much smaller snare drum. The sexual potency inherent to the sight gag is unmistakable, with Arnaz and his Cuban conga drum representing a much fuller phallic authority, whereas Wynn is portrayed as the comparatively emasculated gringo with such a tiny drum to pound.[9] As Arnaz performs on his conga drum, Wynn tactlessly undermines the Afro-Cuban cultural traditions on display, intoning, "Desi, you'll ruin the whole show . . . you play those drums and they'll think its some African show."

As negotiations with CBS for *I Love Lucy* progressed in 1951, Arnaz also took on musical duties for the CBS radio program *Tropical Trip*, a musical quiz show in which the grand prize (with its traces of the Good Neighbor Policy intact) was an all-expenses paid vacation, promoting a different Latin American destination each week. By the fall of 1951, production on *I Love Lucy* commenced. Straddling the music, film, radio, and television industries, Arnaz claimed a uniquely privileged professional vantage — especially for a Latino artist — and his insights onto the life of a working bandleader conveyed an invaluable element of authenticity upon his televised character.

Capitalizing on Arnaz's ascendance as a major television celebrity through the early decade, the music trade magazine *Down Beat* printed a slight profile of the Cuban bandleader in 1953, describing him as "America's Best-Known Leader" (Emge 1953: 3). In the article, Arnaz confesses that his television responsibilities had displaced his earlier focus on music and show-room performances, although he also stresses that his band is not simply a television construct. Indeed, during the program's lifespan the Arnaz band was very much a working ensemble comprising actual musicians, not merely actors playing musicians. With its demanding television production schedule, the orchestra was always relatively well rehearsed and quite capable of playing in clubs or on tour, although it did so intermittently.

Even though *I Love Lucy* was shot on film and was not, therefore, beholden to the performance demands of live television, the musical component of the program maintains an impressive degree of fidelity to the experiences of a working orchestra. In his role as Ricky, Arnaz presented himself as a leader with a commitment to musical perfection (characteristics that were equally evident in his role as the show's executive producer and head of Desilu Studios and, in the final 1959–60 season, when he took the reins as the show's director). With acting and production responsibilities, Arnaz delegated the actual musical direction to Wilbur Hatch, who had conducted the orchestra for Lucy's radio broadcasts of *My Favorite Husband* and other CBS radio shows. In the production credits Hatch is listed as "conducting the Desi Arnaz Orchestra," a role he maintained through the entirety of the series.

The pianist Marco Rizo was also an important contributor to the show. Rizo had worked with Arnaz since his formative stage, when the orchestra first appeared at the Copacabana. He was frequently given lines and a supporting actor credit in the program, but he also drew on his status as an accomplished musician and musical arranger, assisting the composer Eliot Daniel and Hatch, the musical director, in arranging the occasional original selections that were written specifically for *I Love Lucy* (Andrews 1976: 99–100). Rizo's experience as a longtime musical collaborator with the Arnaz orchestra further infused the show's musical sequences with an aura of authenticity as the star and his band demonstrated for viewers the toil and effort of maintaining a nightclub orchestra.

The musical repertoire on *I Love Lucy* was impressive in its scope; episodes commonly featured one or two songs, many of which were original compositions, although one 1954 episode lists as many as nine tunes, while other episodes featured no music at all. In many of the program's early episodes, Arnaz sang Spanish and Cuban songs as well as standard ballads in a highly affected style that enunciated a Latino identity even though the arrangements were often watered-down versions of rumba, conga, or mambo idioms. The music performed on the program emphasized Latin numbers, drawing on rumba tunes (many associated with the Cugat orchestra) such as "Bim Bam Bum," "Cielito Lindo," "El Cumbanchero," "The Lady in Red,"

I Love Lucy, featuring Tennessee Ernie Ford. CBS, 1954. COURTESY OF PHOTOFEST.

"Vaya con Dios," and the Arnaz standard, "Babalu." The show also introduced an abundance of Tin Pan Alley compositions, some that referenced various Latin American nations, including "Cuban Pete/Sally Sweet," "Down Argentina Way," "Granada," "Guadalajara," "I'll See You in C-U-B-A," "In Acapulco," and "In Santiago, Chile" as well as light musical confections such as "Glow Worm" or "Shine On, Harvest Moon." Other songs performed on the show were selected to correspond with the week's comic themes or with a musical guest; for example, on the May 3 and 10, 1954, episodes featuring Tennessee Ernie Ford (appearing as himself) the musical selections conform to Ford's persona as a "hillbilly" artist.

During the orchestra's "performances," Arnaz usually sported an elegant tuxedo, while the band members were dressed in elaborately frilled "rumba" shirts that are associated with a stereotypical image of a mid-century Havana orchestra. On the 1952 "Cuban Pals" episode this debonair and cultivated style is tastelessly juxtaposed against the image of a dark-skinned Cuban dancer sporting naught but a grotesque tribal mask and loincloth. In an atrocity of racial and cultural paranoia, a repulsed Lucy, horrified by the Other before her, is "rescued" from the ghastly specter by Desi — wearing his tuxedo — who personifies the white, urbane, and assimilated Cuban.

Agitating against such sartorial tendencies, however, the Afro-Cuban jazz leader Machito questioned the cultural authenticity of many popular Latin bands, acknowledging that Latin orchestras working in the United States (such as Arnaz's, with Latino and non-Latin American members) were often composed of a hybrid pan-American amalgamation. As Machito explained, "I have always objected to dressing up my orchestras in various kinds of sashes and hats and exaggerated sleeves. It seems to me that these orchestras where the men are of various nationalities and all of them wear what they call Cuban costumes are more like a mixed salad than anything authentic and genuine" (1947: 27). In summoning the concept of cultural and musical authenticity, Machito raises one of the more prominent criticisms leveled at Arnaz whose pseudo-Cuban song renditions were at odds with the urgent rhythmic styles associated with the rapidly surging mambo phenomenon of the early 1950s. Moreover, television itself was regarded as a neutering medium, broadcasting a diluted version of Latin music that misrepresented the torrid sounds of the dance clubs frequented by Latin crowds. For some critics, Arnaz was little more than an experienced poseur whose insipid renditions of Latin music had never adequately outgrown his early Cugat influences. For them, Arnaz served Latin music devoid of taste and absent of spice in order to ensure maximum palatability among an ignorant or undiscerning U.S. audience sector.

Television and Mambo-Mania

The music phenomenon known as the mambo developed in almost precisely the same temporal period as commercial television and, with mambo's rise, producers and musical hosts integrated the rhythms and dance form into their TV shows. While the established dance bands were in a steadily weakening posture after the 1946–47 industry crisis, music critics in the music

I Love Lucy. CBS, 1951–57. COURTESY OF PHOTOFEST.

I Love Lucy. "Cuban Pals," CBS, April 21, 1952. COURTESY OF PHOTOFEST.

trade journals acknowledged that there was a change afoot in the U.S. music sector; Latin music was overtly challenging the supremacy of the popular swing-oriented orchestras. Within a few years, *Metronome*'s influential jazz critic Barry Ulanov (referring to the rising status of Perez Prado) proclaimed, "The swingingest jazz band in this country right now ain't — it's in Mexico. And furthermore it isn't a jazz band; it blows mambo" (1950: 26).

U.S. audiences were long familiar with the rumba genre associated with Xavier Cugat, the Latin "conga" style of Desi Arnaz and others, and with Mexican boleros — beautifully sensitive ballads, some of which had been successfully translated into English — but the mambo introduced a significant new trend that, at least briefly, captured the American imagination and its feet. Addressing the popular appeal of the rumba in U.S. ballrooms and the country's prestige nightspots, the Afro-Cuban artist Machito offered an important set of musical and cultural distinctions, noting, "In Cuba, the conga is a street dance and not at all a ballroom number, while the rhumba is a typical exhibition dance, which until recently was never done by 'nice' people in Cuba" (1947: 26). The mambo constituted another thing altogether with its sharp rhythmic accents and a breakneck tempo that was propelled by congas, timbales, maracas, and the "clave" beat of the wood blocks, fiery piano arpeggios, and fiercely swinging horn sections.

Increasingly called upon by the music press to define their emergent brand of Latin music, several top Cuban, Mexican, and Puerto Rican musicians, including Mario Bouza, Machito, Noro Morales, and Perez Prado, explicitly articulated the importance of Afro-Caribbean aesthetic linkages and the particular affinities between U.S. jazz and Latin American musical forms with an emphasis on the distinctive time signatures associated with traditional rumba, *son*, and guaracha styles (Gottlieb 1947; Machito 1947). The Puerto Rican pianist Morales, for instance, defined the mambo and the driving Latin music of the postwar era as a "merger between the schools of Be-bop and Rhumba" with Latin rhythms inflected by the dance band arrangements of hot swing orchestras with Duke Ellington, Woody Herman, or Stan Kenton being prominently cited (Bach 1947: 22).

Machito also stressed the geocultural distinctions of the Latin sound, explaining that Latin music has "a rhythm and a reality all its own. But both that rhythm and that reality are not well known to people in the United States. This is partly because of the unwillingness of their native musicians to travel and spread the good word of Cuban compositions and orchestrations" (1947: 26). Recalling an earlier discourse of U.S. foreign policy, the jazz critic Ulanov identifies a hybrid musical and dance form with deeper cultural implications in his discussion of mambo: "It is closer to an amalgamation, uniting a couple of related traditions with firmness and finality. This enlightened variation of the Good Neighbor Policy is implicit in the mambo when you see it danced, watching its syncopated movements combine Lindy and rhumba essentials" (1950: 26). Partly out of a sincere interest in musical cross-pollination and partly a result of circumstance (due to the close proximity in New York of various nightclubs that booked U.S. jazz ensembles and Latin orchestras), artists such as Dizzy Gillespie and Stan Kenton integrated gifted Latin percussionists into their bands, boosting the musical wattage and creating exciting new hybrid arrangements.

Even with a solidified position within the music industry, Latin music's audience appeal experienced a dip in 1951, especially in the heartland where "dancehall and ballroom promoters . . . and agency men are advising the Latin-groups to deemphasize their south-of-the-border rhythms and add a wider selection of pop tunes to their music library" ("Limited Dates" 1951: 41). *Variety* reported that New York, where the Spanish Caribbean musical influence was intensely felt, also seemed to be turning away from the Latin sound as clubs and record labels each minimized their investment in Latin American orchestras (although evidence suggests that club activity did not diminish uniformly, with several key showcase night spots maintaining consistent Latin music bookings).

Within only a year, however, *Variety* noted that the record industry was again placing its hopes in Latin music, describing a cyclical process whereby publishers and record labels turned to Latin music "when the U.S. pop output was at a low ebb and they've managed to instill life into the music industry until the big hit came along" ("Music Execs" 1952). Even with the occasional popular crossover hit, frequent radio broadcasts, and positive concert reviews, Latin music was still widely conceived as a marginal cultural force that was associated with the ethnic and cultural Other and accompanying notions of exotica. The powerful allure of Latin music and its potential to generate audience interest and commodity consumption ensured its place within the entertainment sector.

The national fascination with new Latin music logically carried over to television and through the early 1950s TV introduced the mambo to viewers outside of the urban and Latino enclaves where it was most familiar. One example of television's attempt to appropriate Latino signifiers and the emergent mambo can be seen on *The Lorraine Cugat Show*, starring the wife of the bandleader Xavier Cugat,[10] airing on the Los Angeles station KECA-TV in the summer of 1951. The program was a travesty of the Latin style, yet it was among the earliest programs to explicitly foreground Latin music in general and the mambo in particular. The hour-long show featured Cugat ostensibly "conducting" a capable Latin orchestra as it performed arrangements in the Latin mambo style, augmented by the occasional Brazilian number.

Cugat was an undeniably attractive woman, but her musical talents were questionable. She claimed none of her former husband's talent or authority as a conductor nor did she harbor the legitimate musical knowledge of her female contemporaries on television, the bandleader Ina Ray Hutton and her orchestra, Spade Cooley's all-girl band, Ada Leonard, or the "Hormel Girls." The Cugat program owed a debt to each, however, riding on her husband's reputation and his association with the rumba while benefiting from her shapely feminine physique that was almost always on full display and in constant motion. *Variety*'s review of the program's premiere broadcast on July 10, 1951, explicitly cites Cugat's nonstop rumba dancing as one of the key visual elements, summing up the physicality of her persona:

> Someone wise in teevee must have told Lorraine that the medium calls for movement and it's fatal to stand still. Those orders she carried out faithfully and her writhing form was as mobile as Alabama. . . . That she is tempting to the eye covers the male assessment; her sisters under the skin may be more demanding of her art and must have counted the hour well contained. . . . Lorraine was slinking and slithering, which was some help to searching eyes. . . . A little Tabasco in the right places will season it to a tasty tidbit of late evening sight-seeing. ("Lorraine Cugat Show," July 11, 1951)

Opening the September 13, 1951, broadcast, Cugat invites the television viewers on a musical journey, exclaiming, "Let's go flying down to Rio with 'The Carioca.'" When introducing the songs to the audience she provides brief details about the musical style or the songs' countries of origin, reinforcing her associations with South America through a series of strategic references to people, places, or other cultural facets. Her repertoire for the program also aligns with South America, merging the samba, rumba, and mambo as well as including U.S. song standards such as "Embraceable You." Cugat was not always up to the physical demands of her leading role, however, as she illustrates during her opening number, a version of "Bim,

Bam, Bum." Her effervescence seems exaggerated while she "conducts" the orchestra and after a spurt of energetic Latin-infused dancing Cugat can be seen gasping for breath. When she introduces the song "Mambo Boogie," she chirps with excessive enthusiasm: "Now for all you mambo fans, we've added a boogie beat. Let's see what you can do with 'Mambo Boogie.' Yeah!" Later in the program when introducing a mambo number she explains "From big mambos, little mambos grow, and we call them mambolitas." As the band embarks on a fine mambo arrangement, Cugat shimmies seductively in front of the orchestra with her back to them, not remotely concerned with conducting the group.

The Cugat show also suffered from several fatal production shortcomings, including severely inferior lighting and sloppy staging, but despite these glitches and the distractions of the host, the show's orchestra (featuring Ziggy Elman on trumpet who, in 1952, recorded several Latin-influenced numbers, including "Zig's Mambo") performs its mambo numbers well, enhanced on the September 13 broadcast by the clear, silky voice of the Mexican singer Pedro Vargas ("as loved throughout Latin America as Bing Crosby is here"), the De Marlo dancers, and guest musician Joe Carioca. As the program winds to its end, Cugat bids the viewing audience goodnight with the sign-off, "This is Lorraine Cugat saying hasta la *televista.*"

Other minor cultural productions during the early 1950s continued to nudge Latin music into the mainstream. For instance, a performance clip of Perez Prado and his orchestra, produced by Universal Pictures and aired on TV in 1952, offers a basic primer on the artist's spirited style and his band's scintillating mambo arrangements. The clip portrays a nightclub setting with patrons taking in the floorshow (with the band dressed in flamboyant scallop-sleeved shirts and dancers bedecked in feathers and sequins), while Prado effusively grunts and moans, cueing the band, guiding it through the changes. He then sits at the piano, where he demonstrates the instrument's full percussive possibilities as the band churns through one of his many mambo compositions.

Although the mambo was eclipsing it in the cultural realm, the rumba style persevered, showing up in various sectors of the entertainment industry. It was a centerpiece of the 1953 film *Surprising Suzy* (directed by Will Cowan), featuring singer Abbe Lane (who recorded with the Xavier Cugat orchestra and was married to the bandleader at the time) performing "Blame It on the Rhumba." That same year the Bob Bachelder orchestra channeled the rising fascination with both television and Latin music, fusing them in the novelty song "TV Rhumba" released on the independent Mood Records label based in Cambridge, Massachusetts.

Latin music and the mambo in particular attained a new legitimacy in 1953, however, when Carnegie Hall hosted the kick-off performance of the "Mambo Concerto" tour that was scheduled to visit twenty-five cities across the United States. With a forty-piece orchestra led by Gilberto Valdes, the Carnegie Hall performance listed several of the genre's top names, including Tito Puente, Tito Rodrigues, Noro Morales, Joe Loco, and Machito, among others ("Carnegie Test" 1953). Almost overnight, the mambo officially displaced the rumba as the main Latin music export, altering the cadence of U.S. dance styles.

The genre erupted across the entertainment and leisure industries in 1954, which was dubbed "the Year of the Mambo." There was a wave of recordings in the mambo style, with Tito Puente recording almost thirty tracks for Tico Records, while Perez Prado ("El Rey de Mambo") performed in some of the top show rooms in New York and Los Angeles and recorded mambo tracks for the RCA Victor label. Prado's mambo's were also prominently featured in the 1954 film *Mambo* (directed by Robert Rossen), starring Shelley Winters and choreographed by Katherine Dunham (who was also typecast in the film as a dance instructor). A second major mambo concert was held at Carnegie Hall in October 1954 and New York clubs including the Roseland Ballroom aggressively promoted their mambo shows; the Palladium even instated an all-mambo music policy. Demonstrating a pattern that was to continue through the 1950s, television producers latched onto emergent social trends such as the mambo, drawing them into the TV orbit.

The Desi Arnaz orchestra, never considered a serious contender in the Afro-Cuban category, also took up the newer mambo rhythm in 1954, when the pianist Marco Rizo penned "Lucy's Mambo." There were countless mambo-inspired novelty songs that failed to make an impression among audiences, yet there were also many popular/best-selling releases by the "easy listening" artists that dominated early television as program hosts or regular guests. Among the mambo deluge were "Papa Loves Mambo" recorded by Perry Como, Dean Martin, Nat "King" Cole, and others; "They Were Doin' the Mambo" by Vaughn Monroe; Richard Maltby and His Orchestra's "St. Louis Blues Mambo" (also released on RCA Victor by Perez Prado); Rosemary Clooney's "Mambo Italiano" (later covered by Dean Martin, who also had a hit with the mambo song "Sway"); "Mambo Baby" by Ruth Brown (also recorded by Georgia Gibbs); and the famous stage star Sophie Tucker contributing the humorous track "Middle Age Mambo."

The 1954 LP *Rock around the Clock* by rock 'n' roll pioneers Bill Haley and the Comets also included "Mambo Rock" (written by Jimmy Ayre, Mildred Phillips, and Bickley "Bix" Reichner), a track offering little in the way of actual Latin mambo rhythms, despite lyrics with tropical allusions and references to "natives" that "do the crazy Mambo Rock all day." The Brill Building songwriting team Jerry Lieber and Mike Stoller composed an R & B mambo, the "Loop-de-Loop Mambo" (recorded in 1954 by the Robins, The Escorts, and Gary Crosby), and the risqué songstress Ruth Wallis wrote and recorded "Psycho Mambo." Other novelty recordings released that year included titles such as "Oink-Oink Mambo," "Koo-Koo Mambo," "Hillbilly Mambo," and a pair of Christmas-oriented numbers, including Billy May's "Rudolph the Red-Nosed Mambo" and "I Saw Mommy Do the Mambo (with you know who)" by Jimmy Boyd. In a televised performance of the latter song, the child singer Boyd, sporting striped pajamas, pretends to hide on a staircase singing his song while Santa Claus and the child's "mother" dance a tame suburban mambo in front of a decorated Christmas tree. The recording of full-length mambo albums was less widespread than were recorded singles, but in 1954 the idiosyncratic vocalist Yma Sumac released *Mambo* on Capitol Records (accompanied by the Billy May orchestra) and Cal Tjader's Modern Mambo Quintet ambitiously released two LPs, *Mambo with Tjader* and *Tjader Plays Mambo* (each on the Fantasy Records label) within a month of one another.

With its expansion into the mainstream, mambo was posited within an interesting range of discursive patterns. The music magazine *Down Beat* weighed in on the phenomenon, with writer Nat Hentoff offering a historical overview of Latin dance and the mambo's place in a cultural continuum (1954: 2). In an adjacent article, the television dance instructor Mrs. Arthur Murray, who hosted TV's *The Arthur Murray Party*, explains the mambo within the contexts of contemporary social dancing, describing it as a "rhumba with a jitterbug accent," providing an accompanying chart outlining the dance's basic footwork (Murray 1954: 2).[11] In the same issue, Murray's attempts to establish a model for the conventional mambo step are undercut in an interview with Perez Prado, who subtly derides American self-conscious sensibilities, proclaiming, "They could all invent steps of their own. . . . There is no basic mambo step. Every place I travel has different steps. You should dance the mambo the way you feel" ("Prado Tells" 1954: 3).

The music and mainstream press obsessed about the mambo's rapid pro-liferation across the nation, affixing the terms "craze" or "mania" to the phe-nomenon while referring to aficionados and converts as "addicts" who were readily swept up into a mambo-induced "frenzy." Citing the vital role of the club-based orchestras in 1954, a *Life* magazine profile titled "Uncle Sambo, Mad for Mambo," noted the rise of the new dance style: "Having for some months lured large numbers of Americans to dance halls where they wiggle like lizards on a hot slab, a dance called the mambo has started to erupt in a holiday frenzy" ("Uncle Sambo" 1954: 14).

In many instances, the mambo effect was defined in rather cynical and subtle ways as a kind of virus infecting the otherwise refined comportment of U.S. patrons. As *Variety* reported, the mambo contagion was being trans-mitted throughout metropolitan society; "New York is continuing to shake from the hips down as the mambo continues to spread around town. The Latino hop has branched out from the Broadway dancehalls to the east-side plusheries and has crossed the bridge into Brooklyn" ("Yanks Dig That Mambo Beat" 1954: 1). The mambo "fever," it seemed, had immediate and irreducible physical symptoms that were first evident in the hips, rapidly spreading throughout the body as the rhythms took hold.

The dancers who converged on the clubs with impressive verve were also described with a Cold War twist as "namboniks," a "writhing," "wig-gling" or "contorted" assemblage often consisting of Latin men and eager U.S. women who displayed the basic characteristics of an emergent mambo "cult" ("Uncle Sambo" 1954; "Darwin and the Mambo," 1954). Even though the versions of mambo dance and music that were broadcast on television were considerably diluted they still functioned as a conduit for the nation's broader familiarity with Latin music and the dances that accompanied it.

Working within a potent double entendre that associates nondemo-cratic or dictatorial "south-of-the-border" politics with revolutionary tran-sition, Perez Prado expounded on his creative process and his aspirations for mambo in the United States. Expressing a convoluted transposition of the Good Neighbor policy suggesting a revolutionary (if well-intentioned) invasion from Latin America, Prado described his hopes for future Ameri-can bookings and the dissemination of his mambo sound; "Then we can set off a big 'boom'—a revolution. Not the shooting kind, but a musical revo-lution like Benny Goodman's that will bring people of North America and especially those from Latin American countries out to dance together and be happy" (1954: 29).

In the hands of the Latin masters, the orchestral performances of the mambo and, slightly later, the cha-cha-cha were occasions for televisual excitement, although many of the top mambo artists were either unilingual (requiring translators in order to engage with U.S. media) or they spoke deeply accented English that complicated television interviews. With few televised appearances by actual hard-core or authentic mambo artists, pseudo-mambo renditions proliferated on television in 1954–55, performed in genteel contexts by American recording stars and television celebrities such as Perry Como, Frankie Laine, Peggy Lee, Tony Martin, and Dinah Shore. These performances normally maintained a cool emotional air that barely hinted at the original mambo elements, sacrificing much of the energy and excitement of the Latin influence that were embodied by physically expressive performers on the scale of Prado or Puente.

Among the more successful mambo-style recordings of the period was the 1954 hit "Papa Loves Mambo," popularized by TV crooner Perry Como. The song became a standard of music shows with televised performances by Rosemary Clooney, Eddie Fisher, Vaughn Monroe, and Martin and Como. Recounting the genesis of the song in 1955, Como offers a detailed, day-by-day and hour-by-hour breakdown of its composition and recording. In his description, Como unambiguously defines the tune as a "novelty," sidestepping the praise heaped on the Latin bands by the music trade press and by top jazz musicians. Como instead expresses his desire to latch onto the "mambo mania" then sweeping the country and to produce a recording that would capitalize on "the huge teenage craze over the dance" (1955).

Adhering to the established practices of Tin Pan Alley songsmiths or the infamous Brill Building tune writers, the entire process took only eight days from conception to completion in the recording studio. Como's reputed casual style, however, was not particularly well suited to the mambo genre, as he demonstrated on his show's October 13, 1954, broadcast. Stepping onto a set festooned with palms and what looks like a small Mexican courtyard, Como opens with a slight, Latinized version of the Dean Martin hit "Sway" (accompanied by his backup vocal ensemble, The Ray Charles singers), during which it appears that he is reading the lyrics from an off-screen prompter. Later, Como introduces Peggy Lee, who performs a fantastic uptempo mambo version of "I Feel a Song Coming On" that has a scintillating horn chart and some fine rhythmic accompaniment. Como closes the show with a lackluster rendition of his hit single, "Papa Loves Mambo," featuring typically understated vocals. As the show winds down Como takes a couple of clumsy dance turns with Lee, whose proficiency with Latin music was clearly superior. Further undercutting the performance, Como also evidently misgauges the final song's timing (by roughly forty seconds), and he glances down to receive instruction from the off-camera stage manager to sing a brief reprise of the chorus and bring Lee out for another spin.

Tony Martin was considerably more comfortable with a mambo tune than were many of his contemporaries. On the October 11, 1954, episode of the *Tony Martin Show*, the program is structured around the typical musical journey, inviting viewers to a virtual Mexico. Clay pots and sombreros hang on the walls of the set, contributing to the vignette's sense of "south-of-the-border" locale while extras cross the stage wearing sombreros, ponchos, and frilled skirts in a sartorial display intended to reinforce a sense of geocultural place. Performing the song "South American Way" (popularized by Carmen Miranda), Martin is conspicuously not "Mexicanized," maintaining his status as the ever-suave nightclub performer in his dark suit and tie. The tune is arranged in a distinct mambo style with well-defined conga drumming as Martin sings about the "hazy," "lazy" and "kinda-crazy" sensibilities of a vague and generalized southern tier, emphasizing the naturalized relations between tropical heat, dance, and erotic romance. The production later departs from the rustic zocalo setting of the Mexican pueblo and, as the band establishes another credible mambo rhythm with sharp percussive conga shots, the show's vocal ensemble, The Interludes, step onto a set identified as "Club Mambo," where they join Martin, who weaves among extras posing as nightclub patrons performing his rendition of "Papa Loves Mambo." Despite the loose mambo arrangements for which many of his television cohorts were known, the agile orchestral accompaniment on Martin's program is filled with brassy horn shots that hint at the vigor of Perez Prado's or Tito Puente's vibrant orchestras.

While the mambo trend in 1954 led to numerous domesticated renditions, Peggy Lee's performance of a mambo-influenced version of Rodgers and Hart's "Bewitched, Bothered and Bewildered" on the May 23, 1954, broadcast of *Colgate Comedy Hour* provides a slightly different representation of Latin musical form that bridges the hotter elements of an arguably more authentic Latin style and the diluted gringo renditions. Lee handles a mambo extremely well, and with her well-practiced seductiveness she embodies the full possibilities of the Latin style in ways that most of her peers never did. Lee's two numbers on the program present an interesting framework within which to display her ample talents and her openly professed love of Latin music; in the jazz magazine *Metronome* she once describe herself as "a frustrated Latin," insinuating a general emotional disposition and a close affective relationship with her material, based in no small part on her composition and recording of the track "Mañana" (sung with a faux Mexican accent and lyrics tapping into a well of cultural stereotypes) ("Peggy Lee" 1950: 14). Neither of the songs she performs on the program, however, is unequivocally "Latin," yet each adopts a Latin essence, embracing and expressing the "Latin tinge" in the American mainstream.

Offering a counternarrative to the open and unabashed embrace of the mambo and of Latin music more generally, the playwright Noel Coward provided an arch, cynical tune that critically engaged the pervasiveness and influence of the Latin sound. In a brilliant program titled, "Together with Music," Coward and the actress Mary Martin hosted the October 22, 1955, broadcast of the *Ford Star Jubilee*. The artists were each at the peak of their talents and though Martin had plenty of television experience, Coward was a relative neophyte in the medium, with Martin at one point intoning, "Think of all those thousands of people in their clean American homes, crouching over their sets just staring at you."[12]

Coward's plays are renowned for their wry humor and on this episode his art was on full display. The song "Nina" is introduced by Coward:[13] "My next number requires a great deal of turgid tropical atmosphere. . . . This is a song about a lady from South America, a fairly disagreeable lady, who throughout her long and checkered existence, resolutely refused to dance." The band launches into a Latin-tinged mambo arrangement opening with a muted trumpet solo as Coward, with direct and uncompromising lyrics (and his own swaying semidance movements), embarks on a rather complex tale involving a woman who disliked all Latin music and Latin dancing in particular:

Senorita Nina from Argentina
despised the tango
although she never was a girl to let a man go
she wouldn't compromise her principles for sex
she looked with scorn on the gyrations of her relations
who did the conga
and she said if she had to stand it any longer
she'd have to wring their silly necks. . . .

... she said I hate to be pedantic
but it drives me nearly frantic
when I see the unromantic sycophantic lot of sluts
forever wriggling their guts
it drives me absolutely nuts. ...

... after some trial and tribulation
she reached the station and met a sailor
who had acquired a wooden leg in Venezuela
and so she married him because he couldn't dance.

With his lyrics Coward acknowledges the undeniable emphasis on dance within Latin American culture, reserving his harshest criticism for the trends that had swept the United States in this period. In his inimitable fashion, however, Coward remarkably manages to provide derisive commentary on the Latin dance fad while performing a Latin-inflected tune, castigating the trend itself in a way that was neither contradictory nor disingenuous. Como and many of the others swept up in the mambo "fever" seem like hapless opportunists compared to Coward.

As Coward's song implies, the mambo and other Latin musical inflections were not necessarily welcomed in every quarter. Sammy Kaye (of the "swing and sway" brand identity) expressed negative sentiments in an article in *Down Beat* that was sure to be read by many of his contemporaries. Kaye dismissed the musical qualities of the mambo and of the Latin orchestras in general, isolating dancing and not musical performance as the core facet of the mambo's appeal. Referring to the music's "offbeat tempo," Kaye suggests that the mambo "is a novelty that will eventually go the way of all novelties ... into obscurity" (1955: 56). Kaye was not inaccurate in his assessment that the mambo's core popularity was closely associated with its reputation as a dance music, but his indifference to the contributions of Latin American musicians and their influence on American popular culture reflects an extremely limited understanding of both Latin music and the changes in U.S. culture at the time.

Perhaps reflecting how out of touch Kaye actually was with his denouncement of the mambo, the 1955 CBS program *America's Greatest Bands* (a three-month summer replacement for *The Jackie Gleason Show* that was hosted by the bandleader Paul "Pops" Whiteman) featured the orchestras of Xavier Cugat, Perez Prado, Machito's Afro Cubans, and Cu-bop virtuoso Stan Kenton, each of whom played unexpurgated Latin jazz arrangements including uncompromising versions of the mambo. Latin music, it would seem from this program roster, was not some fad or passing anomaly but a crucial and much loved facet of U.S. popular music.

As this chapter's historical analysis of cultural convergence indicates, there was a mutual reliance between U.S. television networks and Latin American musicians. This is obviously not the only tale to tell about this process of collaboration, for the formation of Latin-based independent record companies, increases in Latin immigration, the huge drawing power and appeal of musical showcase clubs, and the success of Latin songs in the jukebox trade, in unison led to further influences of Latin music. Television, however, must be considered in this nexus of convergent factors. The musical performances of Latin Americans may not have overturned the hegemonic relations of racial and ethnic authority on the television screen, but they ensured that the screen was not a monopolized field of ethnic homogeneity.

CONCLUSION

Rocking the TV Conventions

*

We think tonight that he's going to make television history for you.
We'd like you to meet him now—Elvis Presley.
BILL RANDLE, INTRODUCING PRESLEY ON HIS NETWORK TELEVISION
DEBUT, *STAGE SHOW*, JANUARY 28, 1956

In any work of a historical nature, there are decisions to be made, decisions that call the role of the writer into sharp relief when documents and their contents are presented as being factual, as evidence of something larger at work in the social sphere. In his classic tract *What Is History*, Edward H. Carr poses the dilemma thus: "It used to be said that facts speak for themselves. This is, of course, untrue. The facts speak only when the historian calls on them: it is he who decides which facts to give the floor, and in what order or what context. . . . The historian is necessarily selective" (1962: 9). While there are certain historical issues or moments that, through consensus or sheer monumentality are granted supremacy of importance, the general point to take from Carr is that the excavation and display of the past is not always or entirely objective.

Whereas this book is about media convergences and the cultural and industrial forces that turned music and early television toward each other in a particular historical period, most of the themes were not consciously preordained. Rather, they were nominated by the extant quotes and sentiments of the people working in the music and television industries over fifty years ago, gleaned from the articulation of cultural change from the 1930s through the immediate postwar period. I listened to these "voices" from the past as I might in any conversation or debate, discerning the argumentative nuances and noting when and where one voice was louder or more urgent than the others. Obviously, as Carr reminds us, not just any *old* thing qualifies for inclusion and the process involves subjective awareness and reflection about what kind of story one wants to tell.

In this project, some of the historical voices have grown familiar and the stories have become quite special to me, and the pleasure of screening early televised musical performances by artists and celebrities at the top of their game is still a constant thrill. I should disclose, however, that my interests in early television have another, more personal angle: my grandmother, Bertha Forman, was a regular cast member of *Soupy's On*, a late-night comedy show starring the inimitable Soupy Sales that aired on the Detroit station WXYZ-TV between 1953 and 1959. Due to her influence, I have always watched early television more attentively, seeking insight and understanding of the medium's history that might connect me more intimately with this odd and quirky character actress that was my father's mother. Sales's pie-throwing antics and hilarious hackneyed weather reports were fun for a kid such as I, but he always represented a different, more tangible link with television as a workplace and a source of income. This wasn't just entertainment, this was part of our family's livelihood and legacy.

While I was writing this section Sales died, on October 22, 2009. With his passing, the encomiums frequently cited his abiding love of jazz music in particular. According to the *New York Times* music reviewer Ben Ratliff, Sales "knew a lot about jazz and was a pioneer in the history of jazz on American television ... he made Charlie Parker's 'Yardbird Suite' his theme song. He took advantage of all the jazz musicians stopping through town to play local clubs like the Rouge Lounge and the Blue Bird Inn and the Crystal Show Bar. His guests included Duke Ellington, Ella Fitzgerald, Billie Holiday, Stan Getz, Milt Jackson, Charlie Parker and Clifford Brown" (2009). Other jazz artists appearing on his show included Miles Davis and Coleman Hawkins, and the show's studio band included the guitarist Joe Messina and percussionist Jack "White Jack" Brokensha, future members of the renowned Motown session unit The Funk Brothers.[1]

In a roundabout way, by virtue of my grandmother's TV pedigree I am drawn closer to television's musical programming (and to the Detroit soul and the Motown sound that I joyfully indulged through the 1960s and 1970s). As this further suggests, however, we come to understand television's functions — what it means and what attracts us most about it — in circuitous ways, not necessarily directly through the medium itself. This concept brings to mind Keith Negus's statement, "Industry produces culture and culture produces an industry" (1998: 359). Negus explains that industry produces culture in the ways that it sets up "structures and organization and working practices to produce identifiable products and 'intellectual properties'" (ibid.). Culture produces an industry in the sense that "production does not take place simply 'within' a corporate environment created according to the requirements of capitalist production but in relation to broader cultural formations and practices that may not be directly within the control or understanding of the company" (ibid.: 359–60). Television music was and remains an object of social negotiation, situated within an amalgamation of influential factors; in my case, it also happens to have a familial angle.

It is inappropriate to neglect some of the other forces that direct us toward television and that inflect our engagements with it. According to Simon Frith, "The musical moments that we remember are the ones that disrupt the flow, that become *newsworthy*" (2002: 280). This assessment is valid and throughout the years specific televised musical moments have surely attained event status. The epigraph opening this chapter identifies one such newsworthy broadcast.[2] The format of *Stage Show* in 1956 was mundane, described as "a straight vaudeville style vehicle. . . . Just like the 'good old days,' one performer after another appeared on stage, while the Dorsey Brothers and their orchestra filled the moments in between acts with a few musical numbers" (Castleman and Podrazik 1982: 106). It was the momentary divergence from the show's conventional presentation that made all the difference.

Bill Randle's introduction of the "young hillbilly singer" on July 28, 1956, is fascinating for its Janus-like possibilities. Janus, the Roman god of doors or gates, represents exits and entrances, simultaneously accommodating both endings and beginnings. This can be further interpreted as meaning a point of transition where one intellectual orientation or cultural sensibility gives way to another. In his role as MC, Randle offers a pragmatic cue to viewers, informing them that there is a transition on the show from one performer to the next, but his comments also resonate within a wider cultural context. His introductory comments are ultimately a declaration about TV standards and, accordingly, about emerging changes to the routines of audience reception and viewer expectations.

Whereas Elvis Presley's influence on popular music was widely discussed by 1956, it was altogether unclear what his TV performances meant for television.[3] With his introduction of a still relatively unknown artist, Randle (a well-regarded Cleveland radio DJ and an unalloyed supporter of rock 'n' roll) addresses a moment of significance and a point of transition in television's brief existence, proclaiming the event status of the broadcast and the uniqueness of the imminent performance. The introduction serves as a reminder of television's elevated cultural standing at this early stage in its evolution and of music's powerful role within TV's presentational logic. That a musical performance on television in 1956 could realistically be conceived as *historical* is something that should not be overlooked from our present vantage. Randle's statement is actually quite complex, summoning a notion of the future *and* the future of the past, projecting how a young charismatic performer making his television debut will be received and how he will eventually be remembered. That Randle was right in his prediction is not an example of mystical prescience (or a good guess) but an articulation of awareness about television's influence and its reach at this particular historical juncture.[4] Robynn Stilwell suggests that television producers quickly recognized new opportunities after Presley's television year and wasted little time in appropriating rock 'n' roll's allure by writing the musical talents of a young Rick Nelson into the scripts of *The Adventures of Ozzie and Harriet*. Citing Nelson's "sweet face and clean-cut image," Stilwell claims that the young TV and music star occupied a crucial role in television's popularization of rock music: "he brought rock and roll to a mainstream audience in as non-threatening a guise as possible, while also paving the way for other teen idols . . . to parley television success into record success" (2003: 13).

Things of a compelling visual nature — things that *really move* — often make for television's most engaging content; musical performers and TV directors had said as much for years. With his telegenic appearance, his riveting kinetic style, and his upbeat rock 'n' roll tempos, Elvis Presley promised good television; his performances added the requisite action while his multivalent symbolic value attained "newsworthiness."[5] Adding to Frith's observation, I would note that while "disruption" is a crucial aspect influencing our recollections there is also something of a highly personal nature involved, something that encompasses subjective affect and the internal pleasures that can, at times, defy rational explanation. TV events of every magnitude are embedded within a permeating everydayness—what Rick Altman (1986) refers to as "household flow"[6]—and as such they require negotiation between text and context before we ascribe greatness to them.

I recall one particular TV viewing experience as a child, stretched out on the floor in front of my family's faux-birch TV set. This was not of itself out of the norm, yet the conventionality of the moment was disrupted by the fact that along with millions of others I was eagerly watching the 1964 Beatles debut on *The Ed Sullivan Show*, tuned in to the "four lovable mop-tops" (a term that seems ready-made for child consumption). While it was beyond my comprehension, the broadcast was deeply affecting at the time. The Beatles, it seemed, had tapped into my unknown desires, and the multiple meanings and pleasures that they presented in their own unique performative mode were now also internalized and highly personal. I knew that, despite my tender age, the Beatles meant far more to me than did the kid-friendly sequences on the Sullivan show featuring Topo Gigio or Senor Wences. The music sounded fresh and John, Paul, George, and Ringo looked sincere, like they were really having a great time. I was mesmerized and I dragged my mother to a record store where she bought me my first single: the Beatles' "I Want to Hold Your Hand" (backed with "I Saw Her Standing There") and I soon after received a toy guitar (which I "played," pretending I was George). In retrospect, seeing the Beatles on TV had a profound influence on my childhood musical tastes and those of a generation, their performance inestimably altering the expectations of music on television.[7]

The Beatles' TV debut is associated with a period of social transition identified by Thomas Hine as "the populuxe era," a phase that "began with Elvis Presley—sexy, energetic, American. It ended with the Beatles—cute, ironic, foreign" (1987: 174). Just as young viewers responded to Presley after seeing him on television, a second wave of young viewers responded to the Beatles. We became *fans*, and as fans we projected our fantasies and desires onto the band, channeling our emotions in and through the music. In this period, different logics of social cohesion emerged among young people resulting in new cultural affinities or "affective alliances" with alternative "mattering maps" (Grossberg 1992). Whereas these emergent sensibilities provided grounds for defined audience formations they also simultaneously enunciated divergence, most notably between youths and the adult/parent authority structures but also between fans of different musical styles and different artists and, occasionally, between viewers of different television programs.

Roughly concurrent with the Beatles' U.S. television debut, the Fisher Price company introduced its wind-up "Two Tune Giant Screen Music Box TV," a plastic unit shaped like a TV set that played "Row Row Row Your Boat" and "London Bridge" as images scroll across a small screen.[8] While the content of the toy was unambiguously oriented toward small children, the mechanism also functioned as a socializing tool that further normalized TV viewing among very young children. The TV toy and network children's programming in the 1960s each reinforced the point that television is a medium where music and images characteristically converge, introducing children to the most basic aspects of television music reception and reception dispositions.

Nonetheless, this wasn't actually television and the toy's content fell far short of what the Beatles (or any of the other popular music acts on TV at the time) offered. As a young child who was obviously unable to attend concerts or nightclubs it seemed to me that music on television was more *real*, and that any other form of child-oriented visual representation was deficient. This notion of the real, or what popular music scholars today might define as "authenticity" had a powerful influence on viewing patterns but as we know now, such visual representations also affected audience's sense of musical value. How the music was framed and presented was a matter of significance and even very young fans of popular music were capable of making distinctions between different visual regimes and TV's mediated realities.

Televised cartoon music programs (*The Beatles, The Archie Show, Josie and the Pussycats, The Jackson 5,* or *The Groovie Goolies,* as well as nonanimated kid-oriented music shows like *The Banana Splits, The Monkees,* or *The Partridge Family*) debuted throughout the mid-1960s and early 1970s, constituting a viewing destination for millions of preteens such as myself. While the Beatles and the Jackson 5 provided real-life models for animated characters, the other productions were purely TV constructs, with the tunes written by professional songsmiths and recorded by often-anonymous session musicians. Still, Michael Jackson was himself only a kid and like many other juvenile fans I was unduly impressed that someone so young — someone my own age — could have songs on the radio or have a TV cartoon character based on his life.

Scholars analyzing music on television regularly ignore such age-specific inclinations, yet they are of the utmost importance if we are ever to unlock the multiple modes of audience apprehension and diverse viewer pleasures that television music delivers. Despite their dismissal by music journalists and older rock fans at the time, these cartoons and music comedy programs were not benign or empty entertainment but complex cultural forms that introduced another means through which to access popular music, offering an important medium for the exploration of fan desires and honing of musical tastes.[9] To place these childrens' music programs in their proper context, the Don Kirshner musical creation The Archies (an animated TV band that was based on a popular comic book) reached the *Billboard* Hot 100 chart with the song "Sugar Sugar" roughly concurrent with the legendary Woodstock Music and Art Fair (August 15–17, 1969), hitting the chart's number one spot a month later. "Sugar Sugar" was the year's top-selling hit recording.

As rock became more explicitly associated with "sex and drugs" or with radical politics in the 1960s and 1970s, the networks took greater risks and courted controversy far more frequently than they had at TV's inception. Despite mainstream predilections, in their eagerness to sustain and expand their audience base the networks were less inclined to consistently "play it safe" or to stick to a narrow representational model. For one thing, television was no longer new and, thus, it was freed from having to prove itself to audiences and consumers as it did in its early years. The executive tier at the networks and the major advertising agencies had also turned over since the early 1950s and a new management cohort was in charge. A more liberal perspective prevailed in the entertainment industries and it showed in the nation's TV content, reflecting transformations in the broader social and political spheres.

Still, there were many instances of generational dissonance and performances that grated against mainstream sociopolitical sensibilities. Ed Sullivan, who in 1956 was vehemently opposed to hosting Elvis Presley, for example, featured the Rolling Stones and The Doors in 1967, each of which offended Sullivan's personal tastes and ostensibly challenged the propriety of the airwaves much as Elvis Presley had done roughly a decade earlier. *The Smothers Brothers Comedy Hour* (on CBS between 1967 and 1969) famously collided with CBS executives around their musical content and the political commentary of artists including Joan Baez, Harry Belafonte, and Pete Seeger.[10] In many of these broadcasts the modernist aesthetics that dominated in the late 1940s and early 1950s were replaced by an aesthetic forged in the "swinging sixties," including "hip" stage sets and psychedelic imagery or surreal special effects as exemplified by Janis Joplin's March 1969 appearance on *The Ed Sullivan Show*. Whereas tradition and past virtues were commonly prized and privileged in TV's early musical broadcasts, by the 1960s and 1970s the effort to remain current and fresh — to be "now" — intensified.

Through the mid-1960s and the 1970s popular music of all sorts jostled on the airwaves,[11] often within the same shows. Ed Sullivan's weekly program stuck to its proven variety show formula featuring varied musical acts and genres from an array of cultural sectors. In a later example of generic collision, the *Donny and Marie* show (on ABC between 1976 and 1979) featured the Osmond siblings in a song and dance showdown titled "A little bit country, a little bit rock 'n' roll," a musical medley that comprised the show's centerpiece. In another juxtaposition of a different nature, David Bowie was a musical guest on a 1975 episode of the afternoon talk show *Dinah!* hosted by the TV and recording veteran Dinah Shore, where he performed a funky version of "Stay" and engaged in earnest conversation about love and relationships with Shore and Henry Winkler — Fonzie from the retro sit-com *Happy Days*. During this period it was not altogether weird to sit — admittedly stoned — with my parents to watch *The Lawrence Welk Show* before flipping the channels in search of music that was more familiar and age-appropriate. In the mid-1970s music always seemed to be available on TV although it was more consistently structured according to generic and demographic segmentation.

As an adolescent, I relied on television as much as radio for exposure to my favorite musical artists. Radio has the obvious advantage of mobility, but teens wanted to see what the stars looked like too, and the magazines of interest (such as *Rolling Stone*, *Creem*, or *Hit Parader*) only went so far in providing insights about creativity, style, performance, the body (and, I suppose, hair). Televised concerts provided a unique vantage on popular music performances, offering cues about the artists' visual personae and performance styles while introducing a primer on fan behaviors before many teens were old enough to actually attend live shows. In the 1970s *The Midnight Special* hosted by Wolfman Jack (produced by Burt Sugarman on NBC from 1973 to 1981) and *Don Kirshner's Rock Concert* (this syndicated program was on the air between 1973 and 1981 and was based on Kirshner's earlier production, *In Concert*, on ABC the previous year) were essential viewing for teens throughout the United States. Each show featured a remarkably diverse artist roster with the performances amounting to a weekly seminar on stagecraft across the musical genres.

Wolfman Jack reenacted his exuberant rock 'n' roll radio personality when he introduced the acts but by the mid-1970s during disco's reign *Midnight Special* often resembled Dick Clark's *American Bandstand* (a show that seemed tired to me, especially when compared to *Soul Train*, hosted by Don Cornelius, which was far more *fun*), with cameras lingering over cavorting dancers while the artists visibly resorted to lip-synching. *Midnight Special* was clearly a studio production, and it seemed more constrained by television's formal concerns. Among my young friends *Rock Concert* was deemed the more "authentic" program because of the large-stage concert productions featured on each broadcast. The show achieved a documentary effect, the cameras "capturing" the performances in more naturalistic manner, constructing a particular idealized image of audience-performer interaction. With his staid opening monologue, it was evident that Kirshner was a straightforward industry guy—only years later did I learn just how influential the music publisher, producer, and entrepreneur really was (and that he was responsible for both The Archies and The Monkees).

Frith writes, "The fact is that for the vast majority of people—particularly the vast majority of youth (and including the minority who themselves become performers)—rock stars are first seen on television, and what a rock star is meant to be is therefore to an extant defined by television" (2002: 284). *Rock Concert* was for many teen viewers a site of "first contact" with several bands and music genres. The show provided my first glimpse of the makeup-wearing KISS (which I understood as falling somewhere between the cartoon bands of my childhood and the heavier stuff preferred by the tough kids around the way, the ones that smoked) while introducing me to jazz-rock fusion (Mahavishnu Orchestra, Weather Report) and providing a greater appreciation for a tight horn section (Blood Sweat and Tears; Earth, Wind and Fire; Ohio Players; Sly and the Family Stone; or Tower of Power). Both *Rock Concert* and *Midnight Special* also featured many of the soul and funk artists that, despite their impressive record sales and popularity, remained comparatively infrequent TV guests. The audience was absolutely essential to *Rock Concert* with broad sweeping shots of the energetic crowds interspersed throughout the edited performances; radio was never this exciting.

Saturday Night Live, premiering on NBC in October 1975, attracted millions of young viewers not just because of the show's irreverent and timely comedy skits. Like its predecessors *Midnight* Special and *Rock Concert*, SNL's musical guest list spanned the genres, bringing both top celebrity artists and relative newcomers to the screen week after week (with artists as diverse as Anne Murray, Neil Sedaka, Leon Redbone, and James Taylor; the Chieftains, the Nitty Gritty Dirt Band, and the McGarrigle Sisters; Sun Ra, the Preservation Hall Jazz Band, Ornette Coleman, the Meters, and the Stylistics; the Rolling Stones, George Harrison, Frank Zappa, and Peter Tosh). Just as it had at TV's inception, SNL's live element constituted a crucial factor of its allure and, as might be expected, some artists performed brilliantly under such conditions and some stumbled noticeably. With the TV industry's reliance on filmed performances since the mid-1950s, artists were less concerned with nailing the perfect performance, benefiting from multiple takes or postproduction editing. Live television is an anachronism (albeit one that harbors a certain appeal) requiring a shift in viewing attitudes and a general acceptance of the fact that the performances may not correspond with the seamless perfection of most televised music. Watching SNL in the 1970s was something of a spectator sport, presenting young viewers with a context for discussion about stagecraft and performance aesthetics (as well as allowing for speculation about whether or not certain stars were drunk or high during their performances).[12]

The expansion of cable television in the 1980s fundamentally changed the music broadcast landscape, especially with the launch of Black Entertainment Television (BET) in 1980, MTV in 1981, Country Music Television (CMT) in 1983, and VH-1 in 1985. Each of these networks was designed for specific audience demographics and featured what were surely the most carefully constructed music program schedules in the history of television. Tom McGrath (1996) explains how Mike Nesmith of the made-for-TV band The Monkees was instrumental in conceptualizing a music video station but a host of other key industry executives (including players with a solid footing at the major record labels and the TV networks) eventually brought it to fruition. Whereas Nesmith was an early music video artist, the commercial potential of the medium was immediately evident to those in the corporate sector and the operative decisions soon adhered to a strictly commercial and promotional logic.

This is not to suggest, however, that there were not deep industrial concerns about music television and its impact on broadcasting and on popular music. Andrew Goodwin cites modes of "anxiety" that are reminiscent of the postwar period when music and television were first merged, describing some of the same themes; an intensified interest in "videogenic" or good-looking musicians, the dilution of musicians' artistic reputations, a loss of musicians' autonomy and control, or the packaging and commercial promotion of musicians' artistic output (1992: 8). Prior to launching MTV (by far the most influential of the music networks), Bob Pittman, then of the Warner AMEX Satellite Entertainment Company (WASEC)[13] embarked on an extensive research process, "to determine people's tastes. . . . [B]y the time the channel was on the air, WASEC would do four separate surveys, polling potential viewers about everything from what kind of music the channel should play to what the on-air personalities should be like to what the new service should be named" (McGrath 1996: 47). In Goodwin's assessment this research indicates that "MTV had to *construct* an audience for music television. . . . [I]t was the television industry, rather than the record business, that led this development" (1992: 38).

By the end of the 1990s, MTV was far in front of any music television competitors, in no small part due to a continued emphasis on in-depth audience research and its reliance on the nascent teen-trend research model known as "cool hunting" (Hay 1998; Morris 1998). Now part of the Viacom stable of international companies,[14] the MTV brand is indelibly associated with the formal and industrial construct "music television," reaching literally billions of consumers globally. It has had its share of "newsworthy" televised musical moments, including the 1985 *Live Aid* African famine relief broadcasts (and the updated *Live 8* international concerts twenty years later) and various breakthrough video debuts by artists such as Madonna, Michael Jackson, Prince, and Bruce Springsteen and much-watched programs including *Headbangers Ball, Total Request Live, Unplugged,* and *Yo! MTV Raps.* Yet in the United States, where it began, the network is now barely recognizable compared to its earliest days.[15] With a severely reduced music video repertoire and far fewer music-oriented programs, the network now specializes in reality television, game shows, and other pop culture themes, reinforcing Goodwin's early observation that TV rather than music guides the network's program decisions. Even as music slides from the U.S. MTV schedule, other music-oriented networks continue to air videos and concerts and "music television" remains an important object of academic scrutiny, as several more recent publications indicate (Vernallis 2004; Beebe and Middleton 2007; Pegley 2008).

During the late 1980s and early 1990s hip-hop and rap music were amplified through a variety of U.S. TV conduits including MTV's *Yo! MTV Raps,*

The Arsenio Hall Show, BET's *Rap City*, *Saturday Night Live*, and the Fox network's *In Living Color*.[16] Network television (like most commercial radio) has never been particularly welcoming of hip-hop's broader palate (with the exception of program's with a younger viewership like *Saturday Night Live* or the occasional late-night talk show), but the cable programs were absolutely crucial to the genre's success. Cable television transformed an important but still relatively marginal musical form into a major cultural influence, in the process communicating the aesthetics and cultural sensibilities of African American urban artists to a far broader audience cross-section (Forman 2002; Charnas 2010). In the current historical moment hip-hop's television presence has receded yet it remains popular online where retro-videos from the so-called golden age (circa 1988–94) and more recent productions are simultaneously available to fans. Videos posted to the Internet are now also essential to the circulation of new music by emerging hip-hop and R & B artists, as are genre-specific cable channels such as VH-1 Soul.

Over the past decade network television has enhanced its status as a source of new music for viewing audiences. For example, the singer-songwriter Vonda Shepard was written into the scripts of *Ally McBeal* (on the Fox network, 1997–2002) as a lounge singer during the show's first several seasons, and she subsequently released two soundtrack albums from the program. Rock and pop music recordings are standard facets of the soundtracks of televised teen dramas (*Dawson's Creek*, *Degrassi: Next Generation*, *Gossip Girl*, *One Tree Hill*, *The O.C.*), presented in a manner that showcases the songs and artists (as occurred on TV drama programs in the mid-1950s) and the tracks inscribed into the narratives such that the scenes often amount to minivideos comprising the most interesting moments in a show. Placing popular music at the forefront, *Degrassi: Next Generation* even bases the titles of its weekly episodes on iconic hit songs, although copyright and licensing constraints influence the extent to which hits are actually included in the soundtrack.

Program soundtracks are frequently packaged and sold, making them a crucial factor in establishing industry synergy and a lucrative revenue stream. Teen dramas are especially significant in the promotion of newer music; viewers are now familiar with the brief advertisements at the end of broadcasts citing the artists and the songs heard on the program, directing us to the relevant websites, where we can hear more by the artists and download tracks.

Audacious in its original concept merging the stage musical format within the context of a standard TV police drama genre, the ABC show *Cop Rock* was critically panned when it debuted in 1990. Robynn Stilwell proclaims that the program "proves the dangers of generic disruption. . . . What is crucial for one genre is deadly for another" (2003: 18–19). This experiment in genre hybridity (created by cop show wunderkind Steven Bochco) was also a dismal failure with viewers, although several subsequent shows on network and cable TV (*Ally McBeal, Scrubs, Six Feet Under, Oz*) occasionally featured similarly outrageous, campy song-and-dance sequences, breaking the mold of their respective genres while adding a dose of humor to the scripts. Within this aesthetic and generic trajectory, the Fox network's *Glee* (debuting in 2009) reintroduced the hybrid musical-drama concept within a more focused and logical narrative context — the travails of teen students and their high school glee club — to critical acclaim.

The show toys with the universal and timeworn concept of the amateur singer while tapping into some of the visual pleasures of amateur dance, in the process strategically linking *Glee* to the successful Disney film and TV franchise *High School Musical* and to TV's contemporary ratings powerhouses, *American Idol, America's Got Talent, America's Best Dance Crew,* and *So You Think You Can Dance. Glee* is actually a broader generic hybrid encompassing the spirit of amateur competition shows as well as teen high school–based dramas and musicals, casting a wide net in the hope of reaching a vast and varied viewing base. While the show has spawned a large and adoring audience known in the industry as "Gleeks," the praise is not universal; the *New York Times* music critic Jon Caramanica notes, "'Glee' may love music, but it often abuses it, with performances wholly lacking grit" (2010: 19).

Demonstrating its explicit affiliations with actual amateur and school-based glee clubs, the show also sells branded sheet music for "piano/vocal/guitar" and full "choral octavos" published by the Hal Leonard Corporation. The *Glee* soundtrack is a proven audience favorite,[17] with the cast recording of the 1981 Journey song "Don't Stop Believin'" breaking into the *Billboard* Hot 100 chart and selling over a half million downloads via iTunes. *Glee: The Music, Journey to Regionals* reached number one on the *Billboard* 200 top album chart, surpassing previous releases *Glee: The Music, Season One, Volume 1, Glee: The Music, Season One, Volume 2, Glee: The Music, Showstoppers* and *Glee: The Music, The Power of Madonna.* At this writing, the *Glee* enterprise has released six soundtrack volumes and several theme albums. The 2010 national touring production of the *Glee* franchise was sold out, prompting industry analysts to describe the show as a "multimedia cash cow" and "a merchandising bonanza!" (Hedegaard 2010: 44).

Amateur music shows had receded from television's program schedules since the 1950s, although *Star Search* (hosted by Johnny Carson's former *Tonight Show* side-kick Ed McMahon) sustained the genre between 1983 and 1995, returning briefly in 2003 with Arsenio Hall as host. On the air since 2002, the Fox network's *American Idol* is obviously a major TV sensation, regularly topping the Nielsen ratings in the United States and garnering similar audience attention globally with over twenty-five international franchises. Though the music featured on the program generally tilts to the past, relying on established hits in the popular vein, the show has a proven capacity to "create" new celebrity artists; some, such as Kelly Clarkson, Chris Daughtry, Jennifer Hudson, Kellie Pickler, and Carrie Underwood have repeated the patterns of radio and TV talent show winners from decades past, such as Dick Contino, Frank Sinatra, Mel Torme, and Diahann Carroll. In 2011, *Idol* creator Simon Cowell also launched his new amateur talent series *X Factor* in the U.S. market and NBC had a powerful launch with its entrant in the field, *The Voice*.

In a sharp break from the amateur TV shows of the 1940s and 1950s, each new season of *American Idol* opens with detailed attention to the audition process, introducing viewers to the next "idols" and framing those that are destined to fail in their bid for the title as being deluded and inferior. As Alison Hearn notes, "At the level of production, text, and reception reality television shows perform, mine, and enforce a general cultural ethos of humiliation and masochism" (2004). Hearn explains that while providing a point of viewer fascination, the poorly conceptualized or badly executed musical performances are beside the point; the hapless hopefuls on *American Idol* are set up each new season as fodder for the masses, constituting what she terms the "paradigmatic docile bodies" of reality television's "ideological sweatshops of techno-capital" (ibid.).

Conforming to the labor model devised by earlier televised amateur talent shows, however, the *American Idol* brand also sends its young contestants out on the road on extensive national tours, exploiting the attention and familiarity generated by the TV broadcasts while ostensibly offering the young artists opportunities to improve their performance skills and widen their fan base. A branded *American Idol* website allows viewers to continue and extend their AI "experience" by logging on for photos and video clips from the show, as well as accessing more details associated with the participants' all-important personal back stories.[18] The various options available to the show's top finalists — not just its winners — are also part of a churning industry apparatus that, with record deals, merchandising contracts, and appearance fees fill the coffers of the show's young contestants (Wyatt 2010: C1).

Today, television is hardly the first place to which people turn for music or images of their favorite artists. Perhaps the most significant change at this juncture involves the ways that the Internet is evolving as a platform for leveraging music. Indeed, as I type these words I occasionally venture online for additional images or information about specific artists or TV shows, flitting between screens, between songs, between aesthetic sensibilities, between cultural ideologies, between historical eras, between audio and visual content. New media technologies untether us from traditional industry structures with undeniable yet unpredictable implications for our musical reception. This falls within Henry Jenkins's definition of "convergence culture": "By convergence, I mean the flow of content across multiple media platforms, the cooperation between multiple media industries, and the migratory behavior of media audiences who will go almost anywhere in search of the kinds of entertainment experiences they want. . . . In the world of media convergence, every important story gets told, every brand gets sold, and every consumer gets courted across multiple media platforms" (2006: 2–3).

The decline and devastation of bricks-and-mortar music retail stores wrought by the Internet has altered the traditional means of hearing or acquiring music (Jones 2002; Breen 2004; Azenha 2006); it have destabilized established relationships among discrete music industry sectors and between audience consumers and producers. Since the disintermediation effect of Napster's file-sharing service (created by my university's most famous dropout, Shawn Fanning) upended the music industry in 1999, the industrial terrain has shifted and the traditions that prevailed more or less intact since television's inception have been rent asunder. The Internet usurped the authority of the major record labels, record distributors and retailers, radio broadcasters, and television's broadcast and cable networks, granting new autonomy to music audiences and fans. The teen fan cohort now searches news and celebrity websites for details about its favorite musical acts, surfing and downloading songs and pictures at will from the various online sites — both legal and illegal — and, importantly, exploiting the growing number of social networking options in a manner that reinforces bonds across taste preferences or social attitudes and practices.

In Gustavo Azenha's assessment, past precedents indicate that industry upheavals of this nature are generally brief and that the larger corporate players often retain their dominant position: "There may be a time lag in this process of re-consolidation, but over the medium to long term major labels are best poised to exploit the digital music market" (2006: para. 37). In this current period of industrial turmoil we witness the various competing companies scrambling to assert their market dominance, but the major record labels may not, in fact, reemerge at the front of the pack. In the process of music's reintermediation the Apple corporation (via its iTunes online store) has surfaced as an unlikely industry leader, controlling an estimated 25 percent of all music sales at this writing; Walmart is, by comparison, responsible for roughly 20 percent of all CD sales.

The television sector has been spared much of the chaos affecting the music industry, but there are clear signs that TV, too, is increasingly susceptible to the Internet's impact. Roger Beebe and Jason Middleton identify the "neglected difference between music television and music video as a form that can be disseminated through media other than television. As important as the proliferation of channels that devote a substantial part of their programming days to video may be, equally important is the proliferation of other media venues for watching music video" (2007: 2). Television is at risk as never before, with audiences shifting away from TV toward other screen technologies (the computer, smart phone, and iPod, primarily). The interconnected entertainment industries have developed alternative methods of presenting music and performances out of necessity or out of sheer desperation. Even the once-mighty MTV has greatly enhanced its online presence (www.mtv.com), offering music videos and other content that exceed what is available on its cable-casts.

The rapid expansion of domestic high-speed Internet connections and enhanced broadband capacity allow people "using the Net to bypass the customary providers of television programming, along with the ads they show and the fees they collect. . . . Television is escaping the TV set and the cable box. We no longer watch the tube" (Carr 2009: 26). Nick Bilton (2009) also describes evolving consumer desire for greater entertainment autonomy and the effort to disengage from the current TV-cable grid. Separating from established TV content carriers is often a cost-effective solution that relies on interconnectivity involving, in one example, cross-wiring between the Internet, Netflix, and a Microsoft Xbox unit plugged into the screen monitor. Despite its confusing service and customer use options, Netflix continues to explore more efficient means of delivering streaming video content, including musical programming; other competitors are naturally entering this field as well.

As part of this phenomenon, the Google-owned video sharing website YouTube further undermines television's role as a purveyor of popular music as music fans increasingly turn to the website rather than broadcast or cable networks to screen new or popular music videos or to watch other sundry music events such as taped awards ceremonies and "candid" camera clips. Amateur musicians are prominent on YouTube (and on other secondary sites such as MySpace and Facebook), performing in various genres and with varying degrees of skill or talent for tens of millions of viewers, yet this organ sidesteps the more humiliating elements associated with mainstream amateur programs such as *American Idol*. The YouTube brand slogan "broadcast yourself" raises the notion of democratic access while promising an individualized platform for self-representation and self-promotion. The talent brokers of TV (embodied in the 1940s and 1950s by such program hosts as Fred Allen, Dennis James, and Ted Mack, and, more recently, by *American Idol's* Ryan Seacrest and the show's panel of judges), are decentered on YouTube, and rather than the imprecise applause-o-meters, text messages, or other forms of audience measurement employed on televised amateur talent contests, website "hits" indicate a YouTube video's audience appeal and success. As television did in the 1950s, YouTube and Facebook have proven their promotional effectiveness, catapulting Justin Bieber, Colbie Caillat, and Soulja Boy Tellum, among others, into the public's consciousness and into the music industry.

YouTube also presents amazing new opportunities for music and television historians. When this project began, it was necessary that I physically visit archives throughout the country to screen the many shows that are described in the preceding pages. Yet as more and more visual performances are uploaded, a huge swath of the history of music on television is readily accessible at my home or office. Over the intervening years, some of my favorite televised music programs from the early TV era became available on the Internet and on YouTube in particular, allowing me to review the broadcasts and reflect on the music, stagecraft, and aspects of form and production during TV's formative phase. Such enhanced access to archival material allows us to revisit some of television's first musical broadcasts and some of television's most "newsworthy" performances, enabling access to visual evidence that directly challenges John Lennon's intentionally provocative statement, "before Elvis there was nothing." The fact is that there was a universe of forces—including music on early television—that combined to manifest the phenomenon known as "Elvis."

Another contemporary development involving screen technology and popular music is the deployment of songs in such interactive games as *Karaoke Revolution, Rock Revolution, Guitar Hero, DJ Hero, Rock Band, Def Jam Rap Star*, and the music game creations of a growing number of companies including industry leaders Activision, Harmonix Music Systems, and Konami. While not actually television music—the TV screen serves as an inert monitor—music game software still warrants attention as it is situated alongside television in the lives of literally millions of music-loving gamers. Music games offer an extensive song list by dozens of artists (*Rock Band 4* alone includes roughly one hundred songs selected from the past forty years of music recording), presenting players with a competitive context for listening to music and providing an interactive engagement that aligns music fans with the performance aspects of hit songs. The games offer an interesting musical experience since they actually embrace and foreground both performance and reception.[19]

The visual scenarios of a game such as *Guitar Hero* or *Rock Band* construct multiple points of view: the privileged onstage perspective of a cameraman (or someone adjacent to the performer), the vantage of someone immersed in a concert crowd (with an ideal stage view), and an omniscient viewpoint that seemingly takes in the entire "event" from on high. Many of the visual perspectives are entirely standard, owing an aesthetic debt to film musicals since the 1930s and to television production conventions that were developed during the medium's formative period. Popular in bars, college dormitories, fraternity and sorority houses, and the family home (as well as global game play via *Rock Band Special Edition*'s online interconnectivity), *Guitar Hero* and *Rock Band* also introduce a new context for music-oriented sociality; while the music fans can enter into a new relationship with the songs and the artists that perform them the games also bring individual players into more proximate and dynamic relationships with one another. *Rock Band*'s "unison bonus" score, for instance, provides a game metric for group cohesion, further accentuating and rewarding the synchronized performance efforts that inform the game.

There remain several dissatisfying and potentially alienating aspects to these music games, however. For one thing, the limited sonic capacities of most television sets continue to serve the music poorly, as they have for decades,[20] although it is entirely common for gamers to wire their components through stereos or other enhanced audio systems. It also seems to me that in the interactive game format the musicians are problematically dehumanized by their transformation to digital avatars. The cold, steely images fail to evoke the sensation of live or filmed musical performances on TV. They lack even one iota of the vibrant warmth communicated by, for example, Peggy Lee's performance on the October 11, 1954, broadcast of *Caesar's Hour*, and they fall far short of Elvis Presley's 1956–57 TV appearances or his 1968 NBC "comeback special." The avatars are empty of what is perhaps the most crucial element in contemporary popular music performances: *affect*.

Ron Burnett poses the question "Why are games so attractive?," citing what were, over a decade ago, the simplistic, surreal, and two-dimensional quality of game images as aesthetic shortcomings (1995: 206); the graphics have improved drastically since then. Yet he also hints at a response when he observes,

> Images can only be controlled if we are ready to accept our own integration into them. In other words we have to be a part of what we see, and to do that much more is required than acceptance. The energy needed to learn a video game is exacting and requires a mental concentration that shifts the burden almost entirely onto the player. . . . Images, whether fictional or documentary, experimental or a hybrid of many genres, types, styles, don't so much offer experiences as they create the field within which a whole host of possibilities can be generated. (ibid.)

In order to achieve the fullness of the contemporary game experience, then, one must immerse oneself into the game, merging with the avatar and becoming Other to one's own self. With this in mind, it seems that the game participants themselves import and convey the requisite affect as they "perform" the songs while watching the screen and hearing the music. Their gestures and facial grimaces are not simply mimicking the artists but are characteristics of their own expression and performance; popular music's histrionics are, after all, a fundamental part of the viewing experience and the games carry this over when watching someone "play."

Yet, there is more to say about the visual design of music games. On first seeing the Kurt Cobain avatar on *Guitar Hero 5* I was shocked by how grotesque the image is, how sinister it looks and, ultimately, how unlike Cobain it appears (although it does bear a resemblance to the equally unnerving Kurt Cobain plastic action figures, marketed under the names "Kurt Cobain

Teen Spirit Action Figure" and "Kurt Cobain Unplugged Action Figure" by the National Entertainment Collectibles Association). Gone is the air of tangible human vulnerability that seemed to hover over Cobain during his 1993 *MTV Unplugged* appearance and his televised concert appearances. Cobain's widow was also distressed by the image; Courtney Love expressed her typically fierce anger about the avatar's failed design features (despite reportedly having provided Activision with image materials from which they could create the avatar). Cobain's former band mates Krist Novoselic and Dave Grohl were also incensed by the game, but the point of their ire was unconcerned with mere appearances. Rather, they argued that Cobain's avatar was not exclusively "locked" to Nirvana songs and could, thus, be "played" onscreen with songs by other bands. The digital avatar, it seems, can be reassigned as a cover artist or virtual karaoke performer.

The term *synthespians* (and accompanying titles such as "v-people" or "vactors") consequently emerges to address the rising trend in visual entertainment and the culture industries' turn toward avatars and similar computer-generated entities (Landon 2002; Burston 2006). Adopting a labor-oriented perspective, Ted Magder and Jonathan Burston take their critique a step further, suggesting that the industrial proliferation of computer-generated film and video characters — "digital scabs" — constitutes a potentially distressing form of economic expediency and labor displacement (2001: 226). Avatars are consequently bound to songs and images within a corporate rationale as part of a new strategic approach to promote and sell cultural commodities.

Introduced in 2009, *The Beatles: Rock Band* exemplifies the state of the art music game at this writing. The "performances" enacted onscreen by the band "avatars" reproduce conventional TV camera shots — close-up, midshot, full-shot — augmented by long shots or "bird's eye view" perspectives encompassing the full stage, the virtual crowd, and the wider performance spaces. It is obvious that film, TV, and video provide the visual template for the game's design, the virtual renderings being drafted directly from extant footage of the band in performance.[21] The avatars also represent different chapters of the band's career trajectory, corresponding to performances from well-known moments in history. In this regard, then, the game deliberately constructs an element of verisimilitude, entailing "notions of propriety, of what is appropriate and therefore probable (or probable and therefore appropriate)" (Grant 2003: 161).

The game visually reconstructs the Beatles' most iconic performances, including their earliest gigs in Liverpool's Cavern Club, their American

TV debut on *The Ed Sullivan Show* in 1964, the 1965 Shea Stadium shows in New York, and the performance on the Apple Records rooftop in 1969 (which provided some of the most memorable scenes from the 1970 documentary film *Let It Be*), as well as depicting the band's studio recording sessions. If one has seen, for example, *Let It Be*, then the game screen for "I Dig a Pony" will be entirely familiar. The band's evolution is signified by alterations in style and fashion and, notably, there is an unmistakable aging process that is designed onto the avatar faces of John, Paul, George, and Ringo reflecting the actual progression of years that are worn on the physical body. Gamers can, thus, select and "perform" their favorite Beatles song, but they can also inhabit the avatars that are designed to correspond with the song's era, in a sense *becoming* their favorite Beatle in a new mediated fashion.

Cultural tastes in television and music have obviously changed since Dinah Shore's prewar NBC TV experiments, since Lawrence Welk's 1951 KTLA debut, since Elvis Presley's TV year, or since the Beatles' 1964 U.S. television premiere. Yet these singers and musicians and the many others who ventured into television with them left a deep and lasting legacy. Their broadcast performances prepared the nation for music on television, establishing the presentational forms that have influenced subsequent generations of musical performers *and* audience members. As this book and the extant broadcast material illustrate, early television is fraught with clumsy, fumbling performances and with the unassailable brilliance of countless musicians. With all their failings and all of their achievements on full display, television's pioneers learned how to produce and present "television music" (Coates 2007), in the process inflecting art, culture, and life in postwar United States with new meanings.

Now, as the bonds conjoining music and television gradually fray and as new screen-based technologies reconfigure the audience-artist dynamic, we are ideally situated to witness an emergent phase encompassing industrial divergence *and* new alternative forms of media convergence. The forces that unlink music and television are already orienting us toward radically different understandings about the visual reception of popular music as we disconnect our television sets and cable connections and log on to the Internet. This, I think, is the perfect place to end; right at the beginning.

APPENDIX

The following is a representative (but not comprehensive) list of early essays, manuals, and educational guidebooks published between 1948 and 1955 that accommodate musical presentation, TV production techniques, and musical careers in the television industry.

Ace, Goodman. *The Book of Little Knowledge: More Than You Want to Know about Television.* New York: Simon and Schuster, 1955.

Begley, Martin, and Douglas MacCrae. *Auditioning for TV: How to Prepare for Success as a Television Actor.* New York: Hastings House, 1955.

Bretz, Rudy. "TV as an Art Form." *Hollywood Quarterly* 5, no. 2 (Winter 1950).

———. "The Limitations of Television." *Hollywood Quarterly* 5, no. 3 (Spring 1951): 251–63.

———. *Techniques of Television Production.* New York: McGraw-Hill, 1953.

Broderick, Edwin B. *Your Place in Television: A Handy Guide for Young People.* New York: David McKay, 1954.

Burgin, Ralph. "Low Cost Music and Participation Shows versus Film." In *Twenty-Two Television Talks.* New York: Broadcast Music, 1953.

Campbell, Victor F. "Low Cost Music and Specialty Programming." In *Thirty-Two Television Talks.* New York: Broadcast Music, 1955.

Cantrick, Robert B. "Music, Television, and Aesthetics." *Quarterly of Film, Radio, and Television* 9, no. 1 (Fall 1954): 60–78.

Dunlap Jr., Orrin E. *Understanding Television: What It Is and How It Works.* New York: Greenberg, 1948.

Harrington, Ruth Lee. *Your Opportunities in Television.* New York: Medill McBride, 1949.

Hodapp, William. *The Television Actor's Manual.* New York: Appleton-Century-Crofts, 1955.

Hubbell, Richard. *Television Programming and Production.* 2nd ed. New York: Rinehart, 1950.

Kaufman, William I. *How to Direct for Television.* New York: Hastings House, 1955.

Kaufman, William I., and Robert Colodzin. *Your Career in Television*. New York: Merlin Press, 1950.

Minter, Gordon. "Education for Television Jobs." *Hollywood Quarterly* 4, no. 2 (Winter 1949): 193–96.

O'Meara, Carroll. *Television Program Production*. New York: Ronald Press, 1955.

Operation Backstage: Staging Services Handbook. New York: National Broadcasting Corporation, 1951.

Paulu, Burton. "Televising the Minneapolis Symphony Orchestra." *Quarterly of Film, Radio, and Television* 8, no. 2 (Winter 1953): 157–71.

Ranson, Jo, and Richard Pack. *Opportunities in Television*. New York: Grosset and Dunlap, 1950.

Stasheff, Edward, and Rudy Bretz. *The Television Program: Its Writing, Direction, and Production*. New York: A. A. Wyn, 1951.

Tooley, Howard. *The Television Workshop*. Minneapolis: Northwestern Press, 1953.

NOTES

Notes to Introduction

1. *Journal of Communication Inquiry* 10, no. 1 (Winter 1986); Kaplan 1987; Grossberg 1989; Frith et al. 1993; Goodwin 1992.

2. In many instances, the analysis focuses on network practices at the National Broadcasting Corporation. There are two distinct reasons for this: first, NBC was at the forefront of both radio and television broadcasting, exerting a defining influence on broadcasting and mass culture since the network's formation in 1926. Second, NBC's corporate history is more readily accessible than is that of its competitors ABC, CBS, or Du Mont because of the numerous extant papers, memoranda, and other archival documentation assiduously collected, organized, and stored at the Wisconsin State Historical Archives, Madison, Wisc.

Notes to Chapter 1: Music, Image, Labor

1. The Boswell Sisters exhibited their close harmony vocal style in their first one-reel film, *Close Farm-ony* (Aubrey Scotto, director, 1932), soon after the CBS/W2XAB station launch.

2. Raymond Williams notes that radio followed a similar trajectory in its formative stages: "In the early stages of radio manufacturing, transmission was conceived before content. By the end of the 1920s the network was there, but still at a low level of content-definition. It was in the 1930s, in the second phase of radio, that most of the significant advances in content were made" (1975: 28).

3. There were several noteworthy experiments in the 1920s and 1930s that merged music and image for the screen: Thomas Wilfred designed a "color organ" called a Clavilux, introducing an abstract sound-image art form that he termed "Lumia" (Betancourt 2006). Oskar Fischinger reflected the avant-garde aesthetic of the 1930s with his animated short films (such as the 1936 film *Allegretto*) that consisted of wildly pulsating geometric shapes in brilliant hues accompanied by music in the grain of George Gershwin's "Rhapsody in Blue" and performed in a style consistent with that of Paul Whiteman's symphonic jazz (Moritz 2004). In these cases, how-

ever, the music-image dynamic was not reliant on, or inhibited by human presence on the screen.

4. Reflecting the extent of Truman's involvement with the AFM and Petrillo, in mid-June 1954 Truman appeared with Petrillo onstage at the AFM annual convention in Milwaukee, where the two performed a piano-trumpet duet. Petrillo was most polite in a telegraph to the NBC president Pat Weaver, asking that the network arrange to cover the staged event that Petrillo describes as "this matter which is very close to my heart" (Petrillo 1954).

5. Clarence Lea's list of AFM infractions includes the union's recent ban "upon the making of records and transcriptions, the quota system for the employment of musicians, the employment of standby musicians, restrictions on the appearance of members of the American Federation of Musicians on television broadcasts, restrictions on the use of service bans on the air, and disputes between A.F. of M. and NABET concerning platter turners" (1945).

6. A *Good Housekeeping* magazine survey in 1951 reported that among members of TV households, there was a 42 percent decrease in attendance at theater or concert performances, a 50 percent decrease in listening to phonograph records, and an 82 percent drop in radio listening ("TV Set Owners" 1951: 85).

7. On Christmas Day, 1953, ABC-TV broadcast a special feature, *The Musicians' Christmas Party*, described as "the AFM's 17th annual party-benefit for blind musicians." The program offered an opportunity for the union and its incendiary president to demonstrate their understanding of TV. For his part, Petrillo, who it was written, "mellowed for the occasion," introduced his mother on the air ("Musicians' Christmas Party" 1953: 16).

8. Reports suggest that, along with the efforts of unions such as the AFM or AFTRA, artist talent agencies were also important in negotiating for and acquiring residual rights for recorded/filmed screenings. See Glickman 1952.

Notes to Chapter 2: "Hey TV!"

1. Though Stone's initial quintet was moderately successful, the group's greatest success arrived in the late 1950s and 1960s in its configuration as a vocal quartet.

2. Anthony was ultimately convinced that his talents could, in fact, be coordinated with TV's production styles, although he waited until many of the bugs had been worked out of the system. He eventually went on to host *TV's Top Tunes* (a summer replacement for *The Perry Como Show*) in 1954 and in 1956–57 he helmed *The Ray Anthony Show*, occasionally featuring his wife, the bombshell B-movie actress Mamie Van Doren.

3. Monroe also hosted four episodes of the *Vaughn Monroe Show* as a seasonal replacement for the *Dinah Shore Show*, appearing twice in the summer of 1954 and twice in the summer of 1955 (McNeil 1996).

4. The public fiasco produced much media commentary and audience ire and resulted

in a satirical recording "Dear Mr. Godfrey" by the "saucy chanteuse," the cabaret singer Ruth Wallis:

Dear Mr. Godfrey, listen to my plea,
Hire me and fire me and make a star of me
I will be so grateful if it can just be done
Hire me and fire me, Ed Sullivan here I come
Humility, humility, Julius lost his humility.

5. Sinatra and Laine each went on to host their own television programs in the early 1950s and Torme was cohost of *TV's Top Tunes* with Peggy Lee when it premiered on CBS in 1951.

6. Among the nation's amateur talent offerings between 1948 and 1955 were: *Tune Try-outs* on Boston's WBZ-TV; *Junior Talent Time* airing on WPIX-TV in New York City; *Talent Parade* on WATV, Newark; *Juvenile Jamboree* on WRGB-TV Schenectady; *Your Junior Revue* on WNBW-TV in Washington, D.C.; *Starlit Stairway* on Detroit's WXYZ-TV; the *Junior Amateurs* show on Milwaukee's WTMJ-TV; and *Chevrolet Talent Hour* broadcast on Los Angeles station KECA-TV. Chicago was reported to be on an "amateur binge" ("Chi Video" 1950: 30) in 1950, with up to six amateur programs airing on the city's various stations; among Chicago's amateur shows were *Admiral TV Talent Hunt* on WBKB-TV; *McCarthy Gang* on WGN-TV; and *Parade* and *Sach's Amateur Hour*, both on WENR-TV. A Spanish language amateur show, *En Busca de Estrellas*, also debuted on KLAC-TV, Los Angeles, in 1950. One long-standing amateur program, *Star Time*, was lauded in 1955 for "surviving" over five years in the competitive New York TV market despite having bounced between local stations RWPIX, WRCA-TV, WABC-TV, and WABD, and completing a full thirteen-week schedule on the NBC network ("TV 'Star Time' Survives" 1955: 22).

7. Whiteman was a sturdy supporter of youth development initiatives and regarded musical education and training as a central element of the well-formed or "cultured" individual. As he recounts in his autobiography, he started the first teen club in 1947 and gradually created a system of clubs dedicated to "providing good, clean, wholesome fun for thousands of youngsters who need a place for dancing and a planned entertainment program" (1948: 25). His television program was an extension of these efforts.

8. Paul Denis reported that talent shows hosted by Arthur Godfrey, Horace Heidt, and Ted Mack each had "two or three stage units touring" the country in 1949 (1949: 47).

9. In 1950, *Variety* did acknowledge the issue of amateur-versus-professional status, noting of Freddy Martin's show, "First-string finalists will receive salaries for their performances, thus eliminating themselves from the amateur ranks" ("Freddy Martin's 'Band of Tomorrow'" 1950: 24).

10. Among the popular television audience and fan magazines in the 1940s and 1950s

were *Modern TV and Radio*, *Radio Best: The Radio and Television Picture Magazine*, *Radio and Television Mirror*, *TV Show*, and *TV Guide*.

11. Chapel was a regular cast member with Garroway from 1949 to 1951 in Chicago, at which point the show ended and Garroway relocated to New York City. A 1951 *Time* report on the distinctive production innovations featured on *Garroway at Large* refers to a special effects gimmick called "the girl multiplier, that once put 64 identical shots of pert singer Bette Chapel on the TV screen at one time" ("The Magic Carpenters" 1951).

12. In 1963, Kurtz's "Snowflakes" was featured on the soundtrack of the John Cassavetes film *A Child Is Waiting*, sung by the movie's female star, Judy Garland.

13. Landsberg was the West Coast director of Paramount Television Productions from 1941 to 1950, when he was appointed vice president of Paramount's TV arm. Under Landsberg's firm guidance, KTLA distinguished itself as a community-oriented station through its extensive employment of remote broadcasts of breaking news and public entertainment. See Kisseloff 1995: 170–82.

14. For an insightful analytical reading of the KTLA broadcasts by Harry Owens and his Royal Hawaiians, see Williams 1998. For a similarly detailed analysis of Ina Ray Hutton, see McGee 2009.

15. A gifted fiddle player, Cooley personified the urbanized country and western music that was gaining popularity on the many "hillbilly" programs in the early 1950s, including *Ozark Jubilee*, *Grand Ole Opry*, and *Leo Carrillo's Dude Ranch* (the latter being a local Los Angeles production broadcast on KCOP). Cooley's exploits as a TV bandleader in Santa Monica were glorified in the 1950 film *Everybody's Dancin'* (directed by Will Jason), in which he starred as himself in a fictionalized version of his rise as a box office success and a popular TV host.

16. Following Cooley's breakout success, it was reported in 1954 that "every one of L.A.'s seven television stations except KHJ-TV has at least one western-style sponsored show with a top rating" (Holly 1954: 5).

17. Hutton was sufficiently established in the industry, as *Down Beat* acknowledged in early 1948, when it speculated that hers was the model behind the formation of an all-girl touring orchestra sponsored between 1946 and 1953 by the Hormel Company of Austin, Minnesota — makers of the Spam meat product. The Spam band was also briefly featured on its own TV program ("Hormel to Pull a Hutton" 1948: 18). In 1951, Ada Leonard's all-girl orchestra debuted on the Hollywood station KTTV's *Search for Girls*, tapping into the audience interest generated by Hutton (Holly 1951b: 8). See also McGee 2009.

18. For a detailed historical analysis of the phenomenon of "all-girl" bands, see Tucker 2000.

19. It was not until roughly 1954 that the nightclub sector's economic tide began to turn for the better with club operators, talent agents, and booking agents across the country reporting a new prosperity, in part "due to the decrease in the lure of television" ("Nationwide Pickup" 1954: 57).

20. In Boston, along with drooping receipts in the restaurant sector due to the perception of "families grabbing a quick meal at home and then adjourning to the living room for an evening of TV" ("Tele vs. Table d'Hote" 1951: 1), the city's Metropolitan Transit Authority even blamed television for an estimated 30 percent decline in bus and subway riders and diminished revenue figures ("TV the Villain" 1952: 30).

21. In her excellent analysis of "ambient television" and the early placement of television sets in bars and taverns, McCarthy also describes journalistic biases and reportorial tendencies in the mid-century that misrepresent the TV "gawker" and bar or tavern patron: "Journalistic coverage of TV in bars nevertheless describes such sites in very particular terms, as masculine arenas of white, working-class, urban culture. . . . [T]he press's narrow focus on a particular version of the tavern audience does highlight the rhetorical value in associating TV viewing-places with particular configurations of collectivity and sociality as well" (2001: 31–32).

22. An example of television's capacity to incubate talent can be read in *Billboard*'s review of a Kyle MacDonnell appearance in 1950 at Jackie Heller's Carousel in Pittsburgh: "How a star can be built into a big café and theater attraction solely thru the medium of TV is on display here this week with Kyle MacDonnell playing to a capacity house. Seen here on *Hold That Camera* and *Celebrity Times* in this one-station city, fem had a ready audience waiting for her and she didn't disappoint. This is her first nitery engagement but she showed plenty of poise and stage savvy in delivering specially arranged tunes for an average set of pipes" ("Jackie Heller's Carousel" 1950: 37).

23. The editors at *Variety* were evidently tired of the ongoing lament about vaudeville's decline. Under its coverage of the ABC-TV network launch in August 1948, a half-inch column read: "Stop It! It's about time the reviewers and the television bunch stopped crying over vaudeville and the dear old Palace, especially the dear old Palace. Many a lousy bill played the Palace. If you don't think so take a look in VARIETY files."

24. For a detailed history of the jukebox, see Segrave 2002.

25. The *Billboard* jukebox play chart was suspended in 1957.

26. Segrave also describes an instance in 1950 where members of the Music Operators of America discussed the option of coin-operated televisions that offered a free picture but required payment to access the audio. The final consensus was, however, that "the trend toward free video in taverns had gone beyond the point where it could be stopped" (2002: 202).

27. Part of the visual "joke" of Anders's TV performance of "I Like the Wide Open Spaces" occurred when she would turn her back to the camera, revealing her frilly bloomers and bare legs that were concealed behind her riding chaps. Anders's rendition was such a TV sensation that it spawned a Ken Murray Glamour Cowgirl doll cast in Anders's image. In 1953 Ken Murray produced the low-cost B-movie western *The Marshal's Daughter* (directed by William Berke). Anders received top bill-

ing under the name "Laurie 'I-Like-the-Wide-Open-Spaces' Anders," with the film poster describing the Anders character as a "rootin', tootin' straight shootin' bundle of curves."

Notes to Chapter 3: Harmonizing Genres

1. *Omnibus* featured special programs celebrating various musical traditions and artists: Benny Goodman, January 25, 1953; Les Paul and Mary Ford, October 25, 1953; special on jazz featuring Leonard Bernstein, October 16, 1955; *Star of the Family* featured Tony Bennett, October 7, 1951; Benny Goodman, December 2, 1951; Gene Krupa, January 10, 1952; Cab Calloway and Olga San Juan, January 24, 1952; and Les Paul and Mary Ford, June 12, 1952.

2. Jackie Gleason's comedy show *The Honeymooners* closes with an extended "ballroom" performance by the Jimmy and Tommy Dorsey Orchestra on its December 26, 1953, broadcast.

3. The decision to omit several prominent genres is based on the prior availability of solid published accounts of these television formats. While country and "hillbilly" shows, for instance, constituted a very popular TV genre, they have been well analyzed by Jensen (1998) and Peterson (1997), among others (Pecknold 2007). Fenster (1993) also examines country music videos in the 1980s. DeLong (1991), Cox (2001), and Mittell (2004a; 2004b) have discussed many of the more popular hybrid musical versions of the quiz show genre.

4. While a chronology of television's development in the booklet clearly describes the historical evolution of working television and laboratory broadcasting in the early 1900s and details Vladimir Zworykin's successful laboratory demonstrations and NBC field tests through the 1920s and 1930s, television's "official" public launch is ascribed to the NBC network's commencement of regular programming at the 1939 World's Fair at Flushing Meadows, New York.

5. Program titles and descriptions in the memorandum imply that the suggestions were submitted by a Cleveland-based NBC affiliate.

6. At the most basic level, the networks and advertising agencies segmented the audience along gender lines, recognizing that men and women displayed distinct leisure patterns and TV content preferences. The television and advertising executives also recognized class difference as being related to cultural taste distinctions (even the first surveys of television set owners in the early 1940s were keenly interested in class status and television purchase patterns) and they set about offering programs that responded to the desires and expectations of groups within a range of economic and educational backgrounds.

7. While taste distinctions certainly existed during television's nascent stage, it should not be assumed that the character and impact of such distinctions were precisely the same as those of today.

8. Circulating under the headline "Time & Program Information: Sales Success at Seven-Thirty," NBC issued a report in 1955 promoting sales opportunities associated

with packaging of shows hosted by Eddie Fisher, Tony Martin, and Dinah Shore. The report refers to "the audience magic of music at 7:30 (and the *selling power* of music at 7:30)" with a breakdown of program Nielsen ratings including gender and age comparisons (*Time & Program Information* 1955).

9. In a review of Allen's debut on *Judge for Yourself*, *Broadcasting-Telecasting* defines his presence as being "second-fiddle to a gimmick," stating, "Mr. Allen needs a new format which will not only encourage his particular abilities but also give them a chance to be seen. In the cluttered surroundings of *Judge For Yourself* a wit of Mr. Allen's sensitivity is neither stimulated nor observed" ("In Review" 1953: 18).

10. Como, Martin, and Shore were all early television veterans and in recognition of their TV talents they were all nominated for Emmy Awards in 1954; Como won in the Best Male Singer category and Shore won the Best Female Singer award.

11. While Shore enjoyed greater autonomy and independence than many female TV pioneers, she was still positioned within an unambiguously gendered dynamic. Andrea Lee Press explains, "For the most part, on early television women are depicted primarily as *women*. Rarely, if ever, are early television women shown to be mature, independent individuals. Family women in particular are shown to be women whose existence is closely bound up with, and by, others in their family group, particularly their male partners. In addition, family women on early television are consistently pictured almost exclusively in the domestic or private realm" (Press 1991: 29).

12. The dramatic narrative of the revolutionary 1938 Orson Welles/Mercury Theatre radio drama *War of the Worlds* on the CBS network was structured on the conventions of a standard "remote" radio broadcast. The radio drama introduced a faux-broadcast of "the Ramon Raquello Orchestra performing in the Meridian Room in the Hotel Park Plaza," that was interrupted by authentic sounding news bulletins about unusual interplanetary activity. In fact, the notion of a musical remote broadcast was essential to the ruse's success.

13. Guy Lombardo and the Royal Canadians appeared on the debut of *Cavalcade of Bands* on the Du Mont network in 1950 and on its final broadcast in 1951. Lombardo also hosted his own show in 1954 and again, briefly, in 1956.

14. Issuing permission cards was standard practice for remote television broadcasts. In March 1948, NBC issued cards reading: "You are being televised. Portions of this program are being televised by the National Broadcasting Company and recipients of these cards are in direct range of NBC's television cameras. May we respectfully call to your attention the fact that during this broadcast you will be in full view of the television audience. Thank you."

15. Goldstein describes the instrumentation of Waner's twelve-piece ensemble, noting that the band's arrangements are "interesting" and that they encompass popular tunes, jazz numbers, and the occasional rumba or samba rhythms. Included in the program pitch is a brief description of the visual possibilities and layout in the Latin Quarter, including the stage and dance floor positions and mention of the room's draped wall coverings.

16. Accentuating the vaudeville and borscht belt styles, the comedian Art Carney served as Amsterdam's sidekick, portraying the club's disoriented, obtuse maitre'd. A young Jacqueline Susann also appeared as a cigarette girl. Don Russell served as Amsterdam's announcer during the show's tenure at both CBS and Du Mont.

17. Although the program is not well documented, *Billboard* announced the May 1950 *Popsicle Parade* debut with Milton Berle as the leadoff host. Tony Martin is also listed as one of the show's revolving hosts along with Arthur Godfrey, Dick Haymes, Martha Raye, and Paul Winchell. *Billboard* also reported that the show would introduce hosts Fanny Brice and Groucho Marx in their television premieres ("'Popsicle Parade' to Feature Stars" April 22, 1950: 6).

18. Elsewhere in the broadcast Martin digs into the past to perform a rendition of "Toot Toot Tootsie, Goodbye." Describing the number as "an old Al Jolson song" Martin sports a straw hat in a symbolic nod toward the vaudeville era that has virtually no connection to the children comprising the audience.

19. By 1950, MacDonnell had already hosted two WABD music programs, *For Your Pleasure* and *Girl about Town*, both in 1948. She also appeared four times in 1950 on the Du Mont musical variety show *Cavalcade of Stars*.

20. Roberta Singer and Elena Martinez explain the rise and local significance of the Bronx Tropicana: "Prior to opening as a Latin music nightclub, the Tropicana (known as the Tropical Paradise in the Bronx), was the Prospect Pool and traditional Russian/Turkish *shvitzbud* (bath). Later, in response to the change in the neighborhood's ethnic makeup, it was converted to a Latin music nightclub. In 1945, under the ownership of Cuban restauranteurs, the brothers Manolo and Tony Alfaro, the Tropicana became the most glamorous nightclub in the Bronx. Inspired by the glitzy Tropicana Cabaret in Havana, it was the mecca for Latinos seeking floor shows with a chorus line, first-rate dance bands, and first-class Cuban cuisine" (Singer and Martinez 2004: 192).

21. For an additional list of DJ programs in 1950, see Bundy 1950.

22. The West Coast DJ Art Ford identified the performative aspect of televised commercials as a critical facet of the new TV DJ responsibilities. In a special *Billboard* Disk Jockey Supplement, he offered specific suggestions for handling commercials and interacting with the camera (1950: 69).

23. Significantly, an inexperienced young WFIL aspirant named Dick Clark read *TV-Teen Club*'s sponsor announcements (for Tootsie Rolls).

24. The integration of filmed materials into the televised DJ format was certainly not unique; several stations employed Snader and Official musical shorts to fill gaps in their programming (often when the live broadcasts ran too quickly) or they structured shows around the filmed spots. In 1951 Screen Gems announced its intention to develop *TV Disk Jockey Toons* in collaboration with top record labels including Capital, Columbia, Decca, Mercury, and RCA Victor. The show proposed airing filmed episodes in an unorthodox mix of genres encompassing "cartoons, live action, shadowgraphs, etc., cued to actual disks so that the deejay, in playing standard hit

records, will also be able to provide a filmization of the song" ("TV Disk Jockey Toons" 1951: 30; "'TV Toons'" 1952: 76). WEWS-TV in Cleveland proposed a program titled *Tune Time* in 1952 that would involve a "film-jockey" presenting Snader films from an informal living room setting.

25. John Jackson directly implicates WFIL-TV's influential *Bandstand* host Bob Horn in the payola practice: "Horn answered to no one, and it was said around town that the show's martinet 'was courted night and day by pluggers hoping that he'll give their platters a spin.' Although no one outside the pop music industry was aware of it, payments to Horn by local record distributors had increased steadily since 1953" (1997: 27).

26. Catalyzing the sense of a community under siege and magnifying a sense of moral crisis in Washington, D.C., in the summer of 1953, the *Washington Post* reported that "gangs and teenage hoodlums" had "swarmed" the television studio WMAL-TV, where the popular daytime dance program *Bandstand Matinee Club*, hosted by Sherman Butler and Bill Malone, was produced. In the final week of August 1953, the paper was awash in articles describing "kid mobs" and "juvenile gangs," with the WMAL dance program providing a narrative focal point. By late August 1953, Judge Justin Miller, head of the National Association of Radio and Television Broadcasters (NARTB) was receiving letters from unnerved citizens complaining about the situation at WMAL. In a letter dated August 28, a Washington, D.C., resident, J. Nelson Stuart, wrote to Miller stating, "The effect of 'Bandstand Matinee' on the neighborhood is identical to the effect that would be created by placing in the middle of his clean living room floor a decayed piece of meat. In very little time the meat would draw roaches and ants that, combined with the odor, would force the occupants to remove the meat" (Stuart 1953). Miller's response to citizen Stuart's comments acknowledged "the ever-growing task of controlling juvenile delinquency," further explaining that "the police think the program 'Bandstand Matinee' is serving a useful purpose in keeping teen-agers occupied and that it should be continued" (1953).

27. In July 1952, *Variety* pronounced, "TV Disk Jock Comes Into Own," identifying seven East Coast DJ shows on television while somewhat optimistically predicting the genre's influence "in the hit-making process" (1952: 57).

28. Horn's reign at WFIL ended in 1955 when he was implicated in two major scandals, one involving drunk driving charges and the other involving Philadelphia's vice squad and allegations of improper relations with one of *Bandstand*'s female teen club members. Though he was acquitted on the latter charge, he was fired by WFIL brass. His reputation shredded, Horn ignominiously stumbled through the few remaining years of his career, dying in 1966 at the age of fifty.

Notes to Chapter 4: The Look of Music

1. Regarding performance purpose, the theorist Sam Godlovitch explains, "One rehearses to perform and one performs (among other things) to be heard by an audience" (1998: 28).

2. *Life* magazine (April 5, 1948) offered screen shots of the televised proceedings and a brief account of both the NBC and CBS broadcasts ("Petrillo Relents" 1948: 43–44; "Rival CBS Program" 1948: 46).

3. Ormandy's selection of the Rachmaninoff composition was appropriate. Rachmaninoff himself had an extensive history with the Philadelphia Orchestra; several of his compositions received their premieres with the orchestra, and he conducted the ensemble at the Philadelphia Academy of Music in 1909. He died a mere five years before the orchestra's landmark 1948 television appearance.

4. Hal Keith of NBC's production staff provides a detailed account of prebroadcast preparations for the first Toscanini TV performance. These included careful planning of camera positions, scripted cuts, screen dissolves and other basic editing techniques, microphone placement and sound considerations, all coordinated between the orchestra, the network's musical consultant Samuel Chotzinoff, and the studio production team (Keith 1948: 35).

5. In her 1945 TV career manual, Judy Dupuy describes the optimal camera position for capturing a harpist's performance: "The harpist, particularly, can be televised most successfully. Careful camera attention and staging of the recital have added to the pictorial quality of the soloist and the instrument. Close-ups of fingers plucking strings are fascinating to those watching. Because television makes it possible for the audience to actually see the artist's hands, it holds a distinct advantage over the concert stage" (1945: 46). Harpists were depicted in such a manner well into the 1950s as they often are today.

6. On the November 1, 1954, episode of *Your Show of Shows* during the Benny Goodman orchestra's performance of "Sing, Sing, Sing," the camera pulls in far too quickly and closely to the bell of Charlie Shavers's trumpet, casting a dark shadow across his face and almost bumping him. To make matters worse, the shot is poorly timed, coming too soon before his solo. The camera hastily retreats as Shavers looks perplexed and then suddenly zooms back in on the trumpeter when he starts his solo.

7. Andre Kostelanetz criticized such emphasis on the close-up with the comment, "Although it might make an equally intriguing shot to show how a pianist hits the keyboard with his fingers or a violinist works his left hand, these technicalities diminish the final effect of music. They distract and rob the audience of a certain magic and illusion which should be part of a good musical performance" (1952).

8. Prior to receiving its FCC broadcast license and the station identification WABD on May 2, 1944, the Du Mont station in New York was identified as W2XWV (Bergmann and Skutch 2002: 17). Kline's comments come just after this corporate transition.

9. Several *Down Beat* articles addressed technical production or featured interviews with TV producers and music directors offering their experienced opinions about how to most effectively capture music for TV broadcasts. See Wilson 1949; Wilson 1950c; Holly 1951a; Leonard 1953.

10. Waring's problems with the demands of "televising" arose early. In correspondence with David Sarnoff, John Royal, and other executives of NBC television immediately following his debut appearances on the network's 1939 World's Fair telecasts, Waring admitted his shock at the blazing temperature of the studio, noting, "Them lights is terrible" (Waring 1939).

11. The nostalgic discourse was explicit on the October 8, 1950, episode of *the Fred Waring Show*, with Waring wistfully reminiscing about the bygone days of the blackface minstrel show. Nostalgia was also centrally scripted on the September 9, 1951, episode of *The Colgate Comedy Hour* (hosted by Eddie Cantor, featuring guest Cesar Romero), titled "Songs to Remember."

12. Welk's discussion about "cats" continues: "My boys are plenty good. Some of them, though, are 'cats.' And I tell them to get that stuff out of their systems. I tell them to go to their jam sessions, but when they come to work for me, I want them to play my kind of music — the kind that people like" (Freeman 1953: 6).

13. Liberace and his management team were impressed by Klaus Landsberg's musical broadcasts on KTLA-TV, in particular *Korla Pandit's Adventures in Music* (Pyron 2000: 144–46), starring its strange and exotic host on the organ (Williams 1998).

14. Les Paul and Mary Ford's domestic life was depicted on the June 12, 1952, broadcast of *Star of the Family*, hosted by Peter Lind Hayes. On the show, the couple reenact the convergence of their music and home life, introducing the concept of the "Les Paulverizer." The Paulverizer was also introduced when the couple appeared on the September 13, 1953, episode of *Orchid Award*; on the show, Paul is described as "a virtuoso musician and an outstanding electronics engineer rolled into one." The Paulverizer was featured again on the October 25, 1953, broadcast of *Omnibus*, hosted by Alistair Cooke, where Paul first pretends to implement the elaborate machine and then admits the gag, demonstrating the actual multitrack recording process that he perfected and using reel-to-reel tape recorders to perform the couple's hit "How High the Moon."

15. Reviewing the June 1948 premiere of the short-lived *We the People* (featuring as musical guests the Nat "King" Cole Trio and Eden Ahbez, composer of the Cole hit "Nature Boy"), *Variety* took issue with the persistent habit of script reading: "In terms of depicting for home viewers how a radio show is run off, it could probably be classed as a success. But to call it a television show is a complete misnomer. . . . If anything, it pointed up one thing — that scripts eventually must go."

16. After almost six months on the air, *Toast of the Town* had evidently addressed its more egregious production flaws and on December 21, 1948, *Variety* reported, "The technical adjustments are meshing more smoothly than earlier exhibits," resulting in more polished performances.

17. Citing an array of musical propriety issues and taboos that the networks contended with in television's early years, Stan Optowsky is clearly in error when he writes, "Of course, there can be nothing like 'Bewitched, Bothered and Bewildered's' 'wouldn't sleep, and couldn't sleep, until I could sleep where I shouldn't sleep'" (1961: 232).

18. Michael Mashon writes of *Hour Glass*, "The program accentuated star power as the means of drawing the largest audience. *Hour Glass* featured different performers every week, including Peggy Lee. . . . [I]t must have been the curiosity factor that prompted some stars to appear on the show because they certainly were not paid much money" (2005: 1141). See also Von Schilling 2003: 73–74, and Edgerton 2009: 86–88.

19. Ferrer's opinion on Lee's body type was not atypical for the time. A further, if regrettable illustration of this viewpoint is evident in the blunt recollection of the TV analyst and one-time CBS executive Gilbert Seldes in 1950 that "a woman with a pleasing voice was supplanted on the TV version of a radio program by a singer not nearly so good; the radio singer was fat, the other slender" (167).

20. Lee combined her singing and acting talents in several feature films during her early television era: she starred opposite Danny Thomas in the 1952 remake of *The Jazz Singer* (directed by Michael Curtiz), and her performance in the 1955 film *Pete Kelly's Blues* (directed by and starring Jack Webb) earned her an Academy Award nomination for Best Supporting Actress.

21. Industry veterans and consummate professionals, Sauter had once been an ace arranger with the Benny Goodman Orchestra and Finegan formerly occupied the arranger role with Glenn Miller's orchestra. The two joined forces in 1952, releasing their first album, *New Directions in Music* (a ten-inch LP on the RCA label) in 1953.

22. For example, a full-page ad appearing in *Variety* in 1949 promoted The Original Hoosier Hotshots as "the greatest new novelty act in show business . . . a television natural!" (May 18, 1949: 35). The quartet was steeped in the humor and musical dexterity common on the vaudeville stage (playing Dixieland jazz with considerable talent), implementing slide whistles and washboards and wearing funny hats while performing novelty tunes. By 1949, the group was experienced on stage and radio as well as recording 78 rpm disks and appearing in numerous musical Soundies film shorts. Television was a logical progression for the act.

23. Following *The Band of Tomorrow* TV debut, it was reported, "Contrary to advance notices that contestants for positions in the 'Band of Tomorrow' would be expected to turn backflips, do card tricks, dance, or juggle — and possibly because of the snorts of derision that arose from musicians — the six applicants selected by Martin's scouts to compete on the first show were picked essentially on the basis of musical ability" (Emge 1950a: 4).

24. Although in 1949 Lombardo steadfastly refused entreaties to host his own TV program, stating that bands belonged in "'their natural environment' . . . ballrooms and hotel rooms" ("Lawrence Out to Solve" 1949: 6), he intermittently dabbled in television before launching a half-hour show in 1954. Describing his new program, he reasserted his views on the band's "natural environment," stating that on his broadcasts from the Roosevelt Hotel's Grill Room "there's nothing staged . . . The show is not written . . . There are also no gimmick shots" ("Now It's Sweetest Music"

1954: 2). Lombardo and his musical brothers also hosted "Guy Lombardo's Diamond Jubilee" on CBS in spring 1956.

25. For an interesting treatise on the character of embarrassment, see Miller 1997.

Notes to Chapter 5: Music in a "Sepia" Tone

1. Gabbard describes Armstrong's early 1950s film appearances as "strange hybrid roles that combined his public persona with a diegetic character" (1996: 223–24). The trend is also evident in his appearance as himself in the 1956 film *High Society* directed by Charles Walters and starring Bing Crosby.

2. The traces of racial insensitivity are, however, notable. For example, on the February 24, 1952, episode of the DuMont program *Stage Entrance*, after playing with hipster argot that he assumes is associated with bebop musicians and awarding *Down Beat* awards to Dizzy Gillespie and Charlie Parker, the program host Earl Wilson poses the question, "you boys got anything more to say?" The demeaning address elicits a withering glare from Parker who responds, "they say music speaks louder than words, so we'd rather voice our opinion that way if you don't mind."

3. Wendall Hall was a popular white singer in the 1920s, benefiting from radio exposure and his role as program host throughout much of the decade. A composer and interpreter of blues-style numbers, in November 1923, Hall released his most successful recording, "It Ain't Gonna Rain No Mo," on the Victor label. The song was listed as an adaptation of a southern folk song and later transcribed in a "fox trot" style on the Wurlitzer piano roll number 13117 (released in July 1924).

4. In February 1948 Truman introduced a ten-point program that challenged Congress to reinforce the rights of African Americans and to empower the federal government in the protection of those rights. By March of that year, Truman issued Executive Order 9980, which desegregated the government's various branches, authorizing a system of federal review boards to address discriminatory employment practices wherever they arose. Of perhaps even greater importance was Executive Order 9981, integrating the U.S. armed forces for the first time and offering, in the process, a discursive template for subsequent corporate employment policies nationwide. The latter executive order read, in part, "It is hereby declared to be the policy of the President that there shall be equality of treatment and opportunity for all persons in the armed forces without regard to race, color, religion or national origin." The policy and associated rhetoric were gradually adopted by most of America's major corporations and cultural institutions.

5. *National Minstrels* featured Lucky Millinder as host, leading his fifteen-piece orchestra, as well as the vocalist Annisteen Allep, the "blues singer and comedian" Bull Moose Jackson, and the "balladeer" Paul Brecker.

6. Though the minstrel shows were never a great success on early television, they did occasionally appear onscreen. See Macdonald 1992 (chap. 2).

7. In 1950, *The Fred Waring Show* presented a special broadcast featuring negro spiritu-

als, with the CBS press release proclaiming "the exuberant rhythms and contagious joy of negro spirituals have made them one of Fred Waring's favorite expressions" ("Fred Waring Show" 1950). Perhaps capitalizing on CBS's plans to broadcast the television version of the popular radio show, *Amos 'n' Andy* (the show debuted in June 1951) CBS announced on October 2, 1950, that "for the first time in his more than thirty years of show business, Fred Waring will put on an old fashioned minstrel show, with The Pennsylvanians in blackface in the best Mississippi tradition" (broadcast October 8, 1950). As a legitimating factor, it was announced that "this section of the program has been produced with the advice of Lillian Gale, daughter of George Gale, one of the most famous interlocutors of the 'nineties" ("Fred Waring and Pennsylvanians" 1950). Evidently the October 1950 broadcast was reasonably well received, for a year later CBS announced that Waring and his Pennsylvanians would "black up" once again for the October 28, 1951, broadcast with Raymond Massey as guest star, who "told Waring that he, Massey, would like to do a minstrel show, since that was his introduction to show business" ("Raymond Massey to Play" 1951).

8. *Down Beat* reported "a deluge of complaints and threats of picketing" by the NAACP in response to the blackface makeup worn by the musicians on *Dixie Show Boat* ("Protest TV Show" 1950: 8).

9. For a detailed description of NBC's Continuity Acceptance Radio/Television Department and its manager Stockton Helffrich, see Pondillo 2005. For a thorough account of NBC's racial policy and content control between 1926 and 1955 and Helffrich's involvement in the network's "integration without identification" initiative in the early TV era, see Forman 2007.

10. Reflecting standard circumstances for the time, the producers, director, and cameramen for *Club Ebony* were all white.

11. Although reporters, citing a station press release, referred to the show at the time as *The Cats and a Fiddle*, a band member, Clora Bryant, refers to the show in Tucker (2000: 322) as *The Chicks and a Fiddle* and in her own edited compendium as *The Hollywood Sepia Tones*. Bryant also explains that the group was known as "The Queens of Swing" prior to its TV debut, but the station directors changed its name to "The Hollywood Sepia Tones" for the broadcasts (Bryant et. al., 1998: 361–62).

12. Musicians appearing on TV encompassed a range of musical genres and performance styles. Artists included Marian Anderson, Louis Armstrong, Mildred Bailey, Harry Belafonte, Cab Calloway, Thelma Carpenter, Cozy Cole, Nat "King" Cole, Billy Daniels, Sammy Davis Jr., Roy "Little Jazz" Eldridge, Billy Eckstine, Duke Ellington, Ella Fitzgerald, Lionel Hampton, Lena Horne, the Ink Spots, Eartha Kitt, The Mills Brothers, the Billy Williams Quartet, Sarah Vaughn, Teddy Wilson, and many others. All of these artists had extensive concert and television performance experience and several could also claim film experience.

13. Vern Carrier, assistant manager for the Esso Standard Oil Company, addressed a letter to Bob Howard on January 31, 1949, that read in part: "You certainly have put

your back in your work the past seven months for Esso." William D. Edouarde of the Badger, Browning, and Hersey agency wrote to Howard, "We feel very fortunate indeed to have secured two one minute spots in your program on Tuesdays and Thursdays . . . for our client Reed and Barton who manufacture top quality sterling silver" (March 30, 1949). In correspondence with Howard dated April 27, 1949, Allan Black of the Cayton advertising agency wrote, "The sponsor and we at Cayton, Inc. are extremely pleased with your handling of the Polaroid Television Filter. . . . [Y]our sincere delivery and warm personality do a terrific selling job."

14. For a detailed biography of Hazel Scott, see Chilton 2008; see also McGee 2009.

15. The *Red Channels* introduction reads, in part: "Testifying before a U.S. Congressional committee on March 26, 1947, J. Edgar Hoover, Director of the Federal Bureau of investigation, stated: 'The [Communist] party has departed from depending on the printed word as its medium of propaganda and has taken to the air. Its members and sympathizers have not only infiltrated the airways but they are now persistently seeking radio channels.'" Citing a perceived benefit to the communist cause by deploying celebrities such as Horne, Robeson, Scott, and others, the text refers to "The great prestige and crowd-gathering power that derives from having glamorous personalities of radio and TV as sponsors of communist fronts and as performers at front meetings and rallies (which incidentally adds to the performers' prestige)" (*Red Channels* 1950: 1).

16. The reporter Alvin "Chick" Webb of the *New York Amsterdam News* should not be confused with the brilliant drummer William H. "Chick" Webb, who reigned at the Savoy Ballroom through the 1930s.

17. William Howland Kenney defines the black-and-tan lounges of Chicago's South Side: "Black-and-tan indicated a night club in which blacks and whites could interact with one another in certain socially stylized ways, talking, flirting, drinking, dancing, and listening to music. Such activities might lead to much more intimate social contacts thereafter, but those more explicitly sexual relations did not take place in the black-and-tan cafes" (Kenney 1993: 17).

18. In fact, the television industry's conception of "the home" as a primary symbolic space did not in any explicit way encompass the black home. Few, if any, of the earliest promotional campaigns or advertisements for TV sets included images of black families assembled before the screen as whites were portrayed. America's TV homes were quite homogeneously and unproblematically white based on the advertising images circulating at the time.

19. For a fascinating account of the racially infused repercussions following the appearance of Sammy Davis Jr. and the Will Mastin Trio on *The Colgate Comedy Hour* hosted by Eddie Cantor on February 17, 1952, see MacDonald 1992 (chap. 2).

20. The Daughters of the American Revolution adopted a resolution banning performances by blacks at Constitution Hall, built in 1929, as well as forbidding blacks and whites to be seated together. In 1939, the opera singer Marian Anderson was famously denied access to the Constitution Hall stage according to the organiza-

tion's segregation policy, resulting in first lady Eleanor Roosevelt's resignation from the D.A.R. Anderson was instead invited to sing from the steps of the Lincoln Memorial in April 1939, where her performance was attended by 75,000 people on the mall and reached a nationwide audience on NBC radio (Arsenault 2009). In October 1945 the D.A.R. also refused the pianist Hazel Scott permission to perform at Constitution Hall, prompting a dispute between President Harry Truman and Scott's husband, Representative Adam Clayton Powell Jr. (Ferrell 1991: 88–89; Donovan 1996: 147–48). The segregationist policy at Constitution Hall was not repealed until 1952.

Notes to Chapter 6: Maracas, Congas, and Castanets

1. An example includes the performance of "The Tennessee Tango," featuring Latin rhythms and western fiddles, sung by Redd Stewart on a 1953 episode of *The Peewee King Show* broadcast from Louisville, Kentucky, on WAVE-TV.

2. The Hawaiian term *haole* refers to non-Hawaiians or, more specifically, Caucasians. *Hapa haole* translates as mixed racial identity (usually Hawaiian-Caucasian) or a blend of Hawaiian and nonisland cultural traits.

3. For a discussion of television's introduction at the 1939 New York World's Fair, see Becker 2001.

4. Roosevelt's inaugural address of March 4, 1933, reads, in part, "'In the field of world policy, I would dedicate this nation to the policy of the Good Neighbor, the neighbor who resolutely respects himself, and, because he does so, respects the rights of others; the neighbor who respects his obligations and respects the sanctity of agreements in and with a world of neighbors. We now realize as we have never realized before our interdependence on each other; that we cannot merely take, but must also give."

5. As the corporate letterhead for Southern Music International reveals, in 1945 Ralph Peer's publishing empire extended to England, France, Spain, Canada, and throughout Latin America with offices in Argentina, Brazil, Chile, Colombia, Cuba, and Mexico.

6. At a time when ASCAP was moving rapidly into the South American market immediately following armistice, BMI's South American representative Ralph Peer may have compromised its position. In a letter to BMI's Sydney Kaye, NAB's president, Justin Miller, recounts a conversation that cast doubts on Peer's priorities and effectiveness: "Briefly stated . . . opinion is that Peer is not trusted by anyone in Latin America. [The] impression is that Peer is working for his own interests and playing everyone against the other for that purpose. . . . [T]he reputation of BMI has suffered very seriously throughout Latin America because Peer has been BMI's representative" (1945).

7. Delora Bueno, a singer and guitarist, was a native of Dubuque, Iowa, who was educated in Brazil and at New York's elite Juilliard School. Miguelito Valdes was a talented Cuban-born vocalist who performed and recorded on RCA Victor with the influential Havana nightclub ensemble Orquestra Casino de la Playa (a band that

also spawned the mambo innovator Perez Prado) in the late 1930s before relocating to the United States in 1940 to sing with Xavier Cugat.

8. Ned Sublette confirms Winthrop's statement pertaining to the illegality of the conga drum: "It might seem hard to believe now that the conga in a dance band could be daring, much less in Cuba. But the instrument had been the subject of prohibitions ever since its invention. Only now was it liberated. In the new, relatively relaxed environment, it was for the first time OK to play a tumbadora anywhere in public. This innovation happened in the early 1940s because it would have previously been illegal" (2007: 479–80).

9. Robynn J. Stilwell explains, "Drums . . . have powerful connotations of masculinity; drums are military instruments, and in many cultures, only men are allowed to play them. The Afro-Caribbean conga, which was Desi Arnaz's primary instrument, also has more explicit sexual meanings in the roughly phallic shape and the 'sexual' rhythms" (2003: 8).

10. In 1951, Cugat was "made aware" of her husband Xavier's romantic interest in the singer and dancer Abbe Lane. The Cugats were divorced in 1952, and Xavier Cugat married Lane soon after.

11. It was estimated that at one point, Latin rumba and mambo dance styles accounted for up to 60 percent of the client traffic at the nation's Arthur Murray Dance studios.

12. Following the broadcast *Variety* noted that Columbia Records intended to release a recording of the Martin-Coward TV special *Together with Music*, only the second time a TV special had been recorded for album release (the first being a 1953 special featuring Mary Martin and Ethel Merman, released on the Decca label). Two weeks prior to the Martin-Coward TV special, Columbia had also released a recording of Coward's stage show, *Noel Coward at Las Vegas* ("COL in Groove" 1955: 39). The trade magazine also cited "the effect of a tele plug on the disk industry" as Coward's Las Vegas concert release received a noticeable sales bump following the Martin-Coward TV special ("Martin-Coward Spec" 1955: 51).

13. Coward's performance of "Nina" from this broadcast is, at this writing, available for screening on YouTube.

Notes to Conclusion

1. Sales's sons, Tony and Hunt (bassist and drummer respectively), have an interesting entry in the history of popular music and television. Following an altogether pleasant conversation with Dinah Shore on a 1977 broadcast of *Dinah and Friends* (with an amused David Bowie chuckling in the background), a shirtless, fidgety Iggy Pop performs "Sister Midnight" accompanied by the Sales brothers. The rhythm duo recorded with Todd Rundgren and with Pop (appearing on his 1977 *Lust for Life* album and *TV Eyes Live*, released in 1978), later forming the band Tin Machine with Bowie and the guitarist Reeves Gabrels.

2. Elvis Presley's ascent to the pinnacle of the pop music charts and his incursion into the nation's common lexicon were inextricably linked to his twelve television ap-

pearances between January 1956 and January 1957, beginning with his performances on *Stage Show* (hosted by the band leaders Jimmy and Tommy Dorsey) — where he was booked on the program for six appearances over an eight-week period — as well as appearances over the course of the year on *The Milton Berle Show* (two appearances), *The Steve Allen Show* (a single appearance), and *The Ed Sullivan Show* (three appearances). According to John Mundy, "What made Presley different was the rapidity with which his visual persona was constructed, disseminated and consumed. What made the difference was television, and the growing ubiquity of its representational regime" (1999: 113).

3. Confirming TV's promotional effects, Presley's television turn reaped immeasurable benefits as teen consumers responded overwhelmingly to the young sensation. In the wake of his televised performances his record sales leaped, leading Peter Guralnick to conclude, "Television was the key to the deal" (1994: 241) and Philip Ennis to remark, "The personal appearances on television . . . handed Elvis the nation" (1992: 238). Gilbert Rodman articulates the deeper implications of these TV broadcasts: "In the long run, what matters most about Elvis's early television appearances is that they dramatically and irreversibly restructure the perspective that vast numbers of people have on the world in which they live. And in changing the ways that people view their culture, that culture is itself changed" (1996: 153).

4. Revisiting the "social ferment" of the 1950s, David Halberstam writes of Presley: "In cultural terms, his coming was nothing less than the start of a revolution" (1993: 456).

5. Verifying the ongoing desirability of such factors via a more contemporary example, U2's performance on the televised 2002 Super Bowl half-time show was both newsworthy and sensational with the cameras tracking Bono as he literally ran laps around the massive heart-shaped stage while the names of the victims of the September 11, 2001, terrorist attacks scrolled skyward behind the band.

6. For further discussion of the concept of "household flow," see Pegley 2008.

7. Keith Negus describes such phenomena in relation to a 1969 British television appearance by Jimi Hendrix: "Much has been written about Hendrix's stage performances. . . . Yet equally significant were those moments when Jimi inspired 10-, 11-, 12-year-olds in front of the television — inspired them to find out more, to pick up a guitar, to listen to rock music" (2006: 18).

8. Online depictions of vintage "Two Tune Giant Screen Music Box TV" toys illustrate a Canadian patent date of 1964; U.S. versions list a 1966 copyright. In 1966 the company also manufactured a "Peek-a-Boo Screen Music Box TV" that played "Mary Had a Little Lamb."

9. Norma Coates recuperates the relevance of *The Monkees* and *Partridge Family* TV shows and analyzes the disparagement of their female fans. As she explains, rock critics at the time adopted a particularly demeaning discourse, addressing these fans as mere "teenyboppers" or "groupies." See Coates 2003.

10. The saga of *The Smothers Brothers Comedy Hour* is detailed in the 2002 documentary

film *Smothered: The Censorship Struggles of the Smothers Brothers Comedy Hour*, directed by Maureen Muldaur.

11. For a more detailed list of 1960s–1970s television music programs, see Tom McCourt and Nabeel Zuberi's entry on the Museum of Broadcast Communications website www.museum.tv/eotvsection.php?entrycode=musicontele.

12. Still on the air today and still presenting top music acts, SNL's lessons on live television continue, as Ashlee Simpson learned when she ingloriously flubbed her performance while lip-synching in 2004.

13. Pittman has had an almost *Zelig*-like career in relation to popular music and the broadcasting industry since the 1980s. After occupying a founding executive role at MTV and top executive positions at AOL Networks, and Time Warner Enterprises, Pittman was appointed in October 2011 as CEO of CC Media Holdings, overseeing 850 U.S. Clear Channel radio stations, online radio networks, and outdoor advertising.

14. In 2012 the Viacom website lists corporate ownership of MTV, MTV2, MTVU, MTV Tr3s, MTV Films, BET, VH1, VH1 Classic, VH1 Soul, CMT, Logo, Nickelodeon, Nick at Nite, Noggin, Comedy Central, TV Land, Spike TV, Atom, AddictingGames.com, Shockwave.com, GameTrailers.com, Neopets, as well as MTVN International and Paramount Pictures.

15. See Craig Marks and Rob Tannenbaum, *I Want My MTV*.

16. Hip-hop also figured into various minor programs at the time, including the 1984 pilot for *Graffiti Rock*. Hip-hop impresario and producer Michael Holman ultimately failed to secure long-term support for the broadcast project although it was nominated for an Emmy award.

17. Another indicator of *Glee*'s audience appeal resides in the numerous self-produced home videos posted on YouTube featuring fans lip-synching to the show's songs while emulating the cast's dance moves.

18. The *American Idol* brand has spun off numerous products in the United States and Canada including recordings, participant biographies, and a publishing brand hybrid titled *Chicken Soup for the American Idol Soul* that includes "stories from top idols from every season" and "a special foreward by Paula Abdul" (Canfield et al. 2007).

19. Kiri Miller offers a theoretical distinction regarding *Guitar Hero* or *Rock Band* players and authentic musical performances. Employing the term "schizophrenic performance," she writes, "These game performances have proved unsettling to many people in large part because of their schizophrenic character. Audiences come to terms with the original schizophrenia—R. Murray Schafer's term for the split between a sound and its source, made possible by recording technology—by establishing value-laden distinctions between the live and the recorded. These games threaten the sanctity of those distinctions by combining the physical gestures of live musical performance with previously recorded sound" (2009: 400–401).

20. Frith writes, "most people's television sets have poor sound quality. . . . Even now

that digital recording is the norm few people have—or seem to want—good television sound" (2002: 279). Negus rebuts this, however, noting, "For much of its history television has been associated with small, poor-quality speakers. . . . However, it is by no means clear that television sound quality is experienced by the public as an impediment. Here a focus on television provides pointers to more general questions about how people gain pleasure from various listening strategies in different situations" (2006: 12–13).

21. The game tracks for certain songs ("I am the Walrus," "Octopus's Garden," "Lucy in the Sky With Diamonds," "Here Comes the Sun," "Yellow Submarine") employ animated visual graphics reminiscent of the 1968 animated film *Yellow Submarine* (directed by George Dunning), abandoning notions of verisimilitude and enveloping the gamer in a visual environment that contrasts sharply with scenes based on any actual social spaces or musical performances.

BIBLIOGRAPHY

Primary Sources

Ace, Goodman. 1955. *The Book of Little Knowledge: More Than You Want to Know about Television*. New York: Simon and Schuster.

Adams, David. 1949a. NBC interdepartmental correspondence, May 11.

———. 1949b. NBC interdepartmental correspondence, May 31.

Adams, Julius. 1949. *New York Amsterdam News*, December 17, 1.

Adams, Val. 1953. "Guest Relations Is Big Business." *New York Times*, March 1.

"AFM Action to Hypo Set Sale, Better Shows." 1948. *Variety*, March 24, 30.

Allen, Steve. 1952. "Here Are Tips about Writing a Song Hit!" *New York Amsterdam News*, January 5, 18.

Altbush, Hannah. 1955. "Negro TV, Radio Jobs Almost Nil, Survey Finds." *Down Beat*, March 23, 3.

"'B' is for Bombshell." 1951. *Radio and Television Mirror* (September), 12.

Bach, Bob. 1947. "Wha' Hoppeen, Noro? Rhumbop!" *Metronome* (July), 22.

"Bamboo." 1950. *Variety*, April 5, 37.

"'Band of Tomorrow' Will Need a Funny Hat Routine." 1950. *Down Beat*, April 21, 6.

Banks, Dale. 1948. *Radio and Television Mirror* (May), 12.

Basch, Charles J., Jr. 1950. Corporate correspondence with Neil Knox, NBC, September 18.

Bate, Fred. 1943. NBC interdepartmental correspondence, June 7.

"Beer Nursers Jam Bars Having Video." 1949. *New York Times*, October 6.

Begley, Martin, and Douglas MacCrae. 1955. *Auditioning for TV: How to Prepare for Success as a Television Actor*. New York: Hastings House.

Black, Allan. 1949. Letter to Bob Howard, April 27.

Blackburn, Norman. 1949. NBC interdepartmental correspondence with Carleton Smith, October 25.

"Blueprint TV One-Niter 'Circuit' to Aid Singer-Disk Exploitation." 1954. *Variety*, December 15, 59.

Brainard, Bertha. 1930. NBC interdepartmental correspondence, December 16.

Bretz, Rudy. 1950. "TV as an Art Form." *Hollywood Quarterly* 5, no. 2 (Winter): 153–63.

———. 1951. "The Limitations of Television." *Hollywood Quarterly* 5, no. 3 (Spring): 251–63.

———. 1953. *Techniques of Television Production*. New York: McGraw-Hill.

Broderick, Edwin. 1954. *Your Place in TV: A Handy Guide for Young People*. New York: David McKay.

Brown, Harry. 1951. Letter to NBC, February 26.

Brown, Les. 1954. "Polka Biz Jumping Like Mambo." *Variety*, September 15, 41.

Bundy, June. 1950. "TV: The New Home for Disk Jockeys." *Billboard*, October 7, 70.

———. 1956. "TV-DJs' Status Up at Local Level." *Billboard*, November 10, 62.

Bunzel, Peter. 1960. "Music Biz Goes Round and Round: It Comes Out Clarkola." *Life*, May 16, 88.

Burgin, Ralph. 1953. "Low Cost Music and Participation Shows versus Film." *Twenty-Two Television Talks*. New York: Broadcast Music.

Campbell, Victor F. 1955. "Low Cost Music and Specialty Programming." *Thirty-Two Television Talks*. New York: Broadcast Music, Inc.

"Cantor Sees Changes Coming in TV, Warns vs. Studio Audience Ogre." 1950. *Variety*, August 30, 2.

Cantrick, Robert B. 1954. "Music, Television, and Aesthetics." *Quarterly of Film, Radio, and Television* 9, no. 1 (Fall): 60–78.

"Carnegie Test for Latino Package." 1953. *Variety*, December 9, 60.

Chandler, Bob. 1950. "Web's Amateur Talent Binge." *Variety*, July 26, 33.

"Chi Video on Amateur Binge: 60 Acts to Play Circuit Weekly." 1950. *Variety*, July 5, 30.

Chotzinoff, Samuel. 1949. "Music in Television." *Variety*, January 5, 170.

"Chubby Rehearses Good Music, Plus Funny Hats in a 'Return to the People.'" 1949. *Down Beat*, March 11, 1.

"Coast Jocks Canter in TV: Refute Claims That Medium's a Tough Ride." 1950. *Billboard*, April 29, 8–15.

"Coast Tele Sets Displace Talent from Clubs, Bars." 1947. *Variety*, November 19, 1.

Cohen, Joe. 1950. "Fiddle as Talent Burns: Need to Develop More Top %-ers." *Variety*, January 11, 1.

Cohen, Martin. 1954. "Arthur Godfrey's Haleloke Hawaiian Doll." *Radio and Television Mirror* (March), 26.

———.1955. "All the Brothers Are Valiant." *Radio and Television Mirror* (June), 36, 70.

"Coin Machines Combine Radio, TV, and Jukes: Videograph's New Projects." 1947. *Billboard*, October 4, 1.

"COL in Groove with Martin-Howard Spec." 1955. *Variety*, October 26, 39.

Como, Perry. 1953 "I'm a Lucky Guy, Admits Como." *Down Beat*, February 25, 3.

———. 1955. "A Hit Is Born. *Coronet* (February), 67.

"Cooley Lauds TV." 1950. *Down Beat*, June 2, 4.

"Cornseed Crooners Reap B.O. Bonanza as City Slickers Lap Cider-Jug Tunes." 1951. *Variety*, June 27, 1.

"Cuba: Dictator with the People." 1952. *Time*, April 21, 38–46.

"Darwin and the Mambo." 1954. *Time*, September 6, 34.

Denis, Paul. 1949. "The Truth about Talent Opportunity Programs!" *Radio Best: The Radio and Television Picture Magazine* (June), 18, 47.

"DeVol Finds Dramatics an Aid in Being a Coast TV Dance Band Leader." 1952. *Down Beat*, April 15, 6.

"Dinah in Blackface." 1949. *Modern TV and Radio*, 70.

"Dinner Date." 1950. *Variety*. February 1, 32.

"Disk Jockey Move to Video Is Still a Long, Hard Trip." 1954. *Billboard*, November 13, 21.

Dunlap Jr., Orrin E. 1948. *Understanding Television: What It Is and How It Works*. New York: Greenberg.

Dupuy, Judy. 1945. *Television Show Business*. Schenectady: General Electric.

Eddy, William C. 1945. *Television: The Eyes of Tomorrow*. New York: Prentice Hall.

Edouarde, William D. 1949. Letter to Bob Howard, March 30.

Egan, Jack. 1948. "Peggy's Better Stage Presence Impressive." *Down Beat*, September 8, 16.

Emge, Charles. 1949. "Coast Station Launches First All-Negro TV Show." *Down Beat*, October 7, 9.

———. 1950a. "'Band of Tomorrow' Good TV; Has Accent on Music." *Down Beat*, June 30, 4.

———. 1950b. "Band Tieups Next TV Trend?" *Down Beat*, April 21, 6.

———. 1950c. "Thornhill Cold to Video Programs from Ballrooms." *Down Beat*, June 2, 4.

———. 1952a. "H'wd Leads TV Bands Parade." *Down Beat*, April 18, 1.

———. 1952b. "Liberace Leads All among L.A.'s Video Music Favorites As Fall Season Commences." *Down Beat*, October 22, 7.

———. 1953. "America's Best Known Leader." *Down Beat*, May 6, 3.

Engles, George. 1930a. NBC interdepartmental correspondence, December 15.

———. 1930b. NBC interdepartmental correspondence, December 18.

English, Mary. 1951a. "Rose Sees Better Things for Music In TV Future." *Down Beat*, November 30, 4.

———. 1951b. "Welk's Success In Video May Set Off New Trend." *Down Beat*, October 19, 4.

———. 1952. "Harry James TV Series Lays Bomb on 1st Show." *Down Beat*, February 22, 4.

Fairbanks, William F. 1935. NBC interdepartmental correspondence, July 17.

"The Forgotten 15,000,000." 1949a. *Sponsor*, October 10, 24.

"The Forgotten 15,000,000: Part 2." 1949b. *Sponsor*, October 24, 30.

"The Forgotten 15,000,000 . . . Three Years Later." 1952. *Sponsor*, July 28, 29.

Ford, Art. 1950. "Art Ford's P's and Q's for Video Jocks." *Billboard*, October 7, 69.

"For Your Pleasure." 1948. *Variety*, May 19, 24, 42.

Fox, David J. 1948. "Gay Nineties Review." *Television World* September 13, 12.

Frappollo, Deanne. 1952. "I'm a Cinderella Girl." *Radio and Television Mirror* (February), 28.

"Freddy Martin's 'Band of Tomorrow.'" 1950. *Variety*, May 31, 24.

"Fred Waring and Pennsylvanians Put on First Minstrel Show." 1950. CBS *Press Information*, October 2.

"Fred Waring Show." 1950. *Variety*, September 27, 31.

"Fred Waring Show to Feature Negro Spirituals." 1950. CBS *Press Information*, January 6.

"Fred Waring to Present His Annual 'Song of Easter.'" 1952. CBS *Press Information*, April 4.

Freeman, Don. 1951a. "Funny Hats Boys Have Ruined Us, Says Comic-Leader Ranch." *Down Beat*, November 2, 13.

———. 1951b. "Let Others Have Video — I'll Stay in the Ballrooms, Says Anthony." *Down Beat*, December 28, 1951.

———. 1953. "Welk's Act of Defiance Spelled Big TV Click." *Down Beat*, August 2, 6.

Fuller, Sam. 1951. NBC interdepartmental correspondence with Fred Wile Jr., October 30.

———. 1955. NBC interdepartmental correspondence with Richard Pinkham, July 28.

Garlington, S. W. 1948. "Radio Row: Producers Assure Public 'Minstrels' Will Be Okay." *New York Amsterdam News*, June 5, 14.

———. 1949a. "Amusement Row." *New York Amsterdam News*, February 26, 24.

———. 1949b. "Amusement Row." *New York Amsterdam News*, April 23, 24.

———. 1949c. "Amusement Row." *New York Amsterdam News*, August 27, 20.

———. 1949d. "Hymn Time to Swing Time." *New York Amsterdam News*, April 2, 17.

———. 1950a. "The Amusement Roundup." *New York Amsterdam News*, March 18, 19.

———. 1950b. "The Amusement Roundup." *New York Amsterdam News*, April 15, 19.

———. 1951. "Amusement Row." *New York Amsterdam News*, June 9, 23.

"Garroway Today." 1953. *TV Guide*, July 10–16.

"Gimme, Gimme, Gimme on the Old Payola." 1959. *Life*, November 23, 45–48.

Glickman, Dave. 1952. "There's No Business Like TV Talent Business." *Broadcasting-Telecasting*, May 12, 72.

"Godfrey Plugs Push La Rosa to 500,000." 1953. *Variety*, February 25, 44.

Goldstein, Leonard. 1949. NBC interdepartmental correspondence with Ray O'Connell, June 8.

"Gotta Get That Video Plug." 1955. *Variety*, April 6, 41.

Gottlieb, Bill. 1947. "Rhumba Bands May Cut Hot Orks." *Downbeat*, July 20, 10–11.

Graf, Herbert. 1945. *The Artistic Development of Television Programs*. New York: Television Program Department of the National Broadcasting Company, February 26.

Green, Abel. 1948. "TV Pickup Point-Kills Edith Piaf's Preem; Other Customer Problems." *Variety*, September 29, 70.

———. 1949. "Show Biz Cools Off on Video." *Variety*, June 29, 1.

Harrington, Ruth Lee. 1949. *Your Opportunities in Television*. New York: Medill McBride.

Harris, Harry. 1953a. "Around the Dials: Bandstand Celebrates First Birthday." *Philadelphia Evening Bulletin*, October 12, 25.

———. 1953b. "Around the Dials: Bandstand-Disc Jockey Formula for TV." *Philadelphia Evening Bulletin*, January 16, 11.

"Hazel Scott Show." 1950. *Variety*, April 19, 24.

Helffrich, Stockton. 1950a. *The National Broadcasting Company and the Negro National Community: A Roundtable*. New York: Transcript of the National Broadcasting Corporation, October 25.

———. 1950b. NBC interdepartmental correspondence with Jack Hein, February 3.

———. 1951. NBC interdepartmental correspondence with William Brooks, March 2.

Hentoff, Nat. 1954. "Mambo Rage Latest in Latin Dance Line." *Down Beat*, December 1, 2.

"Her Chance of a Lifetime . . . Only 80 Minutes Away." 1954. *TV Guide*, July 17–23, 8–9.

"Hey TV, We're Still Waiting," 1951. *Down Beat*, November 2, 10.

Hodapp, William. 1955. *The Television Actor's Manual*. New York: Appleton-Century-Crofts.

Holly, Hal. 1948. "Cooley's Cowboy Crew Clicks in Video Show." *Down Beat*, August 25, 12.

———. 1950. "Ina Ray Ork Looks Good on TV; Plays Well Too." *Down Beat*, December 1, 13.

———. 1951a. "Producer Tells Sidemen How to Live with Video." *Down Beat*, February 23, 8.

———. 1951b. "Reporter Fails to Trap Ada into Scrap with Ina. *Down Beat*, April 6, 8.

———. 1952. "DeVol Doing a New Book for Video-Tailored Band." *Down Beat*, February 8, 9.

———. 1954. "Rustic Rhythm's California Boom Stemmed from TV." *Down Beat*, March 10, 5.

"Horace Heidt Show." 1950. *Variety*, October 11, 30.

"Horace Heidt Trains Talent." 1951. *TV Show*, October, 19.

"Hormel to Pull a Hutton with Ex-USO Musicians." 1948. *Down Beat*, January 28, 18.

"How to Win with Juan." 1951. *Sponsor*, June 4, 25.

Hubbell, Richard. 1950. *Television Programming and Production*. 2nd ed. New York: Rinehart.

Hutchinson, Thomas H. 1944. "Programming." *Televiser* 1, no. 1 (Fall): 12–13.

———. 1946. *Here Is Television: Your Window to the World*. New York: Hastings House.

"H'wood Eateries Drop Live Entertainment with Tele as Come-on." 1948. *Variety*, January 28, 1.

"Ike Heading down the Hambone Alley." 1949. *Down Beat*, February 25, 3.

"In Review: Judge for Yourself." *Broadcasting-Telecasting*, August 24, 1953, 18.

"Jackie Heller's Carousel." 1950. *Billboard*, December 23, 37.

"Jackie Robinson to Direct New Community Project: WNBC-WNBT Music Foundation." 1953. *NBC Chimes*. New York: National Broadcasting Company (January), 10.

"Juke Op Surveys Video Effect." 1947. *Billboard*, October 11, 110.

"Jukes-vs.-Television in Bars Creates Snarl." 1948. *Variety*, April 28, 43.

"Julius LaRosa, Archie Bleyer Exit Godfrey Show after Big Blowup." 1953. *Variety*, October 21, 1953, 1.

Kanaga, L. W. 1952. "Phonograph Records Make Strong Comeback in 1951." *Radio Age* 11, no. 3 (April): 26, 30.

Kaplan, Mike. 1951. "Tout Television as Talent Tutor; Tube Increasingly Eyes New Faces." *Variety*, May 16, 2.

Kaufman, William I., ed. 1955. *How to Direct for Television*. New York: Hastings House.

Kaufman, William, and Robert Colodzin. 1950. *Your Career in Television*. New York: Merlin Press.

Kaye, Sammy. 1955. "To Heck with the Mambo!" *Down Beat*, April 20, 56.

Keegan, Junie. 1952. "Paul Whiteman's TV Teen Club." *Radio and Television Mirror* (February), 59.

Keith, Hal. 1948. "Symphony on TV." *Broadcasting-Telecasting*, April 12, 35.

Kern, Jerome. 1938. Correspondence with Bertha Brainard, June 11.

Kline, Midge. 1944. "Music for Television." *Televiser* 1, no. 1 (Fall): 14.

Kostelanetz, Andre. 1952. "Music's Potentialities in Television." *Variety*, January 2, 224.

"Krupa All Eyes for Video." 1948. *Down Beat*, July 14, 2.

Landsberg, Klaus. 1951. "Eye Appeal and Music Go Hand in Hand on TV." *Down Beat*, September 7, 8.

"Lawrence Out to Solve TV Band Presentation." 1949. *Down Beat*, April 22, 6.

Lea, Clarence F. 1945. Correspondence from the chairman of the Congressional House Committee on Interstate and Foreign Commerce to the National Association of Broadcasters, February 27.

Lee, Robert E. 1944. *Television: The Revolution*. New York: Essential Books.

Leiter, Robert D. 1953. *The Musicians and Petrillo*. New York: Bookman Associates.

"Lena on Cantor's TV." 1951. *Variety*, February 21, 29.

Leonard, Will. 1953. "TV Cameramen Provide Muddled Look at Music." *Down Beat*, December 30, 12.

Levey, Lawrence. 1949. *Television Opportunities* 1, no. 11 (September).

"Limited Dates for Latin Orchs: Gotta Add Pops as Rhumba Fades." 1951. *Variety*, May 30, 41.

Lombardo, Guy. 1955. "Lombardo Lauds TV." *Down Beat*, April 20, 13.

"Look Out! Hampton's Readying Funny Hats." 1949. *Down Beat*, June 3, 2.

"Lorraine Cugat Show." 1951. *Variety*, July 11.

Mabley, Jack. "Radio and Video." 1955. *Down Beat*, December 14, 46.

Machito. "Latin Music Isn't What You Think It Is." 1947. *Metronome*, August, 26.

Mack, Ted. 1951a. "Memo: to Amateurs from: Ted Mack subject: How to Win!" *Radio and Television Mirror* (February), 29.

———. 1951b. "'Old Bowesies' — The New Assembly Line of Supply for Video Talent." *Variety*, January 3, 98.

———. 1952. "This Wonderful World." *Radio and Television Mirror* (February), 27.

"The Magic Carpenters." 1951. *Time*, May 21, 62, 64.

Mannheim, Mannie. 1950. "Video Dermatitis." *Variety*, July 26, 41.

Martin, Freddy. 1951. "Problems for Bands in Video." *Variety*, July 11, 48.

"Martin-Coward Spec Boosts 'Las Vegas' LP." 1955. *Variety*, November 2, 51.

"MCA, Morris Call the Turns: Talent Agencies Rule Radio, Tele." 1950. *Variety*, September 13, 27.

"MCA, Wm. Morris 'Control' of Talent Faces Early Public Airing in TV Probe as Senate Mobilizes Forces." 1955. *Variety*, June 15, 23.

McGarrett, George. 1951. NBC interdepartmental correspondence with Fred Wile Jr, September 6.

———. 1955. NBC interdepartmental correspondence with John Dodge, August 17.

McMillan, Allan. 1950. "Allan's Alley." *New York Amsterdam News*, December 9, 25.

"Melodiers Dance Band Rhythm Rodeo Champion." 1952. *Philadelphia Inquirer*, December 6, 13.

Merwin, Gregory. 1953. "Godfrey's Mariners." *Radio and Television Mirror* (April), 52.

"Miami's Copa City as Major TV Origination Point for Networks." 1954 *Variety*, November 17, 33.

Miller, Justin. 1945. Correspondence with Sydney Kaye, president, Broadcast Music, December 27.

———. 1946. Correspondence with U.S. Assistant Attorney General Wendell Berge, February 18.

———. 1948. "Statement of Justin Miller, President of the National Association of Broadcasters, before the House Committee on Education and Labor." January 13.

———. 1953. Correspondence with J. Nelson Stuart, August 31.

Minter, Gordon. 1949. "Education for Television Jobs." *Hollywood Quarterly* 4, no. 2 (Winter): 193–96.

Modern TV and Radio. 1948. (December), 12.

Murray, Mrs. Arthur. 1954. "What the Heck Is the Mambo?" *Down Beat*, December 14, 2.

"Music Biz Eyes TV Future." 1947. *Billboard*, August 9, 20.

"Music Execs Again Look to Latin Music to Bail Them out of Business Slump." 1952. *Variety*, July 2, 41.

"Musicians' Christmas Party." 1953. *Broadcasting-Telecasting*, January 4, 16.

Music Performance Trust Fund Trustee's Regulations. 1949. New York: Samuel R. Rosenbaum, Trustees' Office, July 1.

"Music Sells . . . When a Disk Jockey Spins Records." 1947. *Sponsor* (February), 20.

"Nat (King) Cole's TV Guest Shot Pacting." 1955. *Variety*, May 18, 27.

"Nationwide Pickup in Nitery Biz: Ops No Longer Fear TV Competition." 1954. *Variety*, October 13, 57.

NBC and You: Operations and Employee Relations Policies Manual. 1948. New York: National Broadcasting Company.

NBC *Program Policies and Working Manual.* 1934. New York: National Broadcasting Company.

NBC *to Employees.* 1938. New York: National Broadcasting Company, December 8.

"Negro Talent Coming into Own on TV, without Use of Stereotypes." 1950. *Variety,* May 3, 30.

"New Frankenstein?" 1948. *Variety,* June 2, 27.

"New NBC Music Foundation Directed by Jackie Robinson." 1953. *The Baton* (January), 3.

"New Shows Are Added to WFIL Roster." 1952. *Philadelphia Inquirer,* October 13, 19.

Niccoli, Ria. 1951a. "Either Get with TV, or Video Will Create Own Bands: Hamp." *Down Beat,* November 2, 2.

———. 1951b. "Many Contribute to Success of 'Cavalcade of Bands' Tver." *Down Beat,* January 12, 4.

———. 1951c. "Martin Finds TV Formula." *Down Beat,* July 27, 5.

———. 1951d. "Relaxation One Clue to Success of Como Show." *Down Beat,* May 4, 4.

"Nightclubs." 1947. *Life,* December 15, 109–15.

"Nitery Ops, Clipped by Falling Biz, Want to K.O. Talent Doubling on TV." 1953. *Variety,* August 12, 1.

"Nitery Talent and Vaudeo." 1948. *Variety,* September 8, 27.

"No, Not That!" 1949. *Variety,* April 13, 1.

"Nostalgic Palace Vaude Bill Debuts ABC in NY Tele." 1948. *Variety,* August 11.

"Not Every Man a Comedian." 1951. *Down Beat,* April 6, 10.

"Novelty Needed If Bands Want Video Contracts." 1948. *Down Beat,* January 28, 10.

"Now It's Sweetest Music This Side of Iconoscope." 1954. *Down Beat,* January 13, 2.

O'Connell, Ray. 1947. NBC interdepartmental correspondence, November.

"Old Dutch Revue." 1954. *Radio and Television Mirror* (August), 20.

O'Meara, Carroll. 1955. *Television Program Production.* New York: Ronald Press.

"On and Off the Air." 1949. *Modern TV and Radio,* April, 6.

Operation Backstage: Staging Services Handbook of the NBC Television Network Operations Department. 1951. New York: National Broadcasting Company.

"The Operator and Television." 1947. *Billboard,* August 2, 112.

"'Overexposure' Still TV's Biggest Enemy of Top Stars, Sez Tony Miner." 1955. *Variety,* September 7, 26.

"Package Shows Solving Budget Problems for Bistro Circuit." 1949. *Variety,* October 26, 66.

"Paradox in TV 'Brush': Talent Holding to High Fees in Niteries." 1955. *Variety,* April 13, 2.

Paulu, Burton. 1953. "Televising the Minneapolis Symphony Orchestra." *Quarterly of Film, Radio, and Television* 8, no. 2 (Winter): 157–71.

"Peggy Astounds Ciroites with Nitery Showmanship." 1948. *Down Beat,* March 24, 9.

"Peggy Lee Goes South of the Border." 1950. *Metronome,* October, 14.

"Peggy Lee's Progress Shows Flair of Ferrer." 1953. *Down Beat,* January 23, 7.

"Peggy to East for Video, Copa Dates." 1951. *Down Beat*, March 23, 5.

Petrillo, James C. 1946. "Why Members of the American Federation of Musicians Are Not Working for Television and Frequency Modulation Radio." *International Musician* 44, no. 10 (April), 1.

———. 1954. Telegraph to Sylvester "Pat" Weaver, president, National Broadcasting Company, June 14.

"Petrillo Relents." 1948. *Life*, April 5, 43–44.

"Petrillo's 'I Surrender.'" 1948. *Variety*, March 24, 27.

"Philly Wide-Open Payola Town for Disk Jocks among Indie Labels." 1952. *Variety*, November 5, 37.

"'Popsicle Parade' to Feature Stars, Berle First." 1950. *Billboard*, April 22, 6.

Potter, Ralph. 1947. "Audivisual Television." *Hollywood Quarterly* 3, no. 1 (Fall): 66–78.

Prado, Perez. 1954. "Perez Prado—I'm Ready to Touch Off Revolution." *Down Beat*, April 21, 29.

"Prado Tells How Mambo Made It but Not How He Makes It Tick." 1954. *Down Beat*, December 1, 3.

"Pretty Thelma Hoping for a Spot on Television Program." 1950. *New York Amsterdam News*, August 12, 22.

"Protest TV Show Minstrel Makeup." 1950. *Down Beat*, April 7, 8.

"Radio and Television." 1955. *Time*, November 21, 91.

Ranson, Jo, and Richard Pack. 1950. *Opportunities in Television*. New York: Grosset and Dunlap.

"Raymond Massey to Play Minstrel on 'Fred Waring Show.'" 1951. *CBS Press Information*, October 18.

RCA and NBC Present Television. 1940. New York: Radio Corporation of America.

"Recording Companies Find That Tele Does Much to Sell Pops on Disks." 1950. *Variety*, March 1, 41.

"Recordland." 1954. *Variety*, September 29, 30.

Red Channels: The Report of Communist Influence in Radio and Television. 1950. New York: Counterattack.

"Reginald Beane Trio Featured on TV Network." 1950. *New York Amsterdam News*, December 23, 26.

Reid, Mrs. Charles F. 1926. Letter to Radio Corporation of America, March 26.

"Rival CBS Program Featured a Maestro Who Ate Cough Drops." 1948. *Life*, April 5, 46.

Rosen, George. 1948. "TV Adds Stature in Toscy Airing: Poorer Philly Show the Better Test." *Variety*, March 24, 30.

———. 1951. "TV's 'What's Next?' Dilemma: Casualty List Presents Poser." *Variety*, February 14, 1.

———. 1952. "TV's 'Hit and Run' Performers: Sloppy, Careless Video Is Scored." *Variety*, October 1, 97.

———. 1953. "Greatest 'Free' Show on Earth: TV Talent Costs at Record Peaks." *Variety*, October 7, 1.

Roy, Rob. 1954. "Out of the Hearts of Stars Came TV and Radio Bids to Sepia Artists." *Chicago Defender*, January 2.

Royal, John F. 1932. NBC interdepartmental correspondence with Bertha Brainard, December 12, 1932.

———. 1935. NBC interdepartmental correspondence with Janet MacRorie, May 1.

———. 1939. Correspondence with Fred Waring, May 10.

Ryan, J. Harold. 1945. Letter to Justin Miller, president, National Association of Broadcasters, October 17.

Sargeant, Winthrop. 1947. "Cuba's Tin Pan Alley." *Life*, October 6, 145–57.

Sarnoff, David. 1939. "Probable Influences of Television on Society." *Journal of Applied Physics* 10, no. 7: 426–31.

Sarnoff, Robert. 1949. NBC interdepartmental correspondence with Carleton D. Smith, June 30.

Saturday Night Jamboree. 1949. NBC program promotion and sales packet.

Schumach, Murray. 1947. "'Revolution' in Tin Pan Alley: Swing, Long the Nation's Musical Fare, Has Virtually Disappeared, and 'Sweet' Is Very Much in High Favor." *New York Times Magazine*, October 19, 20, 69–71.

"Scott Adapting Quintet for Sight Engagement." *Down Beat*, September 8, 1948, 20.

"See No End to Cornball Cycle: Folk Tunes Held to Be Less Risky." 1951. *Variety*, July 18, 41.

"See Video As No Maker of Hits." *Variety*, September 5, 1951, 55.

Seldes, Gilbert. 1950. *The Great Audience*. New York: Viking Press.

Sellers, T. J. 1953. "Harlem Theme Opera Shown on 'Omnibus.'" *New York Amsterdam News*, April 4, 13.

"Sell Juke Boxes to Homes: Sale of Used Juke Boxes for Rec Room Use Increases along Eastern Seaboard." 1947. *Billboard*, August 2, 112.

Shane, Irwin. 1945. "Television's Untapped Talent and Program Resources." *Televiser* 1 no. 2 (Winter): 9–10.

"Showletter from Television Promotion." 1950. New York: NBC Television Network, July 18.

"Showmanship, New Talent Needed Now." 1947. *Down Beat*, February 26, 10.

Simon, George. 1952a. "The Editors Speak: George T. Simon: The Real Sinatra." *Metronome* (May).

———. 1952b. "Stan Freeman." *Metronome* (October), 30–31.

Sinatra, Frank. 1951. "What I Learned about Television." *Metronome* (May), 11.

"Singing Those Tele Blues: It Hurts Where It Hurts When It First Debuts." 1948. *Billboard*, July 10, 100, 103.

Smith, Carleton. 1949a. Interdepartmental correspondence with Norman Blackburn, October 20.

———. 1949b. NBC interdepartmental correspondence with Robert Sarnoff, July 5.

"Song-Sharks Use Radio-TV as Bait in Feeding on Amateur Cleffers." 1951. *Variety*, September 12, 1.

Sosnik, Harry. 1951. "TV Has Set Music Back 20 Years Because 'Picture' Is Main Thing." *Variety*, September 26, 29.

"Spike Jones Revue Pulls $908,000 in 109 1-Nighters; TV Doesn't Hurt Any More." 1953. *Variety*, May 13, 149.

"Spinning Images." 1949. *Broadcasting-Telecasting*, May 16, 63.

Stahl, Bob. 1954. "Godfrey Snaps Back at 'Untruths.'" *TV Guide*, August 7–13, 13–14.

———. 1955. "Godfrey Talks." *TV Guide*, January 15–21, 13–15.

Stanton, Carl. 1951. NBC interdepartmental correspondence with Sylvester Weaver, December 21.

Stasheff, Edward, and Rudy Bretz. 1951. *The Television Program: Its Writing, Direction, and Production*. New York: A. A. Wyn.

Steffens, Mildred. 1945. "The Case for Visualized Music in Television." *Telescreen* (Spring): 8–12.

Stewart, R. W. 1949. "Report on Saloons." *New York Times*, April 24.

"Strike Up the Bands!" 1954. *TV Guide*, August 28–September 3, 16–17.

Stuart, J. Nelson. 1953. Letter to Justin Miller, president, National Association of Radio and Television Broadcasters, August 28.

Sullivan, Frank. 1948. "Anyway, It's Here to Stay." *New York Herald Tribune*, August 20.

Sullivan, Mady. 1948. "What's New." *Television World*, March 15, 5.

"Sullivan Stops Vaughn Monroe on Murray TV'er." 1954. *Variety*, July 14, 27.

Taubman, Howard. 1948. "Should Conductors Be Seen or Just Heard?" *New York Times Magazine*, April 25, 17.

Taylor, Davidson. 1951. Letter to Carl Byoir, National Broadcasting Company, August 30.

"Teen-Age Dance Bands to Vie in Rhythm Rodeo." 1952. *Philadelphia Inquirer*, October 5, 1.

"Teenage Nitery Idea Spreading in Philadelphia." 1949. *Variety*, October 26, 66.

"Teen-Agers Swarm to WPEN Broadcast." 1949. *Radio Showmanship*, September, 13.

"Teenagers 'Worst' Market to Reach in TV; Radio Up." 1955. *Variety*, March 16, 130.

"Tele Band Remotes Will Right Wrong Ballroom Impressions, Says Greer." 1948. *Variety*, April 7, 45.

"Tele 'On Own' from Here on In: 'Fanaticism' Era Is Over." 1949. *Variety*, July 13, 29.

"Tele's Economy Nips Bands." 1948. *Variety*, September 15, 43.

"Telestatus: Hofstra Surveys Habits." 1948. *Broadcasting-Telecasting*, August 23, 18.

"Tele Still a Headache: Bromo No Aid for Operators Hit by Video." 1948. *Billboard*, July 3, 100, 108.

Television and Youth: Interests, Activities, Hobbies. 1954. Washington: National Association of Radio and Television Broadcasters.

"Television Builds Ina Ray Hutton into Coast Lure." 1950. *Variety*, December 20, 36.

"Television Cuts Down Juvenile Delinquency: Video Lures Kids Home from Street." 1949. *New York Amsterdam News*, April 2, 15.

"Television Developments Demonstrated for Press by NBC and RCA." 1936. Press release. New York: National Broadcasting Company, November 6.

"Television News from CBS." 1949. November 4.

"Television Outlook." 1948. *International Musician*, April 7.

"Television Pay Scales for Musicians." 1948. *Down Beat*, August 23, 12.

"Television Set Owners Cut Amusement Spending Temporarily." 1948. *Wall Street Journal*, October 13.

Television's First Year. 1940. New York: National Broadcasting Company.

"Tele vs. Table D'Hote; It's Now Blamed for Hub Restaurant Fall-Off." 1951. *Variety*, February 21, 1.

"Thank TV for Vaude Revival." 1949. *Down Beat*, June 17, 10.

"That !?*?! Television: TD." 1951. *Down Beat*, June 29, 5.

"Their Lips Move . . . But Do They Sing?" 1954. *TV Guide*, December 18–24, 8–9.

Time & Program Information: Sales Success at Seven-Thirty. 1955. Promotion report. New York: National Broadcasting Corporation, March 2.

"Tired Monroe Has Sub Sing During Rehearsals." 1951. *Down Beat*, March 9, 4.

"The Tony Martin Show." 1954. *TV Guide*, June 18–24, 23.

Tooke, Rolland V. 1951. Letter to Sheldon B. Hickox Jr., NBC Television Station Relations, February 26.

Tooley, Howard. 1953. *The Television Workshop*. Minneapolis: Northwestern Press.

"Too Many A&R Men Already, So Pubs Don't Like Song-Judging AM-TV Shows." 1954. *Variety*, February 17, 41.

"Toscanini Televised." 1948. *Radio Age* 7, no. 3 (April): 21.

"Tradio Unveils Video-Sound Set at Hotel Show." 1947. *Billboard*, November 22, 96.

"Tropic Holiday." 1949. *Variety*, October 5, 28.

"TV a Fulltime Job, Doubling Too Tough, Performers Find Out." 1949. *Variety*, March 30, 1.

"TV Can't 'Make' Bands — Monroe." 1951. *Variety*, May 9, 1.

"TV Costs: Sponsor Pays More, Gets More." 1949. *Sponsor*, April 25, 58.

"TV Danceland." 1954. *Variety*, May 19, 30.

"TV Disk Jock Comes Into Own." 1952. *Variety*, July 30, 57.

"TV Disk Jockey Toons Set for Major Markets." 1951. *Variety*, June 13, 30.

"TV Hex Ups Sex in Mpls. Bistros." 1952. *Variety*, June 23, 52.

"TV High Spots for Your Daily Entertainment." 1949. *New York Amsterdam News*, April 2, 15.

"TV Only Job Hope." 1950. *Broadcasting-Telecasting*, June 5, 18.

"TV's Disk Effect in Brushoff by Ted Wallerstein." 1949. *Variety*, August 3, 37.

"TV's Drain on Acts Cues Bistro Boys to Cushion Their Future via P.M.'s." 1952. *Variety*, January 9, 56.

"TV's Hit-Making Potential Blocked by 'Play-It-Safe' Policy on New Songs." 1954. *Variety*, May 12, 41.

"TV's Musical Math." 1949. *Broadcasting-Telecasting*, April 18, 40.

"TV Set Owners: 'Good Housekeeping' Surveys." 1951. *Broadcasting-Telecasting*, November 5, 185.

"TV Set Price to Hit Skids: Taverns Soon to See Models under $1,000." 1947. *Billboard*, August 30, 104.

"TV 'Star Time' Survives Lots of Hurdles in Kid Contract Problems." 1955. *Variety*, December 21, 22.

"TV's 'Tuxedo Rates.'" 1948. *Variety*, March 24, 31.

"TV the Villain in Hub Transit Slumps." 1952. *Variety*, February 6, 30.

"'TV Toons': Visualizes Music Records." 1952. *Broadcasting-Telecasting*, January 7, 76.

Ulanov, Barry. "El Rey!" 1950. *Metronome*, December, 19.

"Uncle Sambo, Mad for Mambo." 1954. *Life*, December 20, 14–18.

"Uptown Jubilee." 1949. *Variety*, September 21, 32.

"Van Heusen-Cahn 'Our Town' Clicks Tuning Up 'Year of the TV' Scores." 1955. *Variety*, September 28, 53.

"Vaudeville Vanishing from Capitol Oct. 1." 1953. *Washington Post*, August 27, 19.

"Vaughn Monroe Refuses Work." 1950. *Down Beat*, December 15, 1.

"Video Just Possibly Might Aid Musician." 1949. *Down Beat*, March 25, 10.

"Video Opening Its Purse Strings to Lure Top Names." 1947. *Variety*, December 24, 27.

"Video Turns to Coin Biz: Tavern Sets on Increase." 1947. *Billboard*, November 22, 96–110.

"Video Uncertainty Hypo to T. Dorsey Aim to Run '49 Gross over $1,000,000." 1949. *Variety*, April 13, 51.

"Video's Vaude Song-Styling: Favors Simple Lyrics." 1947. *Variety*, February 4, 41.

"Video, Visual Appeal Put Welk in Champagne Class." 1953. *Down Beat*, April 22, 40.

Wade, Robert. 1949. NBC interdepartmental correspondence with Carleton Smith, May 18.

Warfield, Ben. 1952. Letter to National Broadcasting Corporation, January.

Waring, Fred. 1939. Letter to John F. Royal, May 13.

———. "Music on Video — Seen from Two Angles." 1954. *Down Beat*, June 30, 70.

Webb, Alvin. 1953a. "Footlights and Sidelights." *New York Amsterdam News*, May 9, 28.

———. 1953b. "Militant Action Urged in TV-Theatre Fight." *New York Amsterdam News*, August 8, 25.

———. 1953c. "New Faces Would Spark Suggested TV Package." *New York Amsterdam News*, August 1, 126.

———. 1953d. "New TV Presentation Needs Tailor, Scissors." *New York Amsterdam News*, June 27, 25.

———. 1954. "Footlights and Sidelights." *New York Amsterdam News*, April 17, 24.

———. 1955. "Footlights and Sidelights." *New York Amsterdam News*, October 1, 18.

"Webs Brush Off Talmadge Beef." 1952. *Variety*, January 9, 1.

Weekly Newsletter on Television. 1948. New York: Television Broadcasters Association, January 15.

"WFIL-TV Will Increase Power Four-Fold Today." 1953. *Philadelphia Inquirer*, July 22, 32.

"The Wheel Spins." 1948. *Radio and Television Mirror*, May, 44.

Whiteman, Paul. 1948. *Records for the Millions*. New York: Hermitage Press.

"'Wide Open Spaces' First Clear Test of TV's Power to 'Make' a Pop Song Hit." 1951. *Variety*, April 25, 46.

Wile Jr., Fred. 1951. NBC interdepartmental correspondence with George McGarrett, October 8.

"Will Funny Hats Be Savior?" 1948. *Down Beat*, December 1, 3.

Wilson, John S. 1949. "Square Produces Condon TV Shot." *Down Beat*, July 29, 1.

———. 1950a. "Freeman's Talents Blossom on TV." *Down Beat*, August 11, 14.

———. 1950b. "Our Success Due to TV, Says Stone 5." *Down Beat*, June 16, 4.

———. 1950c. "Why TV Music Directors Flip." *Down Beat*, October 6, 4.

Wirth, Wayne. "Telestatus." 1948. *Broadcasting-Telecasting*, December 27, 12.

"Wm. Morris Eyes Bands Once Again, but This Time for Video." 1950. *Variety*, December, 6, 45.

Woods, Bernie. 1948. "1948 Looms as Critical Year for Band Biz." *Variety*, January 7, 193.

———. 1949. "Tele, LP Expected to Have a Big Effect on Sales of Records in the Next Year." 1949. *Variety*, January 4, 173.

"Yanks Dig That Mambo Beat." 1954. *Variety*, June 16, 1.

"'You're out of Business in TV Unless You Get the Teen' (25,000,000 Sets)." 1955. *Variety*, March 9, 1.

Secondary Sources

Altman, Rick. 1986. "Television/Sound." In *Studies in Entertainment: Critical Approaches to Mass Culture*, edited by Tania Modleski. Bloomington: Indiana University Press.

———. 2007. "Early Film Themes: Roxy, Adorno, and the Problem of Cultural Capital." In *Beyond the Soundtrack: Representing Music in Cinema*, edited by Daniel Goldmark, Lawrence Kramer, and Richard Leppert. Berkeley: University of California Press, 2007.

Andrews, Bart. 1976. *Lucy & Ricky & Fred & Ethel: The Story of I Love Lucy*. New York: E. P. Dutton.

Arnaz, Desi. 1976. *A Book*. New York: William Morrow.

Arsenault, Raymond. 2009. *The Sound of Freedom: Marian Anderson, the Lincoln Memorial, and the Concert That Awakened America*. New York: Bloomsbury Press.

Attallah, Paul. 1991. "Of Homes and Machines: TV, Technology, and Fun in America, 1944–1984." *Continuum* 4, no. 2: 58–97.

Auslander, Philip. 1999. *Liveness: Performance in a Mediatized Culture*. New York: Routledge.

————. 2000. "Liveness, Mediatization, and Intermedial Performance." *Degrès: Revue de Synthèse à Orientation Semiologique* (Belgium), no. 101 (Spring): 1–12.

————. 2004. "Performance Analysis and Popular Music: A Manifesto." *Contemporary Theatre Review* 14, no. 1: 1–13.

Austen, Jake. 2005. *TV A-Go-Go: Rock on TV from American Bandstand to American Idol.* Chicago: Chicago Review Press.

Azenha, Gustavo. 2006. "The Internet and the Decentralisation of the Popular Music Industry: Critical Reflections on Technology, Concentration and Diversification." *Radical Musicology* 1, at www.radical-musicology.org.uk.

Baker, David. 2005. "Rock Rebels and Delinquents: The Emergence of the Rock Rebel in 1950s 'Youth Problem' Films." *Continuum: Journal of Media and Cultural Studies* 19, no. 1 (March): 39–54.

Baughman, James L. 2007. *Same Time, Same Station: Creating American Television, 1948–1961.* Baltimore: Johns Hopkins University Press.

Becker, Ron. 2001. "'Hear-and-See Radio' in the World of Tomorrow: RCA and the Presentation of Television at the World's Fair, 1939–1940." *Historical Journal of Film, Radio and Television* 21, no. 4. (October): 361–78.

Beebe, Roger, and Jason Middleton, eds. 2007. *Medium Cool: Music Videos From Soundies to Cellphones.* Durham: Duke University Press.

Bergmann, Ted, and Ira Skutch. 2002. *The Du Mont Television Network: What Happened?: A Significant Episode in the History of Broadcasting.* Lanham, Md.: Scarecrow Press, 2002.

Bergreen, Laurence. 1980. *Look Now, Pay Later: The Rise of Network Broadcasting.* New York: Doubleday.

Betancourt, Michael. 2006. *Thomas Wilfred's Clavilux.* Rockville, Md.: Wildside Press.

Betrock, Alan. 1986. *The I Was a Teenage Juvenile Delinquent Rock 'n' Roll Horror Beach Party Movie Book: A Complete Guide to the Teen Exploitation Film: 1954–1969.* New York: St. Martin's Press.

Bilton, Nick. 2009. "Cable Freedom, Aided by a Mouse." *New York Times,* December 10, B5.

Black, George. 1988. *The Good Neighbor: How the United States Wrote the History of Central America and the Caribbean.* New York: Pantheon.

Boddy, William. 1990. *Fifties Television.* Chicago: University of Chicago Press.

Bogle, Donald. 2001. *Prime Time Blues: African Americans on Network Television.* New York: Farrar, Straus and Giroux.

Breen, Marcus. 2004. "The Music Industry, Technology and Utopia: An Exchange between Marcus Breen and Eamonn Forde." *Popular Music* 23, no. 1: 79–89.

Brown, Judith. 2009. *Glamour in Six Dimensions: Modernism and the Radiance of Form.* Ithaca: Cornell University Press.

Bryant, Clora, Buddy Collette, William Green, Steve Isoardi, Jack Kilson, Horace Tapscott, Gerald Wilson, and Marl Young, eds. 1998. *Central Avenue Sounds: Jazz in Los Angeles.* Berkeley: University of California Press.

Burnett, Ron. 1995. *Cultures of Vision: Images, Media and the Imaginary.* Bloomington: Indiana University Press.

Burns, Gary. 1998. "Visualising 1950s Hits on *Your Hit Parade.*" *Popular Music* 17, no. 2: 139–52.

Burston, Jonathan. 2006. "Synthespians among Us: Rethinking the Actor in Media Work and Media Theory." In *Media and Cultural Theory,* edited by James Curran and David Morley. New York: Routledge.

Caldwell, John T. 1995. *Televisuality: Style, Crisis, and Authority in American Television.* New Brunswick: Rutgers University Press.

Canfield, Jack, Mark Victor Hansen, and Deborah Poneman. 2007. *Chicken Soup for the American Idol Soul.* Deerfield Beach, Fl.: Health Communications.

Caramanica, Jon. 2010. "'Glee' Makes Some Sour Music." *New York Times,* April 11, Arts Review, 19.

Carr, Edward H. 1962. *What Is History?* New York: Knopf.

Carr, Nicholas. 2009. "The Price of Free: What Will Happen to TV If We All Stream Shows from the Web." *New York Times Magazine,* November 15, 26–27.

Castleman, Harry, and Walter J. Podrazik. 1982. *Watching Television: Four Decades of American Television.* New York: McGraw Hill.

Cawelti, John. 1976. *Adventure, Mystery, and Romance: Formula Stories as Art and Popular Culture.* Chicago: University of Chicago Press.

Chafe, William. 1986. *The Unfinished Journey: America since World War II.* New York: Oxford Books.

Charnas, Dan. 2010. *The Big Payback: The History of the Business of Hip-Hop.* New York: New American Library.

Chevigny, Paul. 1993. *Gigs: Jazz and the Cabaret Laws in New York City.* New York: Routledge.

Chilton, Karen. 2008. *Hazel Scott: The Pioneering Journey of a Jazz Pianist from Café Society to Hollywood to HUAC.* Anne Arbor: University of Michigan Press.

Clark, Dick, and Richard Robinson. 1976. *Rock, Roll & Remember.* New York: Thomas Y. Crowell.

Classen, Stephen. 2004. *Watching Jim Crow: The Struggles over Mississippi Television, 1955–1969.* Durham: Duke University Press, 2004.

Coakley, Mary Lewis. 1958. *Mister Music Maker: Lawrence Welk.* New York: Doubleday.

Coates, Norma. 2003. "Teenyboppers, Groupies, and Other Grotesques: Girls and Women and Rock Culture in the 1960s and Early 1970s." *Journal of Popular Music Studies* 15, no. 1: 65–94.

———. 2007. "Filling in Holes: Television Music as a Recuperation of Popular Music on Television." *Music, Sound, and the Moving Image* 1, no. 1 (Spring): 21–25.

Corner, John. 1998. *Studying Media: Problems of Theory and Method.* Edinburgh: Edinburgh University Press.

———. 1999. *Critical Ideas in Television Studies.* New York: Oxford University Press.

Cox, Jim. 2001. *The Great Radio Audience Participation Shows: Seventeen Programs from the 1940s and 1950s*. Jefferson, N.C.: McFarland.

Deaville, James. 2011. "A Discipline Emerges: Reading Writing About Listening to Television." In *Music in Television: Channels of Listening*. edited by James Deaville. New York: Routledge.

Delmont, Matthew F. 2012. *The Nicest Kids in Town: American Bandstand, Rock 'n' Roll, and the Struggle for Civil Rights in 1950s Philadelphia*. Berkeley: University of California Press.

DeLong, Thomas. 1983. *Pops: Paul Whiteman, King of Jazz*. New York: New Century Publishers.

———. 1991. *Quiz Craze: America's Infatuation with Game Shows*. New York: Praeger.

DeVeaux, Scott. 1997. *The Birth of BeBop: A Social and Musical History*. Berkeley: University of California Press.

Dickinson, Kay. 2008. *Off Key: When Film and Music Won't Work Together*. New York: Oxford University Press.

Dienst, Richard. 1994. *Still Life in Real Time: Theory After Television*. Durham: Duke University Press.

Doherty, Thomas. 2003. *Cold War, Cool Medium*. New York: Columbia University Press.

Donnelly, Kevin. 2001. "Music on Television." In *The Television Genre Book*, edited by Glen Creeber. London: British Film Institute.

Donovan, Robert J. 1996. *Conflict and Crisis: The Presidency of Harry S. Truman, 1945–1948*. Columbia: University of Missouri Press.

Douglas, Susan. 1999. *Listening In: Radio and the American Imagination*. Minneapolis: University of Minnesota Press.

Eberly, Philip K. 1982. *Music in the Air: America's Changing Tastes in Popular Music, 1920–1980*. New York: Hastings House.

Edgerton, Gary R. 2009. *The Columbia History of American Television*. New York: Columbia University Press.

Ellis, John. 1994. *Visible Fictions: Cinema, Television, Video*. New York: Routledge.

Ely, Melvin. 1991. *The Adventures of Amos 'n' Andy: A Social History of an American Phenomenon*. New York: Free Press.

Ennis, Philip H. 1992. *The Seventh Stream: The Emergence of Rock 'n' Roll in American Popular Music*. Middletown, CT: Wesleyan University Press.

Epstein, Daniel Mark. 1999. *Nat King Cole*. New York: Farrar, Straus and Giroux.

Erenberg, Lewis A. 1998. *Swingin' the Dream: Big Band Jazz and the Rebirth of American Culture*. Chicago: University of Chicago Press.

Fenster, Mark. 1993. "Genre and Form: The Development of the Country Music Video." In *Sound and Vision: The Music Video Reader*, edited by Simon Frith, Andrew Goodwin, and Lawrence Grossberg. New York: Routledge.

Ferrell, Robert H. 1991. *Truman in the White House: The Diary of Eben A. Ayers*. Columbia: University of Missouri Press.

Feur, Jane. "Genre Study and Television." 1992. In *Channels of Discourse, Reassembled:*

Television and Contemporary Criticism, edited by Robert C. Allen. Chapel Hill: University of North Carolina Press.

Firmat, Gustavo Perez. 1994. *Life on the Hyphen: The Cuban-American Way.* Austin: University of Texas Press.

Fisher, David E., and Marshall Jon Fisher. 1996. *Tube: The Invention of Television.* New York: Harvest.

Fiske, John. *Television Culture.* 1987. New York: Methuen.

Forman, Murray. 2002. *The 'Hood Comes First: Race, Space, and Place in Rap and Hip-Hop.* Middletown, CT: Wesleyan University Press.

———. 2007. "Employment and Blue Pencils: NBC, Race, and Representation, 1926–55." In *NBC: America's Network*, edited by Michele Hilmes. Berkeley: University of California Press.

Friedberg, Anne. 1993. *Window Shopping: Cinema and the Postmodern.* Berkeley: University of Califronia Press.

Frith, Simon. 1996. *Performing Rites: On the Value of Popular Music.* Cambridge: Harvard University Press.

———. 2002. "Look! Hear! The Uneasy Relationship of Music and Television." *Popular Music* 21, no. 3: 277–90.

Frith, Simon, Andrew Goodwin, and Lawrence Grossberg, eds. 1993. *Sound and Vision: The Music Video Reader.* New York: Routledge.

Gabbard, Krin. 1996. *Jammin' at the Margins: Jazz and the American Cinema.* Chicago: University of Chicago Press.

Gabler, Neil. 1998. *Life the Movie: How Entertainment Conquered Reality.* New York: Alfred E. Knopf.

Gandy, Oscar H. 1998. *Communication and Race: A Structural Perspective.* London: Arnold.

Garofalo, Reebee. 2005. *Rockin' Out: Popular Music in the U.S.A.* 3rd ed. Upper Saddle River, N.J.: Pearson Prentice Hall.

———. 2008. *Rockin' Out: Popular Music in the U.S.A.* 4th ed. Upper Saddle River, N.J.: Pearson Prentice Hall.

Gavin, James. 2009. *Stormy Weather: The Life of Lena Horne.* Memphis: Atria.

Gendron, Bernard. 1993. "Moldy Figs and Modernists: Jazz at War (1942–1946)." *Discourse* 15, no. 3: 130–57.

Gilbert, Douglas. 1940. *American Vaudeville: Its Life and Times.* New York: Dover Publications.

Godlovitch, Stan. 1998. *Musical Performance: A Philosophical Study.* New York: Routledge.

Goodwin, Andrew. 1992. *Dancing in the Distraction Factory: Music Television and Popular Culture.* New York: Routledge.

Grant, Barry Keith. 2003. *Film Genre Reader III.* Austin: University of Texas Press.

Gray, Herman. 1995. *Watching Race: Television and the Struggle for "Blackness."* Minneapolis: University of Minnesota Press.

Grossberg, Lawrence. 1989. "MTV: Swinging on the (Postmodern) Star." In *Cultural Politics in Contemporary America*, edited by Ien Angus and Sut Jhally. New York: Routledge.

———. 1992. "Is There a Fan in the House?: The Affective Sensibility of Fandom." In *The Adoring Audience: Fan Culture and Popular Media*, edited by Lisa A. Lewis. New York: Routledge.

Guralnick, Peter. 1994. *Last Train to Memphis: The Rise of Elvis Presley*. Boston: Little, Brown.

Halberstam, David. 1993. *The Fifties*. New York: Villard Books.

Halper, Donna. 2001. *Invisible Stars: A Social History of Women in American Broadcasting*. Armonk, NY: M. E. Sharpe.

Hartley, John. 1999. *Uses of Television*. New York: Routledge.

Hay, Carla. 1998. "MTV Reaches Out to Audience via Research: Viewer Opinions Sought." *Billboard*, September 26: 5.

Hearn, Alison. 2004. "Image Slaves: The Phenomenon of Reality Television Represents the Increasing Trend toward the Corporate colonization of the 'Real.'" *Bad Subjects*, no. 69 (June).

Hedegaard, Erik. 2010. "Glee Gone Wild." *Rolling Stone*, April 15, 42–49.

Herzog, Amy. 2004. "Discordant Visions: The Peculiar Musical Images of the Soundies Jukebox Film." *American Music* 22, no. 1. (Spring): 27–39.

Hill, Constance Valis. 2000. *Brotherhood in Rhythm: The Jazz Tap Dancing of the Nicholas Brothers*. New York: Oxford University Press.

Hilmes, Michele. 1997. *Radio Voices: American Broadcasting, 1922–1952*. Minneapolis: University of Minnesota Press.

Hine, Thomas. 1987. *Populuxe*. New York: Alfred Knopf.

Holt, Fabian. 2007. *Genre In Popular Music*. Chicago: University of Chicago Press.

Horowitz, Joseph. 2005. *Classical Music in America: A History of Its Rise and Fall*. New York: W.W. Norton.

Jackson, John. 1997. *American Bandstand: Dick Clark and the Making of a Rock 'n' Roll Empire*. New York: Oxford University Press.

Jenkins, Henry. 2006. *Convergence Culture: Where Old and New Media Collide*. New York: New York University Press.

Jensen, Joli. 1998. *Nashville Sound: Authenticity, Commercialization, and Country Music*. Nashville: Vanderbilt University Press.

Jezer, Marty. 1982. *The Dark Ages: Life in the United States 1945–1960*. Boston: South End Press.

Johnson, Victoria. 2008. *Heartland TV: Prime Time Television and the Struggle for U.S. Identity*. New York: New York University Press.

Jones, Steve. 2002. "Music That Moves: Popular Music, Distribution and Network Technologies." *Cultural Studies* 16, no. 2: 213–32.

Kaplan, E. Ann. 1987. *Rocking around the Clock: Music Television, Postmodernism, and Consumer Culture*. London: Methuen.

Keightley, Keir. 1996. "'Turn It Down!' She Shrieked: Gender, Domestic Space, and High Fidelity, 1948–59." *Popular Music* 15, no. 2: 149–77.

———. 1998. "Reading Capitol/E.M.I.: Musical Tourism and Industrial Globalization in the Record Industry, 1954–63." Paper delivered at the International Association for the Study of Popular Music (U.S.) meeting, October 16, University of California, Los Angeles.

———. 2001. "You Keep Coming Back Like a Song: Adult Audiences, Taste Panics, and the Idea of the Standard." *Journal of Popular Music Studies* 13, no. 1: 7–40.

———. 2008. "Music for Middlebrows: Defining the Easy Listening Era, 1946–1966." *American Music* (Fall): 309–35.

Kellner, Douglas. 1993. "Popular Culture and the Construction of Postmodern Identities." In *Modernity and Identity*, edited by Scott Lash and Jonathan Friedman. Cambridge, Mass.: Blackwell.

Kenney, William Howland. 1993. *Chicago Jazz: A Cultural History, 1904–1930*. New York: Oxford University Press.

Kienzle, Richie. 2003. *Southwest Shuffle: Pioneers of Honky-Tonk, Western Swing, and Country Jazz*. New York, Routledge.

Kisseloff, Jeff. 1995. *The Box: An Oral History of Television 1920–1961*. New York: Penguin Books.

Knight, Arthur. 2002. *Disintegrating the Musical: Black Performance and American Musical Film*. Durham: Duke University Press.

Koszarski, Richard. 2008. *Hollywood on the Hudson: Film and Television in New York from Griffith to Sarnoff*. New Brunswick: Rutgers University Press.

KTLA: The First Twenty Years (videotape). 1967. Los Angeles: KTLA-TV.

Landon, Brooks. 2002. "Synthespians, Virtual Humans, and Hypermedia: Emerging Contours of Post-SF Film." In *Edging into the Future: Science Fiction and Contemporary Cultural Transformation*, edited by Veronica Hollinger and Joan Gordon. Philadelphia: University of Pennsylvania Press.

Lebrecht, Norman. 2001. *The Maestro Myth: Great Conductors in Pursuit of Power*. Secaucus, N.J.: Citadel Press.

Lhamon Jr., W. T. 1990. *Deliberate Speed: The Origins of a Cultural Style in the American 1950s*. Washington: Smithsonian Institution Press.

Lopez, Ana M. 1997. "Of Rhythms and Borders." In *Everynight Life: Culture and Dance in Latino/a America*, edited by Celeste Fraser Delgado and Jose Esteban. Durham: Duke University Press.

Lury, Karen. 1995–96. "Television Performance: Being, Acting and 'Corpsing.'" *New Formations*, no. 27 (Winter): 114–27.

MacDonald, J. Fred. 1992. *Blacks and White TV: Afro-Americans in Television since 1948*. 2nd ed. Chicago: Nelson-Hall.

Magder, Ted, and Jonathan Burston. 2001. "Whose Hollywood?: Changing Forms and Relations Inside the North American Entertainment Industry." In *Continen-*

tal Order?: Integrating North America for Cybercapitalism, edited by Vincent Mosco and Dan Schiller. New York: Rowman and Littlefield.

Magoun, Alexander B. 2009. *Television: The Life Story of a Technology*. Baltimore: Johns Hopkins University Press.

Mann, Denise. 1992. "The Spectacularization of Everyday Life: Recycling Hollywood Stars and Fans in Early Television Variety Shows." In *Private Screenings: Television and the Female Consumer*, edited by Lynn Spigel and Denise Mann. Minneapolis: University of Minneapolis Press.

Marks, Craig and Rob Tannenbaum, eds. 2011. *I Want My MTV: The Uncensored Story of the Music Video Revolution*. New York: Dutton.

Marling, Karal Ann. 1994. *As Seen on TV: The Visual Culture of Everyday Life in the 1950s*. Cambridge: Harvard University Press.

Mashon, Michael. 2005. "Hour Glass." In *Encyclopedia of Television*, edited by Horace Newcomb. Chicago: Fitzroy Dearborn.

———. 2007. "NBC, J. Walter Thompson, and the Struggle for Control of Television Programming, 1946–58." In *NBC: America's Network*, edited by Michele Hilmes. Berkeley: University of California Press.

McCarthy, Anna. 2001. *Ambient Television*. Durham: Duke University Press.

McCourt, Tom, and Nabeel Zuberi. No date. "Music on Television." *Museum of Broadcast Communications*, http://www.museum.tv/eotvsection.php?entrycode=musicontele.

McGee, Kristin A. 2009. *Some Liked It Hot: Jazz Women in Film and Television, 1928–1959*. Middletown, CT: Wesleyan University Pres.

McGrath, Tom. 1996. *MTV: The Making of a Revolution*. Philadelphia: Running Press.

McNeil, Alex. 1996. *Total Television: The Comprehensive Guide to Programming From 1948 to the Present*. 4th ed. New York: Penguin Books.

Meyrowitz, Joshua. 1990. "On 'The Consumer's World: Place as Context' by Robert Sack." *Annals of the Association of American Geographers* 80, no. 1 (March): 129–33.

Miller, Kiri. 2009. "Schizophonic Performance: Guitar Hero, Rock Band, and Virtual Virtuosity." *Journal of the Society for American Music* 3, no. 4: 395–429.

Miller, Rowland S. 1997. *Embarrassment: Poise and Peril in Everyday Life*. New York: Guilford Press.

Mittell, Jason. 2004a. *Genre and Television: From Cop Shows to Cartoons in American Culture*. New York: Routledge.

———. 2004b. "Quiz and Audience Participation Programs." In *The Museum of Broadcast Communications Encyclopedia of Radio*, edited by Christopher H. Sterling. New York: Routledge.

Mordden, Ethan. 1983. *Broadway Babies: The People Who Made the American Musical*. New York: Oxford University Press.

Moritz, William. 2004. *Optical Poetry: The Life and Work of Oskar Fischinger*. Bloomington: Indiana University Press.

Morley, David. 2000. *Home Territories: Media, Mobility and Identity*. New York: Routledge.

Morley, David, and Kevin Robins. 1995. *Spaces of Identity: Global Media, Electronic Landscapes, and Cultural Boundaries*. New York: Routledge.

Morris, Chris.1998. "MTV Reaches Out to Audience Via Research: Future Divined in New 'Trendsetters Study.'" *Billboard*, September 26, 5.

Mundy, John. 1999. *Popular Music on Screen: From Hollywood Musical to Music Video*. Manchester, UK: Manchester University Press.

Murray, Susan. 2001. "Our Man Godfrey: Arthur Godfrey and the Selling of Stardom in Early Television." *Television and New Media* 2, no. 3 (August): 187–204.

———. 2005. *Hitch Your Antenna to the Stars: Early Television and Broadcast Stardom*. New York: Routledge.

National Survey of Television Sets. 1967. New York: Advertising Research Foundation.

Negus, Keith. 1996. *Popular Music in Theory: An Introduction*. Middletown, CT: Wesleyan University Press.

———. 1998. "Cultural Production and the Corporation: Musical Genres and the Strategic Management of Creativity in the US Recording Industry." *Media, Culture and Society* 20: 359–79.

———. 2006. "Musicians on Television: Visible, Audible and Ignored." *Journal of the Royal Musical Association* 131, no. 2: 310–30.

Newcomb, Horace. 1997. "The Opening of America: Meaningful Difference in 1950s Television." In *The Other Fifties: Interrogating Midcentury American Icons*, edited by Joel Foreman. Urbana: University of Illinois Press.

———. 2005. "Teenagers and Television in the United States." In *Encyclopedia of Television*. 2nd ed. Chicago: Fitzroy Dearborn.

Omi, Michael, and Howard Winant. 1994. *Racial Formation in the United States from the 1960s to the 1990s*. 2nd ed. New York: Routledge.

Optowsky, Stan. 1961. *TV: The Big Picture*. New York: Dutton.

Owens, Harry. 1970. *Sweet Leilani: The Story behind the Song*. Pacific Palisades, CA: Hula House.

Pecknold, Diane. 2007. *The Selling Sound: The Rise of the Country Music Industry*. Durham: Duke University Press.

Pegley, Kip. 2008. *Coming to Wherever You Are: MuchMusic, MTV and Youth Identities*. Middletown, CT: Wesleyan University Press.

Pegolotti, James. 2003. *Deems Taylor: A Biography*. Boston: Northeastern University Press.

Peterson, Richard. 1997. *Creating Country Music: Fabricating Authenticity*. Chicago: University of Chicago Press.

Pondillo, Bob. 2005. "Racial discourse and censorship on NBC-TV, 1948–1960." *Journal of Popular Film and Television* 33, no. 2 (Summer) 102–13.

Press, Andrea Lee. 1991. *Women Watching Television: Gender, Class, and Generation in the American Television Experience*. Philadelphia: University of Pennsylvania Press.

Pyron, Darden A. 2000. *Liberace: An American Boy*. Chicago: University of Chicago Press.

Ratliff, Ben. 2009. "Soupy Sales, Jazz Maven, Brought Gigs to the Small Screen." *New York Times*, October 23.

Ritchie, Michael. 1994. *Please Stand By: A Prehistory of Television*. Woodstock, N.Y.: Overlook Press.

Ritz, David, ed. 2005. *Elvis by the Presleys*. New York: Crown.

Roberts, John Storm. 1999. *The Latin Tinge: The Impact of Latin American Music on the United States*. 2nd ed. New York: Oxford University Press.

Roberts, Shari. 1993. "'The Lady in the Tutti-Frutti Hat': Carmen Miranda, a Spectacle of Ethnicity." *Cinema Journal* 32. no. 3 (Spring): 3–23.

Robins, Kevin. 1991. "Tradition and Translation: National Culture in Its Global Context." In *Enterprise and Heritage: Crosscurrents of National Culture*, edited by John Corner and Sylvia Harvey. New York: Routledge.

Rodman, Gilbert. 1996. *Elvis after Elvis: The Posthumous Career of a Living Legend*. New York: Routledge.

Rodman, Ron. 2010. *Tuning In: American Narrative Television Music*. New York: Oxford University Press.

Rothenbuhler, Eric, and Tom McCourt. 2002. "Radio Redefines Itself, 1947–62." In *Radio Reader: Essays in the Cultural History of Radio*, edited by Michele Hilmes and Jason Loviglio. New York: Routledge.

Sanjek, Russell. 1988. *American Popular Music and Its Business: The First Four Hundred Years*, vol. 3, *From 1900 to 1984*. New York: Oxford University Press.

Sanjek, Russell, and David Sanjek. 1991. *American Popular Music Business in the 20th Century*. New York: Oxford University Press.

Segrave, Kerry. 2002. *Jukeboxes: An American Social History*. Jefferson, N.C.: McFarland.

Shumway, David. 1997. "Watching Elvis: The Male Rock Star as Object of the Gaze." In *The Other Fifties: Interrogating Midcentury American Icons*, edited by Joel Foreman. Urbana: University of Illinois Press.

Singer, Roberta L., and Elena Martinez. 2004. "A South Bronx Latin Music Tale." *Centro: Journal of the Center for Puerto Rican Studies* 15, no. 1 (Spring): 177–201.

Skutch, Ira. 1990. *I Remember Television*. Lanham: Scarecrow Press.

———. 1998. *The Days of Live: Television's Golden Age as Seen by 21 Directors Guild of America Members*. Lanham: Scarecrow Press.

Small, Christopher. 1998. *Musicking: The Meanings of Performances and Listening*. Middletown, CT: Wesleyan University Press.

Smulyan, Susan. 1994. *Selling Radio: The Commercialization of American Broadcasting, 1920–1934*. Washington: Smithsonian Institution Press.

Snyder, Robert W. 2000. *The Voice of the City: Vaudeville and Popular Culture in New York*. Chicago: Ivan R. Dee.

Southall, Brian. 2000. *The A-Z of Record Labels*. London: Sanctuary Publishing.

Spigel, Lynn. 1992. *Make Room for TV: Television and the Family Ideal in Postwar America*. Chicago: University of Chicago Press.

———. 2001. *Welcome to the Dreamhouse: Popular Media and Postwar Suburbs*. Durham: Duke University Press.

———. 2008. *TV by Design: Modern Art and the Rise of Network Television*. Chicago: University of Chicago Press.

Stahl, Matthew W. 2004. "A Moment Like This: *American Idol* and Narratives of Meritocracy." In *Bad Music: The Music We Love to Hate*, edited by Christopher Washburne and Maiken Derno. New York: Routledge.

Stebbins, Robert. 1992. *Amateurs, Professionals, and Serious Leisure*. Montreal: McGill-Queen's University Press.

Sterne, Jonathan. 2003. *The Audible Past: Cultural Origins of Sound Reproduction*. Durham: Duke University Press.

Stilwell, Robynn J. 2003. "It May Look Like a Living Room . . . : The Musical Number and the Sitcom." In *Echo*. 5, no. 1 (Spring): 1–27.

Storey, John. 1999. *Cultural Consumption and Everyday Life*. London: Arnold.

Sublette, Ned. 2007. *Cuba and Its Music: From the First Drums to the Mambo*. Chicago: Chicago Review Press.

Szatmary, David. 1991. *Rockin' in Time: A Social History of Rock-and-Roll*. 2nd ed. Englewood Cliffs, NJ: Prentice Hall.

Torres, Sasha. 2003. *Black and White in Color: Television and Black Civil Rights*. Princeton: Princeton University Press.

Toynbee, Jason. 2000. *Making Popular Music: Musicians, Creativity and Institutions*. London: Arnold.

Tucker, Sherrie. 2000. *Swing Shift: "All-Girl" Bands of the 1940s*. Durham: Duke University Press.

VanCour, Shawn. "Television Music and the History of Television Sound." In *Music in Television: Channels of Listening*. Edited by James Deaville. New York: Routledge.

Vernallis, Carol. 2004. *Experiencing Music Video: Aesthetics and Cultural Context*. New York: Columbia University Press.

Von Schilling, James. 2003. *The Magic Window: American Television, 1939–1953*. New York: Hawthorn Press.

Waggoner, Susan. 2001. *Nightclub Nights: Art, Legend, and Style 1920–1960*. New York: Rizzoli International Publications.

Waksman, Steve. 1999. *Instruments of Desire: The Electric Guitar and the Shaping of Musical Experience*. Cambridge: Harvard University Press.

Waring, Virginia. 1997. *Fred Waring and the Pennsylvanians*. Urbana: University of Illinois Press.

Watson, Mary Ann. 1998. *Defining Vision: Television and the American Experience since 1945*. Fort Worth: Harcourt Brace.

Weaver, Pat. 1994. *The Best Seat in the House: The Golden Years of Radio and Television*. New York: Alfred Knopf.

Weinstein, David. 2004. *The Forgotten Network: DuMont and the Birth of American Television*. Philadelphia: Temple University Press.

Welch, Jim. 1999. "Shaping the Box: The Cultural Construction of American Television, 1948–1952." *Continuum: Journal of Media and Cultural Studies* 13, no. 1: 97–117.

Wertheimer, Alfred. 1979. *Elvis '56: In the Beginning.* New York: Collier Books.

Williams, Mark. 1998. "Entertaining 'Difference': Strains of Orientalism in Early Los Angeles Television." In *Living Color: Race and Television in the United States*, edited by Sasha Torres. Durham: Duke University Press.

———. 1999. "History in a Flash: Notes on the Myth of TV 'Liveness.'" In *Collecting Visible Evidence*, edited by Jane Gaines and Michael Renov. Minneapolis: University of Minnesota Press.

Williams, Raymond. 1975. *Television: Technology and Cultural Form.* New York: Schocken Books.

———. 1977. *Marxism and Literature.* Oxford: Oxford University Press.

Wyatt, Edward. 2010. "'Idol' Winners: Not Just Fame but Big Bucks." *New York Times*, February 24, C1.

INDEX

Page numbers in italics refer to illustrations.

Abbot, Bud, 64, 123, 207, 232

ABC-TV: *Cop Rock* show, 331; *Disneyland* program, 112; *Gay Nineties Revue* program, 191; *The Musicians' Christmas Party* benefit, 344n7; network debut (1948), 220, 347n23; script reading on, 204; shows featuring black artists, 231, 256, 259, 263–64; Paul Whiteman as spokesman for, 216

Academy Awards, 213, 354n20

Adams, David, 74–75

Adams, Val, 94

Adams' Alley, 245, 247

advertising: audience expectations and, 127; for *The Bob Howard Show*, 252–53; disk jockeys and, 157; of drinking establishments with TV sets, 96; for Excelsior accordions, 52, *53*; gender and class distinctions in, 348n6; of Gibson Guitars, *182*; of Latin music, 277; on MTV, 1; race issues and, 271; for TV sets, 34, 45, 357n18; of TV shows to viewers, 124; of world travel and exotic cultures, 285, 289

Afro-Cuban music, 295, 298, 304, 306

Allen, Fred, 64, 129, 158, 335

Allen, Steve, 85, 219, 243, 359–60n2

Al Siegel's Song Shop, 157

Altman, Rick, 193, 323

amateur talent shows: contestants or participants of, 72–73; criticism of, 76–77,

81; difference between professionals and amateurs on, 73, 345n9; exploitation of contestants on, 332–33; host introductions and banter on, 80–82; list of shows from 1948–1955, 345n6; opportunity and optimism of, 77–79, 81; roots in radio programming, 71–72; self-promotion on YouTube, 335; social values of contestants on, 82–83; songwriting contests, 85–86; talent hunt programs, 74–77; winner selection methods and prizes on, 83–84

"ambient television," 108, 347n21

American Bandstand, 2, 167–68, 327

American Federation of Musicians (AFM): ban on TV musical performances, 37–38, 43–47, 71–72; failure to recognize new music, 48–49; *International Musician* newsletter, 52; party for blind musicians, 344n7; President Truman's involvement in, *38*, 38–39, 41, 344n4; recording bans, 36, 42–43, 344n5; residual payments, 48; salary requirements for rehearsal time, 178; television pay scale, 46–47, 87; union rates for ballroom broadcasts, 87

American Federation of Television-Radio Actors (AFTRA), 38, 270, 344n8

American heartland, 109, 151, 196–97, 307

American Idol, 331–32, 335, 361n18

American Society of Composers and Publishers (ASCAP), 281–82, 358n6

"America's housewives," 5

Amos 'n' Andy, 231, 235, 256, 300, 355–56n7

Amsterdam, Morey, 69, 136, 143, 220, *222*;
　Morey Amsterdam Show, The, 128, 137,
　145–46

Anders, Laurie, 110–12, *111*, 347n27

Anderson, Marian, 264, 356n12, 357n20

Anthony, Ray, 60–61, 226, 344n2

"Anywhere I Wander," 112

Apple Corporation, 334

Aragon Ballroom, 87, 92–93, 195–96

Archies, The, 325, 327

Armstrong, Louis: appearance on *Floor
　Show*, 249; appearance on *The Frank
　Sinatra Show*, 211–13, 232, 267; film ap-
　pearances, 355n1; gesturing of, 176, 221;
　recordings by, 192

Arnaz, Desi: on *I Love Lucy*, 151–54, *299*,
　300–304, *305*; musical background of,
　296–300, 306, 310, 359n9

Arthur Godfrey's Talent Scouts, 72, 85

Arthur Murray Party, The, 67, 311

audiences/viewers: and acceptance of Lati-
　nos, 277–78; access to wide range of
　programs, 105; advertising/marketing to,
　124; black, 221, 246–48, 258; cable expan-
　sion's influence on, 109; competition for,
　42; complaints, 165, 241, 243–44; desire
　for exotic Otherness, 286–90; engage-
　ment in nightclub programs, 139, 142,
　146–50, 154; expectations of, 322; famil-
　iarity with performer personae, 197–202;
　gender norms of, 131, 134; genre relations
　and, 116, 125–30, 135; increase in (1940),
　278; Latin music popularity and, 282–83,
　299–300, 307; negative assessments of,
　5; networks designed specifically for,
　328; nostalgia and recall/memory appeal
　for, 190–92; performance appraisal and,
　170–71; performer struggles to identify,
　177–78; production and performance
　glitches and, 58, 212; promoting/mar-
　keting of TV medium to, 34–35; public
　TV set installation for, 94–98, 106; rates
　for Lawrence Welk show, 195, 197; re-

actions to amateur shows, 77, 81, 332, 335;
　reactions to "newsworthy" or compel-
　ling performances, 322–33; reactions to
　vaudeville radio shows, 235–36; sensory
　demands of, 135; southern or racist, 213,
　246, 263–68, 271; Spanish-speaking, 276–
　77; studies on viewing habits, 95; survey
　on musical tastes, 329; teen/young, 159,
　166, 327–28, 330, 333; traditional leisure
　practices and, 58, 93–95, 347n20; virtual
　tours and musical journeys for, 95, 139,
　284–85, 289–92, 308, 314

"audivisual music," 33

Auslander, Philip: on artists' personae, 197,
　202–3; on cultural discourse of watch-
　ing TV, 93; on intimacy of TV, 148; on
　musical artists and cultural forces, 15; on
　performances and perception, 182; on TV
　in the war years, 29

Austen, Jake, 5

avatars, digital, 337–39

Azenha, Gustavo, 334

"Babalu," 287, 294, 298, 301, 303

Baker, Joseph V., 262–63

Baker, W. R. G., 160–61

Ball, Lucille, 102, 151–53, 299–301, *305*

"Ballad of Davey Crockett," 112

ballroom broadcasts: KTLA-TV remote
　productions, 87–93, 115, 195–96; spon-
　taneity and honesty of performances in,
　182, 184

Bamboo, 276, 291

Band of Tomorrow, 224, 354n23

Bandstand, 161–66, 351n25, 351n28. See also
　American Bandstand

Bandstand Matinee Club, 165, 351n26

Beane, Reginald, 258, 267

Beatles, 2, 323–24; *Rock Band* game, 338–39,
　362n21

bebop: aesthetics and presentation style of,
　216–18; Lawrence Welk's views on, 196;
　as a target for mockery, 218–19

Belafonte, Harry, 246–47, 264, 325, 356n12

Bennett, Tony, 85, 112, 348n1

Benny Goodman Orchestra, 191, *222*, 312, 352n6; demise of, 39; members of, 208, 216, 267, 354n21; teen entertainment and, 154, 159

Berle, Milton, 123, 136, 219, 350n17, 359–60n2; host of *The Texaco Star Theater*, 3, 246

Berlin, Irving, 287

Beulah, 231–32, 256

"Bewitched, Bothered, and Bewildered," 207–8, 314, 353n17

Billboard: on DJ programs, 157, 166; on *Popsicle Parade* program, 350n17; ratings on top songs, 102, 112–13, 325, 331; on TV sets in drinking establishments, 96–97; on TV's impact on jukeboxes, 103, 105

Binford, Lloyd T., 266

black actors: organizations and interest groups for, 239, 262, 270; in subservient or support roles, 231–33, 256, 267; underrepresentation of, 14–15

black culture, 135, 219, 238, 272

blackface minstrelsy, 235–36, 243, 353n11, 355–56nn7–8

black musicians: "all-black" televised musical programs, 245–48; and bigotry on radio broadcasts, 234–39; corporate sponsorship for, 238, 241, 247, 253, 262, 271–72; depicted on early TV, 233; discrimination toward, 15, 269–72, 355n2, 357n20; guest appearances by, 249; labor and, 264, 270; as program hosts, 249–50, 252–63; television aesthetics and, 251; typecasting of, 232

black press, 239–40, 249, 262, 269–70. See also *New York Amsterdam News*

Bloch, Ray, 85, 144–45

Boddy, William, 136

Bogle, Donald, 249, 256, 258

Bono, 360n5

Boswell Sisters, 24, 343n1

Bowie, David, 326, 359n1

Boyd, Jimmy, 311

Brainard, Bertha, 19–21, 24, 236

Broadcasting-Telecasting, 127, 349n9

Broadcast Music Incorporated (BMI), 281–82, 358n6

Broadway: entertainment categories of, 123; presentational style of, 18; stage traditions of, 175, 184, 189, 200, 259, 286

Broadway Open House, 112, *222*

Brown, Judith, 138

Bryant, Clora, 247, 356n11

Bryant, Willie, 246

Bueno, Delora, 292–93, 358n7

Burnett, Ron, 337

Burns, Gary, 4

Burston, Jonathan, 338

Byrne, Bobby, 147

cable television expansion, 101, 109, 328, 330

Caesar, Sid, 219, 220; on *Your Show of Shows*, 143, 154, 242

Caesar's Hour, 222, 337

Caldwell, John, 58–59, 82, 204

Calloway, Cab, 85, 159, 221; visual personality of, 9, 32, 259

Camel Caravan, 61, *62*, 65

Candlelight Revue, 229

Cantor, Eddie, 30, 123, 136, 251; civil rights supporter, 243; host of *The Colgate Comedy Hour*, 63–64, 148, 242, 357n19; performance style of, 69, 177–78, 200

Caramanica, Jon, 331

Carmichael, Hoagy, 207

Carnegie Hall, 310

Carney, Art, 128, 350n16

Carpenter, Ike, 223

Carpenter, Thelma, 247, 250–51, 356n12

Carr, Edward H., 319–20

Carrier, Vern, 356n13

Carroll, Diahann, 84, 332

cartoon music programs, 324–25

Cats and a Fiddle, The, 247, 356n11

"cats" jazz reference, 195–96, 353n12

Cavalcade of Bands, 179, 221, 259, 287, 349n13

Cavalcade of Stars, 68, 256, 350n19

Cawelti, John, 119, 121

CBS radio, 252–54, 300–302

CBS-TV: all-black productions, 246–48, 252–56; amateur talent shows on, 85–86; *Camel Caravan Show* on, 61, *62*, 65; *I Love Lucy* on, 296–304, *299, 303, 305*; impact of war years on, 29; *Ken Murray Show* on, 110–12, *111*; KPIX-TV station (San Francisco), 157; Latin musical broadcasts, 274, 276; launch of W2XAB-TV station, 24; press release on *It's Strictly for Laughs*, 227; program redundancy problem, 68; *Studio One*, 113; symphony broadcasts on, 47–48, 171–74; Fred Waring on, 69, *70, 185*, 185–87, 240, 355–56n7; variety shows, 66, 144, 205, 210–11, 225, 325, 345n5; viewer complaints, 243

celebrities: amateur musicians as, 78–79, 81, 332; black musicians as, 246, 249, 261, 270; network competition for, 99; radio broadcasters as, 162; salaries and contracts for, 99–100

censorship, 19, 30, 241, 266–67

Chafe, William, 35, 40

Chance of a Lifetime, 72, 78–80, *80*, 83–84

Chapel, Bette, 83, 346n11

Chevigny, Paul, 36–37, 48

Chicago Defender, 239, 249, 262

Chico Swingtime, 276

children's programming, 128, 324

Chotzinoff, Samuel, 57, 352n4

Chubby Jackson Orchestra, 226–27

Ciro's nightclub, 151, 208

civil rights, 243, 249, 269–70; TV networks and, 241, 254, 261–62

Clark, Dick, 162, 168, 327

class: distinctions in Latin music, 294–95; and ersatz nightclub settings, 142–43; programs for middle-class audiences, 200, 220, 264; status and advertising, 348n6; values of contenders on amateur talent shows, 82–83

classical music, 31–32

Clooney, Rosemary, 85, 199, 310, 313

Club Caravan, 245

Club Ebony, 245, 247, 356n10

Club Mantan (Revue), 247–48

Club Seven, 147

Coates, Norma, 2–3, 360n9

Cobain, Kurt, 337–38

Coca, Imogene, 242–43

"Coffee Song," 289, 293

coin-operated machines, 102–6, 347n26

Cole, Nat "King," 270–72, 353n15, 356n12

Colgate Comedy Hour, The, 60, 263, 267, 357n19; Lena Horne's appearance on, 242–43; hosts of, 63–64, 102, 148, 221; Peggy Lee's appearance on, 207–9, 314

"color organ," 343n3

Columbia Records, 84, 106, 112–13, 359n12

comedy sketches/skits: bebop visual performances and, 217–19; on *The Frank Sinatra Show*, 211–13; funny hats routines, 14, 216, 223–30, 293, 354n22; genre of, 4–5; on *It's Strictly for Laughs*, 55–56, 227; novelty and slapstick in vaudeville acts, 219–21; on *Saturday Night Live (SNL)*, 327–28, 330, 361n12; on *Soupy's On*, 320–21. See also *The Colgate Comedy Hour*; *I Love Lucy*; *Your Show of Shows*

commercial/commodity values, 21–22, 77, 284

Como, Perry, *133*, 148, 214, 316, 349n10; "Papa Loves Mambo" performance, 310, 313–14; performance style and persona of, 130–34, 202–3, 225–26, 271

"conditional professionalism," 78

Condon, Eddie, 124, 128, 205, 249

conga, 292, 298, 314, 359n8; Desi Arnaz's performances, 297–99, 301, 359n9

Constitution Hall (Washington, D.C.), 269, 357n20

consumer groups: Latin-American audiences as, 277; postwar habits of, 201, 285, 289; race issues among, 127, 265, 267; youth/teenagers as, 128, 154–55, 158, 360n3

consumer trends, 108–9

Cooke, Alistair, 248, 353n14

Cooley, Spade, 88–91, *89*, 195, 308, 346nn15–16

"coon song" genre, 236–37

Copacabana Club, 65, 137, 148, 152, 259; Desi Arnaz's performances at, 151, 302; first black performance at, 263

Copa City nightclub, 141

Corner, John, 10, 118, 125

corpsing, 212

Costello, Lou, 64, 123, 207, 232

"covering" songs, 64

Coward, Noel, 315–16, 359nn12–13

Crosby, Bing, 75, 226, 309, 355n1

Crosby, John, 35, 127

Cuban music, 293–95, 298, 301–4, 306

Cuban Pete (Yarbrough), 299, 303

Cuban *son*, 293–94

Cugat, Lorraine, 9, 307–9, 359n10

Cugat, Xavier, 32, 215–16, 306, 308, 359n10

cultural convergence, 295, 317, 333

cultural industries, 114, 171, 272, 321, 338; commercial values and, 22, 74, 155, 223; Latin American music and U.S., 284. *See also* Good Neighbor Policy

cultural transformations, 10, 155, 214–15, 261, 325; Latin music's contribution to, 274–75, 312

culture: black, 135, 219, 238, 272; easy listening music and, 134–35; Latin American, 283, 288–296, 299–300; popular, 118, 161, 188–89, 316; U.S. relations with Latin American, 278–84; values of "middle-America," 142, 197; and values of song standards, 193; youth, 107, 155

Dagmar, 112, 132

dance bands: decline in popularity, 39, 49, 218, 273, 304; Ray Anthony's criticism of TV and, 60–61, 101; Fred Waring and the Pennsylvanians, 12, 28; Latin music influence on, 151, 306, 359n8; Sauter-Finegan band, 209; TV broadcasts of, 37, 87, 91, 141

Daniels, Billy, 259, 356n12

Darcel, Denise, 132, 274

Daughters of the American Revolution (DAR), 269, 357n20

Dave Garroway Show, 83

Davis, Sammy, Jr., 261, 263–64, 357n19

DeCarlo, Yvonne, 211–12

Degrassi: Next Generation, 330

DeLong, Thomas, 161

Delugg, Milton, *222*

Denis, Paul, 76, 345n8

Dennison, H. F., 105

Desmond, Johnny, 85, 166

DeVeaux, Scott, 196

DeVol, Frank, 63, 87, 179–80, 223

Dickinson, Kay: and fabricated nature of the musician, 203; on failure of musical performances, 206; on labor in music and cinema, 11, 57, 229; on practice of doubling, 65; on synaesthesia, 32

Dienst, Richard, 174

digital music market, 334–35

Dinah Shore Show, The, 129–33, *131*, 344n3

disk jockeys (DJs): music shorts on programs, 350n24; as promoters of new music, 158–59; on teen dance programs, 161–68; TV shows featuring, 155–57; visits to high schools, 159

Disk Magic, 67, 156

Doherty, Thomas, 238–41, 244, 267

Don Kirshner's Rock Concert, 2, 326–28

Don McNeill's Breakfast Club, 204

Donnelly, Kevin, 8

Donny and Marie show, 326

Dorsey, Tommy, 39, 75, 179, 321; criticism of TV's impact on concert tours, 100–101

doubling (double-booking), 65, 100

Douglas, Susan, 139

Down Beat: article on *Cavalcade of Bands*, 179; profile of Desi Arnaz, 301; criticism of amateur talent, 71; criticism of Ike Carpenter, 228; on Perry Como's casual persona, 203, 225; and Dave Cooley's influence on western shows, 89; on Ina Ray Hutton's *All-Girl Show*, 90–91, 346n17; criticism of Harry James's performance, 61; on Gene Krupa, 55; on KTLA-TV ballroom broadcasts, 88; on mambo phenomenon, 311, 316; on Tony

Down Beat (*continued*)
Martin, 221, 223; music awards given by, 194, 355n2; on musicians benefiting from ballroom broadcasts, 87; on musicians risking embarrassment, 228; criticism of Fred Nagel, 224; on performance short-comings in postwar era, 215–16; on Kirby Stone group, 56–57; on vaudeville acts, 219–20; comments on Lawrence Welk, 93, 195, 197

DuMont network (New York): Latin musi-cal programs, 276, 291–93; programs featuring black musicians, 254–59; *The Raster* newsletter, 29–30; remote broad-cast programs, 140–41, 146, 182; WABD flagship station, 46, 254, 257, 352n8

Dunham, Katherine, 291, 310

Dunlap, Orrin, 201

Dupuy, Judy, 123, 245, 352n5

Durante, Jimmy, *60*, 64, 69, 143, 220

easy listening music, 130, 134–35, 166, 310

Eddie Condon's Floorshow, 124, 128, 205, 249

Eddy, William, 175

Ed Sullivan Show, The, the Beatles on, 2, 323, 338–39; Elvis Presley on, 359–60n2; Janice Joplin on, 326

Ed Wynn Show, The, 301

Egan, Jack, 208

Ellington, Duke, 85, 251, 264, 273, 306, 320

Ellis, John, 129–30

Emerson, Faye, 243

Emge, Charles, 91

Emmy Awards, 91, 125, 349n10, 361n16

Engles, George, 19–23

Ennis, Philip, 7, 360n3

Erenberg, Lewis, 39, 196

Ertegan, Ahmet, 6

exotic Otherness, 26, 286–90

Fairbanks, William, 25

fan magazines, 76, 78–79, 345n10; *Modern TV and Radio*, 12, 59; *TV Guide*, 83, 133, 189. See also *Radio and Television Mirror*

Fantasia (Disney), 32–33

Farnsworth, Philo T., 24, 27

Federal Communications Commission (FCC), 29

Ferrer, Mel, 209, 354n19

Feur, Jane, 117, 194

film industry, 138, 215, 276; Latin American themes in U.S., 279–80, 299; synchro-nized sound technology in, 23

Finegan, Bill, 207, 209–10, 354n21

Firmat, Gustavo Perez, 152–53, 296–97

Fischinger, Oskar, 32, 343n3

Fisher, Eddie, 9, 214, 225, 313, 348–49n8

Fisher Price TV toy, 324, 360n8

Fiske, John, 117, 120, 124

Flight to Rhythm, 276, 291–94

Floor Show, 205, 249

Ford, Art, 350n22

Ford, Mary, 198–200, *199*, 353n14

Ford, Tennessee Ernie, 112, 303, *303*

Forman, Bertha, 320

For Your Pleasure, 67, 350n19

Fox network, 330–32

Frank Sinatra Show, The, 59, 137, 148, 210–13, 232, 267

Freddy Martin's "Band of Tomorrow," 75, 84, 221, 224, 345n9

Fred Waring and the Pennsylvanians, 25, 28, 32, 355–56n7

Fred Waring Show, The, *70*, 124, *185*, 240, 353n11, 355n7

Freeman, Stan, 228–30

Friedberg, Anne, 284

Frith, Simon, 5, 23, 210, 224, 321

Fuller, Lorenzo "Larry," 248, 258–59

Fuller, Sam, 167

Gabbard, Krin, 218, 232, 355n1

Gabler, Neal, 214–15

Gaillard, Slim, 248

Gale, Lillian, 355–56n7

gamers, 336–39, 362n21

Gandy, Oscar, 277

Garlington, S. W., 246, 249, 255, 259–61

Garofalo, Reebee, 115, 281

Garroway, Dave, 59, 136, 243
Garroway at Large, 83, 346n11
Gay Nineties Revue, 191
gender norms, 131, 348n6
Gendron, Bernard, 218
General Electric (GE), 29, 122, 245
"genericists," 130
genre theory: and audience expectations,
    125–26; as a cultural practice, 117–18;
    discourse on, 120–21. *See also* musical
    genres; television genres
Gershwin, George, 24, 248, 343n3
Gillespie, Dizzy, 85, 157, 194, 307, 355n2
Girl about Town, 67, 350n19
girl bands, 90–91, 308
glamour, 137–38
Glamourlovelies, 110–11
Gleason, Jackie, 256, 316, 348n12
Glee, 331, 361n17
Glenn Miller Orchestra, 228, 354n21
Godfrey, Arthur, 68, 75, 112, 274, 344–
    45n4; support for black musicians, 269;
    as talent show host, 72, 345n8, 350n17
Godlovitch, Sam, 351n1
Goldstein, Leonard, 140, 349n15
Good Housekeeping, 344n6
Good Neighbor Policy, 278–79, 282, 293,
    307, 312, 358n4
Goodwin, Andrew, 328–29
Gould, Jack, 35, 127
Grady, Joe, 159
Graf, Herbert, 122–23
Gray, Herman, 264, 272
Guitar Hero, 336–37, 361n19
Guralnick, Peter, 360n3
Guy Lombardo and the Royal Canadians,
    139, 144, 218, 288, 349n13

Haines, Connie, 192
Halberstam, David, 360n4
Hall, Wendall, 234, 355n3
Hampton, Lionel, 221, 224, 250, 259–60,
    260; performance on *Club Ebony*, 245,
    247
hapa haole music, 274, 358n2

harpists, 173, 352n5
Harrington, Ruth Lee, 175–76, 219
Hartley, John, 170
Hatch, Wilbur, 302
Hawkins, Coleman, 251, 320
Hayes, Richard, 85
Hazel Scott Show, The, 256–58, *257*
Hearn, Alison, 332
Hein, Jack, 242
Hellfrich, Stockton, 241–42, 244, 356n9
Hendrix, Jimi, 360n7
Hentoff, Nat, 311
Herman, Woody, 39, 273, 306
"hillbilly" shows, 115–16, 346n15, 348n3
Hine, Thomas, 323
hinterlands, 136, 141–42
hip-hop, 329–30, 361n16
Holly, Hal, 91
Hollywood, 15, 94, 138, 159, 215; black talent
    in film, 258, 266; Latin themes in film,
    278, 299; Sinatra's success in, 210, 213
Hollywood Sepia Tones, 247, 356n11
Holman, Michael, 361n16
Holt, Fabian, 120
Hopkins, Claude, 248
Horace Heidt Show, The, 75, 81, 345n8
Horn, Bob, 161–62, 165–66, 351n25, 351n28
Horne, Lena, 242–44, 258, 264, 267, 357n15
Hour Glass, 208, 354n18
Howard, Bob, 251–54, *252*, 256n13
Howard, Joe, 191
Howdy Doody, 128
Howell, Wayne, *222*
Hurst, Ed, 159
Hutchinson, Thomas, 116–17, 123, 175
Hutton, Ina Ray, 9, 39, 87, *92*, 308; *All-Girl
    Show*, 90–91, 193, 247, 346n17
"hyperrealism," 146, 150

Ike Carpenter Orchestra, 223
"I Like the Wide Open Spaces," 110–12,
    347n27
"I'll See You in C-U-B-A," 287, 303
I Love Lucy: "Cuban Pals" episode, 304, *305*;
    "Lucy Goes to the Hospital" episode,

I Love Lucy (continued)
102; musical repertoire on, 296–304, *299, 303*; nightclub settings on, 151–54
"image organ," 32
Ina Ray Hutton's All-Girl Show, 90–91, 193, 247, 346n17
International Musician, 45, 52, *53*, 169
Internet, 333–35, 339
It's Strictly for Laughs, 55–56, 227

Jack, Wolfman, 326–27
Jackson, Chubby, 226–27
Jackson, Joe, 1
Jackson, Michael, 324, 329
James, Dennis, 28, 78–80, *80*, 83–84, 194
James, Harry, 28, 39, 61
jam sessions, 196–97, 353n12
Jarvis, Al, 157
jazz: "cats" reference in, 195–96, 353n12; jam sessions, 196–97, 353n12; modern jazz, 217–19; musicians on Soupy Sales show, 320; progressive jazz, 218; similarities between Latin music and, 306–7
Jenkins, Henry, 333
Jewish comics, 235
Jezer, Marty, 40, 164
Johnson, Victoria, 196–97
Jones, Spike, 64, 101–2, 148, 200, 221
Judge for Yourself, 129, 349n9
jukeboxes: coin-operated movies and radios, 104–6; decline of, 103, 108; promotional strategies for, 102–3, 107–8; TV-jukebox hybrids, 105; TV manufacturers and, 103–4
Jukebox Jury, 4, 157
juvenile delinquency, 160–61, 165, 167, 351n26

Kanaga, L. W., 109–10
Kaye, Sammy, 316
Kaye, Sydney, 282, 358n6
KECA-TV (Los Angeles), 308, 345
Keightley, Keir: definition of easy listening music, 130, 134–35; on exoticism of Latin music, 289–90; on symbolic meaning of song standards, 192–93
Kellner, Douglas, 54
Ken Murray Show, The, 110, *111*
Kenney, William Howland, 357n17
Kenton, Stan, 84, 273, 300, 306–7, 316
Kilty, Jack, 156
King of Jazz (Anderson), 286
Kirby Stone Quintette, 55–56, *56*, 227, 344n1
Kirshner, Don, 325; *Rock Concert*, 2, 326–28
KLAC-TV (Los Angeles), 157, 198, 247, 276, 345n6
Kline, Midge, 175, 352n8
Knight, Arthur, 239, 266
Kostelanetz, Andre, 64, 177, 352n7
Koszarski, Richard, 24, 29
Kovacs, Ernie, 59, 136
Krupa, Gene, 55, 57, 216–19, *217*
KTLA-TV (Los Angeles): ballroom broadcasts on, 87–93, 115, 182, 184, 195; *Ina Ray Hutton's All-Girl Show* on, 90–91, 193, 247, 346n17; Latin musical broadcasts on, 274, 276, 290
KTSL-TV (Hollywood), 156–57, 240
KT TV (Los Angeles), 90, 205, 223, 240, 346n17
Kurtz, Marjorie, 86, 346n12
Kyser, Kay, 32, 288

labor: amateur talent and, 72–73, 79–80, 332; Kay Dickinson on music and, 65, 206, 229; displacement of, 338; organization, 36–37, 40; racial relations in, 264–65; relationship between music and, 54–55
Laine, Frankie, 9, 72, 225, 313; on *The Frankie Laine Show*, 192, 345n5; on *The Frank Sinatra Show*, 59, 137, 148
Landsberg, Klaus: on authenticity in broadcasting, 182; as director of Paramount Television Productions, 346n13; as manager at KTLA-TV, 87–88, 92, 184, 290; at W6XYZ-TV station, 119
Lane, Abbe, 309, 359n10

La Rosa, Julius, 68, 112

Latin American culture, 283, 288–296, 299–300

Latino identity, 291, 295–96, 302

Latino musicians: stereotypes of, 276–77, 279, 291, 301; televised musical performances of, 273–78, 287–96. *See also* conga; mambo; rumba

Laytons, The, 255

Lea Act (1946), 40

Lee, Peggy, 9, 65, *207*, 345n5, 354n18; film appearances of, 354n20; performance style and persona of, 9, 132, 207–9, 313–15

Lee, Robert, 30–33

Leiter, Robert, 46

Lennon, John, 335–36

Leo Carrillo's Dude Ranch, 295–96, 346n15

Leonard, Ada, 90, 308, 346n17

Les Paul and Mary Ford Show, 198–200, *199*, 353n14

Lester, Jerry, 112, 144

Lester, John, 86

"Let Me Go Lover," 113

Lewis, Jerry, 64, 124

Lewis, Jim, 269–70

Liberace Show, The, 198–99, 353n13

Life magazine, 39, 68, 168, 312, 352n2

lip-synching, 66, 214, 361n12, 361n17; by artists on *American Bandstand*, 168, 327

Live Aid (1985), 329

Lombardo, Guy, 85, 197, 219, 226, 354n24; and the Royal Canadians, 139, 144, 218, 288, 349n13; music publishing company of, 86

Lopez, Ana, 283

Lopez, Vincent, 139–40, 229

Lorraine Cugat Show, The, 9, 307–9

Love, Courtney, 338

"Love and Marriage," 113

Lury, Karen, 126, 170, 190, 212

Mabley, Jack, 203

MacDonald, J. Fred, 238, 247

MacDonnell, Kyle, 201, 350n19; host of *Hold That Camera*, 67–68, 146, 347n22

Machito (Francisco Grillo), 273, 298, 304, 306, 310, 316

Magder, Ted, 338

mambo: criticism on, 316; "mania" or "craze" across America, 15, 274, 304, 312, 316–17, 359n11; Noro Morales's definition of, 306; nightclubs (1950s), 151; recordings and concerts, 310–11; televised musical performances of, 207, 307–9, 313–16

Mambo (Rossen), 310

"Mambo Boogie," 309

"Mambo Rock," 311

"Managua, Nicaragua," 288

Mann, Denise, 189

Mariners, 269–70

marketing strategies: of black media markets, 266; of Latin music in U.S., 278–84; promotion of new songs, 110, 112–13; promotion of TV shows, 13, 99, 124. *See also* advertising

Martin, Dean, 64, 124, 310, 313

Martin, Mary, 315, 359n12

Martin, Tony, 9, 200, 225, 313; host of *Popsicle Parade*, 144–45, *149*, 350n17; *Tony Martin Show*, 132, 132–34, 142–43, 314

Mashon, Michael, 354n18

Massey, Raymond, 355–56n7

McCarthy, Anna, 96, 284, 347n21

McDaniel, Hattie, 232, 256

McGarrett, George, 143, 202

McGrath, Tom, 328

media convergence, 8, 18, 319, 333, 339

Meredith, Morley, 78

Merman, Ethel, 99, 359n12

Metronome: advertisement for Gibson Guitars, *183*; photograph of Gene Krupa, *217*; article on Peggy Lee, 315; criticism of Vaughn Monroe's TV debut; on popularity of mambo, 306; review of Frank Sinatra, 211

Mexican musical performances, 290, 294–96

Meyrowitz, Joshua, 285
Midnight Special, The, 2, 326–28
Miller, Justin, 44, 282, 351n26, 358n6
Miller, Kiri, 361n19
Millinder, Lucky, 240, 355n5
Miner, Worthington "Tony," 68
minstrel shows/skits, 235–37, 240, 353n11, 355nn6–7
Miranda, Carmen, 279, 293, 314
miscegenation, 246, 266–68
Mittel, Jason, 121
modernist aesthetic, 136, 138, 189–90, 194, 325
modernity, 54
Modern TV and Radio, 12, 59
Monkees, The, 324, 327–28, 360n9
Monroe, Vaughn: appearance on *The Arthur Murray Party*, 67; club and theater performances, 65–66; headliner of "Rhythm Rodeo," 163; host of *Camel Caravan*, 61, 62; *Vaughn Monroe Show*, 344n3
Morales, Esy, 274, 290–91
Mordden, Ethan, 285–86
Moreland, Mantan, 248
Morey Amsterdam Show, 128, 137, 145–46
Morley, David, 278, 285
Morrow, Liza, 205
Mottola, Tony, *183*
MTV (Music Television), 1–4, 329–30, 338; corporate ownership, 361n14; online presence, 334
Mundy, John, 3, 126, 359–60n2
Murray, Susan, 220
musical accompaniment, 23, 98, 130
musical genres: award shows to help define, 125; bebop/jazz as, 218; cable TV influence on, 330; classical music broadcasts as, 171–72; contemporary, 12; and definition of easy listening music, 134–35; emergence of patterns/categories, 120–21; general analysis of types/classifications, 115–19, 124; of Latin music, 273–74, 277, 283, 291–92, 297–98, 306, 310; and performance style, 130, 134; rock 'n' roll as, 6, 42, 327–28; Tin Pan Alley and

"coon song" as, 237; vaudeville and musical halls as, 58, 191
musical integrity, 221, 223–27
music and television convergence, 2, 8, 18, 55, 130
music critics: of aesthetic and performance weakness, 215; of *Glee* show, 331; of jazz musicians, 218; of Latin music, 304, 306, 316; of the mambo, 306–7; of rock, 360n9. See also *Billboard; Down Beat; Metronome; New York Times; Variety*
music games, 336–39
music halls, 14, 191, 253, 286
"musicking" and televising, 180–82, 184–87
music licensing, 281–82, 330
Music Operators of America, 106, 347n26
music video, 2–3, 328–29, 334–35
My Favorite Husband, 300, 302

NAACP (National Association for the Advancement of Colored People), 239, 270, 356n8
Nagel, Fred, 224
narratives/program announcements, 139, 145–46, 285, 291
National Association of Broadcasters (NAB), 44, 281–82, 358n6
National Minstrels, 240, 355n5
NBC radio: Continuity Acceptance Radio/Television Department, 237, 240–42, 244–45, 356n9; *National Minstrels* program, 240, 355n5; photograph of Pickens Sisters on, *27*; racial insensitivity on, 234–37, 239; racial policies manual, 237–38
NBC-TV: amateur talent programs on, 74–75; black program hosts on, 249, 264, 271–72; blue-pencil specialists (script editors) at, 241, 263; Continuity Acceptance Radio/Television Department, 237, 240–42, 244–45, 356n9; disk jockey broadcasts on, 156, 158, 167; experimental broadcasts, 25–28, 339; first censorship case (1944), 30; foundation for the poor, 261; founding of Kyle MacDonnell's

career, 67–68; history of, 343n2; impact of AFM TV ban on, 43; impact of war years on, 29; implementation of props for vaudeville acts, 221; initiatives with RCA records, 73–74; Latin-themed broadcasts, 276, 280, 283; launch at World's Fair (New York, 1939), 28–29, 36, 278, 348n4; launch of first daytime program, 201; nightclub broadcasts, 140, 143–44; permission cards for televised audiences, 349n14; practical working conditions at, 27–28; premiere of *Saturday Night Live*, 327; Elvis Presley "comeback" special (1968), 2, 337; program definitions/types, 121–22, 126; Program Department, 19–21, 119, 129, 236–37; programming strategies, 94, 128; promotional publications for, 275; racial policies, 234, 237–38, 262–63; relations with Southern market/audiences, 265, 268; salaries for top talent, 99; sponsors and sales performance, 201–2; staff members with TV sets at, 171; survey on audience viewing patterns/preferences, 127, 129; symphony broadcasts on, 48, 171–72, 352n4; technical production/camera skills of, 172–74; telegenity or visual standards for talent, 19–21, 23

Negro Actors Guild, 239, 262

Negro spirituals, 355n7

Negus, Keith, 3, 130, 321, 360n7, 362n20

Nelson, Rick, 322

Nesmith, Mike, 328

Newcomb, Horace, 3, 156

New York Amsterdam News: on all-black TV productions, 245–46; on Amanda Randolph's TV show, 255; on black stereotypes, 248–49; on Horne's performance on *Your Show of Shows*, 242; on networks' exclusion of top black talent, 261–62; on racial degradation on radio shows, 239–40; on Reginald Beane Trio, 258; on TV's effect on youth, 160

New York Herald Tribune, 35, 97, 127

New York Times: critique of *Glee*, 331; on demand for tickets to variety shows, 94; on public acceptance of TV genres, 127; reaction to televised musical performance, 174; on revolution in music, 188, 215; tribute to Soupy Sales, 320

Niccoli, Ria, 203

nightclubs: audience engagement in, 146–50; competition for booking artists, 98–100; drop in attendance, 39, 346n19; ersatz settings and staging for, 137, 143–50; featured on *I Love Lucy*, 151–54; iconic cultural status of, 137–38; owners of, 66–67; radio broadcasts from, 139; remote TV broadcasts from, 139–42; themes, 142–43; TV's impact on, 93

Night Life, 141, 246

"Nina," 315–16, 359n13

950 Club, The, 159, 167

Nipper's Record Shop, 157

nostalgia, 188–90, 192, 353n11

O'Connell, Ray, 43, 140

Old Dutch Revue, 137, 148, 150

Old Knick Music Hall, 150–51

Omi, Michael, 261

Omnibus, 115, 248, 348n1, 353n14

one-nighters, 63, 65, 101, 141

"optical accompaniment," 33

Optowsky, Stan, 353n17

Original Amateur Hour, 5, 72, 75–78, 82–83, 242

Original Hoosier Hotshots, 354n22

Ormandy, Eugene, 47, 171–73, 176, 178, 352n3

Owens, Harry, 87, 274

Page, Patti, 113, 191

Palladium Ballroom, 87, 151, 185, 310

"Papa Loves Mambo," 310, 313–14

Partridge Family, 324, 360n9

"pastiche numbers," 286

patriotism, 296

Paul, Les, 198–200, *199*, 353n14

payola, 159, 162, 351n25

Peer, Ralph, 281, 358nn5–6

performance style/aesthetics: of bebop and modern jazz, 216–19; double-booking (doubling) schedules, 65–67; of Elvis Presley, 6, 8–10, 322; funny hats routines in, 14, 216, 223–30, 293, 354n22; marketability or salability of, 21–22, 201–3; metacommentary and banter as part of, 212–13; musical integrity and, 221, 223–27; novelty and slapstick in, 219–21; performance modification for TV, 182; performer personae, 131–34, 198–202; physicality and dance in, 308; and risk of public embarrassment, 228–30; script reading in, 204, 353n15; use of prerecorded vocal tracks, 214; weak or inadequate, 204–13, 215

Perry Como Show, 68, 129–34, *133*, 175, 202–3, 344n2

Peter Potter's Party, 156

Petrillo, James C.: and ban on TV musical performances, 37–38, 43–47, 71–72; demands on corporate radio broadcasters, 40–41; failure to recognize newer music forms, 48–49; friendship with President Truman, *38*, 38–39, 41, 344n4; and payouts for music in movies, 48; and recording bans, 36, 42–43; remark on development of TV, 12

Philadelphia: DJ/teen dance TV programs in, 159–61, 163–68; independent record companies in, 162

Philadelphia Inquirer, 162

phonograph recordings, 29, 33, 36, 110, 344n6

Piaf, Edith, 140, 274

Pickens Sisters, 27, *27*

Picture Platters, 156

Pittman, Bob, 329, 361n13

Plainsmen, 295

polka music, 274

Pop, Iggy, 359n1

Poppele, J. R., 44–45

Popsicle Parade, 144–45, *149*, 350n17

Potter, Peter, 156–58

Potter, Ralph, 33

Prado, Perez, 306, 309–14, 358–59n7

presentational style: camera errors and spatial miscues in, 178–79, 205; camera shots of classical musicians, 173–74, 352nn5–7; critics of, 172–73, 215; Elvis Presley's influence on, 6, 8–10; intimacy and proximity in, 26; modernist aesthetic of, 136, 189–90; psychedelic imagery in, 326; rehearsals and performance preparation, 178–80, 206; and struggles to identify the audience, 177–78; visual shortcomings/gesturing of performers, 175–77; visual standards for, 19–21, 24, 216, 221. *See also* performance style/aesthetics; television production

Presley, Elvis, 5–6, 360n4; performance style of, 8–10; television appearances, 322–23, 325, 337, 339, 359n2, 360n3; TV viewing habits of, 6–7

Press, Andrea Lee, 349n11

program announcements, 139, 145–46

programming strategies: competition for artists, 64–65; competitive program scheduling, 246; emphasis on foreign travel and exotic Otherness, 288–91; Internet's impact on, 334; novelty and familiarity requirements in, 190–91, 193–94; overexposure and redundancy in, 63–69; prejudiced booking patterns and, 250; program distinctions and distinguishing traits in, 131–34, 348n7; segregated programming, 245–48, 262–63, 267–68; sequential organization in, 129–30; structured around tradition and nostalgia, 188–93; viewer preferences and patterns in, 126–28, 348n6

Puente, Tito, 310, 313–14

Pyron, Darden, 198

race relations: black-and-tan lounges, 265–66; cultural rules of, 264–65; onscreen miscegenation, 246, 266–68; politics and, 261–62. *See also* civil rights

racism: blackface exploits, 235–36, 243, 353n11, 355–56nn7–8; segregated pro-

gramming, 245–48, 267–68; of south-
ern/white audiences, 213, 246, 263–68,
271; stereotypes, 233, 237, 244, 248, 257
Radio and Television Mirror, 79, 150, 269,
345–46n10
radio broadcasting: of amateur talent
shows, 71–72, 76, 85, 332; audiences/lis-
teners, 33, 95, 167, 234, 241, 344n6; black
hosts and musicians on, 245–46, 251–52,
254–56, 259–60; DJ shows/personalities,
155–59, 162, 166, 327; easy listening music
and, 135; formative stages of, 343n2;
Latin American-themed shows, 274, 301;
music licensing in, 281–82, 330; performance skills, 176, 204; racist and lewd
content on, 234–37, 239–40; of R & B
musicians, 6; remote broadcasts, 138–40,
154, 349n12; shift to television, 8; stereotyping in, 239; TV's emergence from,
17, 21, 25, 54, 127; union contracts and
negotiations for, 36–38, 40–42, 46–47;
WPEN radio, 159, 161, 167
Radio-Keith-Orpheum (RKO), 21, 116,
296
Radio Showmanship, 159–60
Raibourn, Paul, 94–95
Ranch, Harry, 227
Randle, Bill, 321–22
Randolph, Amanda, 254–56
rap music, 12, 329–30
Ratliff, Ben, 320
Ray Anthony Show, 344n2
Ray Bloch Orchestra, 144–45
RCA (Radio Corporation of America), 22,
119, 128
RCA Victor records: jukebox singles, 107;
Elvis Presley's contract with, 5; record-
ings, 113, 310, 355n3, 358n7; record sales
(1951), 109–10; strategy for acquiring
new talent, 73–74
Recordland, 166
record sales, 108–10, 112–13
*Red Channels: The Report of Communist
Influence in Radio and Television*, 258,
357n15

rhythm and blues (R & B), 6, 42, 128, 155,
162, 330
Ritchie, Michael, 119
Rizo, Marco, 302, 310
Roberts, John Storm, 151
Roberts, Shari, 179, 299
Robinson, Jackie, 261
Rock Band (music game), 336, 338–39
Rock Concert, 2, 326–28
rock 'n' roll, 311, 325, 327; Elvis Presley and
the emergence of, 5–8, 322
Rodman, Gilbert, 360n3
Rodman, Rod, 153
Rogers, Richard, 28
Roosevelt, Franklin Delano, 258n4, 278–79
Rose, Dave, 147
Rosen, George, 171–72, 211
Ross, Lanny, 190–91
Roy, Rob, 262
Royal, John F., 12, 19, 236–37, 280, 353n10
rumba: Desi Arnaz's performances, 297–
98, 302, 304; emergence of bands in
America, 273–74; performances in film,
309–10; popularity in dance studios,
359n11; televised musical performances,
287, 293, 308; in U.S. ballrooms, 306
Russell, Don, 146, 350n16

Sales, Soupy, 156, 320
Sanjek, David, 4, 21, 42
Sanjek, Russell, 4, 21, 42
Santa Monica Ballroom, 87–89
Sargeant, Winthrop, 298
Sarnoff, David, 20–21, 234, 272, 275, 280,
353n10
Sarnoff, Robert, 171
Saturday Night Dance Party, 124, 143–44
Saturday Night Live (SNL), 327–28, 330,
361n12
Sauter-Finegan Orchestra, 207, 209–10,
354n21
Schumach, Murray, 134
Schumann, Walter, 112
Scott, Hazel, 254–58, *257*, 357–58n20
Search for Girls, 90, 346n17

Segrave, Kerry, 96, 347n26
Seldes, Gilbert, 180–81, 354n19
sepia revues ("all-black" music programs), 245–48
Shaver, Charlie, 352n6
Shearing, George, 218, 229
Shepard, Vonda, 330
Shore, Dinah, 28, 41, 71, 113, 214, 349n10; *The Dinah Shore Show*, 129–33, *131*, 198, 344n3; *Dinah!* show, 326, 359n1; performance style of, 9, 134, 200, 225–26, 313, 349n11
Simon, George, 211
Sinatra, Frank, 28, 41, 71, 113, 289, 345n5; *The Frank Sinatra Show*, 59, 137, 148, 210–13, 232, 267; Paramount Theater concerts, 154–55
Sing It Again, 252, 254
Skutch, Ira, 67
Small, Christopher, 180–81
Smith, Carleton, 171, 221
Smith, Kate, 24, 148, 201–2
Smothers Brothers Comedy Hour, The, 325, 360n10
Smulyan, Susan, 235
Snader and Official musical shorts, 162, 350n24
Snyder, Robert, 235
Songs for Sale, 85–86
"song sharks," 85
song standards, 110, 192–93, 197, 308
Sosnik, Harry, 206
Soul Train, 2, 167, 327
soundtracks (TV), 330–31
Soupy's On, 320
Soupy's Soda Shop, 156
Southernaires, The, 254
Spade Cooley Show, The, 89–91, 195
Spaeth, Sigmund, 85
Spigel, Lynn: on imaginary travel ventures of TV, 285; on modernist aesthetics of early TV, 136, 190; on TV's distinguishing characteristics, 26; on TV's "hyperrealism," 146–47, 150
Spinning Images, 156

Splatter Party, 167
Sponsor magazine, 41, 253, 265, 277
sponsors: announcements on shows, 130; Armour meat company, 202; for Billy Daniels program, 259; for *The Bob Howard Show*, 253, 256n13; favoring established musicians, 69, 71, 197–98; and marketable performances, 201–2; Popsicle company, 144; *Red Channels* incident and, 258; southern attitudes/threats and, 263, 265, 268, 272; Spam meat company as, 346n17; support for black musicians, 238, 241, 247, 253, 262, 271–72
Stafford, Jo, 28, 66, 214, 225
Stage Entrance, 194, 355n2
Stage Show, 319, 321, 359–60n2
Stanton, Carl, 144
Star of the Family, 115, 353n14
Star Search, 332
Star Time, 345n6
Statley, Ralph, 292–93
St. Clair, Sylvie, 46, 145
Stebbins, Robert, 73, 78
Steffens, Mildred, 32–33
Sterne, Jonathan, 24
Stilwell, Robynn, 322, 331, 359n9
Sublette, Ned, 359n8
Sugar Hill Times, 246–47
Sullivan, Ed, 67, 124, 246, 325; *The Ed Sullivan Show*, 2, 263, 323, 326, 339, 359–60n2; *Toast of the Town*, 64, 128, 205, 208, 264
Sullivan, Frank, 97
Swift Show, The, 190
swing music, 39, 218, 273, 306
synaesthesia, 32
synchronized sound technology, 18, 23
"synthespians," 338

Taft-Hartley Act (1947), 41–42
talent recruiting, 19–23
talkies, 23
Talmadge, Herman, 267–69
Taubman, Howard, 174
Taylor, Deems, 33

Ted Mack's Original Amateur Hour, 5, 72, 75–78, 82–83, 242

Teen Canteen, 156

teen dramas, 330–31

teen entertainment: DJ visits to high schools, 159, 167; radio listening rates, 167; televised dance programs, 161–68; TV dramas, 330–31

Teen Twirl, 167

televised concerts, 326–27

Televiser, 116, 175

television, early developments: artist exploitation in, 67; audiences of, 34–35; content demands in, 63–65; critical studies of, 3–6; experimental programming in, 24–28, 117; mainstream or homogenous programming of, 30; opportunities and risks for performers in, 52–62; overexposure and redundancy in, 63–65; program expenses, 71; promotional strategies, 34–35; roots in Broadway and cinema, 286; set designs and aesthetics in, 135–36; sound quality in, 30–31; visual effects of, 32–33; visual limitations, 59. *See also* programming strategies; television genres; television production

Television Broadcasters Association, 44, 126

television genres: amateur talent programs as, 72, 77–78, 84, 331–32, 335; award shows to help define, 125; critical studies on, 3–5; definitions/categories in early TV, 122–23; disc jockey/teen platter shows as, 155–57, 159–60, 163–68; emergence/evolution of, 14–15; ersatz nightclubs as, 135, 137, 147, 154; function of, 124; hybrids/mixing of, 331, 348n3, 350n24; variety shows as, 123–24, 190, 326; and viewer preferences, 127–30, 135

television/media critics: of all-black TV productions, 246, 248, 263; arguments for and against TV, 58–59; on character and content on TV, 136–37; on incompatibilities between musician and TV producers, 187–88; on Lawrence Welk's conventional style, 195; on NBC's technical production, 172–73; on Perry Como's performance style, 203; racially intolerant critics, 269; of *Revue* premiere broadcast, 248; of Sinatra's TV performances, 210–12; of teen-oriented content, 160; of TV's influence on touring musicians, 100–101; on visual shortcomings of artists, 176–77; on weak performances by top musical artists, 206–7, 211. *See also* *Billboard*; *Downbeat*; *Variety*

television production: advances and experimentation in, 119–20; formula and format definition in, 120–21; musicking and televising compatibilities in, 181–82, 184–87; organizational structures and responsibilities in, 186–87; program definition or typology in, 121–22; technical and presentational problems in, 58, 123, 203–6, 209–10. *See also* programming strategies

television sets: advertising for, 34, 45, 357n18; coin-operated, 106; cost of (1939), 29; household ownership rates (1940), 278; placement in public establishments, 94–98, 347n21; repairs, 96; sales of, 35, 108; sound quality of, 31, 336–37, 362n20

Television World, 95, 191

Texaco Star Theater, 3, 246

Thaler, Al, 291

Thornhill, Claude, 184–85

Three Stooges, 211–12

Tico Records, 276, 310

Time magazine, 187, 284, 346n11

Tin Pan Alley, 15, 25, 191–92, 237, 303

Tjader, Cal, 311

Toast of the Town, The, 64, 128, 205, 208, 264. *See also* *The Ed Sullivan Show*

Tommy Dorsey Orchestra, 28, 321, 348n2

Tony Martin Show, *132*, 132–34, 142–43, 314

Too Many Girls (Abbott), 296–97, 299

Torme, Mel, 72, 112, 345n5

Toscanini, Arturo, 48, 128, 171–73, 178, 352n4

Toynbee, Jason, 150
Tradio, 105–6
travelogues, 26, 285–86
Tropicana (Bronx), 152, 350n20
Tropic Holiday, 290–91
Truman, Harry, *38*, 38–39, 41, 344n4, 357–58n20; racial policies of, 238, 355n4
Tucker, Sophie, 59–60, *60*, 311
"tuxedo rates," 47
TV a-Go-Go (Austen), 5
TV Danceland, 166
TV Guide, 83, 133, 189
TV Land, 15
TV Teen Club, 72, 75, 83–84, 161, 350n23

Ulanov, Barry, 306–7
union/labor organization, 36–37, 40
union musicians. *See* American Federation of Musicians (AFM); American Federation of Television-Radio Actors (AFTRA)
Uptown Jubilee, 246
U.S. armed forces, 355n4
U.S. foreign policy, 15, 306
U.S. State Department, 282

Valdes, Miguelito, 292–94, 297–98, 358n10
Variety: on AFM TV ban, 46–47; on amateur shows, 72, 81, 345n9; review of Laurie Anders's TV performance, 110–11; on artists double-booking, 65; Samuel Chotzinoff's letter to, 57; on costs of top TV talent, 34, 67, 98–100; criticism of *Old Knick Music Hall*, 150–51; on gesturing in musical performances, 176; on jukebox competition with TV, 106; on juvenile delinquency, 167; on mambo phenomenon, 274, 312; on musicians transitioning to TV, 63; on network ratings, 99; on nightclub broadcasts, 140–41; criticism of Peter Potter, 156; on record listening habits, 109; reviews of all-black productions, 245–46, 250; reviews of Latin musical performances, 276, 291, 307–8; on revitalization of Tin

Pan Alley, 219; review of Hazel Scott, 256; on script reading habit, 353n15; on struggles of union musicians, 41; on the success of Ina Ray Hutton, 90; on technical inexperience, 205, 353n16; on TV set placement in public establishments, 94; on TV's power to promote music, 112–13; on Fred Waring show, 187; on weak performances and substandard stagecraft, 205–6, 211
variety shows: comedies, 4, 58, 190; black musical celebrities on, 249; featuring all-black casts, 245–48; references to different countries/cultures on, 286–88; structure and patterns of, 123–24; tradition and nostalgia trends on, 188–90
vaudeville: blackface exploits in, 235–36; decline in popularity, 102, 235, 347n23; as a showcase for modern art, 190; traditional performance style of, 128, 143, 191, 219–21, 350n16, 354n22
Vaughn Monroe Show, The, 61, *62*, 344n3
Viacom, 329, 361n14
Videograph Corporation, 105–6
viewers. *See* audiences/viewers
visual effects, 32–33
Von Schilling, James, 29–30

WABD-TV (New York), 46, 145, 256–59, 352n8
Wade, Robert, 221
Waggoner, Susan, 142
Waksman, Steve, 200
Wallerstein, Ted, 109
Wallis, Ruth, 311, 345
Wall Street Journal, 94
Walters, Lou, 66–67, 140
Waring, Fred, 12, 30, 69, 186–87, 353n10; *Fred Waring Show, 70, 124, 185,* 240, 353n11, 355n7; and the Pennsylvanians, 25, 28, 32, 355–56n7
Warner AMEX Satellite Entertainment Company (WASEC), 329
War of the Worlds, 349n12

Washington Post, 102, 351n26
Waters, Ethel, 249, 255–56, 258, 264
WAVE-TV (St. Louis), 245, 358n1
WBKB-TV (Chicago), 128, 166–67, 345n6
WCBS-TV (New York), 276, 291
Weaver, Sylvester "Pat," 94, 127, 144, 344n4
Webb, Alvin "Chick," 248, 261–64, 357n16
Weber, Joan, 113
Weinstein, David, 141, 254
Weitman, Robert, 263
Welk, Lawrence, 9, 87, 326, 339; appeal to "middle America," 197; reference to jazz "cats," 195–96, 353n12; remote ballroom broadcasts, 92–93, 184, 195; as a television pioneer, 194
Wertheimer, Alfred, 7
western music shows, 89, 110–11, 295, 346n15
WEWS-TV (Cleveland), 148, 150, 156, 274, 350–51n24
WFIL-TV (Philadelphia), 161–66, 168, 351n25, 351n28
Whiteman, Paul, 216, 286, 316, 343n3; host of *TV Teen Club*, 72, 75, 83, 161, 345n7
white supremacists, 265, 267–69, 271
Wilfred, Thomas, 32, 343n3
Williams, Mark, 88

Williams, Raymond, 343n2
Will Mastin Trio, 263, 267, 357n19
Wilson, Earl, 355n2
Wilson, John, 56–57
Winant, Howard, 261
"window on the world" expression, 284
WJZ-TV (New York), 191, 220, 254
WMAL-TV (Washington, D.C.), 165, 351n26
WNBT-TV (New York), 156, 261, 290
World's Fair (New York, 1939): children's programming at, 128; Fred Waring's debut at, 12, 186, 353n10; NBC television launch at, 28–29, 36, 278, 348n4
WOR-TV (New York), 150, 157, 247–48, 254, 276
WPEN radio, 159, 161, 167
WRGB-TV (Schenectady), 122, 156
W3XPF-TV (Philadelphia), 27

Xavier Cugat Orchestra, 297, 302, 309, 316

Your Hit Parade, 4–5, 94, 184
Your Show of Shows, 112, 143, 154, 242–43, 352n6
YouTube, 16, 335, 361n17

Zworykin, Vladimir, 24, 348n4

Murray Forman is an associate professor of Media and
Screen Studies at Northeastern University.

Library of Congress Cataloging-in-Publication Data
Forman, Murray.
One night on TV is worth weeks at the Paramount : popular music
on early television / Murray Forman.
p. cm. — (Console-ing passions: television and cultural power)
Includes bibliographical references and index.
ISBN 978-0-8223-4998-3 (cloth : alk. paper)
ISBN 978-0-8223-5011-8 (pbk. : alk. paper)
1. Television broadcasting of music — United States — History — 20th century.
2. Television and music — United States — History — 20th century. 3. Popular
music — United States — History — 20th century.
I. Title. II. Series: Console-ing passions.
PN1992.8.M87F67 2012
791.45'65780973 — dc23   2011041900